Northern Ireland, the United States and the Second World War

Northern Ireland, the United States and the Second World War

Simon Topping

BLOOMSBURY ACADEMIC
LONDON • NEW YORK • OXFORD • NEW DELHI • SYDNEY

BLOOMSBURY ACADEMIC
Bloomsbury Publishing Plc
50 Bedford Square, London, WC1B 3DP, UK
1385 Broadway, New York, NY 10018, USA
29 Earlsfort Terrace, Dublin 2, Ireland

BLOOMSBURY, BLOOMSBURY ACADEMIC and the Diana logo are trademarks
of Bloomsbury Publishing Plc

First published in Great Britain 2022
This paperback edition published 2023

Copyright © Marilyn Dunn, 2022

Simon Topping has asserted his right under the Copyright, Designs and Patents Act, 1988, to be identified as Author of this work.

For legal purposes the Acknowledgements on pp. ix–xi constitute an extension of this copyright page.

Cover image: Private Milburn Henke, who was presented to the press as the 'first' United States soldier to step ashore, salutes as he lands at Dufferin Quay, Belfast, Northern Ireland. © Imperial War Museum (H 16847)

All rights reserved. No part of this publication may be reproduced or transmitted in any form or by any means, electronic or mechanical, including photocopying, recording, or any information storage or retrieval system, without prior permission in writing from the publishers.

Bloomsbury Publishing Plc does not have any control over, or responsibility for, any third-party websites referred to or in this book. All internet addresses given in this book were correct at the time of going to press. The author and publisher regret any inconvenience caused if addresses have changed or sites have ceased to exist, but can accept no responsibility for any such changes.

A catalogue record for this book is available from the British Library.

Library of Congress Cataloging-in-Publication Data
Names: Topping, Simon David, author.
Title: Northern Ireland, the United States and the Second World War / Simon Topping.
Description: London; New York: Bloomsbury Academic, 2021. | Includes bibliographical references and index.
Identifiers: LCCN 2021038589 (print) | LCCN 2021038590 (ebook) | ISBN 9781350037595 (hardback) | ISBN 9781350037618 (pdf) | ISBN 9781350037601 (ebook)
Subjects: LCSH: World War, 1939-1945–Northern Ireland. | Northern Ireland–History. | Americans–Northern Ireland–History–20th century. | Civil-military relations–Northern Ireland–History–20th century. | United States–Relations–Northern Ireland. | Northern Ireland–Relations–United States.
Classification: LCC D760.8.N6 T67 2021 (print) | LCC D760.8.N6 (ebook) | DDC 940.53/416–dc23
LC record available at https://lccn.loc.gov/2021038589
LC ebook record available at https://lccn.loc.gov/2021038590

ISBN: HB: 978-1-3500-3759-5
PB: 978-1-3502-5771-9
ePDF: 978-1-3500-3761-8
eBook: 978-1-3500-3760-1

Typeset by Deanta Global Publishing Services, Chennai, India

To find out more about our authors and books visit www.bloomsbury.com and sign up for our newsletters.

To Bill Riches, John Campbell and Bob Fawcett

Contents

List of illustrations	viii
Acknowledgements	ix
List of abbreviations	xii
Introduction: 'The Ties of Kinship'	1
1 'Céad Míle Fáilte': One hundred thousand welcomes!	9
2 'Uncle Sam's Stepping Stone to Berlin': The US military in Northern Ireland	21
3 'Absolute and executive jurisdiction': Policing and managing the Yanks	37
4 'If you can't see the hills': Occupying the occupiers	53
5 'My own country overrun': Irish nationalism and the American presence	77
6 'To clear this territory of such forces': The IRA and the Americans	99
7 'Developments in Northern Ireland': The Belfast consulate and the war	111
8 'Johnny Doughboy Found a Rose in Ireland': Women and the Americans	121
9 'The Dusky Doughboys': Jim Crow racism in Northern Ireland	135
10 'A testy old gentleman': David Gray, hyphenated-Americans and partition	149
11 'Ulster Had a Hand in the First Independence Day': Ulster-American revivalism and the Second World War	167
12 'Letters from Ulster': Propaganda, memory and the Americans	181
Conclusion: 'Without Northern Ireland'	199
Epilogue: 'Gray's Great Illusion'	207
Notes	211
Primary sources	279
Bibliography	285
Index	297

Illustrations

Figures

1.1	People watching members of the first contingent of the New American Expeditionary Forces	14
2.1	Children standing in front of a soldier	32
3.1	Sir Basil Brooke, prime minister of Northern Ireland, 1943–63	47
4.1	The American Red Cross Club, Belfast	55
4.2	American Soldiers and Sailors and their friends, New American Red Cross Building, Belfast	56
4.3	'Hull Warning to Neutrals', *Stars and Stripes*, 12 April 1944	60
4.4	Navy and Marine Shore Patrolmen at Londonderry railway station	65
4.5	US sailors sightseeing in the Dunluce Castle	73
4.6	The Jive Bombers swing band	74
4.7	Marine Pipers	75
5.1	Francis Matthews, Joseph Cardinal MacRory, David Gray and others	90
8.1	Dance at Kircassock House, Magheralin, County Armagh	128
9.1	'More fighting men for Ireland', *Chicago Defender*	140
9.2	American Red Cross dance held at Cookstown	142
9.3 and 9.4	2nd Battalion, 28th Quartermaster Regiment, Cookstown; October 1942	145–6
11.1	Thomas T. Wright, Scotch-Irish Society of America	170
11.2	Robert Bonner, Scotch-Irish Society of America	171
12.1	Landing anniversary	193
12.2	General Eisenhower at Belfast City Hall, 24 August 1945	197

Maps

0.1	US military bases in Northern Ireland, 1942–5	xv
0.2	USAAF bases in Northern Ireland, 1942–5	xv

Acknowledgements

Back in the old days before the knowledge of the world was a click away, I was trawling through the voluminous *New York Times* index as part of my PhD on the Republican Party and civil rights in the 1930s and 1940s. Slightly curious and slightly bored, when I arrived at 1944, I decided to see what references there were to Northern Ireland and Belfast in America's paper of record. On 25 May there was a fifty-word report at the bottom of the third column on page four, sandwiched between advertisements for a baby carriage and a dress, about the imminent execution of an American soldier, Wiley Harris, for the murder of a man in Belfast. I had a shamefully vague notion that the Americans had been stationed in my homeland during the war; indeed, in a box of family photographs was one, sadly lost, of my dad as a teenager and some of his friends posing cheerfully with a 'Yank' on a Belfast street. Curiosity piqued, my research soon revealed that the victim was a local man named Henry Coogan and that Harris was a 'coloured' soldier, a revelation which immediately complicated things and made me wonder how African American servicemen and the people of Northern Ireland responded to each other. From there the topic mushroomed, encompassing American race relations, unionist and nationalist responses to the Americans, how the government at Stormont managed the 300,000 Americans who passed through, the impact on cross-border and transatlantic politics and how it was to be remembered.

My family history is bound up in the war. My parents experienced the conflict as children; the areas of Belfast where they grew up suffered badly in the 1941 Blitz, which killed nearly a thousand people in the city. My paternal grandfather, Ernest, a father of five, lost his job at a linen mill due to 'enemy action'. A character reference from his employer, still in my Auntie Doreen's possession, stressed this as the reason for his unemployment and praised his good work ethic to help him find something else. My dad was evacuated to Fermanagh, where he harvested potatoes before making a long trek to school, experiences he rarely spoke of, beyond calling it 'slave labour', and a far cry from the images of happy evacuees with their square gas mask boxes and short trousers boarding trains for a big adventure. He loved Fermanagh, but suffered little nostalgia about his time there. He rarely spoke of the war, even to his historian son, but did recall when, as a Boy Scout, he transported a Lewis gun on his bicycle for the Home Guard, which struck me as a thoroughly unhealthy enterprise when in Belfast plenty could have found nefarious use for his cargo. As an aside, in 1950, he turned up in Berlin (his one and only trip abroad) as a Territorial Army soldier in the North Irish Horse to defend Western civilization from communism, another story tantalizingly half-told. Amid the hardships and the continued threat of air-raids in the aftermath of the Blitz, my maternal grandparents, Jean and Sam Berry, adopted a baby girl, my Auntie Jean, who represented a beacon of love and hope within the bleakness. In a time of rationing, if Sam saw a queue, he would join it, joking to my mum that there must be something good at the end of it; otherwise why would people be queuing? On VE Day, the *Belfast Telegraph* printed a picture of Boundary Street, where the Berrys lived, of children at a street party. There is some comfort in the fact that my family came through the war intact if not unscathed. My mum remains an unwitting folk historian of Belfast, but when my dad died a few years ago, his untold and half-told tales were lost. It brought to mind a saying I picked up from folklorist Bill Ferris in Mississippi about the history bound up in the lives of ordinary people: 'when an old person dies, it's like a library has burnt down'.

Every family in Northern Ireland will have its own library, with holdings both heart-breaking and heart-warming, and many who remembered the Yanks shared their memories with me. While most of these stories have not found their way into the book, I remain hugely grateful to all of those who took the time to write to me, as far back as 2011, including Éamon McGale (Omagh), Pat Grimes (Ardboe), the MacDermott family (Derry), Annie Purdy (Belfast), Michael Carvill (Bangor), P.J. McKay (Newcastle), Gerry Murphy (Newry) and Éamonn McBride (Ballymoney). I am acutely aware that each was already elderly when they contacted me and that many will have died in the intervening years taking their libraries with them; it is a source of enormous regret that I did not keep in touch with each and that they will not see this book, but I hope that their families may do.

Two other correspondents do feature, however, for their particular pertinence, poignancy and humanity. John Campbell recalled how as a seven-year-old he and his mates, making nuisances of themselves, were chased by the police from the air-raid shelter – not far from my dad's home – where Harris stabbed Coogan. Among his vivid wartime recollections, John remembered being wary of African American troops, but white GIs lived up to their friendly and generous reputation. John, who unbeknownst to us when we made contact, knew my dad; he later became a poet, novelist and chronicler of his beloved 'Sailortown'. The second is Bob Fawcett, a teenager in Antrim during the war who ran errands for African American troops stationed in the town. He befriended an intermittent sergeant who had a tendency to get busted to private, so he kept two jackets, one with stripes the other without, telling Bob, 'it saves sewing!' Bob also told me of 'less pleasant episodes', including when he heard the shots which wounded a white GI as African American soldiers sought vengeance for the killing of a comrade by US military police. He recalled, too, the sound of smashing glass one night, and his family, for reasons which will be explained, came downstairs to find an African American soldier on their living room floor. John and Bob (who died in 2012) could have little idea that their memories, perhaps dormant for over sixty years, would shed considerable light onto the experiences of African American troops in Northern Ireland. It is an honour to dedicate this book to both of them.

I have accumulated numerous debts in writing this book. Colleagues, friends within academia and experts on the period have taken the time to read portions of the manuscript when they had far more pressing matters demanding their attention. I am especially grateful to Claire Fitzpatrick and Alicja Syska, history colleagues at Plymouth, in this regard, and also to Leanne McCormick, Sam Edwards and Kris Allerfeldt, who were all kind enough to offer their insights and knowledge on chapters. I doorstepped various authorities on Ireland and the war asking for their assistance, and Brian Hanley, Brian Girvin, John Day Tully and Christopher Norton unhesitatingly offered their services. I greatly appreciate their enormously useful, and ultimately reassuring, comments. The ideas, arguments and conclusions are, of course, my own, but they were undoubtedly improved by the input of everyone who read chapters. Huge gratitude is due to Clive Moore, who has accumulated a wonderful online photographic record of the Yanks in Northern Ireland (https://www.flickr.com/photos/usani4245/), and I am enormously grateful to him for supplying many of the images which appear in the book. Very special thanks also to Jamie Quinn of Plymouth's geography department for readying these and other images for publication and for creating the maps I have used.

I am fortunate to work in such a collegial and supportive environment within the history team at Plymouth. I have benefited from the generosity of the Faculty of Arts' R-1 research fund, which has funded research trips to the States, allowed me to present the research for this book at numerous conferences over the years and granted sabbaticals in 2015 and 2020 to enable me to complete the book and articles related to it. Even as this project became much bigger than anticipated, my history colleague and chair of our R-1 research committee Professor James Daybell has remained hugely supportive, and I am very appreciative of his patience. The Roosevelt Study Center (now the Roosevelt Institute for American Studies) in the Netherlands awarded me several grants to carry out research in its holdings, and I am grateful for the support of Leontien Joost, Giles Scott-Smith, Cornelius van Minnen and Hans Krabbendam and everyone at the institute over many years. My thanks too to archivists at the Public Record Office of Northern Ireland, the Belfast Newspaper Library, the National Archives and Records Administration (Washington, DC), the National Archives in London, the American Heritage Center at the University of Wyoming and the Cardinal Ó Fiaich Memorial Library in Armagh. I am extremely grateful to Abigail Lane and Emily Drewe at Bloomsbury for their tolerance as several deadlines came and went.

I am very lucky to have a network of friends within and beyond Plymouth who, whether they realize it or not, have provided invaluable support throughout the writing process and especially in the circumstances of six months before submission, so love and thanks to Alana (and 145), Jon, Patrick, John C., Hannah, Steve, Sam, Leighton, Jim, JT, Miguel, Deborah, Gavin, Mark, Rich C., Dena and Leslie, along with my brothers Phil and Andrew, Andrew's wife Emma and my nieces Lucy and Eve. I could add many more to this list, and I hope those missing will forgive its brevity. Along with John Campbell and Bob Fawcett, I am also dedicating this book to William Riches, my undergraduate tutor at the University of Ulster, for his unwavering faith and support as I progressed from BA to MA to PhD. I genuinely could not have done this without Bill.

Abbreviations

ABC-1	American-British-Canadian Committee
AEF	American Expeditionary Force
AFIN	American Friends of Irish Neutrality
AFN	American Forces Network
AP	Associated Press
ARC	American Red Cross
ARP	Air Raid Protection
ATS	Auxiliary Territorial Service
BBC	British Broadcasting Corporation
BO	*Ballymena Observer*
BT	*Belfast Telegraph*
BTNI	British Troops Northern Ireland
CID	Criminal Investigation Division
CFU	Crown Film Unit
DGP	David Gray Papers
DJ	*Derry Journal*
DO	Dominions Office
DR	*Down Recorder*
ENSA	Entertainments National Service Association
ETO	European Theater of Operations
ETOUSA	European Theater of Operations, United States Army
FO	Foreign Office
FDRP	President Franklin D. Roosevelt Office Files (Franklin Roosevelt Papers)
GAA	Gaelic Athletic Association
HO	Home Office
IN	*Irish News*
IP	*Irish Press*
IRA	Irish Republican Army
JAGD	Judge Advocate General Department

JCM	Joseph Cardinal MacRory Papers
LS	*Londonderry Sentinel*
MO	Mass Observation
MOI	Ministry of Information
MPs	military police
NARA	National Archives and Records Administration
NEA	Newspaper Enterprise Agency
NIBC	Northern Ireland Base Command
NIBS	Northern Ireland Base Section
NILP	Northern Ireland Labour Party
NL	*News Letter*
NW	*Northern Whig*
NYT	*New York Times*
OSS	Office of Strategic Services
OWI	Office of War Information
PRO	Public Relations Officer
PRONI	Public Record Office of Northern Ireland
PSIS	Pennsylvania Scotch-Irish Society
RAF	Royal Air Force
RIO	Regional Information Officer
RN	Royal Navy
SISA	Scotch-Irish Society of America
SOS	Services of Supply
SPOBS	Special Observer Group
SS	*Stars and Stripes*
SSL	*Stars and Stripes* (London edition)
TNA	National Archives
UPL	Ulster Protestant League
USAAF	United States Army Air Force
USAFBI	United States Army Forces in the British Isles
USAFNI	United States Armed Forces Northern Ireland
USO	United Services Organization
UTV	Ulster Television
VFA	Visiting Forces Act

WAAF	Women's Auxiliary Air Force
WES	*Washington Evening Star*
WRENS	Women's Royal Naval Service
WVS	Women's Voluntary Service
YMCA	Young Men's Christian Association

Map 0.1 US Military Bases in Northern Ireland, 1942–5.

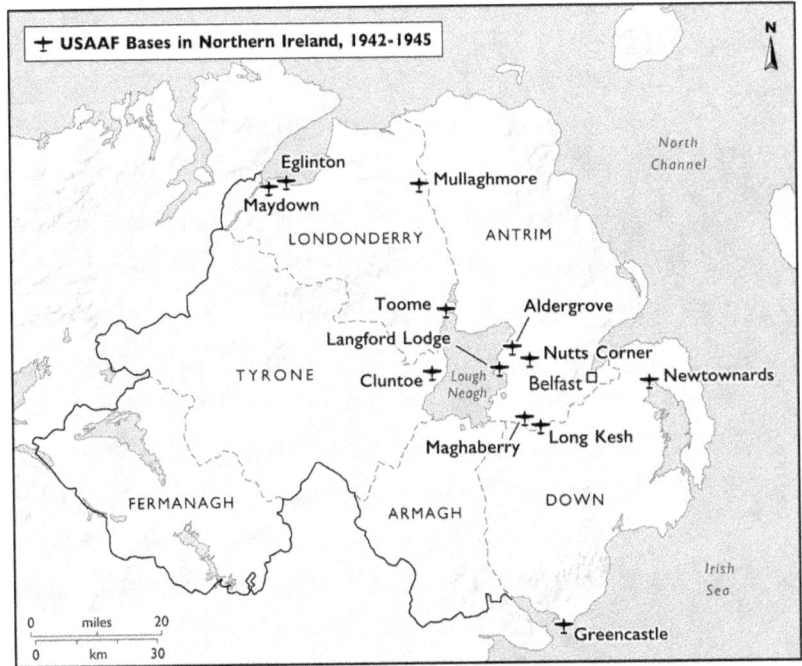

Map 0.2 USAAF Bases in Northern Ireland, 1942–5.

Introduction

'The Ties of Kinship'

On 26 January 1942, less than six weeks after the Japanese attack on Pearl Harbor, American troops descended gangways at Belfast's Dufferin Dock to become the first Doughboys to set foot in Europe since the Great War. Some 300,000 would eventually pass through, bringing their music, gum, nylons, movies and sports; not to mention their generosity, their *joie de vivre*, their charm, but also their racism, arrogance, criminality and seeming inability to hold their drink. They left Northern Ireland's people changed, but not necessarily transformed, a little less insular and conservative, perhaps, but they triggered no social revolution or lessening of communal animosities. The war and the American presence were, however, transformative in other ways as Northern Ireland's devolved government at Stormont projected an image which emphasized its Britishness, its links with the United States and its pivotal wartime role, entrenching partition but ignoring the nationalist minority in the process. At the conclusion of the conflict in Europe in May 1945, Winston Churchill described Northern Ireland as a 'faithful sentinel' which had stood by Britain's side in the darkest hours of the war, a description which closely aligned with Stormont's own assessment. When General Dwight D. Eisenhower, the Supreme Commander of the Allied forces in Western Europe, made a triumphant visit to Belfast shortly after VJ Day, he was similarly effusive, declaring that 'without Northern Ireland' the American forces could not have prepared for the invasion of Europe. An accident of geography had facilitated this indispensability, partition reinforced it and grim wartime realities ensured that it became what one writer would call the 'life-line to freedom' as the desperate struggle to protect supplies from the United States ensued.[1] Northern Ireland, or more accurately unionism, ultimately, had a 'good' war, and the Americans were absolutely central to this.

This study deals with a tangle of interlocking themes related to the American presence. As the first part of the UK to host American troops, Northern Ireland became a testing ground for solving the problems which accompanied the Yanks, but this was complicated by its very specific circumstances. For a start, it was the only part of the UK with a land border, a border with a potentially vulnerable neutral country and a country which had a territorial claim over Northern Ireland and was hostile to its very existence. Northern Ireland was riven with sectarian tensions, its government discriminated against its Catholic minority in every aspect of civic life; yet its place within the union often felt tenuous, at times unwelcome, making it quite different to the rest of the UK and superficially the last place to send American troops.

This book functions as a regional study of the impact of the Americans in the UK, one of the few of its kind, but crucially it acts also as a 'national' or 'sub-national' history, given Northern Ireland's status as a devolved region with its own government responsible for the day-to-day handling of the Americans and as a place apart within the UK (and increasingly within Ireland). It works in a number of additional ways. It is diplomatic and high history, examining transatlantic, cross-border and internal UK history from the perspectives of governments, politicians, diplomats and generals. It deals with various intergovernmental relationships, between Belfast and Washington (via the US consulate in Belfast and the legation in Dublin), Belfast and London, and Belfast and Dublin. The latter was indirect given Dublin's refusal to engage at any formal level with Belfast, while the war, and the American presence, heightened divisions between the two states. As far as the American forces and partition were concerned, the book also considers Dublin's relationship with Washington, personified by Éire's Taoiseach (prime minister) Éamon de Valera and David Gray, the American minister in Dublin. It is not a retread of the often fraught relationship between Éire and the United States during the war, which has been dealt with in numerous excellent histories, but merely how this related to Northern Ireland. This study demonstrates how unionists endeavoured to create a low-level, largely informal, bilateral relationship with the United States, based upon the welcome bestowed upon the Americans and a shared history. This was done independently of a London government which, terrified of the Irish-American lobby, preferred to keep quiet about the existence of Northern Ireland.

The war and the Americans proved politically useful to unionism as they helped to integrate Northern Ireland within the UK, and enhanced its sense of 'Britishness', while camouflaging its internal problems.[2] This Britishness was otherwise illustrated largely through shared wartime hardships, such as the Blitz or rationing, but hosting the Americans was also significant. The American presence, moreover, was often also framed in terms of the unity of 'English-speaking peoples' in winning the war and an implicit Anglo-American mission in which Northern Ireland was integral, allowing Stormont to further reinforce the province's Britishness. Yet this enhanced sense of Britishness becomes a missed opportunity to reconfigure Northern Ireland's sectarian dynamics.

It is a social history of the period, dealing with race and gender in some detail, and more tangentially with class and religion, but it is not local history, in that it does not assess the impact of the Americans in specific towns and villages, nor is it an 'any gum chum?' popular history of the Americans.[3] My earlier work on African American soldiers, one of the first academic studies of race in Northern Ireland, is revisited here, while I have tried to add something to Leanne McCormick's excellent research on women in Northern Ireland during the war. The religious conservatism of the Catholic and Protestant churches and how they handled the influx of tens of thousands of young men are discussed largely through the prisms of race and gender, but there is clearly a class element to this, relating, for example, to the 'type' of girls who associated with Americans. The Americans threatened to disrupt the centrality of religion to local life for both Protestants and Catholics, but partition and fears about the importation of a foreign and liberal culture and its attendant threat to morality via dancing, music and cinema created additional anxieties for the Catholic Church.

The political dimension to the American arrival led to unionists and nationalists quickly repurposing default positions on their respective links to the United States. Prior to the war, nationalists saw Americans as natural allies, as many were in the fight for Irish independence, and this made unionists instinctively wary of American intentions. Unionists hastily resurrected dormant links with the United States, reviving a diasporic narrative which predated the latter's revolution. This was to be celebrated uncritically, through claiming a dozen presidents for Ulster, a crucial role in the American Revolution, and the philosophical architecture for the creation of a new, and a new kind of, country. This led to what is described here as 'Ulster-American revivalism', where Presbyterians in particular highlighted the centrality of their forebears in the creation of the American republic. The paradoxes of this Ulster-American revival were obvious but scarcely addressed by its most forceful advocates; its flaws and contradictions were secondary to their contemporary political utility. These efforts also offered the hope that if Americans understood Ulster's part in their history and the fact that many had Ulster ancestry, they would be sympathetic to its battle with Éire and help offset the influence of Irish-America.

Protestants were pro-American, partly because their presence strengthened the war effort, but this also fortified the union. If nationalists were at least ostensibly anti-American, it was because the Yanks legitimized partition. The latter were philosophically hardwired to resent the Americans but at a practical and personal level found them difficult to dislike. A minority within the nationalist community saw the war as an opportunity to destabilize the state in 1942 when the Irish Republican Army (IRA)-fomented unrest was rhetorically linked to the Americans.

As will be demonstrated, Stormont's strategy was primarily to promote good relations between the Americans and the local population, but Protestants in particular. Doing so would minimize problems the Americans brought, and this would reflect well on the government and aid the war effort. American troops were, therefore, made enormously welcome by Stormont, and it must be emphasized, by both communities on the whole, and the government endeavoured to ensure that this welcome was publicized, nurtured and memorialized, while downplaying the tensions it created. Closely aligned to this were formal and informal attempts to ingratiate Stormont with the Americans, by being a good ally and indulgent host, offering a marked contrast with neighbouring Éire and constant reminders of America's historic bonds with Ulster. Sometimes, uncomfortable compromises were made with American racism and the imposition of US military justice, done so for the sake of the transatlantic alliance and the immediate need to manage a tricky domestic situation. Yet the pragmatic approach adopted, particularly by Sir Basil Brooke, served Northern Ireland well and arguably worked better than anywhere else in the UK.

The US government was represented by its consulate general in Belfast. The role of the consul, particularly Parker Buhrman from early 1942 until the spring of 1943, offers a useful perspective on Northern Ireland's domestic wartime politics. Buhrman's reports dealt with many topics and how they impacted both directly and indirectly upon the Americans, so beyond discussing responses to the troops, the impact of the

IRA campaign of 1942 and the behaviour of the Yanks, he offered assessments of life more generally, examining sectarian tensions, industrial unrest and what he saw as a lackadaisical war effort. This, hopefully, provides an additional dimension to Francis M. Carroll's history of the consulate. The pivotal American political influence was to be found, however, over a hundred miles away in Dublin with David Gray. Gray arrived in 1940 with a self-assigned brief to end partition but quickly realized that irredentism in Dublin was more of an obstacle to this than a 'Bourbon' unionist clique in Belfast. He was also acutely aware that what happened in Ireland could impact American domestic politics. He was concerned – obsessed even – with Irish-Americans, hyphenated compatriots of supposedly questionable loyalty, who he believed would work with de Valera after the war to undermine the Anglo-American alliance and inject partition into American politics. Gray made it his mission to prevent this.

The broader threads of Northern Ireland's history are essential to understanding the American presence, meaning that partition looms large. The position taken here largely coincides with the views of Bowman (among others) that partition was the only practicable, pragmatic solution to an otherwise intractable problem in 1921. For nationalists, as Bowman states, 'the price of independence was partition itself'; the British hoped that it might be temporary and portrayed it, according to Jackson, as a 'transient evil' which a subsequent Boundary Commission would render unviable, and this helped convince Irish negotiators to accept it.[4] That the border was ham-fistedly drawn to adhere to county boundaries, at unionist insistence, rather than reflect the loyalties of those, mainly Catholics, who would end up on the wrong side of it, created a sense of nationalist grievance that festered, enabling them, Bowman argues, to 'easily ignore any merits in an Ulster unionist case for *some* border'.[5] The debates which raged in Dáil Éireann (the parliament set up in Dublin by abstentionist Sinn Fein MPs in 1919), on the treaty signed with the British, focused on an essentially symbolic oath of allegiance to the British monarch rather than partition, and the reluctance of nearly half of the Dáil's members to ratify the treaty hinged on the oath. Within six months of the treaty's ratification by the Dáil in January 1922, the new Irish Free State descended into a civil war in between pro- and anti-treaty forces, eventually won by the former by mid-1923. Sectarian violence, as bad as anything seen in the 1970s, raged in Ulster and particularly in Belfast from 1920 until 1922. Amid this Northern Ireland was created by the Government of Ireland Act of November 1920 and came into existence in May 1921, and, crucially, ahead of negotiations between the British and the Dáil's representatives.[6] Northern Ireland would technically be part of the new Irish Free State but was given an opt-out, which its exclusively unionist parliament quickly and unambiguously exercised in December 1922.

It was only in the years after partition that it became a major issue in the Free State's politics and its dealings with Britain and Northern Ireland. Partition became the retrospective and unspoken original sin of the Free State's inaugurators, functioning as a rallying point for Irish nationalists both within and beyond Ireland, and something for which they believed British and unionists bore sole responsibility. In the midst of the bitter schisms within the new state, and among the abandoned Catholics of Northern Ireland who fully understood its implications from the outset, the innate wrongness of partition was something upon which all could agree. Resentment at the division of Ireland was undoubtedly genuine, but Southern nationalism was guilty of complicity in acquiescing to partition, under British pressure admittedly, compounded by being outwitted in Anglo-Irish negotiations, and agreeing in good faith to an ultimately toothless Boundary Commission. It proved easier to blame the British than admit this; thus, the idea of partition solely as a British imposition was routinely deployed as a unifying injustice and a convenient reminder of the British capacity for perfidy and was repeated frequently throughout the Second World War but particularly after the Americans arrived. Nationalists may have subsequently claimed that they were duped or coerced into agreeing to partition, but it did not alter the fact it was enshrined in a treaty that the newly independent Irish government had signed and then fought a civil war to protect, while, in 1925, the border was recognized by the Dáil. Moreover, tentative reconciliation between Northern Ireland and the Free State during the remainder of the 1920s was undermined by the election of de Valera, who opposed the treaty and railed relentlessly against partition, in 1932. The negative consequences of partition for Northern Ireland's Catholic population are beyond dispute as the new unionist government discriminated against them at every level and created mechanisms to exclude them from political life. Yet the realities of partition for Catholics north of the border sometimes seemed rhetorically secondary to the political usefulness of the existence of the border to politicians south of it. Ultimately, politicians in Dublin had simply no practical or reasonable proposals to end partition, and many, not least de Valera, realized this but persisted with strategies which might as well have been designed to foster unionist anxieties, perpetuate partition and thus further entrench the political and psychological division of Ireland.

Northern Ireland's history is not solely a prelude to the sectarian strife from the late 1960s and until the 1990s; however, Stormont's treatment of the Catholic population risked an eventual reckoning. This troubled history has, of course, been well documented, and it existed largely as a single-party, Protestant-dominated state, which, from its creation in 1921 until Stormont's collapse fifty years later, discriminated against its minority Catholic population and gerrymandered electoral boundaries to secure overwhelming Protestant representation at Stormont and on local councils. It is difficult to escape the conclusion that it defined itself, first and foremost, as Prime Minister James Craig infamously declared In 1934, a 'Protestant Parliament for a Protestant State'.[7] Brooke, one of his successors, had proclaimed the previous year that 'he had not a Roman Catholic about his own place', urging his supporters to employ 'Protestant lads and lassies'. This was both opportunistic bigotry and political expediency by Brooke, and not aberration: he repeated and defended these sentiments.[8] These are seemingly the only two quotations either man is ever associated with, offered with no other context than the bigotry of each, and they have ultimately defined in both popular and historical memory.[9] There is, nevertheless, no escaping that most members of the unionist government, Craig included, were members of, or closely associated with, the sectarian and anti-Catholic Orange Order. None of this was lost on the powerful Irish-American lobby or critics closer to home. By the 1930s, unionist attitudes towards Catholics increasingly rankled with London; however, during the war, overt anti-Catholicism from Stormont was rare, with fear of alienating the Americans providing an implicit restraint. For their part, nationalist elected representatives refused to recognize the legitimacy of Stormont or take their seats – those which could not be gerrymandered in favour of unionists – leaving Catholics with no formal political voice within the state.

Other factors in the pre-war period beyond sectarianism are vital in understanding and contextualizing the American presence. Northern Ireland's divisions were also characterized by class, even if this was not readily accepted or articulated by either unionists or nationalists, but the latter were clearly worse off, which could be blamed upon partition. The 1930s were pockmarked by sectarian violence; however, in 1932 Protestants and Catholics briefly united in protest against their shared hardships, yet this collaboration proved fleeting. By 1935, sectarian violence and troops had returned to Belfast's streets, and the metaphorical orange and green trenches of sectarianism were soon dug even more deeply. Stormont refused to genuinely reach out to the minority population and instead actively pitted the two communities against each other. Prior to 1939, moreover, Northern Ireland suffered from some of the worst unemployment and poverty and the highest infant mortality rate in the UK. Then, when war came, Belfast's heavy industry was disproportionately wracked by strikes and poor productivity, leading to considerable private criticism in London about Northern Ireland's lacklustre war effort. Disputes between London and Stormont over responsibility for defence left Northern Ireland ill-prepared for war, compounded by the assumption that it was beyond the range of German bombers, rendering Belfast virtually defenceless when the Luftwaffe arrived to devastating effect in April and May 1941.

At the start of the war, Stormont was still consolidating in the face of what unionist leaders saw as internal threats from the Catholic minority and extremist Protestant groups and external pressure from both Dublin and, more problematically, London, its nominal and often disinterested guarantor. Stormont suffered from an ongoing existential crisis over Northern Ireland's place within the union, with London's questionable commitment painfully illustrated in June 1940. As France fell, Prime Minister Neville Chamberlain tried to trade Northern Ireland to Éire in return for the latter's full participation in the war, and London attempted to coerce Stormont into settling for the best deal possible for the ending of partition. In the event, it came to nought, but London's willingness to offload Northern Ireland emphasized the union's precariousness and made fostering good relations with the Americans imperative. Serendipitously, the British return of the so-called 'Treaty ports' to Éire in 1938, in effect ensuring that it would not be dragged into any future Anglo-German conflict, actually made Northern Ireland absolutely crucial to the war effort. With the return of the ports and the fall of France leaving Britain's supply chain very dangerously exposed, Northern Ireland became the first line of defence in the Battle of the Atlantic. Éire's neutrality gave Stormont leverage in the maintenance of the union which Éire's participation in the war would have eliminated, while de Valera's rejection of the offer to end partition served to buttress Britain's often ambivalent commitment to Northern Ireland. Northern Ireland was suddenly indispensable.

Alongside analysing the American presence in Northern Ireland, I hope that this book will fill important gaps in studies of the impact of the Second World War on both the UK and Ireland, from Barton, McCormick and Carroll's works specifically on

Northern Ireland to excellent recent studies of Anglo-Irish relations, including those by Cole, Ollerenshaw and Girvin. It also dovetails neatly with historiography about the 'Emergency' in Éire and American-Irish relations, for example, Wills and Fisk's classic studies, and the work of Dwyer, Duggan, O'Halpin and others, while ideally finding a place alongside Gardiner's classic work on wartime Britain and Reynolds' definitive study of the Americans in the UK.

Terminology and sources

Terminology is chosen and used quite deliberately. 'Northern Ireland' and 'Ulster' tended to be employed interchangeably by unionists; however, by and large, here Ulster describes the province prior to partition; it is also deployed in certain circumstances to denote the Ulster of contemporary unionist imaginations, but only occasionally synonymously with Northern Ireland. 'Stormont' is used as shorthand for the government of Northern Ireland. I make a distinction between 'Ulster-Scots' and 'Scotch-Irish'. Here, 'Ulster-Scots' defines those who moved from Ulster to settle in North America in the eighteenth century and those in Northern Ireland who emphasized these links in the twentieth century. 'Scotch-Irish', essentially an American term, describes these same immigrants from the American side of the Atlantic and subsequent American-born generations seeking a link to their ancestral homeland. 'Unionists' and 'Protestants', and 'nationalists' and 'Catholics' are largely used interchangeably, while I have opted for 'Londonderry' rather than 'Derry' unless quoting. I have decided to use 'Éire' to describe the (now) Republic of Ireland, while recognizing it as a historical relic which would be anachronistic in a modern setting. Éire came into common usage after the Irish Free State created a new constitution in 1937, renamed itself 'Ireland' in English and 'Éire' in Irish, and asserted a territorial claim over Northern Ireland. 'Éire', to the dismay of Dublin, quickly became synonymous with the twenty-six counties of the former Free State in Washington, London and Belfast (interestingly at Stormont, 'Free State' generally fell into disuse with Éire usually adopted by officials), and this was reinforced by Dublin's preference for the term in diplomacy. Éire is appropriate here as it avoids confusion between the state claiming 'Ireland' as its official name and the geographical island of Ireland inhabited by two states, one at war and one neutral. Although not always used at the time, I have retained the accent in Éire throughout. I use 'Irish-American' when referring to Americans with Irish ancestry and 'American-Irish' when discussing bilateral relations between the United States and Éire. Like much else in Irish history, nomenclature is highly contentious, but I hope that whatever the imperfections of my choices I at least use them consistently. Finally, the Americans are variously referred to as 'Yanks', 'GIs', 'Doughboys' and the 'AEF' (American Expeditionary Force). As an alumnus of the University of Mississippi, I am fully aware that sensitivities regarding terminology are transatlantic. In the American South, whites resent being called 'Yanks', but the subtleties of this were lost on the British public and all Americans became 'Yanks', regardless of which side of the Mason–Dixon line they hailed from.

The bulk of my primary research was carried out at the Public Record Office of Northern Ireland (PRONI) in Belfast and the National Archives and Records Administration (NARA) in Washington, DC. Much material from NARA, unavailable online when I started my research, is now accessible via https://www.fold3.com/. I have used Fold3 extensively but not made a distinction in my endnotes between what I found physically at NARA and what I located online; they are, however, listed separately in my sources. For simplicity's sake, I have not included 'PRONI' or 'NARA' for every reference from either, rather any document with a 'CAB' (Cabinet) prefix is from PRONI and anything beginning with 'RG' (Record Group) is from NARA. Sources from either archive with a different prefix are identified as such. I examined material relating to David Gray at both the Roosevelt Institute for American Studies (RIAS) in the Netherlands and at the American Heritage Center at the University of Wyoming. The material held at RIAS is part of the Franklin Roosevelt collection (FDRP), while the David Gray Papers (DGP) are held in Wyoming. There is some inevitable duplication, but I have opted to reference one or the other collection rather than both. Other collections, such as those held at the National Archives (TNA) in London or the Joseph Cardinal MacRory Papers (JCM) at the Cardinal Ó Fiaich Memorial Library in Armagh, are identified throughout.

1

Céad Míle Fáilte

One hundred thousand welcomes!

At the visitor centre of the Lake Superior Railroad Museum near Duluth, Minnesota, is a fading newspaper clipping from 1998 reporting the death, aged 79, of an unprepossessing man, from an unremarkable town, who subsequently led a life notable largely for its ordinariness.[1] During the Second World War, however, he found momentary fame as the first GI to officially arrive in Europe. On 26 January 1967, Milburn Herman Henke, of Hutchinson, Minnesota, returned to Belfast as the guest of honour on the twenty-fifth anniversary of the moment he, the *Belfast Telegraph* enthused, 'marched into the history books' when American forces arrived in Northern Ireland.[2] Henke, now a restaurateur, always hoped to return, and Ulster Television (UTV) furnished that opportunity, flying him in for a special edition of its *Flashpoint* programme.[3] Docker Mick Gallagher vividly recalled the precise moment Henke faced the poised flashbulbs of eager pressmen: '[s]ure I remember that fellow coming off. The Americans threw cigarettes and chewing gum to us from the ship. They all looked like a bunch of cowboys as they attempted to march down the quay'.[4] General Dwight D. 'Ike' Eisenhower, Supreme Allied Commander in Europe during the war and twice a wartime visitor to Northern Ireland, sent greetings to Prime Minister Terence O'Neill, 'to assure you and the gallant people you lead of the appreciation of every American who was privileged to enjoy the hospitality of Northern Ireland during that conflict. All of us remember that experience with gratitude and affection'.[5] The arrival of Henke and the Yanks proved a defining moment in the war and eased British gloom of the previous two years, as suddenly the war appeared winnable. It also marked a turning point for Northern Ireland, fleetingly putting it on the world stage, making it absolutely vital to the Allies and marking a rare moment of positivity in its otherwise troubled history.

Churchill and Roosevelt agreed to send US forces soon after the Japanese attacked Pearl Harbor on 7 December 1941, when they met at the Arcadia conference in Washington, DC, on 23 December. This was, however, hardly unpredictable, nor, indeed, was it even a spontaneous reaction to changed international circumstances. The Americans had been building bases in Northern Ireland throughout 1941 and as early as October, Churchill privately requested Roosevelt send two American divisions, including one armoured, 'of course at the invitation of that Government as well as of his Majesty's Government', to relieve the British garrison. Churchill was forthright about the diplomatic and strategic benefits of such a move: 'the arrival of American troops in Northern Ireland would exercise a powerful effect on the whole of Éire, with favourable consequences which cannot be measured. It would also be a deterrent upon German invasion schemes'.[6] Reconciling this with America's continued neutrality was not explained, but a precedent had been set with the Americans occupying Iceland, replacing the British in June 1941, despite both the United States and Iceland being neutral, which Northern Ireland pointedly was not. On 16 December Churchill repeated his request, stating that American divisions could finish training and deter any lingering German ambition of invading Ireland.[7]

Roosevelt was reputedly wary of sending a large force to the UK, but Churchill arrived in Washington to find the president persuaded of its merits. Churchill credited Roosevelt with the idea, but General George C. Marshall, the American Chief of Staff, and Churchill's own memoir demonstrate that it originated with Churchill.[8] Both strategic and political factors prompted the decision. The strategic element was obvious, freeing British troops, allowing American troops to become battle-ready while the symbolism of Americans on European soil would be obvious to the Nazis.[9] It was, Churchill recalled, 'an assertion of the United States' resolve to intervene directly in Europe', and they wanted the Germans to be fully aware of the deployment, in the hope that the threat of an early invasion of France would tie down German divisions there that could otherwise have gone to the Eastern Front or North Africa.[10] Yet this strategic need was offset by the deteriorating situation in the Pacific, meaning that the two divisions originally assigned went there to shore up American defences. Known as *Operation Magnet*, four waves, totalling 32,000 men, arrived in Northern Ireland during the first half of 1942.[11]

Northern Ireland was already heavily militarized. With the fall of France, tens of thousands of British troops poured in to fortify the border amid concerns that Éire could be the backdoor to a German invasion of Britain. By the end of 1940, 70,000 British troops were in Northern Ireland (a number only exceeded by Americans in early 1944) on an active war-footing, blocking border roads, preparing bridges for demolition and making contingency plans to repel a German invasion of Éire. The historic connotations were not lost on nationalists, who predominated in border areas, or the troops, who viewed nationalists (and Éire) as pro-German. This created 'a state bordering panic' among local nationalists in June 1940 according to Éire's police.[12] The changed shade of khaki heralded by the Americans, therefore, relieved one set of tensions by replacing the British garrison but created another, admittedly abstract, by endorsing partition and disrupting traditional American-Irish relations; but crucially, it made an American border incursion potentially more palatable for Éire. Considered in this way, the replacement of British with American troops becomes a strategic, diplomatic and political masterstroke.

On 6 January, Roosevelt announced that American forces would go to the UK, generating speculation all over Ireland that their destination was Northern Ireland.[13] London simply informed Stormont of the decision, consulting it only about the arrangements; however, far from being insulted at seemingly being taken for granted, the unionist government delightedly welcomed hosting the Americans. Churchill summoned Northern Ireland's prime minister John M. Andrews to London, with the unionist leader telling only his deputy why.[14] Andrews (and Northern Ireland's official war historian John Blake) amplified this consultation, portraying a heroic Ulster ready to do its bit and somehow a full partner in the discussions, but despite being suddenly centre stage and indispensable, suspicion about London's motives and the security of the union lingered.[15]

In London, Andrews told the Defence Committee of the War Cabinet that he was 'most anxious that no impression should be given that we were handing over responsibility for the defence of Northern Ireland to the United States. Irresponsible or wrong-minded people might misinterpret this as the first step to handing Northern Ireland over to Éire'.[16] The Americans were replacing a substantial British garrison, but this irrational fear was probably due to residual bitterness over London's 1940 offer to end partition if Éire joined the war, accentuating existing unionist paranoia, and particularly Andrews' own. Yet there was also a concern that Irish republicans might use the situation to stage an armed insurrection, as they had in the Great War, having already committed acts of terrorism in the current conflict. Andrews' unease also reflected the persistent unionist view that all nationalists were not only disloyal but also a potential fifth column. Alan Brooke (Sir Basil Brooke's uncle and an Ulsterman), the chief of the Imperial General Staff, implicitly agreed to the retention of some British forces to handle any sectarian violence.[17] Sir Alexander Maxwell, the permanent undersecretary at the Home Office, offered explicit reassurance, declaring that 'a proportion of British troops' would stay to respond to 'civil disturbance' as 'it would be preferable if these troops were British'.[18] The last phrase implies calling upon US forces in extremis, an eventuality not discussed with America; the Americans, however, were acutely aware of Northern Ireland's divisions and had no desire and made no plans to involve themselves. Keeping some British troops, to be deployed as necessary, reassured Andrews, but the Americans' sole strategic priority remained defending all of Ireland, not policing local enmities.[19] The practicalities of the American presence were agreed by the British and American militaries, the latter in mufti, at the Grand Central Hotel in Belfast from 22–25 January.[20]

In the immediate aftermath of Pearl Harbor, Churchill tempted Éire's prime minister (Taoiseach) Eamon de Valera with an impetuous, ambiguous (but entirely sober) offer on partition, declaring it 'now or never'. Rightly suspicious, de Valera tentatively followed up the message, but Churchill denied it suggested ending partition, and nothing came of it.[21] With American troops en route to territory claimed by Éire, the Allies considered how to tell de Valera. The War Office in London proposed informing de Valera in two ways, either when it was clear that the Germans knew or when the force was no longer in danger of attack, 'whichever was the earliest', and he would be told in person. Britain wanted its representative in Dublin (in effect, an ambassador) Sir John Maffey to inform de Valera on behalf of the British and Americans.[22] The Allies were sending a clear message to a leader whose attitude towards the war Roosevelt and Churchill viewed as duplicitous, as in public he refused to differentiate between the war aims of the Allies and the Axis, even though his private actions favoured the former. He also used residual Anglophobia and coded sectarianism, usually in relation to partition, within Éire to help maintain his domestic political dominance.[23] According to Davis, sending the troops was intimately linked with existing American-Irish tensions, which Pearl Harbor merely exacerbated.[24] The *New York Times* soon suggested that the Americans were employing 'a subtle form of pressure, using Irish-American sympathy to get what Éire has thus far been unwilling to grant' – in other words, Allied access to the so-called Treaty ports, ceded by the British to Éire in 1938.[25] The troops became a public source of irritation for de Valera, and his predictable protest was predictably condemned by unionists and equally predictably welcomed by nationalists.

The United States was not wholly blind to Éire's feelings, naming the force 'United States Army Forces in the British Isles' (USAFBI). The *New York Times* rationalized this, as 'calling it the American Expeditionary Force would have likely affronted independent Éire', although this was how the US press referred to it.[26] The USAFBI, later the 'European Theater of Operations, United States Army' (ETOUSA), was activated on 8 January 1942, commanded by Major General James E. Chaney, with a subordinate force called the United States Army Forces Northern Ireland (USANIF) activated on 24 January under Major General Russell P. 'Scrappy' Hartle, pending Major General Edmund L. Daley's arrival.[27] The appointment of Daley, a Catholic of Irish descent, as commander represented another nod to the delicate local sensibilities and the hope of fostering good relations with Éire.[28] Daley, however, never arrived. He was eventually relieved of command on 7 May 1942 by Marshall, 'following a series of reports from a number of directions, all indicating an identical reaction to your method of exercising command and its effect on morale'. Added to this was the insinuation of an alcohol problem. The decision to relieve him was, Marshall explained, based upon 'a unanimity of opinion that it would be most unwise to continue you in high command', a damning indictment of any officer.[29] Hartle assumed permanent command of USANIF; Chaney was eventually recalled to Washington in June and replaced by Dwight D. Eisenhower as commander in the ETO.[30]

The recently arrived US consul in Belfast, Parker M. Buhrman, reported rumours of the impending arrival, but initially thought that Andrews' London visit concerned relations between Northern Ireland, Éire and the United States.[31] Soon, well-informed sources gave 'color to the reports that American troops might be expected at any time' as stories, 'believed to be accurate', were circulating that some British forces were leaving their barracks apparently to accommodate them. Buhrman's tone, talking of their 'alleged arrival', suggests a degree of cynicism about the plausibility of these rumours.[32] The choice of Northern Ireland, and the Iceland precedent, did not surprise some. Helen Kirkpatrick, of the *Chicago Daily News*, speculated that the bases built by the American technicians the previous year were to house US forces. She also hoped that 'Irish-American history is such that the establishment of United States troops in Ulster would have great significance for the Irish and might lead to the solution of the hitherto unsolvable Irish dilemma'.[33] The German minister in Dublin, Edouard Hempel, ascribed rumours of the Americans' imminent arrival to the fevered imaginations of journalists and, like Buhrman, was shocked at their appearance.[34]

'Where's Sgt. York?': Gangway to history

Local authorities had a day's notice to prepare for the troop ships. Beyond the greeting at Dufferin Quay, they needed to arrange road and rail transportation to enable the Doughboys to reach their billets, but these practical aspects went smoothly.[35] The *Strathaird* and *Chateau Thierry*, too large for Belfast harbour, docked in Bangor and transferred men to Pollock and Dufferin docks by tender. The hastily assembled welcome ceremony was nonetheless carefully choreographed; it was rather spoiled when, as the Royal Ulster Rifles' band struck up the 'Star Spangled Banner' to greet Henke, other Americans, having disembarked too early from a different ship, marched past.[36] 'The "first" man was duly publicised', noted an official historian; 'he was in fact about the 501st'.[37] In actuality, the first Americans arrived in Londonderry on 18 January 1942 on the damaged trawler *Albatross*, while the next day a seven-man photographic unit landed.[38] Other American fighting men arrived on 21 January, when four American destroyers docked in Londonderry, an arrangement dating back to November 1941. The Royal Navy (RN) was keen to provide an appropriate welcome but did not trust the local authorities to do this if 'left to their own devices'. The RN wanted a representative of the governor general to greet them, 'a generous sum of money' set aside to entertain Americans, the creation of 'a volunteer organisation which will help with looking after future visitors' and ideally a welcome from the King, recommending 'a really big effort' for 'what will be a tremendous event'.[39] The docking of these ships was ultimately low key and did not overshadow Henke and his comrades.

Henke was chosen at random, but his German-born father and mother with German ancestors symbolized the unity of the American 'melting pot' against a common foe, making him the ideal all-American ambassador.[40] Having descended the eleven steps of the gangway, Henke had a microphone thrust under his nose and confessed only dim awareness of where he was; he had heard rumours, but confirmation came when a British sailor identified the Irish coastline.[41] Henke vowed to 'give the Germans hell' and quickly became a minor celebrity, receiving some 300 items of fan-mail.[42] These glamorous newcomers, with their dapper uniforms, self-assurance and sunny dispositions, had an unquestionable novelty value and raised the morale of a war-weary population, but, declared the *Northern Whig*, they 'are not the jaunty boasters and cocksure war winners you might expect'.[43] One was called Goering, and another, Silas Johnson of South Dakota, 'with the brightest smile of all, was a young man, a full-blooded Indian, one of the Sioux race'.[44] George Fleming, a former professional baseball player, decided 'winning the war was more important job than finishing top of a baseball league'.[45] One docker shouted, '[w]here's Sgt. York?' at a soldier wearing a cowboy hat and boots; another docker offered to sell him a horse.[46] News of the exotic arrivals spread, and the crowd of curious onlookers increased throughout the day. The Associate Press's (AP) Rice Yahner reported that for security reasons there 'was no flamboyant welcome', but the realization that troops were American 'brought townspeople streaming to the curbstones' to watch.[47] Singing 'Marching Through Georgia', the Americans headed to their barracks (Figure 1.1).[48]

Figure 1.1 'Northern Ireland. People watching members of the first contingent of the New American Expeditionary Forces as they march to their trains after disembarking from transports'. Library of Congress.

They were largely Midwesterners, mainly of Scandinavian or Polish ancestry, with some Germans like Henke, but the unionist press, especially the *Whig*, was keen to canvass some Irish-Americans on partition and Éire's neutrality and secure a useful soundbite.[49] The best the *Whig* managed was a soldier with Irish ancestry, who declared: '[w]hy should Mr de Valera worry what is going on in Northern Ireland as long as [the Americans] don't land in his country?' As far as de Valera, partition and neutrality were concerned, concluded the *Whig*, 'most of the soldiers did not understand it, and had no desire to be enlightened'.[50] The Yanks may not have known where they were going until land was in sight; however, they had sufficient sense to avoid anything resembling an opinion on local politics.

Andrews officially welcomed the Americans and Roosevelt to the fight against 'ruthless barbarianism', calling it an endorsement of the 'principles of human liberty for which the British and American peoples stand'.[51] In what became a central theme in the unionist narrative about the Americans, he quickly acknowledged the 'close kinship that has long existed between the United States and Ulster'.[52] He then underscored this at Stormont, noting the 'many bonds that can never be broken – bonds created by kinship and language, identity and outlook, and a common faith in democracy', and the many Ulster immigrants who settled in America. The Americans, he continued, would soon enjoy 'the warm-hearted hospitality that is so characteristic of our people'. As almost all nationalists abstained from Stormont, opposition was largely limited to two Northern Ireland Labour Party's (NILP) MPs, Harry Midgley, who later joined the ruling Ulster Unionist Party, and Jack Beattie, an anti-partition Protestant, with Beattie welcoming the Americans 'on behalf of the working class people of Northern Ireland'.[53]

Belfast's triumvirate of unionist newspapers, *Belfast Telegraph*, the *News Letter* and the *Whig*, all intimately linked with Stormont, along with the unionist *Londonderry Sentinel* added their voices to Andrews' effusive welcome. The *Telegraph* proclaimed that prior to Pearl Harbor Roosevelt 'was never neutral in mind or heart'.⁵⁴ It also immediately contrasted the huge and positive press coverage in Britain and America with 'the Dublin papers, cramped no doubt by the Censor's blue pencil, [who] have dismissed the historic event in less than thirty lines'.⁵⁵ The *Whig* gloated about de Valera receiving 'flattering comment' in German propaganda, which praised his 'manly attitude' in maintaining Éire's neutrality.⁵⁶ The *Sentinel*, like Andrews, lauded Ulster's 'many ties of kinship ... with the great Republic of the West' and Ulster immigrants' role in building it.⁵⁷ It heralded 'a new chapter' between the British Empire and America, and 'especially this most loyal patron of it in Ulster'.⁵⁸

Nationalist newspapers, primarily Belfast's *Irish News* and the *Derry Journal*, invariably took the opposite stance, condemning the arrival as an endorsement of partition and an insult to Ireland's nationhood and supporting de Valera's protest. The *Journal* questioned the need to send the troops and slammed 'the mushroom show of specious regard that the Six County Ascendancy has now conceived for the American Republic'. De Valera, it continued, would have been 'false to the historical and indefeasible principles on which Irish nationhood is based' had he remained mute.⁵⁹ Nationalist politicians were similarly scathing, comparing the Americans, among other things, to the Germans occupying Norway.⁶⁰ If anything, the isolationist and Anglophobic Irish-American press reaction was more intemperate. Doubly blindsided, first by Pearl Harbor and now American troops in Northern Ireland, it resorted at times to anti-Protestant bigotry and argued that American troops were needed in the Pacific.⁶¹ Newspapers in Éire largely ignored the arrival, publishing only the Americans' official communique, de Valera's protest and no editorial comment.⁶² Many Irish-American leaders were privately furious and considered public protests about the landing, but ultimately thought better of it, as, reported Robert Brennan, Éire's minister in Washington, 'in the present mood of the public, would do more harm than good'.⁶³ This was wise; Pearl Harbor demonstrated Irish-American patriotism to the United States and, as Wills notes, the severance of lingering sentimental ties with Ireland and emphasized the primacy of the 'American' dimension of their dual identity.⁶⁴ Indeed, anything other than unflinching patriotism could have reignited anti-Irish and anti-Catholic nativism within the States.

'Indefensible as aggression against small nations': de Valera's protest

Having claimed the entire island as the 'national territory' with Éire's new constitution of 1937, de Valera faced the harsh reality that his irredentism rendered him precisely no jurisdiction beyond the border and a national aspiration which America felt no obligation to respect or even acknowledge. The Americans' arrival reinforced extant realities, which de Valera, for all his bluster about partition, was keenly aware of, but it necessitated a response even if only to maintain his fictive leadership of all of Ireland. Thus, as 'everyone knew', Britain had imposed partition, 'despite the expressed will of the Irish people', and 'to partition the territory of ancient nation is one of the cruellest wrongs that could be committed against a people'.⁶⁵ This was at best a highly simplistic reading of partition, compounded by his repeated tacit, and practical, endorsement of it. As Dwyer notes, he reinvented the acrimonious debates in the Dáil over the Anglo-Irish treaty 'to generate the impression that partition had been a central issue in the dispute', when it was basically irrelevant. He had even been the first person in the Dáil to suggest the necessity of partition, while his suggested changes to the treaty 'included the partition clauses verbatim'.⁶⁶ Now, however, he offered analogies with 'the former partition of Poland' and Abraham Lincoln's desire to maintain the American union, 'even at the cost of fighting one of the bitterest civil wars in history'.⁶⁷ He complained that his government 'had not been consulted', that Northern Ireland's existence was contrary to Woodrow Wilson's principle of national self-determination and that partition was 'as indefensible as aggressions against small nations elsewhere', which the Allies sought to end.⁶⁸ He could do little else than protest, even if it invited American ire. Yet he also revealed his implicit hostility towards unionists, claiming that American troops were propping up a 'Quisling government': comparing his supposedly fellow countrymen to Nazi collaborators was unlikely to induce them to join an all-island state.⁶⁹

It was not an official protest, which would have involved delivering it to the American legation in Dublin and triggering a formal diplomatic incident, as de Valera was canny enough to realize that this escalation would have only antagonized the Americans further and incited diplomatic, economic or military pressure. He maintained to the American, British and Canadian representatives in Éire that his statement was not a protest, but according to the Canadian minister, John D. Kearney, he 'felt obliged' to say something lest 'silence be interpreted as acquiescence in the status of partition'. De Valera also feared, he noted, that the American presence would worsen American-Irish relations.⁷⁰ De Valera's rationalization was hardly persuasive and ignored the possibility it might provoke violence across the border. Discomforting realities exposed the emptiness of his, and others', irredentist rhetoric and publicly demonstrated that Northern Ireland was patently not part of the 'national territory' and the Americans needed not even his tacit consent to enter it. His powerlessness, however, would have been exacerbated by silence, so he had to say something even at the risk of angering the Americans.⁷¹ It did, however, provide a pretext for continued claims on Northern Ireland during the war.⁷²

David Gray, the American minister in Dublin, certainly regarded it as a protest, believing it is a cynical face-saving ploy, and even suggested imposing sanctions on Éire as a response.⁷³ Fisk argues that the protest 'achieved no purpose and was not expected to', but de Valera underestimated American resentment, especially the inference of moral equivalency between the Allies and Axis.⁷⁴ Roosevelt, reported Brennan, stated that 'he was sorry Mr. de Valera had made the statement he did but, of course, he knew he had to make a protest if only for appearance sake'.⁷⁵ As if to underline this, as de Valera made his protest, an American pilot in the Royal Air Force (RAF) having become lost violated Éire's neutrality by landing at Dublin airport. He was permitted refuel and depart when theoretically he should have been interned.⁷⁶ This confirmed to Gray that the protest was to maintain face rather than born of any real outrage.⁷⁷ Roosevelt viewed the protest with disdain. Brennan informed

Sumner Welles, undersecretary at the State Department, that Irish people viewed it as 'official sanction of the partition of Ireland', but the Americans were unmoved.[78] Welles, according to Brennan's conveniently self-regarding interpretation, 'regretted misunderstanding which had arisen over Expedition. Action was not at all intended as sanction or otherwise of partition. It was merely movement of troops in accordance with needs of war'. Welles was also shocked at the insinuation that it was the prelude to an invasion, calling this 'preposterous' and 'inconceivable'.[79] Invasion rumours created an existential crisis for Éire; Roosevelt, at Welles' suggestion, assured de Valera that the Americans had no intention of invading, but facetiously told colleagues that 'he only wished they would'.[80] The secretary at Éire's Department for External Affairs, Joseph Walshe, demanded that Brennan continue to 'emphasise essential historical, moral unity of Ireland' and 'Britain's immoral and undemocratic position there' and that he repeatedly stress the American presence was seen by nationalists as endorsing partition.[81] Walshe claimed to Éire's minister in Vichy France that the Americans had realized they had made 'a mistake in flouting the moral claims of the Irish people to their sovereignty over their whole territory'.[82] This is unlikely. Had the Americans actually believed they had made a mistake, they would not have repeatedly flouted this 'moral claim' by sending a total of 300,000 troops to Northern Ireland and continue sending them long after the possibility of a German invasion had evaporated.

Andrews savoured the chance to assail de Valera and could very effectively contrast Northern Ireland's steadfastness with Éire's neutrality. The 1920 Government of Ireland Act, he argued, meant that Éire and de Valera had lost any rights regarding Northern Ireland; he also blamed partition and cross-border tensions on de Valera, presenting the perfectly reasonable judgement that '[i]t is they who, by their policy and actions both before and since the outbreak of war, have widened the gulf'. 'No less danger of invasion', Éire, he concluded, 'may choose to stand aside. But Northern Ireland is in the fight for freedom, and intends to see it through'.[83] Sir Frederick James Simmons, the 75-year-old unionist Mayor of Londonderry, left his sickbed to simultaneously welcome American officers and berate de Valera's 'impudent protest'. Such a complaint 'from a neutral source' was in 'utterly bad taste', and Britain was simply 'adhering to the bargain' made in 1920.[84] 'Apparently', he declared sarcastically, 'the new order will not depend much on Mr de Valera's help'.[85] At a civic reception in the city's Guildhall, he greeted the Americans in Gaelic, a language generally shunned by unionists, with the Irishman's welcome of 'Céad Míle Fáilte' (a hundred thousand welcomes).[86] He assured the Americans that they were 'welcome guests' and could ignore the protests. Simmons' effusive welcome would have rankled with the city's Catholic majority, as his position relied upon rampant gerrymandering, which ensured unionist domination; he refrained, perhaps conscious of the irony, from talking about shared values of liberty and democracy.

In a letter to the *Sentinel*, Professor Douglas Savory, an English-born Unionist Westminster MP and historian, methodically deconstructed de Valera's argument, declaring its misrepresentations 'so extraordinary that it was hard to believe that it was authentic'. Analogies between countries conquered by the Nazis or the American Civil War and the 'voluntary severance' of Éire from the UK stretched credulity, and he concluded that the protest was 'so extravagant that it scarcely deserves to be taken seriously'.[87] Valid or not, no one in Dublin challenged criticism by these three senior unionist figures, and, in any case, none of this was reported in Éire's press, under the guise of strict, but selective, censorship. Besides, Éire's political establishment's interaction with unionists rarely went beyond pillorying Stormont, partition and 'Orangism'; thus, even challenging Andrews, Simmons or Savory would tacitly acknowledge their state's existence, if not its legitimacy. As Murphy argues of the 1930s, 'irredentist sentiment, devoid of any real understanding of the Northern Ireland situation, was ardent and universal in the Southern state', and global conflict clearly did little to change this.[88] De Valera's protest gave unionists a chance to attack him and Éire without fear of a rebuttal which relied on partition having much traction in the States. Yet this bravado masked the reality that Northern Ireland was geographically a vital British territory, and technically the Americans no more needed Stormont's permission to station troops there than they did de Valera's. Willing pawns they may have been, but unionists were pawns nonetheless.

This was illustrated when Savory failed to secure a public British condemnation of de Valera at Westminster.[89] Savory also sought support from the Dominions Office, but the official line was, in effect, to leave well enough alone: '[t]he United Kingdom government did not and do not consider it necessary or desirable for them to issue any reply to that statement. By refraining from doing so, they do not consider that they are in any way ignoring the position of Northern Ireland.'[90] This reiterated the stance taken in 1937, when the Irish Free State adopted its new constitution claiming the whole island and adopting 'Éire' and 'Ireland' as the state's official names. The British government, the Dominions Office stressed, denied that this 'involves any right of territorial jurisdiction' over Northern Ireland, and 'this remains the position'.[91] A public reiteration would have been as welcome as the private one was reassuring, but it did point to London's pragmatism whereby sensitive ongoing and informal military cooperation with Éire was preserved, with the prospect of greater future assistance. A crowd-pleasing official outburst from London could have jeopardized this.

Some Irish-American congressmen weighed in. The *Whig* reported Republican Joseph J. O'Brien of New York's support for the landing as he urged de Valera to act in his own self-interest as 'if Britain and America should fall, Éire will be at Hitler's mercy'. Éire should remember its traditional friendship with America, O'Brien argued, and overlook its historical grievances with Britain for the war's duration.[92] The *Derry Journal* offered an alternative, with another Congressman demanding troops meet the crisis in the Philippines as 'Britain had 3,500,000 men armed to the teeth', with the subtext that political rather than military needs dictated sending troops to Northern Ireland.[93]

'One of those small little trouble spots of the British Empire': Reactions to the arrival

There was plenty of positive newspaper and newsreel coverage in the States.[94] This was accompanied by reports that the arrival had been leaked and that 'the entire city of Belfast knew the Americans were coming'.[95] It was clear to the press that the Americans would garrison Northern Ireland, train there, protect Ireland from German invasion and eventually invade Europe. The AP hoped Éire would view the American troops 'with considerably more tolerance, if not favour', than they would British.[96] As for the constitutional issue, the *Washington Evening Star* editorialized: '[i]n theory, the whole island may be one nation, yet in terms of practical fact it is and long has been two separate and distinct communities', each with discrete loyalties.[97] The *New York Times* counselled caution, as American conscripts had 'set foot upon a troubled land', and somewhere without conscription. Northern Ireland was 'one of those small little trouble spots of the British Empire. It is industrial, mountainous and Tory – a British controlled foothold on the island of Ireland'. It was 'a strange country . . . proud and loud in its declarations of fealty to Empire' but plagued by unemployment and in desperate need of war work.[98] This was a gloomy, but largely accurate, assessment of an impoverished, insular and divided society; it challenged the indomitability projected by Stormont and warned the Americans of the problems they could confront.

Other American publications were highly critical of Éire. America's neutrality, only recently and involuntarily ended by Pearl Harbor, was forgotten as its press demanded that Éire unilaterally abandon its own neutrality. The *New York Herald Tribune* condemned de Valera's 'gratuitous piece of impertinence'. It claimed that Éire had been 'treated very tenderly in this war', noting that '[t]he devastating raids on Belfast appear to have gone unrebuked in Éire, but when the United States troops landed in what is certainly de facto belligerent territory, the protests came in battalions'.[99] *The Nation*'s entire issue of 31 January 1942 dealt with Ireland. Americans', and *The Nation*'s, previous backing of Irish independence was invoked, and if Éire remained neutral then it 'must inevitably forfeit American sympathy and support and take its place, when the war is over, with the anti-democratic nations at the peace table'.[100] In the next edition, an article entitled 'Irresponsible Neutrality' condemned de Valera's 'churlish' attitude and warned Éire that 'old grievances blind it to present dangers'. Partition, it argued, would only end with the agreement of Northern Ireland's Protestants, 'unless it is prepared to wage civil war and kill, imprison, or deport 600,000 recalcitrants'.[101] Not only was Northern Ireland absolutely vital to the war effort, but it was also 'very probably responsible for Britain's continued existence', which fortified Britain's commitment to it, and therefore partition.[102] The irony of the United States entering the war only when attacked, and now demanding Éire join without this provocation, was highlighted by Irish commentators.[103]

The practical consequences of the American presence were of greater interest to ordinary Protestants and Catholics than the constitutional, although its political significance was apparent to both. A June 1942 Mass Observation report found that Protestants believed that the Americans brought victory closer but also saw them 'almost unconsciously as a strengthening of the forces of order against the constant fear of Catholic (Nationalist) trouble'. Catholics, on the other hand, were 'largely antagonistic, although it is only a minority who are strongly so, many individual Catholics are thoroughly in favour of the Americans'.[104] The Ministry of Information (MOI) reported the following year that 'with a few honourable exceptions . . . [t]he welcome given to the Americans has been overwhelming on the part of the Unionists and Protestants – those loyal to the British Crown and resolved to maintain the British connection'.[105] Buhrman's analysis tallied with the MOI. Both communities were welcoming, and 'the initial general hospitality accorded to our troops was greater than could be expected'; if anything, it was a little too fulsome. This cut across sectarian lines, as 'on its face the troops were received with goodwill only by the Unionist group, actually they were received just as heartily by Nationalist groups'.[106] Buhrman observed the Belfast press closely in making his conclusions and fretted endlessly about the Americans' behaviour and the ever-present fear that local problems would eventually involve them, as either victims of or converts to violent Irish republicanism, this was, therefore, relatively rare positivity about the impact of the arrival of American troops.[107]

Unionists, from politicians to the press, proffered the idealized loyal, homogeneous Ulster of their imaginations, doing its bit for the war, free of the inconvenient realities of a divided society with a disenfranchised and rightly disgruntled minority. The unconfined joy of unionists and the feigned outrage of nationalists were reserved very much for the first American deployment, however. There was still interest when the next batch arrived in March, followed by an armoured division and the first African American troops in May, but even when they flooded back in late 1943 the celebrations that greeted Henke were absent.[108] Both sides had made their points, but equally the US military did not want or need the fanfare, and its presence soon became normalized, and, besides, there was more important war news from elsewhere.[109] Northern Ireland adjusted to a new wartime routine in which the Americans became a familiar presence, a routine punctuated by industrial unrest but never directly threatened again by the conflict. Its comparative security, particularly after the Battle of the Atlantic, meant that Northern Ireland would become something of a diplomatic and strategic sideshow.

2

'Uncle Sam's Stepping Stone to Berlin'

The US military in Northern Ireland

'We're going to regret every damn boat we sent to Ireland', recorded General Dwight D. Eisenhower angrily in his diary on 30 January 1942: '[d]amn 'em, I tried, but I don't wear 45s. So the hotshots can sneer at me'. He at least succeeded in reducing the numbers sent but cursed the fact that vital transport 'could have taken a bunch of anti-aircraft to Australia. It now lies in the dock. Hell'.[1] At the war's end 'Ike' visited Belfast and fulsomely praised Northern Ireland's wartime contribution and hospitality to American soldiers, but his initial fury was understandable in military terms. He believed, and the facts bore him out, that the immediate strategic and practical need for American troops was the increasingly desperate situation in the Far East, and the symbolism of Americans in Belfast undermined the war effort in this theatre. Yet, symbolic or not, to Roosevelt and Churchill the arrival demonstrated a commitment to victory on both fronts, and while few in number, the troops created the likelihood of a second front in Western Europe, and this relieved a modicum of German pressure on the Soviets. Roosevelt and Churchill realized that the troops' geopolitical importance greatly exceeded their intrinsic military value, even if Eisenhower did not.

Henke's disembarkation formally began the American deployment, yet it was long in the making, predating Pearl Harbor by almost a year, involving Anglo-American liaison (with only tangential consultation with Stormont) and political and diplomatic sleights of hand by Roosevelt. Roosevelt's pro-Allied stance increased exponentially after France's surrender and his re-election in 1940, and friend and foe alike believed that 'if' America entered the war was being supplanted by the inevitability of 'when'. This was amplified after he signed the Lend-Lease Act in March 1941 granting aid to Britain and exchanging American destroyers for British bases in the Caribbean and elsewhere. To Roosevelt's critics, this represented provoking the Axis to manufacture a crisis obliging the United States to join the war. To his domestic supporters and the British, fighting alone from Dunkirk until the Germans invaded the Soviet Union in June 1941, he was the last hope for rolling back Nazism, maintaining democracy in Britain and restoring it in Europe. By 1941, a de facto Anglo-American naval alliance existed in the North Atlantic, with the Americans garrisoning Iceland, replacing the British and Canadians, to protect convoys but without technically violating their own neutrality. Lacking Éire's ports, Northern Ireland was a logical potential hub for the US

Navy if America went to war; therefore, arrangements were needed in anticipation of this. This could be done under the guise of Lend-Lease, maintaining the convenient fiction that preparations were solely for British benefit, but if American ground and air forces were deployed, Northern Ireland would be ready to accommodate them.

Proposals for US bases began as early as January 1941 and talks continued initially until March, with the ABC-1 (American, British, Canadian) agreement.[2] This made several recommendations, including creating the US Special Observer Group (SPOBS) in London and a British Joint Staff Mission in Washington to pool ideas and resources.[3] It was also agreed that if Britain had to shift troops from Northern Ireland to bolster the Far East, then American forces would replace them, including taking over Londonderry's naval base.[4] US representatives visited Londonderry in late April, and by May increasing Anglo-American naval cooperation led to secret discussions formalizing US use of bases in Northern Ireland and Scotland.[5] These bases used Lend-Lease materials to construct destroyer and flying boat facilities in Londonderry and Lough Foyle, respectively, while Belfast was to be a repair base.[6] An official stricture reflected their sensitivity: 'Washington has emphasised the vital importance of keeping these projects secret until news of them is officially released by the President.'[7] The Americans were constantly updated (learning, for example, that the Belfast blitz had slowed progress), and the bases were unquestionably for eventual American use.[8]

By June rumours in America claimed that the bases had been, or were about to be, built.[9] Both the British and Undersecretary of State Welles unconvincingly dismissed his assertion.[10] The 1940 Republican presidential candidate, Wendell Willkie, met Roosevelt and suggested American bases in Northern Ireland and Scotland would more effectively defend shipping than those in Iceland. Willkie was a maverick and rare internationalist in a largely isolationist Republican Party, which remained justifiably suspicious that Roosevelt was determined to drag America into the war.[11] Arthur Krock of the *New York Times* insisted the idea was Willkie's, despite it emerging immediately after his meeting the president.[12] The following day's front page reported 'US technicians and laborers are in loyalist Northern Ireland', rather undercutting Krock's analysis and rendering further denials pointless.[13]

Roosevelt had brushed off accusations that these Americans worked for the British with his approval but stressed their legal right to do so. His typically casual response to criticism, however, masked his strong suspicion that his actions were illegal, privately telling US Catalina flying boat pilots sent to train the RAF in Fermanagh, for example, that 'if Congress finds out, I will be impeached'.[14] Almost immediately the British announced officially that US technicians were indeed in Northern Ireland. Roosevelt's strategy was potentially risky as, regardless of increasing pro-Allied American sentiment, stiff isolationist opposition remained and the news heightened isolationist misgivings. Republican Senator Burton K. Wheeler declared that their presence had 'been an open secret that for several weeks'.[15] Furthermore, one technician claimed he worked for the Navy Department, not the British, and was compelled to go, telling Wheeler:

> [H]e was not just an ordinary workman making a contract with the British Government. In effect, he was a member of the [US] armed forces. He was ill

and did not want to go, but he was given no choice. While ostensibly he was to be attached to the American Embassy in London he was really assigned to build a base in Northern Ireland.[16]

Another isolationist Republican, Senator Robert Taft, claimed knowledge of the plan weeks before Willkie's remark and that it would release half a million British troops and put a similar number of 'American boys into the British Isles'.[17]

The American public were not the only people kept in the dark. An unnamed British official recalled a summons to 'a hush hush conference held behind closely guarded doors' where he was 'introduced to some very pleasant quaintly dressed, drawling voiced gentlemen'. It quickly became clear that they 'were representatives of the US forces on the look-out for sites for depots and installations the required magnitude of which fairly captured the imagination'.[18] Andrews had some knowledge, shared with a few colleagues, but, as noted, neither his input nor his acquiescence was required by the British and Americans. It was June before Stormont received details, and soon a meeting of ministers and officials chaired by Sir Basil Brooke, Minister of Commerce, and attended by British military figures and a senior American naval engineer discussed war construction work.[19] The British and Americans at least recognized that work within Northern Ireland required Stormont's assistance, meaning that public relations and security were devolved to a degree.[20]

Official war historian Blake regards the meeting as useful, as Stormont felt involved and consulted, while 'the Americans were enabled to grasp more thoroughly the constitutional position of Northern Ireland within the United Kingdom'.[21] Thus, the unionist perspective on partition and differentiating Northern Ireland and Éire was impressed upon the Americans. Unoffended by no prior consultation, Stormont wholeheartedly embraced the scheme and devoted considerable energy and resources to it.[22] Unionist sentiment invariably favoured the notional bases, with the *Sentinel* welcoming Willkie's statement and Andrews pledging to 'do everything possible to facilitate the proposal'.[23] The *Sentinel* condemned Republican isolationists' 'public utterances [which] jeopardise the lives of Ulster people, because they direct the attention of the Nazis to an American activity'.[24] The *Sentinel* criticized Taft for comments about 'this phantom naval air base' and conflation of Éire and Northern Ireland. It condemned his indiscretion as provocative as it drew the attention of the Axis legations in Dublin while ignoring the lack of discretion from any other quarter.[25]

Éire's inevitable complaint did not come until October and was couched in the politest of terms but assumed that the United States would 'show consideration and respect for the very special position, generally acknowledged, which the Irish Government occupy in regard to the territory'.[26] The message was ignored.[27] Brennan soon stridently demanded an official explanation from the State Department. 'The Partition of Ireland', he declared, 'was effected and is being sustained against the expressed will of the great majority of the people of Ireland and that the restoration of the integrity of the national territory of Ireland' was the goal of 'Irish people everywhere'.[28] The reference to 'Irish people everywhere' was, of course, a veiled threat about the Irish-American vote. Welles refused to even acknowledge the 'very special position' asserted in the earlier memo, and his response demonstrated the reality of Northern Ireland's sovereignty and American disinterest in Éire's grievances.[29] He replied matter-of-factly that Brennan's enquiry related 'to territory recognized by the Government of the United States as part of the United Kingdom' and was 'obliged to suggest that the inquiry in question should be addressed by the Irish Government to the Government of the United Kingdom'.[30] Roosevelt annotated his copy with 'very good'.[31] This was a precursor to protests about American forces arriving in January 1942, and the reference to the Irish-American lobby was a recurring theme in Éire's diplomacy and nationalist complaints.

The technicians were, then, theoretically employed by the British under Lend-Lease; therefore, it was not strictly a violation of American neutrality. Northern Ireland's ports, primarily Londonderry, were essential to protecting Atlantic convoys, and this was the Americans' strategic priority.[32] Unable to use neutral Éire's ports, Londonderry was the Allies' gateway to the Atlantic and the most convenient base to combat the German U-boat threat, making fortification of the city's port, as well as Lough Erne in County Fermanagh, an absolute necessity[33]. The Royal Navy had already begun work at Lisahally and the old dock at Mulville near the city, but on 12 June 1941 the UK government signed a contract with a New York construction firm enabling American technicians to take over and expand these projects.[34]

The first 500 technicians arrived in Londonderry via Scotland at the end of June, crossing the Atlantic on a Canadian troopship.[35] Supposedly a secret, their clothes and accents made them difficult to conceal. Indeed, the technicians, reportedly recruited from the Pacific North West's lumber regions, wore, according to the US press, 'the gaudy checked shirts and the high-laced boots of the American lumberjacks'.[36] The *Telegraph* commented: '[t]hey are a colourful lot, their yellow jerkins, multi-coloured shirts, and green corduroy trousers attracting much attention in the streets'.[37] This made blending in tricky and in reality, little effort was made to camouflage their presence. Pictures appeared in local papers, while Robert Montgomery, an actor serving as assistant naval attaché at the US embassy in London, inspected a project, illustrating that neither the British nor the Americans were trying to hide the bases or America's role in building them.[38] A further 400 technicians arrived in July, with both the local and the American press helpfully reassuring readers that none had ancestors 'of Axis or pro-Axis descent'.[39] The technicians were told not to talk to the press; they were 'as closed as clams', according to the *Telegraph*, which also wondered if they were actually building a naval base, speculating that they would soon be assembling tanks and planes.[40] The *Telegraph* did conclude, nonetheless, that they were not under military control. In September, however, an American journalist met uniformed technical personnel (indicated by their insignias), who maintained they were volunteers, on their way to London.[41]

Although supposedly civilian volunteers, there is no doubt that, as part of America's preparedness programme, they would be ready as America joining the conflict became increasingly likely. The *New York Herald Tribune* noted that the Londonderry base was 'nominally' for British use but easily transferable to the Americans.[42] The 1,000 or so technicians, supervised by their own engineers, were supplemented with 3,000 local workers, and the huge project was largely complete, including rebuilding Lisahally dock, building a ship maintenance base, a radio station and ammunition depots, by January 1942.[43] It was to many of these bases, built by their countrymen, that US troops were sent.[44] If the bases were insufficient evidence of America's war-footing, more was discovered by a civilian working in a warehouse full of American uniforms in Londonderry.[45] When the US Navy eventually arrived, settling in could prove difficult, but it was still preferable to their previous posting. According to one American, 'Londonderry, a stronghold of strict Irish Presbyterians, offered bluejackets [US sailors] slight recreation on the Sabbath, but seemed like Coney Island after Reykjavik; and the green Irish countryside was heaven compared with the barren wastes of Iceland'.[46] That said, the *Telegraph* reported in March that technicians were leaving because of the weather; the Americans were still a long way from either Coney Island or heaven.[47] Londonderry, codenamed 'Base One Europe', remained the main American naval base in Europe throughout 1942.

American indiscretion, which went far beyond individual loose-lipped servicemen, periodically caused concern, with the perception that the US military preferred boasting about its achievements than maintaining security. Prior to Pearl Harbor this bravado was highly provocative; afterwards, it was potentially extremely dangerous. The British press marvelled at American ability to erect facilities in double-quick time; British officials, by contrast, worried about their almost equal capacity to brag about this ability, ignoring the decorum necessitated by wartime security. It made little difference in one sense as the German minister in Dublin had already reported the Londonderry base to Berlin in August 1941.[48] The Royal Navy had complained in June that news coverage 'was just asking for air attack on Londonderry and Lisahally, and mine laying approaches to Lough Foyle'.[49] This concern was further illustrated with the official opening of the Londonderry base in 1942, with a detailed *Telegraph* article noting that it 'wasn't on the map' a year before.[50] Buhrman reported that ministers had 'sharply criticized' this publicity as 'a direct invitation to bombing'. The American (and British) authorities' decision to publicize it, without consulting Stormont, Buhrman continued, was viewed as needless incitement barely a year since the Belfast blitz. Buhrman added that this exposure circumvented censorship rules and endangered Londonderry's people.[51]

Similarly, in February 1943, *Stars and Stripes* detailed the work of the Lockheed Corporation at Langford Lodge aerodrome, again drawing criticism from the local authorities, who, according to Buhrman, suggested that a base in America within range of German planes would not be publicized.[52] He commented that they attributed this to 'our exaggerated publicity complex, and to the instability of the American public which apparently requires this sort of publicity to keep up its morale'. He linked it directly to the earlier coverage about Londonderry and strongly advised that American propaganda pay more attention to local sensibilities.[53] Arguably, Anglo-American actions in 1941, from employing an American firm and workers to the publicity about the bases, were a deliberate provocation to the Germans, inviting an attack only months after the Blitz, which – if Americans were killed – could pull the United States into the war. In theory, moreover, workers could have been recruited without controversy from, say, Canada or elsewhere in the Commonwealth.[54]

Special Observer Group: Preparations

In April 1941, the War Department sketched out a proposed deployment to the UK, the 'Rainbow-5' plan, anticipating sending some 87,000 troops, with 26,300 going to Northern Ireland.[55] General Chaney was appointed to head SPOBS in May and, based at the US embassy in London, monitored the UK and assessed America's needs if it joined the war. Chaney had arrived in the autumn of 1940 and after the failure of the Blitz and believed that Britain would not be defeated.[56] He made his first visit to Northern Ireland in July 1941 and estimated a 36,000-strong American garrison soldiers, an increase on the recommendation in the earlier 'Rainbow 5' plan.[57] Members of SPOBS inspected again in September and October, especially anti-aircraft provision, and advised the construction of facilities under Lend-Lease 'as soon as practicable'.[58] One of Chaney's subordinates, Lt. Col. Homer Case, visited Dublin hoping to secure bases should America become a belligerent, amid Anglo-American fears of invasion through Éire. Gray informed him that the bases would not be forthcoming, exacerbating worries that neither Éire nor Northern Ireland was adequately prepared for invasion.[59]

Ireland's importance to America's war effort was emphasized when a British officer addressed SPOBS on 19 December 1941, stressing that German-occupied Ireland would have U-boat bases to attack the Atlantic and be a staging ground to invade Britain. This justified sending the first major contingent of American troops to Northern Ireland and paralleled the thinking of Chaney, who, two days before, had again recommended that troops go to both Northern Ireland and Britain.[60] On 2 January 1942 the War Department informed SPOBS that American forces would arrive as part of *Operation Magnet*. This had been agreed by Roosevelt and Churchill during their first wartime meeting in December 1941 when they decided that the Americans would garrison Northern Ireland, as Chaney had advised, allowing British forces to shift to North Africa. An initial force of 14,000 men became 4,100, and the remainder was redirected to the Pacific.[61] The Americans were also earmarked to provide fighter cover against future German bombing, initially shadowing the RAF; however, pressures elsewhere saw this amended in October 1942 to using Northern Ireland for training only.[62]

The logistics of readying Northern Ireland fell to the Office of the Assistant Chief of Staff, known as G-2, under the auspices of SPOBS. Headed by Case, activated on 8 January 1942 and headquartered at Wilmont House in south Belfast, it handled the practicalities of the American presence, from press relations to censorship. Case was, however, very conscious that 'the security problem was complicated by religious and political intrigue', both from the IRA and the German legation in Dublin, and the belief that Northern Ireland was infested with spies.[63] The advance guard of eighteen officers and eighteen enlisted men arrived, like the technicians before them on a Canadian troopship and in mufti, docking on the Clyde on 19 January. Most of the officers headed to London and the enlisted men to Glasgow to be fitted out in civilian clothes. As the American military's subsequent history of their forces in Northern Ireland noted, the Yanks were hardly inconspicuous: 'it would not have required the instincts of a Gestapo to sense something unusual at the sight of eighteen American youths all wearing new clothes of British design and walking heavily in United States Army service shoes'.[64]

Despite its many virtues, Northern Ireland was, the American official history noted, 'not a good training area'. Because as much land as possible was dedicated to agricultural production, there was insufficient space for manoeuvres for either the Americans or the British. In addition, the terrain 'was especially unsuitable for exercises which required that heavy vehicles leave the roads, due to spongy soil, peat bogs, lowlands and marshes'.[65] American tank crews, therefore, found conditions difficult, with one commander stating that even tops of the hills were boggy. One journalist noted, rather presciently, that 'the country actually resembles that of Normandy which the Germans found excellent for tank warfare'.[66] Anglo-American manoeuvres carried on regardless, with the first major exercise occurring in March 1942 and others, sometimes including Canadians and even General Władysław Sikorski's Poles, in the summer. Training and large-scale American manoeuvres continued until D-Day. [67]

One of the war's most famous American units – the First Ranger Battalion, better known as 'Darby's Rangers' – was formed in Northern Ireland during the summer of 1942. Impressed by the Royal Marine Commandoes, Major General Lucian Truscott proposed a similar unit to General Marshall, who agreed.[68] Truscott put Major William O. Darby in charge; he then recruited suitable candidates from other units and began training at the old Sunnylands military base in Carrickfergus in June. The Rangers took their name from a unit from the French and Indian (or Seven Years') War, 1745–63, rather than the Pennsylvania Scotch-Irish Ranger units of the American Revolution.[69] Darby was the consummate diplomat, liaising closely with civilians, and rewarded with his first citation for merit in July for his 'tact and demeanour, which contributed much towards the exceptionally pleasant relations existing between the American troops and the citizenry of Northern Ireland'.[70] The Rangers departed for Scotland and were among the first Americans to see combat in occupied Europe during the disastrous Dieppe raid of August 1942. They served in North Africa and Italy but most famously scaled the cliffs of Pointe du Hoc in Normandy on D-Day. Darby was killed in Italy on 30 April 1945. The German surrender in the country had been agreed the previous day and came into effect on 2 May, making Darby one of the last casualties of the campaign.[71] Of the original 500 Rangers, only 87 survived the war.[72]

'Closing the ring': Aircrew and aerodromes

Northern Ireland also proved vital to the development of wartime American air power. There were aerodromes dotted around the country, but, flying boat squadrons in Fermanagh aside (manned by the RAF rather than Americans), these were for training, assembly and repair rather than staging combat missions.[73] Much of this infrastructure had to be built from scratch. In March 1941, and without explicit reference to the Americans but perhaps with a nod to its tardy preparedness, Churchill pressurized Stormont to 'accelerate the completion of certain aerodromes', which the cabinet vowed to do.[74] The Americans saw the possibility of needing air bases during planning in 1941 and that summer outlined their expected requirements to the British, which may have prompted Churchill's note. The most important facility would be Langford Lodge, some twenty miles west of Belfast on the shores of Lough Neagh. The site was designated as a repair centre and was given priority over all other construction in Northern Ireland by the ministries of Labour and Home Affairs; it was built in secret and within four months, rather than the planned six, by August 1941.[75] The base was the ultimate responsibility of the Ministry of Aircraft Production in London, but this 'could have made little or no headway with the help and guidance of the authorities in the province', according to Blake.[76]

In May 1942, the War Department signed a contract with the Lockheed Overseas Corporation, and almost exactly a year after Chaney's initial visit, Langford Lodge was completed and handed over to the US Army Air Force.[77] Bombers flew from either the States or Canada (via Iceland or Prestwick in Scotland), were given final checks at Langford Lodge and then flown to East Anglia, the hub of the Allied air campaign. Smaller planes such as fighters were un-crated and assembled at Belfast docks before taking the short flight from Sydenham to Langford Lodge for completion.[78] The proximity of Belfast's port to an airfield made it ideal, as an American officer recalled: 'the problem was to find a port in the United Kingdom where there were facilities for the aircraft to be flown almost directly from the ships. This scheme was first tried in Belfast and proved successful. By this method thousands of man-hours were saved'.[79] Langford Lodge had some 2,600 civilian Lockheed technicians and included a seaplane facility on Ram's Island in the lough. It reduced the strain on similar facilities in England and was reasonably safe from German bombing.[80] The VIII Army Air Force began arriving in late 1943 when Langford Lodge and other aerodromes came into service, and, by 1944, around 20,000 US personnel were training at Long Kesh, Langford Lodge, Toome, Greencastle, Cluntoe, Maghaberry, Mullaghmore, Eglinton and Maydown, all of which were transferred to the Americans between July and December 1943.[81] Combat crews would rest here after missions or train the new recruits.[82] When the invasion of Europe began, operations were reduced; Langford Lodge closed in August 1944 and was eventually handed back nearly a year later, formally ending the American presence. Northern Ireland's contribution was demonstrably vital in the air war over Europe.

Aircrew faced more peril than any Americans in Northern Ireland. Prior to Pearl Harbor American volunteers ferried planes from Canada, timed to land between dusk and dawn, and with a single red light acting as a beacon.[83] Around 140 quite inexperienced United States Army Airforce (USAAF) aircrew died in accidents, some having negotiated the transatlantic trip only to crash on arriving or flying blind to airfields surrounded by hills and mountains.[84] The two most serious crashes involved B-17 Flying Fortresses. On 2 October 1942, B-17 41-24451 departed Newfoundland destined for Prestwick; however, the rookie crew became lost, crashing into Slieveanorra Mountain in County Antrim, killing eight of the ten onboard.[85] A few days before D-Day, B-17 42-97862 en route from Newfoundland to the Nutt's Corner airfield in Antrim crashed on Belfast's Cave Hill, killing all ten crew. In 1991, a local man found a gold ring near the crash site; he discovered that it had belonged to Staff Sergeant Lawrence Dundon and eventually returned it to his widow. The story inspired the film *Closing the Ring* (2007), directed by Richard Attenborough.[86] Another serious crash involved a B-26 bomber, 41-18150, which went down on a training mission over the Mournes in April 1944, killing all five crew.[87] The dead from all three planes were initially interred in the American cemetery at Lisnabreeny in East Belfast, and locals created simple memorials at the crash sites. Not every incident ended in disaster; after a non-stop flight from the States and a forced landing in Eden, near Carrickfergus, the local Women's Voluntary Service (WVS) fed the ten crewmen as they awaited pick-up.[88] Eight parachutists bailing out of a stricken plane caused a mildly comedic response in Fermanagh in January 1944. Brooke recorded that the Home Guard mobilized to pick-up the airmen initially unsure whether they were Allied or German. Some of the Home Guard brought their rifles, while instructing their wives to put the kettle on, as Brooke noted, 'they said no matter who it was they would probably want tea'. Identified as Americans, the airmen were duly plied with tea.[89]

Ireland's border was hugely complicated to police at ground level, and it was just as tricky to prevent Allied planes straying over it or landing in neutral Éire. Aircrew landing Éire should have been interned for the duration of the war, but this almost never happened to Americans. The first test of this occurred two days after their arrival in Belfast, when, as noted in Chapter 1, an American piloting an RAF Hurricane landed at Dublin airport and was refuelled and sent on its way.[90] The State Department and Gray pressured Éire to release their personnel, hinting that American public opinion would not tolerate the internment of its airmen. Éire's authorities were hugely cooperative, even without Gray's unsubtle threat, provided this cooperation remained secret. The diplomatic charade concocted to avoid internment involved crews claiming that they were on training, or non-operational, rather than combat (operational) missions, and were lost or suffered engine trouble. Éire's authorities allowed planes to refuel or took crashed crews to the border or exercised virtually non-existent security at the Curragh internment camp outside Dublin.[91] The most serious incident occurred in January 1943, when General Jacob Devers and three other generals crash-landed in County Galway when travelling from North Africa to London on a clearly operational flight. The general's party wined and dined with Irish army officers before being delivered to Fermanagh, but this took Gray's intervention after Hempel got wind of the crash.[92] One crew was unaware that they were to claim to have been on a non-operational flight, yet even they were released.[93] An exception to the general rule of not interning Americans was Roland Wolf. Serving with the RAF, he was interned in November 1941 but absconded after Pearl Harbor only to be returned to Dublin for violating his parole and jeopardizing arrangements between the Allies and Éire.[94]

'Don't argue religion; Don't argue politics': GI guidance

The Americans trudging towards their billets in January 1942 were accompanied by much speculation on either side of the border that their mission extended beyond simply defending Northern Ireland. The obvious conclusion was that they would invade Éire, either to repel a German invasion or to seize the Treaty ports. Buhrman reported the gossip: '[i]t is common talk ... not only in the American army itself, but among the general population that the purpose of the American Army in Northern Ireland is to take over the whole of Ireland'.[95] The president emphasized that the Americans had no intention of invading Éire; however, hints of invasion reminded de Valera of continued Rooseveltian displeasure at his outwardly uncooperative neutrality and were a mischievous diplomatic ploy to foster paranoia in Éire. Invasion was certainly considered by the American military, and seemingly not just to repel the Germans. A high-powered American delegation consisting of presidential emissaries Harry Hopkins and W. Averell Harriman, as well as General Marshall, visited US troops in April 1942. Back in Washington, Hopkins reported that the Americans could be in Dublin 'in seventy minutes' if the Germans violated Éire's neutrality.[96] The British and Americans recognized privately that the latter's forces might have to 'move into South [sic] Ireland for the defense thereof', something diplomatically difficult, if not impossible, for the British to do.[97] Éire's armed forces made the same calculations and were split between those on its southern coast – ready to face the Germans – and those on the border – to resist the Allies if necessary.[98]

Liaison between Britain and Éire's militaries had already tacitly accepted that if the Germans invaded, then the two would cooperate, and the same was true of the American garrison. Even with a German invasion, the historical connotations of British troops crossing the border would have been hugely problematic; therefore, having the Americans poised to assist Éire made much more sense.[99] Yet contingency plans considered a unilateral American invasion with an altogether more sinister edge, including the brutal suppression of any opposition. The US military attaché in Dublin reported that Éire's generals reckoned on holding out for forty-eight hours against the Americans.[100] The intelligence officer of the 1st Armored Division argued that an invasion would confront only 'token resistance' from a 'poorly equipped' military, fighting mainly 'to satisfy honor'. This might not, however, subdue the country, and guerrilla warfare was anticipated; therefore, 'military justice must be swift, certain and harsh', and resistance crushed. This included placing priests under surveillance and no fraternization with the population because 'under these conditions the SOUTHERN IRISH are the most treacherous people on earth'.[101] This was highly alarmist analysis, possibly based partly on Britain's experience in the Anglo-Irish War, but it suggested that the worst-case scenario involved conquest and subjugation. The 'American Note' of February 1944 demanding the removal of the Axis legations in Dublin triggered an invasion scare in Éire, and its armed forces were put on high alert; however, there was no prospect of the Americans invading, and invasion rumours were largely manufactured by de Valera for domestic political consumption.[102]

There was no avoiding that the Yanks were in a contested land, and the original arrivals' boots had barely scratched Belfast's damp cobbles before they were being asked their opinions on Irish politics. A little belatedly, in June 1942, Major Boyd Shriver, the Americans' adjutant general in Northern Ireland, produced 'A Few Tips' for distribution to all servicemen. This marked the first formal attempt to help US personnel understand their surroundings, with the warning that local divisions were none of their business. Some troops received similar advice on the way over, so this was for those not yet briefed on the peculiarities of their new posting. By this point, the third landing had taken place, and instructions not to talk to newspapers about local politics had been largely heeded. 'You are now stationed in Ireland', Shriver began, before listing various presidents and famous Americans of Irish descent, then trying to contextualize Northern Ireland geographically and politically ('it is part of Great Britain').[103] 'The Irish Free State, officially called Éire' was neutral and independent, although many of its citizens enlisted with the British. 'And now, frankly', he continued, 'here are a few good tips which will help make your stay in Ireland a pleasant one'. He stressed: '[d]on't forget you are a visitor in a foreign land. The Irish that have gone to America have been a credit to their homeland; let us be a credit to ours'. Americans should keep 'an open mind' about Ireland, not be critical of its customs, and remember that the Irish were well-informed about America 'because they helped to build it. So don't brag'.[104]

Then came the crucial part: 'Ireland has its religious and political differences, just as the United States or any other free country has. Those differences don't concern you. Prejudice and politics have never concerned the American fighting man. We are fighting side by side, regardless of race, creed, or social background, for a common purpose – the defeat of Hilterism.' Engaging in religious or political discussion hindered the American mission and 'the relationship between Great Britain and Ireland does not concern America'. If Americans '[l]isten more than [they] talk', then needless offence could be avoided, and they should always remember that they represented all America stood for.[105] A necessarily general overview based on some questionable assumptions, Shriver was unconcerned with the subtleties of Irish politics, making no reference to political factions, denominations or why Ireland consisted of two states. It was sufficient to stress that the historical origins of these divisions were irrelevant to their job, and the best approach was ordering Americans not to talk about them (Figure 2.1).

The impulse behind Shriver's 'Tips' was expanded into the *Pocket Guide to Northern Ireland*, published in October 1942, one of many American pocket guides distributed in various theatres of the war and the first in the United Kingdom.[106] This thirty-seven-page booklet attempted a potted history of Ireland's divisions and customs and sound advice on how, and how not, to behave. Too late to influence the first wave, now mostly departed for North Africa, its counsel would be useful when the Americans eventually returned. A similar pamphlet had already been distributed to British troops, which viewed Northern Ireland's population as largely homogeneous and loyal, and while the American version offered at least some nuance, its analysis of thorny questions relied upon fairly broad generalizations.[107] The *Guide* adopted an informal, colloquial tone and, as Kelly argues, recognized that its audience was young men, with an average age of about nineteen, who had likely never been away from home before, certainly not travelled abroad but had now been plonked into 'a culture both alien and familiar'.[108] It emphasized sidestepping local tribal disputes, but it also stressed not squandering people's goodwill through poor behaviour: '[i]t is common decency to treat your friends well; it is a military necessity to treat your allies well'.[109]

There were 'two Irelands', with the Shamrock, St Patrick's Day and the colour green attributed to Éire, whereas Northern Ireland 'treasures its governmental union with England'. It added nine Revolutionary War generals to the ubiquitous signatories of the Declaration of Independence and presidents of Ulster stock. The booklet recognized that many soldiers had Irish ancestors, but it recommended 'two excellent rules of conduct for the American abroad. They are good rules anywhere but they are

Figure 2.1 'Children standing in front of [a] soldier, Ulster, Ireland, 1942'. Photo by David E Scherman/The LIFE Picture Collection via Getty Images. The soldier is Milburn Henke, the first American to officially disembark.

particularly important in Ireland: (1) Don't argue religion; (2) Don't argue politics.'[110] 'Irish history', it suggested, 'is endlessly complicated', a dazzling insight with which the locals would doubtlessly have nodded in agreement.[111] The *Guide* offered tips about the climate ('damp, chilly, rainy'), the geography, history – both recent and ancient – currency and so on. It also dealt with border politics, noting that Éire's neutrality might seem strange 'when the grave issues at stake in this war are considered'. It acknowledged de Valera's desire for a single state but argued that most people in Éire wanted an Allied victory.[112] Despite this, the Axis legations in Dublin, and the potential for enemy eavesdroppers crossing the border, meant 'Éire's neutrality is a real danger to the Allied cause'.[113] Interestingly, it ignored the recent IRA campaign and its rhetorical threats against the Americans.

The *Guide* paraded various hackneyed stereotypes; Ulster folk were 'serious minded', hardworking and 'exceedingly thrifty', due to their Scottish roots, but it recognized the economic dimension in a poor country. It offered guidance on pub culture and the avoidance of poteen, bemoaned the lack of nightlife, Sunday opening (or lack thereof), and warned against 'even mild profanity'. As for religious divisions, Protestants and Catholics tended not to socialize, and the Americans' job was not to bring them together.[114] Boasting was to be avoided, for example, claiming that the Americans won the Great War, and respecting the British fighting man was encouraged because 'Hitler wants you *not* to get along.'[115] Americans should remember that they were much better paid than their British counterparts and civilians, so '[d]on't be a spendthrift. Don't be a dope.'[116]

A Short Guide to Great Britain, published in 1943, also recognized that Irish-American soldiers might recall ancestral injustice. It warned that it was 'No Time to Fight Old Wars':

> you may think of the English as persecutors of the Irish, or you may think of them as enemy Redcoats who fought against us in the American Revolution and the War of 1812. But there is no time today to fight old wars over again or bring up old grievances. We don't worry about which side our grandfathers fought on in the Civil War, because it doesn't mean anything now.[117]

Some individual Yanks tried to make sense of their posting. In 1944, Keith T. K. Pitzer wrote and illustrated a booklet entitled 'And They Called It Ireland', describing it as 'a caricatured portrayal of an American soldier's life in Ulster', complete with cover drawing of a GI trudging through rainy countryside towards a Nissen hut. It was 'To the Irish – begorrah!' and 'respectfully dedicated because they have done so much to make us feel at Home – away from home'. Pitzer wanted to 'make the booklet contain information about Ireland which normally would take a soldier ten letters to write home', calling it an 'unpersonalized diary' of life in Ulster.[118]

This was all good advice, but how much it was heeded is another matter. The Yanks avoided making political statements which could be then published in the local press and steered clear of sectarian disputes. Squabbles with British soldiers and attitudes towards women proved harder to police, but the *Guide* put the American military on record regarding expectations of its soldiers (and created a bureaucracy to police this) and publicized it both within Northern Ireland and in the States, featuring in *Stars and Stripes* and the *New York Times*.[119] The *Times*'s report focused mainly on the elements regarding Éire, noting its populace's support for the Allies but warning of the dangers of its neutrality and cross-border security.[120] *Stars and Stripes*, being a soldiers' publication, was more interested in its advice about women, but the idea of 'two Irelands' and pub arguments involving, according to the *Guide*, 'not only pig-stealing but actual treason' were also highlighted.[121] The booklet also attracted de Valera's attention, and he took exception to the claim that Éire's neutrality was detrimental to the Allied cause.[122] The guidance was timely. As discussed elsewhere, August to October 1942 saw four killings by Americans (two civilians, a British soldier and an African American GI), a spike in brawling with the British, an upsurge in IRA violence, in which both the terrorist group and unionist papers attempted to involve the Americans, and Cardinal Joseph MacRory's resurrection of the earlier nationalist protest. Buhrman was concerned about his compatriots' behaviour generally, even without the complex local context, and he believed that ordinary GIs would be inevitably dragged into Northern Ireland's difficulties, so the *Guide*'s sensible counsel was to be welcomed. When the Americans returned the following year, each was armed with the *Guide*; the problems and solutions it identified were unchanged, but they were to be played out on a much larger scale.[123]

The vast majority of American troops left in the autumn of 1942 to participate in *Operation Torch*, the Allied invasion of North Africa; the bulk of the air force went to East Anglia with only a small portion remaining.[124] In July 1942, the Americans reduced their command structure from a full-fledged Base Command to a Base Section; in December, this was further reduced and re-designated as the 'Northern Ireland District of the Western Base Section'.[125] Andrews confessed that he had 'no idea' the Americans were leaving but wrote Hartle of his 'great pride' in welcoming the Americans and forging strong ties with the United States. Hartle thanked Andrews for his 'fine friendship' and declared himself 'a loyal supporter of Ulster and its hospitality'.[126] The year 1943 was perhaps the quietest of the war for Northern Ireland. The Americans had largely gone, and the air-raid threat was negligible; the ports of Belfast and Londonderry remained busy, but the Battle of the Atlantic was all but won by May. Most of the forces there were British yet with little likelihood of a German invasion of Ireland, even this command, British Troops Northern Ireland (BTNI), was disbanded. The rapid American departure may have taken Andrews by surprise, but Brooke was fully aware that they would be returning and in much greater strength; however, this time he had readied the groundwork. If the first deployment was about preventing or resisting a German invasion and relieving British troops for other theatres, then the second was solely focused on the liberation of Europe. The resumption of *Operation Bolero* from late 1943 was smoother for several reasons. The careful preparations laid down by the military authorities in liaison with Brooke were easily and speedily reactivated, while victory in the Atlantic – to all intents and purposes – allowed more troops to be transported more quickly.[127] Northern Ireland Base Section (NIBS) was reactivated in October 1943, commanded by General Leroy Collins and subdivided into four districts: in Belfast, Ballymena, Portadown and Omagh.[128]

Upon their return, alongside the *Guide*, the Americans distributed 'The Day Ulster Became Uncle Sam's Stepping Stone to Berlin', an eight-page pamphlet from the *Telegraph* reprinting stories and pictures from the newspaper commemorating the American presence.[129] It described 'the murky January morning that grew into a day to remember', which '[i]f it was a thrill for Ulster folk, it was no less a thrill for the new arrivals'.[130] The first anniversary celebration, '[t]he most brilliant military spectacle to be staged in the British Isles since the outbreak of World War II', was covered in detail, accompanied by pictures, and others of GIs, including African Americans, and one of Eleanor Roosevelt's visit in November 1942. It also included a warning not to brag or underestimate the locals and to remember why they were fighting.[131] In December, the American Forces Network (AFN) broadcast a fifty-minute radio programme entitled 'Welcome to Northern Ireland' to aid the newcomers' acclimatization.[132]

By early 1944, there were some 100,000 Americans in Northern Ireland, training in almost every part of the country and for almost every kind of warfare, with tank and infantry divisions, paratroopers, service troops, the navy and the air force all present.[133] The US top brass put in appearances, with Eisenhower making a flying inspection visit in April and General George S. Patton, also in April, greeted at a parade in Armagh by soldiers batting inflated condoms into the air during his speech.[134] The Americans' departure was even more swift, and clandestine, than their arrival. By May, they were moving to disembarkation points in southern England and seemed to disappear overnight.¹³⁵ The *News Letter* reflected on VE Day that Belfast Lough had contained 'the largest concourse of American ships ever seen in a United Kingdom port' but almost emptied in a single day.¹³⁶ On 15 June 1944, NIBS once again became the North Ireland Base District, West Base Section, and by early July the last American troops were going directly from Belfast to France, bringing an effective end to the US Army's stay.¹³⁷ The MOI's assessment of the Americans in June 1942 was equally appropriate exactly two years later:

> [i]t should be made perfectly clear, however, that in view of the extraordinary internal difficulties in Ulster, the American occupation of certain strong points has been carried out with a noteworthy lack of friction. No one could have done what the Americans have had to do without generating some antagonism and bad talk. The amount, in this case, is much less than might have been anticipated.¹³⁸

3

'Absolute and exclusive jurisdiction'

Policing and managing the Yanks

As an American soldier awaited execution for murdering a civilian in 1944, Northern Ireland's governor, the Duke of Abercorn, under public pressure to intervene, asked for cabinet advice on broaching clemency with the US military. The cabinet had little to offer: 'if this were a case in which the Northern Ireland authorities had jurisdiction, the governor would be recommended to exercise the prerogative. In the circumstances it is thought that His Grace might feel disposed to intimate this to the United States army authorities informally'.[1] This was as much as the cabinet could do. London, and therefore Stormont, had willingly ceded criminal jurisdiction over American personnel with the Visiting Forces Act (VFA) in 1942, even where British civilians were involved, leaving Stormont powerless in cases such as this. There were many good reasons for this approach, but it illustrated the difficulties in managing the American presence, further aggravated in Northern Ireland by additional complexities absent elsewhere.

From the outset, the unionist government understood the importance of creating a good impression, even flying the American flag at Stormont on special occasions.[2] Brooke, in particular, recognized the political capital in contrasting Northern Ireland with Éire as well as being an exemplary host. These efforts, led by Brooke, were largely successful, although it meant underplaying some problems the Americans brought, including crime, while making an uneasy accommodation with other issues, notably segregation, and ceding legal jurisdiction over American troops to achieve this. At worst, particularly in serious criminal cases, Stormont was a bystander, but it also established mechanisms making the American sojourn as peaceful as possible and, while there was undoubtedly serious disruption to life, handled this commendably. It did so, furthermore, despite the latitude officially granted to the Americans by London. The American military knew that troops had to behave, but it essentially had free rein over them, only involving the local authorities where sensitivities or practicalities dictated. Stormont responded pragmatically regarding archaic local attitudes – for example, Sunday opening of cinemas was amended, if not entirely abandoned. As importantly, Brooke created a hospitality system giving Americans plenty to do, with structured activities, from dances to visiting local homes, helping to keep the Yanks out of trouble. Its success was testament to Brooke's organizational skills. The public's broadly positive perception of the Americans made Stormont's task easier, with obvious caveats around dating, drunkenness and nationalist antagonism.

'As wide a jurisdiction as practicable': The law and the Americans

The VFA of July 1942 exemplified the discretion granted to the Americans and the contentiousness of criminal jurisdiction. The Home Office hastily tried to develop British policy as the AEF was mid-Atlantic. This urgency, and the insistence that American service tribunals had exclusive jurisdiction, was hampered by the unavailability of American officials to discuss the tribunals' scope or crime generally. In lieu of this, the Home Office wanted an ad hoc policy 'to prevent incidents occurring which might embarrass future negotiations', revisable when the Americans provided greater clarity. Such were the political sensitivities that the British permitted the Americans the freedom they demanded, but there remained discomfort over murder, rape and manslaughter committed against British civilians.[3] The Home Office passed this advice to Stormont.[4] Northern Ireland's Attorney General, John MacDermott, noted that Stormont, with its limited jurisdiction, would not be a party to whatever the Americans and the Home Office agreed, despite having a greater immediate interest in this than elsewhere in the UK. This was, MacDermott explained to colleagues, for three reasons: firstly, regarding Northern Ireland's 'internal jurisdiction', where the Americans were concerned. Secondly, he anticipated a higher proportion of Americans in relation to the population. Finally, the local political context was potentially hugely problematic due to the 'the presence of a subversive element and the sharp differences in political opinion make a vigilant and careful administration of the law a matter of outstanding importance'. MacDermott believed, therefore, that granting American courts-martial 'as wide a jurisdiction as practicable', but retaining a 'valve' to have trials in civil courts 'where expedient', best served the public interest.[5]

Initially, American service tribunals had jurisdiction over all crimes committed by Americans except rape, murder and manslaughter of non-Americans.[6] The VFA, however, willingly relinquished jurisdiction over American personnel, who would face courts-martial rather than civilian courts even for crimes committed against British citizens. Foreign Secretary Anthony Eden at least ensured that courts-martial involving civilians would be public.[7] MacDermott discussed the bill in cabinet in June 1942. Briefed by London, he identified its key component as 'the withdrawal ... of any criminal jurisdiction' over American personnel, giving the Americans 'an absolute and exclusive jurisdiction' over their men. He again advocated retaining some ability to prosecute Americans, used judiciously and pragmatically, if local feelings ran high and the Americans saw the benefits of a civilian trial.[8] MacDermott's analysis was good, but even if the American military recognized the virtue of public trials in capital cases, these remained courts-martial, binding civilians to military procedures. Furthermore, controversial judgements gave Stormont no recourse, for example, if a court-martial judgement contradicted an inquest after a civilian death or if justice was not seen to be done, including the perception that sentencing was too severe. From the perspective of Anglo-American relations, not hauling Americans before British civilian courts also avoided diplomatic discord and negative publicity in the States but it threatened to create frictions between Yanks and civilians.[9]

Concessions were additionally problematic as rape was a capital crime under US military law, potentially carrying the death sentence, but not in British law. The death penalty, although available in the UK, Northern Ireland included, was used comparatively sparingly, whereas the American military more routinely enforced it during the war, often inviting accusations of racism. There was logic to American jurisdictional demands. It reflected suspicion of the ability of the British and other foreign legal systems to treat Americans fairly, yet its rationale transcended mere nationalistic prejudice and judicial insularity. The purpose of military justice was maintaining discipline and morale, rather than a civilian concept of justice; therefore, as American conscripts were an involuntary army, and permanently on duty, they had to be subject to American military, rather than British civilian, law.[10] The Americans were aware of the sensitivities this created, warning that 'this arrangement imposes an obligation upon all unit commanders to see that our own military law is promptly and efficiently enforced' and cases are prepared 'with meticulous accuracy' to avoid any inference of undue leniency.[11]

The extent political priorities took precedence over legal ones was confirmed shortly after the VFA's passage when the Lord High Chancellor, Viscount Simon, confirmed to MacDermott that the 'project is not the Lord Chancellor's but comes from the Foreign Office'. He declared that without the 'diplomatic considerations' he would be 'very much opposed to any surrender of criminal jurisdiction on British soil', but the Americans were insistent. He saw, however, considerable merit in MacDermott's call for flexibility and communicated this to the Foreign Office.[12] This deference is a good example of Lilly and Thomson's 'imported context' whereby 'judicial culture is brought in from the outside, a process not unlike the importation and imposition of cultural hegemony by a colonial power', and this was evident in the UK during the war.[13] Northern Ireland assumed a particular importance in this regard as the first place to host the Americans, seeing the first court-martial for the killing of a civilian, the first British soldier killed by an American, the first convictions for the manslaughter of civilians and the first racial killing within US forces. The VFA gave Stormont little option beyond deferring to the Americans in each case, but the Americans acknowledged the public relations value of open trials after civilian deaths, where justice could be visibly served. Yet discrimination against African Americans showed how American military justice reflected its civilian counterpart, and Stormont and London were essentially powerless to object. As with every aspect of the American presence, Northern Ireland's sectarian divisions further complicated law enforcement. With nationalists ostensibly viewing the Americans as an illegal occupying force, crimes against the minority could be particularly problematic and conceivably trigger sectarian conflict. This context made the political implications of prudent management, good policing and careful jurisprudence even more important.

The British had practical concerns about policing. The US military warned officials that conscription would mean that, according to Stormont's understanding, 'the proportion of criminals' in the American population 'will be reflected in the ranks of the American Army' and that the American military police (MPs) lacked 'the training, experience or toughness' to handle these criminals.[14] Consequently, a Federal Bureau of Investigation (FBI) 'posse' would accompany American forces, but plainclothes 'G-men' could only be permitted if they worked 'in the closest co-operation' with local police. The police could, for example, arrest and return deserters (a particularly contentious area), but this would drain already strained policing resources.[15] It seems unlikely that actual G-men ever arrived, but the army's Criminal Investigation Division (CID) was present and investigated crimes, in cooperation with local police, with the former interviewing GIs and the latter civilians.[16] US MPs in Belfast, trained by local police, eventually policed 'important corners' in 1943.[17] There were also rumours that Americans were posted abroad to avoid punishment – for example, the belief that a soldier who stabbed a Belfast policeman in 1944 was redeployed – adding further confusion about jurisdiction and increasing resentment about the administration of justice.[18]

While in Northern Ireland, American soldiers killed five civilians, one British soldier and one American soldier, and two were executed for their crimes.[19] They committed many other offences, mainly vandalism and brawling, often under the influence of alcohol; sexual assaults, no doubt common, were rarely reported; Americans were also often victims of civilians or British servicemen.[20] The numbers of Americans in Northern Ireland make this unsurprising; indeed, so few deaths are more noteworthy as are five of the seven that occurred in 1942, four from August to October. While American servicemen could not be tried by local courts, they could be nevertheless arrested and then handed over to the American military authorities for court-martial, and civilians could be compelled to give evidence. In early August 1942, the American military explained, according to the *Dromore Leader*, 'the chief differences between British and American courts-martial are that in the American Courts penalties are heavier, and decisions and sentences are announced immediately'.[21] In September 1942 a Summary Court was established in Belfast to deal with arrests by American MPs, with the 'numerous cases of drunkenness and disorderly conduct' blamed on overcrowding, the lack of entertainment and scarce hotel beds.[22] These rules also covered American civilians; however, technicians, who often had a worse reputation than the military, could face civilian courts as other foreign nationals did.[23] Technicians' poor behaviour, especially in Londonderry, reflected badly on the military and concerned both Stormont and the American authorities.[24] Policing American civilians was further complicated as neither Stormont nor the American consulate was entirely sure who had jurisdiction or even if they could cross the border.[25]

American military justice was first tested in April 1942, prior to the VFA, when Sergeant William Clipsham shot and killed bus driver Albert Rodden near Dungiven in County Londonderry. Rodden's bus found itself in an American convoy, cutting off the final scout car which then repeatedly tried to overtake him. As the car finally drew alongside the bus, the vehicles collided side-on and shots were fired from the American vehicle, killing Rodden and causing the bus to crash. It was not revealed at the inquest or court-martial that the convoy carried General Marshall and other high-profile military and civilian figures.[26] As Rodden was a civilian, his death required a coroner's inquest which occurred before Clipsham's court-martial: if they reached different conclusions, this created the potential for conflict between the locals and the Americans. If their judgements broadly aligned, however, then this possibility reduced. Rodden was a Protestant and likely sympathetic to the Americans and the war effort, yet his death caused significant anger and the *Londonderry Sentinel* described his funeral, attended by some Americans, as 'the largest ever seen in the Limavady district'.[27] Moreover, resentment, and the feeling that the shooting was no accident, was such that it has been blamed on nearby Londonderry being put out of bounds to US personnel. This, however, related to an increase in IRA violence and attacks on Americans in the city, and Americans feared Rodden's death would further aggravate tensions, but it could also reflect the (unfounded) American suspicion that the terrorist group had attacked the convoy.[28]

At the inquest, bus conductor Frederick McMichael claimed they tried to 'signal down' the American vehicle, which could not pass owing to oncoming traffic. When the scout car drew level, he heard a shot and 'saw Rodden fall over the wheel'.[29] The coroner declared the death accidental and returned an open verdict, partially assuaging local feelings before the court-martial.[30] The public court-martial demonstrated the Americans' desire for transparency, thus negating bad publicity about, and resultant ill-will towards, troops. The local press noted, for example, the thoroughness of proceedings, while British military representatives were present to witness the UK's first court-martial of this kind.[31] Rodden believed the entire convoy had passed him, but he separated it from the last vehicle, Clipsham's scout car. Several Americans testified that Rodden appeared to block the road deliberately, preventing Clipsham from rejoining the convoy; it was also reported that the bus had knocked the car into the kerb, triggering the machine gun. After examining technical evidence, the unanimous verdict declared the gun faulty and activated by the vehicle hitting the kerb. Clipsham was duly cleared of manslaughter.[32]

The American military was extremely conscious of civilian scrutiny, meaning courts-martial could treat servicemen more harshly than civilian courts may have, but this maintained the military's reputation. Here, however, Barton implies a cover-up by claiming that Clipsham, fearing an attack, shot Rodden deliberately; despite the trial's openness and technical evidence, questions remain.[33] Clipsham's court-martial, as noted, predated the VFA; it predicted, however, its operation as Stormont would be effectively an onlooker as American military justice took its course. Yet both the civil and the military powers had to deal these decisions' fallouts; from the perspectives of each, Clipsham's trial performed a valuable public relations purpose, as it highlighted the apparent rigour of American justice.

Only in August 1942 did the police begin collating monthly reports for the cabinet on the Americans, and these emphasized positivity, noting that relations between Americans and civilians were 'generally . . . very good'. County Inspector Ewing Gilfillan conceded to Sir Robert Gransden, the Cabinet Secretary, that initially relations in some areas 'were not as harmonious as they might have been, mainly as the result of rumour and prejudice and the boisterous conduct of American troops'.[34] Civilians and Americans fought in Carrickmore, County Tyrone, and technicians had been troublesome in Londonderry, for example, but things had improved. Relations between

British and American troops were 'good but not so cordial as between the Americans and the civil population', attributed by Gilfillan to pay and American popularity with women.[35] Gilfillan stressed that the Americans were far from home and 'quartered in small towns where they find it very difficult to find recreation and amusement during their leisure hours', creating an acute need for recreational facilities.[36] The official police view was, therefore, largely positive, even when serious incidents occurred, although the monthly reports did reflect fluctuating views of American behaviour.[37]

Two fatalities in 1942 exposed schisms within the US forces and between the Americans and the British, and represented different problems for Stormont than civilian deaths. In August, a Scottish soldier named Owen McLoughlin was stabbed to death by an American at a dance in Randalstown, County Antrim. The coroner eliminated premeditation, and the inquest jury decided that McLoughlin was killed by 'a person unknown'. Private William E. Davis was subsequently court-martialled, cleared of murder but convicted of manslaughter, receiving an eight-year prison sentence and dishonourable discharge; two British soldiers faced court-martial separately, receiving three years' penal servitude.[38] Officials underplayed this and similar but relatively trivial non-fatal incidents and often kept them out of the press, wary of fuelling nationalist or Axis propaganda about conflicts between British and American forces.

Neither Buhrman, who blamed British troops for Randalstown, nor Gilfillan was especially worried about the long-term impact of this killing.[39] Gilfillan's September report noted a 'fair amount of drunkenness' among the Americans because individuals bought whiskey by the bottle, but 'any unpleasantness is usually among themselves and does not involve civilians'. He recounted 'some minor incidents – drunken brawls, etc. – between US troops and ours', but only two were serious, the shooting of a British soldier by a drunken American at a dance and McLoughlin's death. He remained phlegmatic, however, having 'little ground for complaint about the conduct of the troops considering the numbers involved and the fact that they are on active service away from their native countries'.[40] He was effectively making allowances for misbehaviour. Even after the killing of a civilian, Edward Clenaghan, he maintained that 'generally there is little cause of complaint' regarding American behaviour.[41] The police, therefore, privately conveyed reassurance and optimism and maintained that they were managing well. McLoughlin proved the only fatality between British and American troops in Northern Ireland, but it may have triggered a conference between both militaries and the unionist press about how newspapers handled such events.

Private William Jenkins' death exposed the simmering racial tensions in the American military when, on 30 September 1942, in Antrim town he was shot by white MPs and his body was left handcuffed to railings.[42] His enraged comrades raided their armoury and sought revenge on white soldiers, shooting one white American before the situation was brought under control. Jenkins' death went unpunished; however, Private George McDaniels was given five years for wounding the white soldier. Such was American concern about racial violence that General Benjamin O. Davis, the first African American general, investigated the problem, but African American newspapers largely dismissed his report as a whitewash.[43] McLoughlin and Jenkins were tangentially linked: British and African American troops got on well, which exacerbated tensions between each group and white Americans. As Gilfillan noted: 'coloured US troops get on well with the British but the fact that they mix well does not tend to help relations between our troops and other Americans who do not fraternize with the negroes at all'.[44] British troops' apparent racial tolerance heightened tensions between them and the (white) Americans, together with ongoing racial problems within the US military, creating another headache requiring Stormont's careful management. The death of Jenkins also pointedly demonstrated the lack of American judicial vigour where the victim was black.

Concerns about the consequences of American crime against the Catholic community arose on 21 September 1942 when two drunken soldiers, Privates Herbert Jacobs and Embra Farley, killed a publican named Edward Clenaghan in Aghalee, County Armagh. The soldiers argued with Clenaghan after he refused them further service, and he left to complain to their commander. When he failed to return, his brother found him in a ditch with a fractured skull and his bicycle gone. He died later that evening. The official civilian response to Clenaghan's death occurred quickly with the coroner's inquest, attended by American military officials, held the following day. The police reported complete American assistance, while the family's solicitor stifled any anti-American antipathy by saying, reported the *Telegraph*, 'he was sure the police and military authorities would do all in their power to bring the perpetrators of the outrage to justice'.[45] Yet not everyone was so generous. Father Daniel Pollen, the priest at Clenaghan's funeral, practically demanded revenge in his eulogy: 'this young man, in the prime of life, was brutally murdered by cowardly assassins and left to die by the roadside. . . . If ever a crime called out to Heaven for vengeance this one did'.[46] Pollen may have rhetorically left retribution to the Almighty, but he risked legitimizing an earthly response. That said, he may have misjudged his immediate audience; members of Clenaghan's Air Raid Protection (ARP) unit attended his funeral, as did an American chaplain.[47] Within days, however, Cardinal MacRory complained about Northern Ireland being 'overrun' by American and British troops, increasing fears about attacks upon them.[48] An IRA terrorist had recently been executed for murdering a policeman, and the group had threatened the Americans, so Clenaghan's death, and Pollen and MacRory's exhortations, risked increasing tensions.

Two weeks after the funeral the one-day court-martial of Jacobs and Farley took place. The two, despite their defence lawyer's claim of reasonable doubt, were identified by several witnesses as the culprits, meaning the main question was whether they were guilty of manslaughter or murder.[49] The trial was again open, but very brief, with neither defendant taking the stand, and after a short recess, the court returned a verdict of manslaughter and sentenced each to ten years' imprisonment.[50] According to the *Telegraph*, the pair 'appeared to be overjoyed' with several witnesses congratulating them on avoiding death sentences.[51] Jacobs and Farley could consider themselves extremely lucky with the verdict's comparative leniency. With justice seen to be served, the court-martial was a public relations success. The police agreed, soon reporting that 'considerable resentment' had now 'subsided owing to the vigorous action taken by the American authorities in assisting in the investigation'.[52] This assessment appears overly optimistic, although it was similar to earlier deaths; moreover, the VFA's application in Northern Ireland had overcome its first, potentially tricky, test, but another would quickly follow.

Between Clenaghan's death and the court-martial of Jacobs and Farley, another drunken American killed another civilian. Inebriated after drinking whiskey in his barracks in Castlewellan, on 4 October 1942, Private Lawrence McKenzie went to the nearby home of Mary Jane 'Minnie' Martin, a deaf-mute aged forty-eight and known prostitute. McKenzie wrote on a piece of paper that he wanted sex, and the two agreed a price. As they began to have intercourse, the bed collapsed, causing Martin to panic; McKenzie attempted to quieten her but succeeded in strangling her. Her body was discovered some days later and reported in the press on 9 October, the day of the Clenaghan verdict.[53] McKenzie considered fleeing to Éire, but after initially trying to cover his crime by retrieving his note and gloves from Martin's home, and giving away his boots, he visited a local priest before voluntarily confessing to police.[54] The initial murder charge was downgraded to manslaughter, and McKenzie received ten years' hard labour. Fortunately for McKenzie, neither the court-martial nor the coroner's inquest nor the US military's review of the sentence found any evidence of malice-aforethought or sexual violence and accepted that he had been extremely drunk.[55] Drunkenness was not regarded as mitigation, but it, and the lack of evidence of sexual violence, probably saved him from the gallows. That Martin was a known prostitute, and not a necessarily sympathetic victim, may also have had some bearing on the verdict, given how such women were viewed more generally.

This cluster of deaths, their overlapping publicity, inquests and trials also concerned the American and local authorities as they coincided with upsurges in IRA terrorism and sectarian tensions. Stormont's efforts to minimize problems were hamstrung not only by the lack of legal jurisdiction but also by the absence of formal liaison between the Americans and the police. When the Americans had arrived, Gransden and the Inspector General (Chief Constable) Sir Charles Wickham advocated appointing a police liaison officer to work with US forces; they opted instead, however, to observe American interaction with the population. By August and McLoughlin's death, the police's role remained unclear; therefore, Gransden again advocated direct contact between Wickham and the Americans via a police liaison officer.[56]

Regardless of these efforts, drunkenness and its violent consequences continued with the second deployment. In March 1944, Private Wiley Harris, an African American soldier, stabbed Henry Coogan to death outside a north Belfast air-raid shelter in a drunken row over paying a prostitute named Eileen Megaw. Harris's court-martial attracted considerable publicity and, his guilt established and with no reduction from murder to manslaughter, he was duly sentenced to death. The Harris case is instructive for many reasons; first of all, his race meant more to the Americans than civilians or the local press, whose attitudes were broadly colour-blind; indeed, some questioned the trial's fairness, while unions, Protestant churches and ordinary people demanded clemency. The court-martial and subsequent review showed how narrowly the American military defined premeditation: Harris was not the initial aggressor, but his disproportionately violent response and the fact that he was deemed to have been armed sealed his fate.[57]

The Harris court-martial also reemphasized Stormont's helplessness under the VFA. Appeals to Brooke and Abercorn urged commutation, and both were privately sympathetic but officially could do nothing. Stormont had no scruples about the death penalty in principle but could not publicly intervene to save Harris. Abercorn sought cabinet guidance; it would, as noted, have recommended mercy and urged him to stress in his private appeal to General Collins that a civilian court would have probably spared Harris.[58] General John C. H. Lee's response, on Collins' behalf, was robust to the point of rude. The American public viewed death or life imprisonment for such crimes as 'requisite and appropriate', he asserted, maintaining that mitigating factors were always considered. Harris was given 'every protection' afforded by the Constitution, including a review, but due to 'the brutality exhibited in the commission of this crime, the execution of this sentence was deemed requisite to justice'.[59] Harris was undoubtedly guilty, but the rationale for the death penalty was explicitly demonstrated when the military wrote to Coogan's brother. It assured him that '[t]he punishment awarded will deter others from like action and evidence to you and your community the severe punishment which the military courts of the United States Army may award in cases involving such atrocious crimes committed by its personnel'.[60] Harris's execution on 26 May, therefore, fulfilled the underlying purpose of American military justice by serving as an example to others, but it also reassured civilians that Americans would pay for their crimes. Stormont's official silence also helped it preserve good relations with the Americans.

In September 1944, after most Americans had left, William Harrison, of the USAAF, raped and murdered a seven-year-old girl in Killycolpy, County Tyrone.[61] Harrison was an alcoholic with mental health issues, a troubled, pathetic figure utterly unsuitable for the military and who should have been discharged when his problems were identified. He had attempted suicide, but also been released three months early having gone absent without leave, and should have been in prison when he committed his crime.[62] The victim and her family knew the murderer quite well, and, where other cases were possibly crimes of passion, here premeditation was evident. The police stated that the murder 'has somewhat strained the relations between the Americans and the civilians in that area. As the offender has been made amenable, this will not be serious and will pass over in due course', demonstrating that, as with Clenaghan, they believed that resentment would be short-lived.[63] Harrison was convicted of murder and sentenced to death in November, but, unlike Harris (and similar cases elsewhere), he had proper defence counsel who requested clemency and appealed his conviction, delaying his execution until April 1945.[64] Where Harris might have reasonably been convicted of manslaughter, there was no mitigation enabling Harrison to escape the noose.

Four of the Americans' five local victims were Catholics, a statistical anomaly given that roughly two-thirds of the population was Protestant but reflecting that the Americans were often stationed in predominantly Catholic districts. The apolitical nature of each case, with only the killer of Rodden – the single Protestant – being on duty, and all the others drunk and off-duty, prevented resentment becoming a focus for nationalist discontent, even with demands for vengeance at Clenaghan's graveside. The police reported the initial anger quickly subsiding after each death, because justice was seen to be swift and decisive, and, the Rodden case aside, no hint that the Americans were protecting their own. In a sense, too, Stormont's lack of jurisdiction was a blessing as it depoliticized these killings: local courts clearing the killers of Catholics could have been portrayed as a refusal to administer justice fairly to the minority and confirmation of institutional sectarianism. The comparative leniency of local courts, therefore, could have been a major disadvantage, if perceived as trying to curry American favour.

'Strengthen further the understanding between our two peoples': Hospitality committees

In a 1944 magazine article, the MOI's Tom Harrisson sardonically characterized Northern Ireland's prime minister as the 'suave, intelligent Sir Basil Brooke, famous for his anti-Catholic outbursts ... [and] considered, by some of his party, dangerously advanced and liberal'.[65] Unfounded accusations of liberalism aside, Brooke had proved an effective Minister of both Agriculture and Commerce and was universally recognized as the government's most able member. When Brooke became prime minister in April 1943, for example, Buhrman reported that he 'has the reputation of being unusually active and energetic and forthright in his actions. He has worked unusually diligently in building up wartime industries'.[66] Brooke was the obvious choice to handle the Americans. In London in January 1942, Churchill personally requested he oversee hospitality, a challenge Brooke readily accepted.[67] Brooke recognized that US servicemen had to be both entertained and managed; the Americans, however, initially eschewed such assistance, deciding in February that the army would look after on-base welfare, while the American Red Cross (ARC) would handle leave arrangements.[68] Andrews and Brooke recognized 'the necessity for liaison', but Brooke understood that 'the Americans are rather afraid of any interference by a British mission'. Stormont was thus side-lined officially, although its efforts to look after the Americans continued, as did those of well-meaning civilians, but a formal scheme would not begin until the autumn.[69] The Americans made their decision although, or possibly because, their presence could prove controversial, meaning that nationalist threats were taken sufficiently seriously to require a modified approach to other theatres (Figure 3.1).

Keeping the Americans entertained was particularly vital in Northern Ireland, according to a June 1942 MOI report, due to 'the rather peculiar psychological, social and economic atmosphere of the area'. Bored and fed-up troops and their 'subsidiary effects' would have particularly wide repercussions in the delicate Ulster set-up'.[70] It also advocated more and better propaganda 'to offset and protect against the present one-sided, word-of-mouth antagonistic propaganda emanating from a minority', and it was crucial that the Americans better understood 'the delicate environment in which they are working'.[71] The problems the Americans brought, their increasing numbers and the potential to become caught-up in local enmities required hands-on intervention by both Stormont and the regional MOI. It was not until August, however, during a spike in bad behaviour, particularly between British and American troops, and renewed IRA activity, that formal arrangements were made. This saw the creation, with American cooperation, of a committee on troop welfare and hospitality and unofficial and private guidelines for unionist newspapers on dealing with problematic stories.

Andrews put Brooke in charge of the new committee, and he soon secured 'a free hand in arranging the hospitality schemes' from the MOI in London (where he also

Figure 3.1 Sir Basil Brooke, prime minister of Northern Ireland, 1943–63. Photo by Keystone/Hulton Archive/Getty Images.

sought advice on racial tensions).[72] The regional MOI's close links with Stormont are revealed by the ministry's regional history of the war. Written by Yorkshireman C. L. Frankland, Regional Information Officer (RIO) based at Stormont at the war's end, who stressed that the intimate connection between the two 'cannot be overemphasised'. Northern Ireland, he continued, had no regional commissioner as this job could be, and was, taken on by the government, with the small MOI staff in Belfast largely seconded from Stormont.[73] Stormont press officer F. M. Adams, formerly editor of the *Whig*, served as the MOI's local RIO from 1940 to 1944, highlighting this closeness; the MOI in Belfast was effectively an arm of the government. All of this gave Northern Ireland control over hospitality not enjoyed elsewhere, including the ability to massage reports to London.

Brooke was a decorated Great War veteran and moved easily in military circles, developing personal relationships with many Americans, including officers who routinely dined at his home, Colebrooke, in County Fermanagh. In this informal setting he discussed the American presence and gained valuable insights into their needs.[74] Brooke, Gransden and Adams agreed that hospitality committees should 'not run on political lines', although what this meant is not entirely clear.[75] Brooke appointed Lady Gladys Stronge, chair of the WVS, to lead the hospitality committees. As with other aspects of managing the Americans, this also asserted unionist control as Lady Stronge's husband, Sir Norman, was a government minister, while Protestant clergymen led some committees and unionist MP Dehra Parker chaired one.[76] Adams noted that committees included 'very few members of the Catholic-Nationalist minority', demonstrating a most definite political element that, at best, discouraged Catholic participation and avoided American exposure to nationalist influences.[77]

Emphasizing this point, A. Dalzell, regional chair of the Entertainments National Service Association (ENSA), soon warned Brooke that 'no time should be lost' in founding hospitality committees as a form of 'countersubversive propaganda'. 'Hospitality and entertainment by the loyal people of the province' were urgently required to offset efforts to corrupt Americans who were 'being invited, and inveigled, into places where no opportunity is lost to disseminate certain views'.[78] Later in the war, a correspondent expressed similar sentiments, warning Brooke that a Catholic priest in Newtownbutler, County Fermanagh, was 'continually entertaining officers and men of the American army and giving plenty of intoxicating drink to any who will take it'. He called it a 'grave danger' and urged Brooke to stop it.[79] Unionist bias in hospitality committees was overlaid with class, as middle-class women, such as the WVS, had the time and the means to participate, which working-class women, especially in rural areas, simply did not.[80] This reinforced both unionist control of these committees and their conservative moral outlook.

The parochial political dimension meant greater urgency in successfully protecting and entertaining the Americans; a devolved government, therefore, was a distinct advantage as the required bureaucratic infrastructure was easily mobilized in a small self-governing area.[81] Brooke's Welfare Committee debuted in September 1942, attended by senior British and American military figures alongside Gransden, Adams and police chief Wickham.[82] Brooke stated that Minister of Information Brendan Bracken had specifically requested devolving hospitality to Stormont. One of the first issues Brooke had discussed with Bracken was 'position of coloured troops in relation to the white British troops and the civilian population'. Bracken 'intimated . . . that there must be no discrimination between white and black troops', but Brooke believed that committees wishing to host African American troops should 'seek the advice of the local American commander'. The committee supported Sunday cinema opening in Londonderry and Belfast for soldiers, with the military wanting this extended to civilians.[83] Brooke approached the Lord Mayor of Belfast; he, however, refused to countenance opening for civilians; he raised no objections to opening for troops but warned that even this relaxation of Sabbath observance could end up in the courts.[84] Brooke, Adams and Stronge worked tirelessly to establish, manage and monitor hospitality committees, with the first formed in Lurgan and Lisburn in October 1942 and numerous others following until January 1943.[85]

Brooke worked quickly and effectively and by the end of 1942, as Reynolds argues, had created 'a bureaucratic structure for dealing with the Yanks that was more co-ordinated and high-powered than its counterpart in Britain'.[86] By this point, however, most of the Americans were gone, but Colonel Alexander Smith Turnham, the Assistant Adjutant General of BTNI, had told Brooke that 'we shall certainly fill up again', and Brooke informed the committee that '[i]t was anticipated that there would be a considerable number of American troops – more or less permanently' returning.⁸⁷ He reported to Bracken in March 1943, noting the original committee's ad hoc nature and the invaluable work of the WVS; although the Americans had largely gone, the organization was being maintained in anticipation of their reappearance.⁸⁸ Brooke kept responsibility for hospitality after becoming the prime minister, such was its importance. When huge numbers of Americans returned from October 1943, the committees were easily revived and many new ones created, making Northern Ireland much better prepared than previously. In November, Brooke created a subcommittee, the 'Northern Ireland Troop Welfare Committee', dealing with welfare, which 'would knit together the detailed working of the various organisations dealing with hospitality', to monitor the committees and handle problems promptly.⁸⁹ Chaired by Gransden, it would not set policy but would be a conduit between Brooke's committee and the hospitality committees.⁹⁰

Ahead of the second deployment, Brooke, General Collins and officials from hospitality committees met to organize entertainments for both British and American forces. Brooke suggested to Collins the shifting of provision from the Red Cross to local committees. Collins agreed, noting that Americans were 'lonesome and homesick', and argued that invitations to homes most effectively overcame this. Conscious that the Red Cross had simply insufficient capacity, he was amenable to a larger role for the local hospitality committees.⁹¹ American military authorities wanted troops to avoid Belfast as it lacked enough beds to cope with demand; doing this, Collins believed, 'falls in very well with the Local Hospitality Committee programme. With your help the smaller places can be made attractive enough'.⁹² Consequently, passes to Belfast were only given to those with overnight accommodation; day trips were encouraged, but the official preference was for troops to use local hospitality committees, which had greatly improved facilities in smaller towns.⁹³ Brooke agreed, also recognizing its political benefits as 'the successful organization of hospitality will strengthen further the understanding between our two peoples' and would bode well for post-war Anglo-American relations.⁹⁴ When the Americans returned, the problems of their initial sojourn accompanied them. Whether Brooke's processes prevented a repeat of the spate of killings in August and September 1942 is difficult to determine, yet lessons were clearly learned, and, as noted, there were only two more killings of civilians. This was partly down to better management but undoubtedly involved a large element of luck, as brawling, drunkenness, racism, casual criminality, prostitution and Anglo-American animosity continued.

Local hospitality did not always include Stormont. Amid much fanfare, in July 1942 an American officers' club, funded collectively by London, the Royal Naval War Amenities Committee and the Ulster-American Hospitality Committee, was opened by Abercorn at the Midland Station Hotel in Belfast.⁹⁵ In January 1943 an Allied officers club in Londonderry was opened as a gift from the UK government to the American forces in return for the hospitality to British servicemen in America.⁹⁶ Another scheme generated by London, which benefited Northern Ireland, was the formation of an Anglo-American Army Relations Committee in August 1943 to combat 'mutual criticism and jealousy' between British and American troops and 'sterilise rumours and exaggerations'. It rationalized that closer cooperation meant fewer problems, therefore 'some social programmes' were organized. One, inaugurated in November

1943, was for 'the inter-attachment of personnel', a worthwhile scheme which saw troops spending two weeks with the other army, with mail censorship reports from Northern Ireland reflecting more positive British perceptions of the Americans.[97]

Brooke's efforts were such that on the eve of D-Day Northern Ireland had forty-five local hospitality committees.[98] Brooke's endeavours drew praise; in March 1943, for example, Bracken lauded the hospitality given to the Americans.[99] A year later, the Foreign Office confirmed that Brooke's system was largely successful. There was 'close collaboration between American Service authorities and various departments of the Northern Ireland government. In main, relationship between American forces and civil populations is good. There have been some incidents, but effect on local opinion only temporary', although problems at dances, prostitution and overcharging of Americans remained the main concerns.[100] The Foreign Office's judgement reflected upbeat police assessments; indeed, the wording suggesting that the 'effect on local opinion [was] only temporary' is almost verbatim from police reports. This raises questions about whether Stormont, via the MOI, underplayed the difficulties the Americans brought and hints too at the Foreign Office's uncritical acceptance of these reports.[101]

Looking after the Americans also meant ensuring minimum disruption for civilians. Censorship reports on civilian mail after the first wave departed identified variations in perceptions of the Americans, with the cover note to one file revealing that 'it is noteworthy that the favourable extracts were written to people in the US, while the rude ones were written to people in England. Manners making the man'.[102] This implied civilian reluctance to portray the Americans negatively to their countrymen. One correspondent writing to New York already pined for the Americans as 'they were such nice fellows. They were much nicer than the English. Omagh is quite lonely without them, they created such fun in the town'.[103] 'You've got the impression along with a great many other people', wrote a Belfast resident in a letter found in a military censorship report, 'that the Americans are up to no good, but believe me you're entirely wrong, as they're a very fine race'.[104] A County Down correspondent, writing to Hampshire, was glad to see the back of them, however, as 'they were no good for anything here but drinking and wrecking any place they would get into', also noting their poor performance in combat in North Africa.[105] It is difficult to extrapolate much from these few reports, other than that more people liked the Americans than did not, and the Americans' reputation, if not their behaviour, was often questionable, as the religious or political loyalties of the correspondents are absent.

'Great discretion': Press management

Stormont and its newspaper allies did their utmost to acclaim the Americans, predominantly to aid the war effort but also hopeful of a post-war political dividend in the States. There was also a perception, often borne out, that those running propaganda in London were disinterested in or embarrassed by Northern Ireland, or even hostile to its very existence. This meant unionists cultivating their own account of the war, promoting the province's role and fighting to have it heard. The American presence was vital to this and utilized to create a narrative to counterbalance Irish nationalist propaganda and British neglect. Yet this was ultimately stymied as Stormont relied on London to provide an outlet for it in the United States, where British officials refused to countenance any challenge to Irish-America.

Positive reporting by unionist newspapers, over which Stormont had some influence, reflected Stormont's desire to ingratiate itself with the Americans. BBC coverage, by contrast, was viewed suspiciously. In 1938, for example, the governing Ulster Unionist Party created a 'Propaganda Subcommittee', 'to consider ways of countering adverse propaganda regarding Northern Ireland'.[106] This committee had six members, including representatives from Belfast's three unionist papers, and was born of a concern, as Ollerenshaw puts it, that the 'BBC did not report the news as impartially as it might'.[107] The cabinet appointed Adams as publicity officer in November 1939 to write newspaper stories about Northern Ireland and the war, emphasizing its place in the UK and to refute propaganda from Éire and misrepresentation in the British press. He would also liaise with the MOI and the Ulster Office, Stormont's publicity bureau in London.[108] In addition, the Canadian-born Sir Ernest Cooper, formerly of Stormont's Ministry of Commerce, was appointed Director of Information Services with the explicit responsibility of securing 'increased publicity for Northern Ireland'.[109] All of this assumed an enhanced importance when the Americans arrived.

The unionist press was often, like the MOI, an adjunct of Stormont. Adams, as noted, formerly edited the *Whig*; Major William Baird, managing director of the *Telegraph*, had close associations with the government, while the family of Commander Oscar Henderson, Abercorn's private secretary, owned the *News Letter*. These papers played a vital role in how the Americans were perceived. The steady stream of good news stories, covering the Americans' history, preparedness and interactions with locals, could not avoid their criminality and poor relations with British forces. These were problems not, of course, unique to Northern Ireland but they required urgent solutions as friction was increasingly problematic for the police and could ignite sectarian tensions or generate negative propaganda exploitable by the Axis or nationalists. Two weeks after McLoughlin's death, the editors of Belfast's triumvirate of unionist dailies, Stormont representatives and the MOI press censor F. M. Quintrell were briefed by Colonel Theodore Arter, the public relations officer (PRO) of US forces in Northern Ireland, and British Colonels Turnham and Lander, the latter from BTNI's Intelligence Branch.[110] The *Irish News* either declined to attend or, more likely, was simply not invited, nor, it would seem, were the *Sentinel* or *Journal*, despite particular problems in Londonderry.

The American military was eager to avoid the negative publicity caused by Anglo-American hostility and growing racial friction within its own ranks. Turnham asked the editors not to highlight trivial incidents 'which by undue publicity could be played up by their enemies in order to strain the relationships between the two armies' and praised the editors' hitherto 'great discretion', hoping that they would continue to foster good relations.[111] Lander warned that incidents could be 'enlarged' by enemy propaganda 'to create dissension', and, with little current war news, these became disproportionately newsworthy. The editors agreed and assured Turnham that they would do everything 'to encourage a better understanding between the two forces and would deal with great discretion with stories that might occur regarding friction between the two armies'.[112] Unionist editors needed no official encouragement to provide upbeat coverage of

American troops and did so long before this meeting, but this pep talk demonstrated the importance of formalizing the policy. Equally, the nationalist press, perhaps having a vested interest in highlighting tensions, chose not to; indeed, the only paper routinely reporting bad behaviour was the staunchly unionist *Sentinel*, which, of course, was not at the briefing.

Unionist press reports were largely divided between good news stories about American soldiers and those repeatedly emphasizing historical connections between Ulster and the United States, while ignoring inconvenient aspects of either. This approach saw papers celebrating the immediate context of the American presence, together with formal and informal efforts to memorialize it by underscoring Ulster's wartime role and crucial place in American history, creating understandable crossover between the two. The process began the moment Henke stepped ashore, which the *Telegraph*'s weekend paper, the *Belfast Weekly Telegraph*, marked with a souvenir edition, while the daily edition soon had a 'Home News Corner for Americans in Ulster'.[113] Each pointed out mutual culture shock, promoted an understanding of America and provided GIs with an unproblematized overview of local differences.

Press coverage, necessarily and practically, was aimed primarily at a domestic audience as Stormont lacked the means to disseminate publicity in America. There was no 'Ulster office' in the United States to do this directly, and the efforts of the Ulster Office in London, however, were limited by its dependence on the embassy in Washington to transmit propaganda. The Foreign Office's general attitude was to leave well enough alone; in other words, the less said about Northern Ireland, or anything reminding Irish-Americans about partition, the better. Indeed, both London and Stormont were paranoid about Irish-American influence on US politics; the British routinely criticized Éire's neutrality in the States, but refused to openly challenge Irish-America.[114] Stormont's efforts relied upon soft diplomacy whereby Americans returned home with happy memories, and positive messages, but this was unlikely to change broader perceptions either among the American public or in Washington. American generals such as Hartle and, particularly, Edmund Hill developed strong relationships with Brooke and other officials, yet this carried little clout in post-war America.

4

'If you can't see the hills'

Occupying the occupiers

Floyd Wilson complained bitterly to his mother about his posting: 'let some of those stay-at-homes who presume to accuse AMERICANS in NORTHERN IRELAND come over and live as we do with absolutely no amusement these long evenings when it is pitch dark at six o'clock, let them live in this depressing climate, tense war conditions, blackouts and all the other things we have to put up with'. Drinking, he noted, was one of the Americans' few pastimes.[1] The excitement the Americans brought was, therefore, not always reciprocated, and many found the place exceedingly dreary: '[g]ee, Rostrevor's swell, but why the hell don't they bury their dead?'[2] This grousing had some validity. The lack of entertainment (cinemas were initially shut on Sundays) and the paucity of suitable radio programming added to the boredom.[3] Open cinemas, however, were only marginally better than closed: *Stars and Stripes* commented that when 'you go to an Irish movie anything may occur' and films not already shown in America were rare; moreover, cinemas were uncomfortable and shabby. On the plus side, '[y]ou can smoke all you want', but '[s]ometimes it's best to wear a gas mask'. As for the 'Way Out', '[t]hat's where you go when you're way out of patience'.[4] Maintaining morale was, therefore, a constant problem, especially in the early days, with the grim weather ('if you can't see the hills, it's raining; if you can see the hills, it's about to rain') compounded by the early winter sunset and the blackout.[5]

With the concerns of officials from all sides about behaviour and morale, it would be easy to overlook that the American experience was largely positive. The soldiers were bored and homesick, but the majority made the best of it, without inevitably turning to alcohol and women of negotiable virtue, and recalled their sojourn fondly.[6] One American, reflecting in *Yank* in September 1942, articulated the joys and complexities of being in Northern Ireland:

> The effect of Yank troops on the Irish citizenry varies considerably with the citizen's age and sex. The children are nuts about us, to slip into the vernacular. We get along very well with the girls, a fact which isn't calculated to endear us to the boys, and the older people take us pretty much as we come. The Visiting Fireman aura which we had upon arrival has worn off now, as has our novelty, and life has settled down to what it was before we arrived.[7]

What is most striking here is how quickly the American presence became normalized, as their 'Visiting Fireman aura' disappeared and they integrated into the wartime routine. Life for the Yanks was largely dictated by training, but they found many ways to fill their spare time. Newspapers are littered with upbeat stories about the Americans helping local communities or arranging exhibitions of their art and crafts. Americans brought their sports but seemed immune to the charms of local games, and their bases were 'little Americas' with whatever home comforts the military could provide. This, of course, was utilized for morale and propaganda, with *Stars and Stripes* the principal outlet.

The MOI's secret 'Report on Americans in Ireland' of June 1942 quite quickly and accurately identified the problems, and recognized that the Americans 'like the Irish and Ireland', but unless carefully managed, trouble would arise. 'The Protestant Sunday enforced throughout Ulster' was bad for morale; the Americans lacked news, finding local newspapers 'quite unsuitable and largely unintelligible', while the BBC was 'unsophisticated, dull and amateur'.[8] There was no American radio station, and US newspapers arrived weeks late, and this threatened to dampen the Yanks' enthusiasm. Improvement, it argued, was 'a matter of immediate urgency'. Social provision had to be greatly enhanced, with up-to-date films and better sports facilities, otherwise Americans would focus on the 'pub and the pick-up'.[9] The MOI suggested educating the Americans about whiskey and crucially 'a confidential explanatory booklet', dealing with their culture shock. It also recommended a weekly paper, in fact, 'from the morale point of view this should receive priority consideration'.[10] The GIs, their commanders and local officials recognized these problems and instituted solutions, often impractical in 1942, for the second deployment in late 1943.

'A little bit of America': the Red Cross

The American Red Cross represented the civilian dimension to the US presence which, liaising with the military and local organizations, looked after soldiers off-base. The ARC provided accommodation and entertainment for those on leave and steered them away from less than savoury pastimes. Operations establishing the ARC began in February 1942; Marcia Mackie, eventual director of the Belfast club, recruited American women living locally as volunteers, and by March personnel arrived with the second contingent of *Operation Magnet*, to set up clubs.[11] Abercorn opened a Red Cross Welfare Centre at the Northern Counties Hotel in Portrush in April 1942, and like subsequent clubs it was designed to be a 'little bit of America'.[12] At the same time, the Red Cross acquired the Plaza, described by *Stars and Stripes* as 'Belfast's swankiest dance hall and amusement center' (before its destruction in a fire the previous year). These became the first Red Cross clubs in the UK.[13] By June, the Plaza, on Chichester Street near the City Hall and the US consulate (and Amelia Street, a haven for prostitutes), had a hostel and a games room.[14] Created by seventeen Americans and 450 locals, working alongside the Young Men's Christian Association (YMCA), Ulster Tourist Development Association, the British Red Cross and the Salvation Army, it boasted 1,600 beds and a further 450 'stretcher cots', but could sleep up to 3,000.[15] After delays, the new club was formally opened by Hartle, alongside Abercorn and Andrews, in October, with the *Telegraph* declaring it the 'finest in Britain'.[16] Edwin T. ('Lefty') Martin, its director, announced that it 'will include one of the largest dance floors in the city' and would host dances, movies, various classes and basketball games.[17] Northern Ireland eventually had twenty-six clubs run by Americans, assisted by local volunteers (Figure 4.1).[18]

The Americans' bad behaviour was a constant problem and Louise Farrand, assistant director of the Belfast club, publically blamed the lack of recreational facilities. Addressing unionist women, she declared that if Americans 'were drunk or going around with the wrong sort of girls, remember they had nothing else to do', and 'if they could give the soldiers something else to do there would be less rowdiness'. She 'appealed for more tolerance of American troops', stressing that troublemakers were the exception, attributing their behaviour to boredom, high pay and the inability to 'handle the bad liquor in this country. I think you call it poteen'.[19] This resulted in money spent on drink and women, or given to children ('a bad thing for the children'), and she wanted Americans invited to homes as 'they were very homesick. They did not want meals, simply somewhere to sit in front of the fire and talk'.[20] Brooke liaised with Farrand, suggesting in their first meeting that hospitality would be 'quite easy

Figure 4.1 The American Red Cross Club, Chichester Street, Belfast, 10 October 1942. The club was on the site of the Plaza Ballroom. National Records and Archives Administration (NARA). Image courtesy of Clive Moore.

to arrange' using women's organizations and the ARC, and emphasizing that 'the one main consideration was to maintain good relations'.[21] He did not always find Farrand especially accommodating, once noting that 'she is alarmist and some of her comments were right off the point', but both recognized the urgency of looking after troops off-base.[22] The Red Cross, therefore, tried to keep Americans out of trouble by providing wholesome distractions and regulating their free time, largely through sport and dances.

The Red Cross hosted regular dances, and initially, the Americans brought their own girls; however, Farrand reported that the 'result was not particularly desirable' and replaced this with its own hostess list.[23] Girls accompanying Americans were subsequently carefully vetted.[24] Red Cross Clubs drew praise from the acerbic pen of columnist Henry McLemore. He thought they were run by men 'who felt that "shucks" and "darn" were cusswords. Or, by some girls who looked as If they had taken up spinsterhood as a profession at an early age and wore horn-rimmed glasses on the outside chance it would improve their looks'. This was until he visited clubs throughout the UK, finding great food and 'swell' hosts and hostesses. He noted that female guests had to be approved – to initial grumbling among troops – but the clubs held the best dances with the best bands, had great sports facilities and looked after the men, even those who had been brawling (Figure 4.2).[25]

Figure 4.2 'American Soldiers and Sailors and their friends enjoying dance at the opening of New American Red Cross Building, Somewhere in the British Isles, October 10, 1942. Belfast, Ireland'. NARA. Image courtesy of Clive Moore.

Other ARC activities kept the Americans busy. St Patrick's Day 1943, for example, offered a particular occasion for celebration with 'Shamrock Parties' and 'special Gaelic dances' held.[26] In September 1943, the ARC took over the Ormeau baths, a short distance from Chichester Street.[27] In March 1944, around 6,000 people attended an art and hobby show in Belfast featuring over 500 paintings and 'works of craft' produced by GIs, many stationed locally. Abercorn, who attended many similar events, was again present, alongside General Collins.[28] Shortly after D-Day, the ARC held an exhibition of murals created by an infantry unit, depicting the 'humorous side of army life along with picturesque harbour scenes'.[29] The clubs, however, accentuated privileges not enjoyed by British troops and added to friction. When British servicemen flooded the Londonderry club, for example, it instituted a policy of 'guests by invitation only'.[30] The club's director described relations between British and American servicemen as 'more or less deplorable'. When asked about joint socials with British forces, the American answer was always 'don't for God's sake!' as these events were more trouble than they were worth.[31]

As the Americans began returning in late 1943, the US military addressed problems identified during 1942, for example, regarding passes, furloughs and accommodation, particularly in Belfast. A new seventy-three room Red Cross Club opened at the Kensington Hotel in Belfast, easing the strain.[32] In addition, the military introduced rules denying accommodation in Belfast to anyone stationed within twenty miles of the city (prioritizing those from further afield) and anyone with an overnight pass could not leave base without proving they had somewhere to stay.[33] Overcrowding continued, however. At the Officers' Club in Belfast (not run by the Red Cross), which had several thousand members, the situation became so bad that its chairman, British Colonel Arthur Chitty, restricted access to members, their wives and daughters and 'privileged guests'.[34]

Beyond boredom, inebriation and turpitude, Red Cross Clubs had to negotiate American military segregation. It had created some twenty-three 'Colored Clubs' in the UK by February 1944, with two in Northern Ireland, in James Street South, Belfast, which had overnight accommodation, and another in Antrim's Protestant Hall. Clubs for white enlisted men were designated 'EMW Enlisted Men' (white staffed) or 'EMN Enlisted Men' (Negro staffed) for African American personnel.[35] The organization was officially forbidden from discriminating against African American troops where no 'colored' facilities were available and formally maintained that '[w]e have no negro [sic] clubs. We have no white clubs. We have negro staff[ed] clubs and white staff[ed] clubs. Any negro in this Theater is welcome to any club we have. Any soldier whether he is white or black is the same'.[36] The reality was often different, for example, when military police prevented black troops from entering clubs and, occasionally, white troops from entering 'Negro' clubs.[37] African American troops, though resenting segregation, appreciated having somewhere to stay, even if it was 'separate but equal': one wrote home, saying '[t]hey have a nice Red Cross for soldiers to stay over night with two brown skins from the good old US running the place'.[38] While the Red Cross was ostensibly independent from the military, the distinction was often blurred, certainly from the troops' perspective, leading to friction – invariably instigated by white Americans.[39] The military's official position, endorsed by Eisenhower as early as July 1942, forbade discrimination and supposedly granted black and white troops identical privileges: 'wherever it is not possible to provide separate accommodations, the Negro soldiers be given the same accommodations in the clubs on the same basis as White soldiers'.[40] Demonstrating this, a Good Conduct Committee set up among black and white Non Commissioned Officers (NCOs) in Antrim in 1942 stated that the Red Cross 'will show no partiality' and would operate on a first-come first-served basis.[41] Collins, in October 1943, conceded that some African American Red Cross workers would be sent with the second wave, yet attempts to improve things for African Americans proved largely tokenistic.[42]

Red Cross Clubs became hubs for Americans, including those returning to Northern Ireland on leave.[43] The Belfast and Londonderry clubs were also calling points for celebrities, from Eleanor Roosevelt to the various entertainers who passed through. Red Cross management of American behaviour was pragmatic. In one sense it was old-fashioned, policing the kind of women it welcomed, but clubs were also somewhere where troops could buy prophylactics, demonstrating a flexible morality reflecting wartime realities. The clubs and the Red Cross more generally maintained American morale and were hugely important in keeping GIs occupied and out of trouble by providing positive distractions and outlets for their youthful energy.

'Somewhere in Northern Ireland': *Stars and Stripes*

Keeping Americans overseas updated on the war and news from home was also vital to morale. In early March 1942 General J. H. Dahlquist was tasked with producing a weekly newspaper for Americans in the UK; he in turn put Major E. M. Llewellyn in charge of the project, and within six weeks, on 18 April, the first weekly issue of *Stars and Stripes* appeared.[44] The paper took its name from a similar publication in France during the Great War and was printed by *The Times* in London. The initial circulation was 5,000, but by October it was 48,000 and by November it became a daily; by September 1943, daily circulation was 125,000, comparable to a metropolitan American newspaper, and had regional editions wherever the Americans were stationed.[45] The paper maintained a good degree of editorial independence from senior military commanders, and Generals Eisenhower and Devers were supportive of this ensuring, notwithstanding copy from professional war correspondents, it was written for and by soldiers.[46] It reported regularly from 'Somewhere in Northern Ireland', with the first issue including a guide on 'What to do in Ireland', highlighting the province's main tourist attractions.[47] Further reports noted training, the Americans' interactions with civilians, general morale, available entertainment and local history. Such stories were invariably soft news pieces about dances and sports, local customs and the Americans' determination to win the war. This attention reflected the greater numbers of American servicemen in Northern Ireland than elsewhere until mid-1942.

Under an agreement between the US military, Stormont and the *Belfast Telegraph*, *Stars and Stripes* began publishing a local edition on 6 December 1943, using the *Telegraph's* presses, with Collins launching the print run.[48] The US authorities felt that the day's delay in the London edition arriving in Belfast, and the number of troops anticipated for Northern Ireland, justified the local edition. Major H. A. Harchar, Llewellyn's second in command, became editor, and it was linked to London via a 'special teletype and courier connections' with a specific reporting staff assigned to Belfast.⁴⁹ The inaugural paper was dubbed the 'North Ireland edition', how Americans tended to refer to Northern Ireland, but, doubtless after a word or two from the authorities regarding sensitivities about nomenclature, it subsequently became the 'Northern Ireland edition' (it used 'Northern Ireland', 'North Ireland', 'Ireland' and 'Ulster' interchangeably in articles).⁵⁰ It served a similar, but ongoing, purpose to the *Pocket Guide to Northern Ireland*, with general information and occasional history lessons, the latter, like stories in the unionist press, emphasizing Ulster-American links, and it made conscious – and simplistic – efforts to differentiate between Northern Ireland and Éire for the troops' benefit. It included an 'Ulster Round-Up' of quirky stories about Americans; however, crime was not reported, nor was any hint of tensions with civilians. *Stars and Stripes* also ignored sectarianism, discrimination against Catholics and politics in Northern Ireland more generally. The first issue published essentially a tourist guide, including a map of Northern Ireland and suggestions for places to visit. It noted that 'Ulster is not big. It is only slightly largely than the state of Connecticut.... But everywhere there are spots of beauty history and legend to interest the sailor, soldier or marine'.⁵¹ It later declared of the capital that '[i]nstead of grace and tradition, Belfast has vigor and ambition', and adhering to the unionist narrative of Ulster-American history, noted 'associations dating back to the Pilgrim times' and the inevitable thirteen presidents of Ulster descent.⁵²

Stars and Stripes contained the occasional morality tale to remind Americans of their privilege and the war's purpose. In December 1943 it published 'An American soldier's Credo'. This parable originally appeared in the London edition a year earlier, but reprinting it was worthwhile, with Americans flooding back into Northern Ireland.⁵³ An American trying to buy black market eggs from a 'peasant' woman discovered someone better informed about the war than himself, causing reassessment of his own disinterested perspective: '[t]hat stopped me. Here I was – a typical American wise guy, knew all the answers and all the angles, nobody's sucker – and I was getting this from a humble Irish woman who probably hadn't been more than 30 miles from Banbridge in her life'. The soldier now felt guilty about 'bumming eggs' from people grateful to have American protection.⁵⁴

Rising American-Irish tensions over the Axis legations in Dublin highlighted the paper's propaganda value. In March 1944, it reported the 'American note' crisis extensively, explaining American hostility to Éire and de Valera. *Stars and Stripes* followed the American line that this was a 'request' (instead of the rather strident demand that it was) made 'because the presence of Axis representatives in Éire constituted a danger to the lives of American soldiers and the success of Allied military operations'.⁵⁵ It published both the full text of Secretary of State Cordell Hull's message to Éire and de Valera's reply.⁵⁶ It did not, however, editorialize against de Valera or Éire until a month after the crisis had subsided, when Hull spoke about neutral nations more generally. *Stars and Stripes* now talked of Éire's 'stubborn neutrality', declaring that 'de Valera's Shangri-la found itself in the center of a maelstrom'.⁵⁷ It provided a map of the British Isles and northern France, with the captions 'Border Trouble',

'Coastal Trouble' and 'Espionage Trouble', around Ireland and 'Invasion Springboard' on the south coast of England, the latter caption claiming that 'Ireland's strategic place overlooking England brought crisis'. It offered a potted history of partition and the Treaty ports, seeing the former in binary religious terms, separating 'Catholic Éire from the Protestant six counties of the north' and being 'tortuous and difficult to watch'. This border, it continued, 'irritates Éire because it cuts off an arm which de Valera says belongs to his country'. It was its first open criticism of Éire, asserting that '[s]ome believed that America's entrance into the war would soften Dublin's attitude. They were wrong. De Valera protested the US troop landings in Ulster' (Figure 4.3).[58]

On 8 July 1944, with the post-D-Day departure of most American forces, *Stars and Stripes* ended the 'short-lived but useful existence' of its Northern Ireland edition. The final 'Ulster Round-Up' commented on the 'close ties have been formed which will never be broken' and quoted William Baird of the *Telegraph*, who declared that 'firm friendships' developed had created solid foundations for 'cordial relationships in the post-war years'. *Stars and Stripes* declared that '[w]e feel privileged to have been on the scene when these relationships were cemented'.[59] *Stars and Stripes* had an important, dual function in Northern Ireland: firstly, it relayed war news and, secondly, it reported specifically on the American forces stationed there. It eschewed politics, and with the exception of the 'American Note' ignored Éire, concentrating

Figure 4.3 'Hull Warning to Neutrals Revives Question of Éire', *Stars and Stripes*, 12 April 1944. Courtesy of Stars and Stripes Archives and Library

on heart-warming stories on American relationships with the people. Like other publications, *Stars and Stripes* presented an unproblematized view of Northern Ireland as homogeneous, hospitable and pro-American, without obvious internal problems and rarely acknowledged that it bordered a neutral state. The London edition would continue to report from Belfast periodically, for example, Eisenhower's visit in August 1945. The Northern Ireland edition had been invaluable, but now *Stars and Stripes*, like the war, moved on.

The Americans' other main news source was the forces' weekly magazine *Yank* launched in June 1942. *Yank* differed from *Stars and Stripes* as it was directly controlled by the War Department, with editorial material coming from New York and regional editors allowed only four pages of local material, even if its contributors were predominantly servicemen (alongside syndicated material and stories culled from news agencies).[60] It resembled a current affairs journal, such as *Time*, with lengthy articles on the war and the enlisted man's role within it; it printed soldiers' letters (and grumbles) and was a source of pin-ups. It reported only occasionally from Northern Ireland, primarily in 1942, covering baseball, culture shock and the odd morality tale.[61]

'Kippered banshee and leg of leprechaun': The American press

Both unionist and American newspapers enjoyed printing quirky and heart-warming stories about the Yanks and their interactions with the locals. The *Stars and Stripes* variously reported an American leaving his false teeth in a Red Cross Club, cycle races and shooting contests with British troops, and even GIs saving lives with their quick thinking.[62] *Yank* described some Americans raiding a locked wine cellar in a castle by fishing bottles out through a window and drinking the lot. This ingenuity came at the cost, however, of hangovers and 'a bill for $954. Each man's pay was docked $106'.[63] The *Telegraph* reported troops being billeted with a ghost.[64] In May 1943 a rare *New York Times* report told a story with both mildly comedic and somewhat sinister undertones. American soldiers arranged a boxing tournament in Belfast which was double-booked with a 'Green Cross' dance. The soldiers decided to share the hall assuming that the Green Cross was the Irish branch of the Red Cross; they generously arranged a collection for the organization not realizing that it was a fund-raising group for jailed IRA members. The bout was attended by police officers and British servicemen who were 'astounded' by the collection but apparently paid 'without a word'.[65]

American syndicated columnists provided amusing anecdotes, wry observations and lazy stereotypes, reinforcing assumptions about Ireland and making little distinction between unionism and nationalism or Protestant and Catholic but noting the two Irish states. Many emphasized Northern Ireland's backwardness and how the war exacerbated this – for example, reliance on horses, used occasionally to pull taxi cabs due to fuel shortages, and the general culture shock, boredom and discomfort faced by the Americans. These columns were interspersed with reports, usually via the AP, about Northern Ireland's war effort, history and differences with Éire, with sympathies firmly in favour of the former.

Many well-known American journalists and columnists spent time in Northern Ireland.[66] Some arrived prior to Pearl Harbor, observing the war effort and Éire's neutrality. Writing for the Newspaper Enterprise Agency (NEA), Paul Manning, a CBS journalist and associate of Edward Murrow, followed the technicians to Northern Ireland. In September 1941 he declared that the 'American population' continued to grow and that 'Belfast and North Ireland have an American accent these days'. He reported American ferry pilots, 'in Fifth Avenue slacks', milling around one of the city's main hotels, American workers visiting villages and even the occasional sighting of US sailors. Commenting on the war effort generally, he compared British troops to settlers in the old west, waiting 'eagerly for the opening gun that was to send them racing across the Plains to a new homestead'. The troops, however, were poised 'for the signal that will send them racing across the Irish border'. Contrasting wartime Belfast with neutral Dublin, he asserted: '[j]ust as in England, too, there are reminders, which you don't see in Dublin that a war is on. The people have the tightening expression you find on the faces of the men and women of Coventry, Bristol, London, Plymouth and Southampton'. The people were more like the English than the 'south Irish' and would fight on regardless: '[a]nd so wherever you go, go there is a great war effort'. He repeated the claim that German agents crossed the border to inspect damage after the first air-raid, before relaying information to the Luftwaffe, making the second attack much more effective.[67]

With little else to report from Europe directly involving the Americans in 1942, Northern Ireland attracted a degree of attention which dissipated as the war progressed and more GIs arrived in mainland Britain or saw action in North Africa. AP staff writer Rice Yahner, who landed with the first detachment, remained until July 1942 and reported African American troops arriving and Northern Ireland 'learning American ways' and 'liking it'.[68] This included 'trying to make coffee to suit American tastes' and prepare French fries and 'to serve them crisp, brown and hot instead of the usual soggy, cold chips'. In June he declared that relations 'were friendly from the start, but there has been a definite growth of cordiality with the passing months'. As a British officer told him, things had improved from when the locals were 'hearing too much and knowing too little about the Americans'.[69] Other stories from American journalists followed a similar pattern. In May 1942, for example, Frederic J. Haskin, another syndicated columnist, called Northern Ireland 'a mixture of history, scenery, song and ships and linens'.[70]

Quentin Reynolds, the associate editor of *Collier's*, was a key pro-British propagandist in the States. He narrated the films *London Can Take It* (1940) and *Christmas under Fire* (1941) (writing the latter), both produced by the MOI's Crown Film Unit (CFU) to rally American audiences to the Allied cause. He visited in the autumn of 1942, publishing two soft-focus pieces to reassure American parents and counter negative publicity regarding racial, Anglo-American and intra-organizational frictions. Reynolds reported, contrary to the military and local authorities' findings, that everything was marvellous. There were no racial problems: the African American troops adored their officers, and the locals, initially thinking they were Native Americans, loved these troops. A white Texan officer took umbrage at the very suggestion of conflict claiming 'they are the best disciplined troops I ever commanded. They're good boys, and if the rumourmongers will leave us alone, my boys will get along fine here'. Reynolds warned that 'sooner or later' fifth columnists would spread rumours of trouble between African American troops and locals, or their white comrades, 'but it'll be bunk'. He reported shortly after General Davis's investigations demonstrated that American race relations were not nearly as rosy as Reynolds claimed, although relations between African Americans and civilians were generally good. Reynolds saw no signs of friction between British and American troops; on the contrary, they mixed splendidly, a judgement based on the generosity of Americans towards a Cockney soldier attached to their unit, when, as with racial problems, the reality was often very different.[71]

Hartle, he reported, citing military efficiency, forbade parking near farmhouses, as troops were invariably invited in for tea and he did not want the locals squandering rations on their guests. He contrasted the ancient with the modern with an American tank parked outside Downpatrick's cathedral, one of the purported burial sites of Ireland's patron saint. He was unimpressed with Belfast, however, describing it as 'a rather dreary town and I defy any Ulsterman to say otherwise. In fact, Ulstermen are the first to admit it', but it, and particularly Grand Central Hotel bar, was popular with Americans on leave. The Americans were also 'mildly intrigued' to find pictures of thirteen former presidents at the Ulster Museum.[72] The second piece saw him attached to the US Navy and Marines in Londonderry. The Americans quickly adopted local naming conventions: 'it didn't take them long to learn all about their new home and call it "Derry" as the natives do, for no one in Ulster ever calls it "Londonderry"'. He reported rumours of Axis spies operating from just across the border ('to all intents and purposes enemy territory'); this embittered many Irish-American troops 'toward the land of their forefathers' as they believed they were being watched by 'invisible Nazi eyes from Donegal'.[73] He repeated the falsehood that de Valera and Éire sheltered German spies operating 'under the guise of diplomats'. Ultimately, Reynolds appreciated Northern Ireland's war effort and defiance of the Axis, which he pointedly contrasted with Éire's neutrality: 'Ulster, unlike her fat sister to the South, never professed to be neutral. She paid for it when Nazi bombers gave Belfast hideous Blitzes; but she thinks the price was worth it. She has her self-respect and intends to keep it'.[74]

Henry McLemore was in Northern Ireland from March to July 1943, when there were relatively few American servicemen there. His columns certainly played upon stereotypes to amuse his readers and were intended as good natured. McLemore made his name as a baseball correspondent, but his journalism had had a sinister edge when he was one of the principal newspapermen demanding in the most demagogic language the internment of Japanese-Americans after Pearl Harbor.[75] His comments on the Irish and Ireland were benign by comparison. He recounted, for example, that no city 'as many odd means of transportation as Belfast. There is no certainty what you will get when you call for a taxi', which included 'a smart cart pulled by a fat donkey' and 'combination horse automobile taxi with the horse pulling the car and the driver holding the reins sitting astride the hood'.[76]

He was accused of 'smuggling' after travelling to Éire and was told by friends that if he informed customs officers that he was American, '[t]hey'll treat you like a long lost brother'. He took the train from Dublin, where 'a first-class ticket only gets you a seat in a third-class coach, usually between a woman who has been digging peat and a man who has been digging for the woman who has been digging for peat'. McLemore tried telling customs agents that he knew de Valera, but to no avail. His goods were confiscated, and he was fined.[77] Next was a ride on an Irish jaunting cart, an experience only slightly less dangerous than the chariot race in *Ben Hur*, followed by a 'hair-raising' trip to a Belfast barbershop, which interrupted his lunch of 'kippered banshee and leg of leprechaun'.[78] Some would doubtless take offence at how he depicted the Irish (the columns were not available in Ireland) mining their supposed backwardness for cheap laughs but may have found some small consolation from similar stereotyping occurring wherever the Americans went.[79]

Radio was vital for the Americans, and the BBC tried to accommodate this need, but this consisted largely of concerts by US military orchestras and occasional talks about the Americans on either the 'Home Service' or the 'American Forces Network' (which ran through the night).[80] Ulster-born poet Louis MacNeice was tasked with writing and producing programmes and plays about the war and Britain's allies, as he had lived in the States in 1939 and 1940, and his work reflected his great affection for the country.[81] Only one of his many BBC programmes directly concerned the Americans in Northern Ireland, when 'Halfway House: The AEF in Northern Ireland' featured on the Forces Network on 25 September 1942 (and later on the BBC's North American Service).[82] Elsewhere, in late May 1942, the BBC broadcast a talk by historian A.J. Tulip on 'American Presidents of Ulster descent', while in October 1943, a programme was broadcast directly from a factory to the States featuring a recorded message by Brooke.[83] In early 1944, Brooke made another broadcast entitled 'East and West through an Ulsterman's Eyes', dealing with Ulster-American history and the Anglo-American alliance.[84] As the Americans returned in December 1943, the Forces Network broadcast a fifty-minute programme entitled 'Welcome to Northern Ireland'.[85]

'A fair amount of drunkenness': Guinness, whiskey, poteen . . . Coca-Cola

Alcohol was both vital for morale and the source of many problems the Americans brought; however, there were few attempts to restrict its purchase (beyond under the counter poteen) and, in fact, the military ensured that troops had a steady supply. The Americans had the misfortune to arrive amid one of history's lesser Anglo-Irish quarrels, the so-called 'Guinness crisis'. This occurred when brewers in Éire refused to supply pubs across the border, leading to a shortage of beer, compounding an ongoing spirit drought. The AP observed that pubs had 'nothing but sympathy to offer their thirsty customers' and warned wryly of 'street demonstrations' if the crisis persisted.[86] The impact of the lack of beer on British troops' morale was sufficient to force the UK government to supply Éire with much-needed wheat and coal, allowing the *Telegraph* to declare 'Guinness Crisis Over' in March.[87]

Beer shortages recurred periodically, often due to a scarcity of bottles, leading the Americans to increase their men's allowance of soft drinks.[88] The Americans took matters into their own hands in December 1943, during another bottle shortage, decreeing that 'beer will be handled in bulk or draft on the basis of seven (7) pints per man per week', purchased through authorized local brewers.[89] The *Guide* advised that 'most people drink stout, ale, and porter which they call "beer"', and American beer, in other words German 'lager', came only in bottles. The fact that beer was not served cold was another hurdle, but the *Guide* warned not to criticize the beer (or the food or cigarettes), and Americans became used to it.[90] A correspondent to *Yank* warned, however: '[i]t's strong, heavy beer, that the boys from the States are not accustomed to and shouldn't drink, but try and stop them'.[91] Americans were not quite sure what to make of Guinness, the most unique of national drinks: several stationed in Belleek bought an unwanted donkey from a farmer and tried to get it drunk on Guinness; another would bring a horse into McCleary's Bar in the town and give it a basin of the 'black stuff' (Figure 4.4).[92]

The *Guide* recognized that 'the male social center in Ulster is the tavern or public house' and advised about the round system, where everyone in a group buys the others a drink over the course of an evening and where 'etiquette demands that all stay until the last of the . . . rounds has been bought'. Offence would be taken if this custom was not respected.[93] One compensation found in pubs, as the *Yank* noted, was the 'charming novelty' that some had barmaids rather than the surly bartenders they

Figure 4.4 Navy and Marine Shore Patrolmen on duty next to a Guinness advert at Londonderry railway station near US Naval Operations Base. Photo by David E. Scherman/ The LIFE Picture Collection via Getty Images.

were used to.[94] American troops sometimes crossed the border, especially to drink in Donegal as the pubs, like the cinemas and much else, in Northern Ireland shut on Sundays.[95] Traversing the border was straightforward with some Americans simply putting a civilian overcoat over their uniforms, while others, out of uniform and with longer passes, made it as far as Dublin.[96] Those apprehended by military police at the border were usually on their way back into Northern Ireland.[97]

If beer was relatively benign, spirits were not. Whiskey was expensive, leading locals to drink beer, but this was no impediment to well-paid Americans.[98] The inaugural meeting of Brooke's Welfare Committee in August 1942 expressed concern about the easy availability of whiskey; the police, however, while reporting 'a fair amount of drunkenness amongst the US soldiers due to their habit of buying whiskey by the bottle', believed that 'any unpleasantness' tended not to involve civilians.[99] The resident magistrate in Londonderry urged price controls for whiskey to combat drunkenness.[100] Even worse was poteen: the *Guide* warned that 'up in the hills you may be offered an illicit concoction known as "potheen" [sic]. This is moonshine whiskey made out of potato mash. Watch it. It's dynamite'.[101] The Londonderry Red Cross Club's director reported American sailors returning from patrols with little else to do than get drunk, often from liquor which was 'part poisoned, driving them temporarily insane'.[102] There was also a sectarian subtext. A Mass Observation report alleged that a pub in Londonderry, 'like many others, was run by Catholics who tend to dislike or despise the Americans', sold poteen to the Yanks in branded bottles. According to the report, '[o]ne of the leading surgeons in Belfast . . . (and as he was a Protestant and a reputable citizen the story may well be true)' claimed that three Americans had died from drinking.[103] Local sectarian stereotypes tended to associate alcohol with Catholics, while Protestants, especially Presbyterians, viewed it as a social evil, hence demanding Sunday closing of pubs. This was, of course, a gross oversimplification, reflecting middle-class, as much as religious, prejudices against working-class pastimes.

Most American crime, from vandalism to brawling, sexual assault and murder, involved alcohol, usually whiskey, so it undoubtedly caused huge problems which cannot be dismissed as simple high spirits. Locals sometimes felt, however, that the US military police's response to drunkenness was heavy-handed and intervened to prevent arrests for minor infringements. This made the newspapers in June 1942 and was reported by Buhrman. He stressed not giving 'undue importance' to this kind of intervention, as interfering with the police was 'not an unusual occurrence' in Belfast where 'hooliganism is common'. He also noted continued fights between the Americans and locals, but there was no evidence of an 'unduly dangerous anti-American sentiment'; it was simply the consequences of quartering troops in cities.[104]

A less troublesome beverage making a transatlantic trip was Coca-Cola. Available in the UK since the early twentieth century, it was far from ubiquitous and remained a (comparatively) luxury product. While not as important to the Yanks' morale as beer, General Chaney, when preparing for the American deployment, was keen to secure a plentiful supply.[105] Coca-Cola sometimes served as an alternative when beer supplies ran low but faced the same problems with bottle supplies; therefore, in late 1943 units were limited to a week's supply 'on the basis of two bottles and 1/12 cases per man per week'.[106] Coca-Cola quickly saw the commercial possibilities of supplying American forces overseas; in 1941, company president Robert Woodruff declared that 'every man in uniform gets a bottle of Coca Cola for 5 cents wherever and whatever it costs'.[107] It found a champion in Eisenhower, who took up Woodruff's offer in 1943, and by 1945 bottling plants had been established in almost seventy locations, including Northern Ireland.

Coca-Cola also developed specific advertisements for American publications such as *Life* reflecting, in often stereotypical and condescending ways, many of the places Yanks were stationed, positioning the drink a global ambassador for American friendship.[108] Its effort in Northern Ireland included the tagline 'Have a "Coke" = Céad Míle Fáilte . . . or how Americans make friends in Ireland'.[109] It featured an idealized Rockwell-esque scene painted by Norman Price, of GIs sitting on a stone wall, sharing the drink with a local man, complete with abundant whiskers, flat cap and green jumper, and using the drink to befriend a local colleen carrying a lamb. This was against the backdrop of a thatched cottage, a family in a horse and cart, and a Nissen hut. Coke, then, was another way to foster good relations (and pick up girls). The purpose of the advertising was to sell Coke to Americans at home and abroad, rather than to the locals, but as the Americans are often shown sharing the drink, it was promoting a part of the American Dream, which could be sold to the world after the war.[110] In this case, it also reinforced to an American audience what they thought Ireland looked like.

'This screwy game of cricket': Sport

American journalist Hugh Fullerton Jr., whose father exposed the fixing of the 1919 baseball World Series, wrote that 'American soldiers are taking their sports along wherever they go, thereby adding greatly to the confusion of world affairs'.[111] Sport was integral to American life and proved vital to maintaining morale, interacting with the locals and engendering goodwill, for instance, invariably donating the proceeds of exhibition games to charities. Baseball was a good example of this. The first game was staged by the technicians' Welfare Organization at the Brandywell stadium, the home of Derry City football club, in November 1941, in aid of local charities.[112] In April 1942, two units played in Belfast, with the air force benevolent fund given the gate money; a league was started with a crowd of 1,000 witnessing the season's opening game, and General Hartle delivering the first pitch.[113] As part of the 4th of July celebrations in 1942, Windsor Park, the home of the Linfield and Northern Ireland football teams, hosted the Kentucky Wildcats and the Mid-West Giants, and a journalist serving with the American forces provided the *Telegraph* with a guide to the rules, history and traditions of the game.[114] Andrews, Brooke and Abercorn attended, with the latter throwing the first pitch. Brooke regarded the experience as 'most entertaining, although I don't know some of the points of the game'.[115] The proceeds were donated to the Belfast branch of the Soldiers', Sailors' and Airmen's Families Association.

Later in July the Americans staged a match at Ravenhill, the Ulster rugby team's ground, in aid of two children's charities, the Belfast Hospital for Sick Children, on the Falls Road, and the Ulster Hospital for Children and Women in East Belfast.[116] This may have been a conscious effort at even-handedness, by supporting institutions in

Catholic and Protestant areas, but the Americans may simply have wanted to aid those with the greatest need. On the game itself, the *Whig* commented that '[i]n America a baseball match is quite a social event, and it is hoped that it will catch on'.[117] A crowd of 6,000, including many Americans, saw the California Eagles (as the 'Giants' were now known) defeat the New York Lions. 'It is absolutely essential', reported the *Whig*, 'that spectators should be noisy, partisan and disrespectful – in a good-humoured way, of course – and it is to be hoped that the last vestiges of "cricket behaviour" will soon vanish from crowds at Ulster ball games', noting how crowds routinely insulted umpires and players. The Abercorns and Hartle attended what was regarded as a better game than the earlier one at Windsor Park.[118]

Baseball and softball leagues were organized throughout Northern Ireland, with the *Telegraph* publishing the fixtures, but when the season ended, attention turned to American football or 'gridiron'. Previously, declared the *Telegraph*, the game could be accused of simply 'a test of brute strength', but it was, in fact, 'a highly technical business' which locals would appreciate.[119] Thanksgiving was central to the American football calendar, and a game between 'Hale' and 'Yarvard' (reflecting its popularity as a college sport) at Ravenhill attracted 8,000. It included a running commentary from an American officer and was broadcast by the BBC.[120] Pennsylvania provided most of Yarvard's players, while Hale's came largely from West Virginia, Wisconsin, New Jersey and New York.[121] The locals, an American sergeant reported, seemed distinctly underwhelmed, thinking it 'uninteresting and slow because they were unable to follow the game'.[122] In January 1944 two army teams competed for the 'Irish Potato Bowl', the championship of Northern Ireland.[123] Basketball was then the poor relation among professional American sports, but, designed as an indoor winter game, it proved incredibly popular as a participation sport among the Americans with leagues organized in Londonderry, Belfast and elsewhere.[124]

Baseball became a truly national American pastime during the Civil War, supplanting cricket, as Union forces played it wherever they were stationed and was also exported it to, for example, Cuba by 1900 as America acquired overseas territories.[125] This cultural imperialism failed in Northern Ireland due to the brevity of the American stay and entrenched local sports. Some Americans did try 'this screwy game of cricket', very much a middle-class sport, playing against a Belfast team, but they proved largely immune to the lure of native games.[126] There were only a couple of reports of them playing football (soccer), for example, technicians challenged a Londonderry team called 'Arsenal' in November 1941 and *Stars and Stripes* reported a match between two units in July 1942.[127] Rugby does not seem to have been embraced even at any semi-organized level, a surprise given its similarities to gridiron. Rugby and football were perceived by nationalists as 'unionist' or 'planter' sports and support for, and participation in, each was largely, but far from exclusively, Protestant. Both sports' authorities, as noted, put their main stadia, Ravenhill and Windsor Park, at the Americans' disposal. Gaelic Athletic Association (GAA) games – hurling and Gaelic football – were not covered in unionist papers, and as the Americans were ignored by the nationalist press, it is difficult to gauge their participation in Gaelic games. Moreover, the GAA banned 'foreign' games (in effect, the 'British' sports of rugby and football) at its grounds, which technically included baseball and gridiron, and established 'Vigilance Committees' to ensure these bans were maintained.[128] As with football and rugby, individual Americans probably tried Gaelic games, particularly those of Irish extraction or who attended Mass, but the GAA's close alignment with Irish nationalism and the Catholic Church (clubs tended to be organized by parish) likely would have seen participation discouraged by both the American and unionist authorities, and possibly the association itself.

'A special time like the present': Religious worship

American engagement with local culture could, as with almost everything else, reveal tribal animosities. Jack Beattie, one of Stormont's two Labour MPs, claimed in October 1942 that some Americans wanted to learn Irish, viewed as the preserve of nationalists by unionists and seen as a worthless and essentially dead language by many of the latter.[129] The *Sentinel* was soon reporting this 'alleged interest' in Strabane, County Tyrone, but claimed that investigations found no demand among Americans to learn Irish (but some for modern languages). Students only took Irish, the *Sentinel* asserted, as it was compulsory for Éire's civil service, contemptuously dismissing it as 'not worth learning', further claiming that there was 'no standard Irish', and the 'accent has been lost', reflecting broader unionist hostility.[130] The language was also seen as seditious, with the *Whig* alleging that IRA was infiltrating Irish classes, another reason for Americans to avoid it.[131]

Religious observance was readily facilitated in an outwardly pious society like Northern Ireland. The *Guide* warned, however, not to discuss religion or politics as 'religious differences and political differences are inseparable', and 'Protestants usually do not mingle with Catholics nor Catholics with Protestants'. Americans were warned not to 'try to bridge this chasm' and, if asked their religion, were to answer truthfully and then change subject.[132] Internecine bigotry was not suspended during the war; indeed, the virulently sectarian *Ulster Protestant* newspaper was freely available, if Catholics in the American forces wished to know how extremist Protestants viewed their religion, and its content greatly exercised David Gray.[133]

Americans, although well-served with their own chaplains, were not discouraged from attending local churches. This was unproblematic for Protestant denominations, and particularly welcomed by Presbyterians, but potentially less straightforward for the Catholic Church. Irish nationalist objections to the Americans and occasional rhetorical attacks did not prevent the Catholic Church, however, from happily ministering to their spiritual needs. These efforts went largely unremarked in either unionist or nationalist papers, but *Stars and Stripes* periodically covered them, serving as a rejoinder to the hard-line of Cardinal MacRory and a few other clerics, and as reassurance to Americans themselves.[134] MacRory, nonetheless, recognized his responsibilities to his American co-religionists and appointed Bishop of Derry Neil Farren to the role of Vicar Delegate to the US forces, drawing praise from Gray.[135] In November 1942, a Nissen hut at the Londonderry base was repurposed as a chapel, with Farren celebrating its first Mass.[136]

A Nissen hut was not the most unlikely place celebrating Mass, with an Orange Hall in Portrush pressed into service for three Christmas Day Masses in 1943. Minister of Home Affairs William Lowry subsequently crassly 'joked' in Stormont that the hall required fumigation, for which he later offered Farren a rather vapid apology.[137] Farren was awarded the US Medal of Freedom in 1947 in recognition of his excellent job looking after the Americans' spiritual well-being, the only recipient from Northern Ireland of such an honour for wartime service.[138] MacRory conducted Mass for 300 Americans at St Patrick's cathedral in Armagh in December 1943; unable to resist restating his resentment at their presence, he stressed that 'he had no desire to see other than Irish soldiers in Ireland'. He conceded, nonetheless, that 'a special time like the present' meant that if other troops came, then 'none would be more welcome than those of the United States, a land that had given so many Irish boys and girls happy homes'.[139] A notable effort to forge links with the Catholic community came in May 1944 when an American chaplain delivered five sermons to over 20,000 locals at Novena devotions in Belfast's Clonnard Monastery.[140]

The Catholic Church's attitude had a broader cultural dimension. Conservative Catholic Ireland was already fighting a culture war against American influence, be it film or music or dancing, to preserve the nation's Catholic soul and protect its young from foreign practices.[141] Now the purveyors of this apparently alien, debased and corrupt culture had arrived on their shores – invited by the occupier no less – with their lascivious dancing and lax sexual attitudes heightening Catholic anxieties. An Office of Strategic Services (OSS – the forerunner of the Central Intelligence Agency (CIA)) report from early 1943 offered a jaundiced and exaggerated assessment of the church's attitude, arguing that American movies, lifestyles and the 'vulgarity' of its music were all 'proofs of our wickedness, and now that thousands of those "wicked" Americans are occupying Northern Ireland the suspicion and hostility of the Irish Roman Catholic Church have reached an all-time high'. The church was, it continued, 'much more preoccupied with fear of the moral infection from the American armed forces in Northern Ireland than it is with the possibility that these Americans may physically invade the rest of the Island of Ireland'.[142] To some, it seemed, American cultural infection was more pernicious than British and more dangerous than military occupation.

An odd encounter with the extremes of Ulster piety occurred in Easter 1942. Protestants were wholeheartedly behind securing victory, but there were those whose commitment did not include violating the sanctity of the Sabbath. Along with cinemas and pubs, therefore, just about everywhere else ground to a halt on Sunday (Northern Ireland was not unique in this respect as the same was true in much of Wales and Scotland).[143] This was eventually eased, but not without objections from conservative Protestants. Three small incendiary devices exploded in the Royal Hippodrome cinema recently vacated by American and British servicemen, and it seemed initially that the IRA, which had murdered a policeman in West Belfast that afternoon and had previously attacked cinemas, was now targeting Americans. The Hippodrome attack was timed for after the audience's departure, but several devices failed to ignite and were dealt with by staff. American journalists in Belfast did not report what they considered a minor incident and unrelated to American troops, but reports, seemingly originating from Reuters, claimed that the IRA was responsible, and these were published in American papers.¹⁴⁴ The 'German-type incendiary time bombs exploded harmlessly', reported the *Washington Evening Star*, and had been planted like 'Easter eggs'; the *Pensacola News Journal* cautioned, however, that there was 'no ostensible connection' between the attack and violence earlier in the day.¹⁴⁵

Buhrman initially reported that the police had blamed the IRA, but stressed that irrespective of the veracity of this, it had 'no bearing whatever' on the Americans as it was 'directed as usual against British sovereignty'. He then outlined what appeared to be an outlandish theory doing the rounds locally, that the culprits were actually 'fanatical religionists', in the form of Protestant ministers, who objected to cinemas opening on Sunday.¹⁴⁶ Buhrman thought this unlikely but was concerned about 'exaggerated reports' in American papers being 'instigated for political purposes', to pressurize Éire. These reports possibly originated in 'highly colored' letters sent by American troops relating their 'fictitious adventures', which made good newspaper copy.¹⁴⁷ In this case, the most absurd theory also appeared quite plausible. The British military had recently requisitioned the Hippodrome for Sunday use by troops, against the wishes of Belfast city council, and drawing a resolution from Protestant churches condemning the 'grievous hurt to the conscience and sentiments of a vast multitude' of Britain's 'most loyal, law-abiding and devoted subjects'.¹⁴⁸ The perpetrators, therefore, may have been Protestant ministers objecting to this affront to the Sabbath.¹⁴⁹

'A foine St Paddy's day to yez': Holidays and celebrations

American national holidays were honoured, but the 4th of July generated a degree of awkwardness for unionists. St. Anne's Church of Ireland Cathedral in Belfast hosted a special service, while Chaplain William T. Brundick spoke at the US headquarters at Wilmont, subsequently broadcast in America, and later at the McCracken Memorial and Grosvenor Presbyterian churches in Belfast. The Americans' history recorded that '[t]hese invitations were significant of the cordial relationship' between civilians and the Americans.¹⁵⁰ Stormont made a fuss, with Andrews issuing a special Independence Day message and various events organized, including the baseball game at Windsor Park.¹⁵¹ Presbyterian and Methodist ministers were encouraged to make the 4th of July the theme of their sermons, while a 'Britain-America Circle' was formed 'to promote a closer understanding between the two peoples'.¹⁵² The latter was needed, observed the *Down Recorder*, as a 'gentle reminder that the Americans' annual festival is a celebration of the day they left the Empire'.¹⁵³ Unionist newspapers carried plenty of the 4th of July coverage, but the circumstances of American independence were largely ignored or explained away.¹⁵⁴ On 6 July Ulster poet and actor Jack McQuoid spoke on the BBC about Charles Thomson, a 'pioneer for American freedom', who left Ulster as a child to become a Pennsylvania patriot leader and secretary of the Continental Congress, which declared independence in 1776.¹⁵⁵ The day was ignored by the nationalist press and the Catholic Church, drawing comment from Buhrman. This, he mused, revealed how closely aligned the church was to nationalism, with both regarding the American presence 'as in some way jeopardizing Irish Independence'.[156] This was hardly very insightful but reflected his binary understanding of Northern Ireland's divisions. The 4th of July in 1943 garnered much less press attention, with some sports events, dances and radio broadcasts, demonstrating the few Americans still there and their lack of novelty, and by July 1944 most had departed.[157]

Other holidays proved simpler to negotiate. Thanksgiving 1942 provided another opportunity to show gratitude to 'the great Republic of the West'. Abercorn sent a message to Collins, hoping that the friendships established 'will be thoroughly cemented for all time'. American troops were not granted a day off, however, with one officer stating that 'we will observe no holidays until the war is won'.[158] Londonderry's mayor hosted a dance at the Guildhall; Omagh staged a theatre show; and Armagh, Downpatrick, Bangor and Larne held other events, while the Ministry of Education requested that '[l]essons on the history and significance of Thanksgiving were given in all Protestant schools'.[159] The Americans in turn embraced St Patrick's Day. *Yank* reported several privates 'wearing the green [and] [t]hat night they joined in drowning the shamrock in Irish whisky'. One of them commented: '[w]e'll all become Paddy Murphys on this day. We will an' bejabbers'. *Stars and Stripes* wished 'a foine St Paddy's day to yez', another piece – in supposedly Irish vernacular – about St Patrick's Day events across Northern Ireland and beyond (Figure 4.5).[160]

As Christmas 1942 approached, American servicemen and Lockheed technicians, the latter providing $10,000 worth of gifts, put on parties for 4,000 youngsters at both Catholic and Protestant churches and a party for 200 more at the Red Cross Club in Belfast.[161] The *Telegraph* praised the technicians fulsomely: 'separated from their own families, they feel they can best interpret the spirit of the season by doing unto others what they would wish for their own children. It is a big, generous idea which does them credit'.[162] The following year, these technicians made toys from scrap wood and salvaged metal, while the YMCA wrapped 25,000 sticks of candy for parties at the Red Cross Club and churches throughout Belfast for 5,000 youngsters.[163] Londonderry's technicians held a Christmas party for 900 local children, while on Christmas Day in Portrush, men of the 82nd Airborne Division took jeeploads of kids to Barry's amusement arcade.[164] The Americans were conscious of the publicity value of this kindness and sought coverage of it in the US press.[165] Such generosity during rationing and perpetual shortages meant that it was often children who remembered the Americans most fondly.[166]

To help overcome loneliness and boredom for the remaining Americans in late 1942, Brooke obtained invitations to local homes. He was responding to Alderman Thomas Henderson, High Sheriff of Belfast, who had observed: '[o]ne of the most pathetic sights of Belfast is to see soldiers wandering about the streets with nothing to do'.[167] It should be noted, however, that hospitality committees fretted over extending these invitations to African American soldiers, with the Moneymore committee arranging a pre-Christmas party for black troops and Christmas Day visits to homes for white.[168] Christmas 1942 also enabled reflection on nearly a year of the American presence, while Brooke's seasonal message in 1943 declared that 'although you are thousands of miles from your homes, I want you to feel this Christmas that you are not exiles but members with us of one great family'.[169]

Figure 4.5 'US sailors sightseeing in the Dunluce Castle ruins in Northern Ireland'. Photo by David E. Scherman/The LIFE Picture Collection via Getty Images.

'The Ulster hep cats': Music, entertainment and the Yanks

The Yanks formed numerous swing bands, a hugely popular genre at the time. *Stars and Stripes* reported that the 'Ghosts of Benny Goodman, Louis Armstrong, Count Basie and other very-much-alive American swing artists are haunting a town hall in one Northern Ireland village' and claimed that '"Boogie Woogie" [was] putting "Danny Boy" in the shade'. With few recreational facilities in the unnamed village, soldiers started an eight-piece orchestra and were 'jitterbugging as only they know how'.[170] Other swing bands formed elsewhere, including the 'Jive Bombers' and an orchestra of technicians.[171] Two sergeants turned a former Orange Hall into a dance hall for a swing orchestra; 'they call the entire movement the Ulster hep cats', reported *Yank*, and it had 400 members, with membership cards for local girls.[172] By August 1942, the *Stars and Stripes* declared an outbreak of 'Jitterbug fever'.[173] Americans took jitterbugging very seriously: '[t]hey look so unhappy when they're dancing', remarked one woman, but *Yank* reckoned dancing was a sure-fire way to 'entice the local colleens', who were 'developing into quite proficient jitterbugs and are very eager about it'.[174] The GAA and Catholic Church, in their ongoing efforts to resist foreign, and especially American, cultural incursions, viewed jitterbugging suspiciously and endeavoured to ban apparently immoral modern dancing from their halls.[175] They regarded dance halls generally as dens of iniquity which encouraged young people to engage in what the Bishop of Clogher denounced as 'unchecked pleasure' (Figure 4.6).[176]

During the Great War 'The Yanks Are Coming' became the Doughboys' unofficial anthem in Europe, and several attempts were made to pen a similar hit in the Second World War. 'Roll Out the Barrel', a Czech polka tune adapted with English lyrics, became an unlikely favourite sing-a-long for the Americans, but they needed their own anthem.[177] One effort was the sentimental 'Johnny Doughboy Found a Rose in Ireland', a big hit for Kay Keyser and his Orchestra in March 1942 and re-recorded by ten different artists.[178] Technician Jack Schafer wrote 'The Yanks in Ireland' as a conscious attempt to replicate 'The Yanks Are Coming', hoping, according to *Stars and Stripes*, that it 'will become the modern counterpart to the last war's favourite'. 'The Ambassadors of Swing' created an arrangement for the song, released in July 1944, and the BBC planned to include it in a recording to be rebroadcast in the States. The song's only direct reference to the Irish, however, was to declare them 'swell'.[179]

Marines in Londonderry discovered perhaps the most curious way to pass the time by founding a Scottish highland band, complete with bagpipes. In conversation with a marine officer, a local policeman, perhaps tired of hearing about how the Americans, and particularly the marines, could turn their hands to anything, suggested that they could never learn the bagpipes. The next day, so the legend went, a marine sergeant was dispatched to Scotland, where he purchased twelve sets of bagpipes at $90 apiece and

Figure 4.6 The Jive Bombers, a swing band made up of technicians from the Lockheed Overseas Corporation perform at the American Red Cross Club in Belfast. NARA. Image courtesy of Clive Moore.

eight drums.[180] *Stars and Stripes* followed the marines' progress, starting in December 1942 with a picture of a bagpiping, kilted marine, and soon reported their plans to have a band by Easter 1943.[181] The band was taught by 'an Ulster ex-serviceman and their base music sergeant', and it led the parade marking the first anniversary of the marines' arrival in May.[182] The band took third prize in the Dromora pipers' contest that month and in July made its Belfast debut at a baseball game in Ravenhill; it also participated in 'Salute the Soldier' events in 1944.[183] The band's stated ambition was to march through Berlin and participate in the eventual victory parade on 5th Avenue but had to content itself with the Navy Day parade in Washington, DC, in October 1944.[184] The *Washington Evening Star* commented on the band's origins and joked how the 'whole project almost blew up in mutiny once when an overzealous officer suggested going the whole hog by outfitting the boys in kilts'.[185] The bandsmen might have drawn a line at kilt wearing, but they became known as 'the Irish Marines' and created their own shoulder patch incorporating an eagle, the corps' emblem, and a green shamrock (Figure 4.7).[186]

A steady stream of American celebrities visited with the United Services Organization (USO) to entertain the troops; for example, Merle Oberon, Al Jolson, Patricia Morrison, Allan Jenkins and Frank McHugh visited for ten days in late August and early September 1942.[187] Oberon and Morrison had tea with Brooke, who found

Figure 4.7 Marine Pipers. 'Éire and the Yank Pipers "Jam Session" . . . with a "wee bit 'o Scotch" thrown in, these lads who are members of bands competing at a recent bag pipe band contest in Dromora, Ireland, get together for a little live session on the pipes. The producers of the hot licks are (left to right) James McManus of Dromora, North Ireland, James Donnan of Saint Field, North Ireland, Private Robert C. Rozelle, US Marine Corps, of Wauseon, Mount Vernon, Ohio, and Malcolm Graham of Sydenham, North Ireland'. NARA. Image courtesy of Clive Moore.

them 'very nice and not a bit hard-boiled as I thought they might be'.[188] Bob Hope came on his last wartime European USO tour in the summer of 1943.[189] Comedian Billy Gilbert, a favourite on the USO 'Spam Circuit', performed at the Red Cross in Belfast in December 1943; he and his wife Ella MacKenzie, also an actor, then visited her relatives in Ballymena.[190] The highlight was Irving Berlin and his all-soldier musical 'This is the Army' in January 1944.[191] Demand was huge, with thousands queuing at Belfast's Grand Opera House for tickets, limited to four per person, with even a US colonel refused extra.[192] A third of the tickets were reserved for US and allied military personnel, and such was the show's popularity that it was extended by a week.[193] Glenn Miller put in a belated appearance in August 1944, playing at the Red Cross in Belfast, Langford Lodge and even Gartree parish church which found itself within Langford Lodge's perimeter; here he treated worshippers to traditional hymns and his wartime classic 'In the Mood'.[194] Some of the stardust was even sprinkled in the distinctly unglamorous direction of Andrews when he discovered that actor Bob Montgomery, who had inspected American technicians 1941, was his cousin.[195]

5

'My own country overrun'

Irish nationalism and the American presence

Tom Harrisson, head of Mass Observation (MO) surveys, offered an early assessment of the Yanks' impact with the 'Report on Americans in Ireland' in June 1942, adding the caveat that it was based on only two weeks of truncated research. Catholics were, he believed, 'largely antagonistic though it is only a minority who are strongly so, and many individual Catholics are thoroughly in favour of the Americans'. That said, '[t]he presence of imported American troops is something of an insult. Highly suspicious and over-sensitive, as the result of centuries of trouble, the Catholics react to the feeling that the Americans may really be there to ensure partition and possibly even invade the south'.[1] Opportunities for conflict were intensified by some Americans being in places with 'an appreciable undertone of IRA'; conversely, this did not cause disorder – in fact, quite the opposite. Harrisson stressed: 'it should not be thought from the above that even in the dominantly Catholic areas the Americans are hated', because their behaviour made them 'difficult people to hate, even if you are a violent Nationalist of the narrowest kind'. Also noteworthy was that, thanks to nationalist propaganda, and no counter-narrative, antagonism was more prevalent 'where there are no Americans in the immediate vicinity'. He recommended remedying this.[2]

The protests of nationalist politicians, notably de Valera, were aimed at the US government and its tacit endorsement of partition and Stormont, rather than the GIs. This shaped initial negativity from ordinary nationalists, yet despite resentment about the principle behind their presence, Americans were generally welcomed. For example, in June 1942 James G. Walsh was sentenced to a month's imprisonment for urging a crowd to attack two American soldiers in Divis Street, Belfast. Sentencing him, the magistrate remarked: 'I am glad to hear you were not able to get any people in that district to assist you.'[3] Americans, especially those in Londonderry and west of the River Bann, were often in areas with nationalist majorities, but according to Harrisson, this lessened hostility; moreover, unionist fears of nationalists either attacking Americans or seducing them with their ideology never materialized. The Catholic Church ministered to the Americans, Catholic women were as likely to marry Yanks, with similar disapproval from Catholic and Protestant menfolk, while kinship ties with

America softened antipathy. With occasional exceptions, therefore, the Americans were bystanders observing local peculiarities with a mixture of curiosity, apathy and ignorance. Ultimately, to borrow Harrisson's phrase, the Americans proved as difficult to hate as to ignore.

Ambivalence was the overriding nationalist attitude towards the war. The experience of the Great War played a part, whereby nationalist Ireland rallied to the British cause, suspending agitation for Home Rule and believing that wartime loyalty and military service would deliver self-government at the war's end. Unionists made similar calculations, believing loyalty would prevent Home Rule; the British, however, made promises to neither. Nationalists had the added motivation of liberating 'Catholic Belgium', but the sense that German atrocities had been exaggerated generated the view that they were being similarly overstated in the current conflict, and again to serve British propaganda.[4] The Great War did not deliver Home Rule; rather, it brought the execution of Irish patriots, the threat of conscription and a bitter war against, and incomplete independence from, Britain. Most Irish nationalists wanted an Allied victory, but Éire's joining the Allies would have hugely, and violently, divided nationalism, potentially even triggering a second civil war in the state. The 'crime of partition', therefore, offered a convenient rallying point for non-intervention. Making neutrality about partition allowed nationalism to avoid taking a moral stand on the war, but for Éire specifically (rather than nationalists across the border) the unity it instilled prevented the IRA from exploiting perceived sympathy for Britain. Neutrality united Éire in a way that even partition failed to, and any deviation was quickly quashed, as Fine Gael's deputy leader James Dillon discovered when expelled from his party in 1942 for advocating, in effect, joining the Allies.[5]

After a statement on the war by nationalists in Northern Ireland in 1940, Peadar Murney, one of their foremost spokesmen, asserted that '[w]e in the North regard partition as Ireland's supreme grievance'.[6] In April 1941, weeks after the first air-raid on Belfast, F. H. Boland, assistant secretary in Éire's Department of External Affairs, wildly exaggerated when he declared that '[t]he vast majority of nationalists in the six-county area were absolutely pro-German on account of their unjust treatment by the British government and its Belfast puppet'.[7] Such attitudes might have been deliberately magnified to expose sectarian inequality, yet they were hard to subsequently explain away when the Allies revealed the full horrors of Nazism. As Wills notes, scepticism about British propaganda and strict internal censorship meant that many in Éire were slow to accept the scale of the Holocaust.[8]

There were doubtless those favouring a German victory simply because it was Britain's enemy, and an extreme minority were sympathetic to fascist ideology. Nationalist attitudes throughout Ireland must be seen both in terms of the adage 'England's difficulty is Ireland's opportunity' and, argues Staunton, 'in the context of the admiration displayed towards fascist ideas in Ireland at that time'.[9] The *Irish News* praised the Nazis in 1939 for 'restoring Germany's absolute sovereignty. Their determination to persecute religion cannot be justified, yet they remain the greatest political bulwark against communism', with the inference that anti-Semitism was excusable in the pursuit of anti-communism and implicitly conflating communism and Judaism.[10] In August 1940 three leading nationalist politicians from Northern Ireland,

Senator Thomas McLaughlin (a close acquaintance of MacRory), John Southwell and Murney, met Hempel in Dublin to put the province's Catholics under Axis protection.[11] In November Eamon Donnelly, a founder of Fianna Fáil from Armagh and Westminster MP for the Falls district of Belfast from 1942 until his death in 1944, secured a German commitment to attack partition via Axis radio propaganda.[12] Dublin, aware of these contacts, kept them secret from Britain, lest they jeopardize Anglo-Irish cooperation, including intelligence sharing.[13] Pearl Harbor complicated matters as nationalist Ireland's ostensive staunchest friend was now allied to its oldest enemy, and the former would soon garrison that portion of the island still 'occupied' by the latter, in a very public diplomatic recognition of partition.

A crucial difference between Northern Ireland and elsewhere in the UK was, despite Stormont's wishes, the absence of conscription. The spectre of conscription during the Great War had galvanized opposition to British rule, and the merest hint of it after 1939 promised the same; quite simply, nationalists did not regard themselves as British and felt no compunction to serve Britain in wartime. In addition, conscription would disproportionately burden the Catholic community as many Protestants worked in reserved occupations, itself a consequence of discrimination, making Protestants more likely to be exempt, while most volunteers for military service were also Protestant, further shrinking the number available for conscription.[14] Conscription was a 'reserved' Westminster power, and over unionist protests, it refused to extend it to Northern Ireland.[15] The matter was revived periodically, as much as a nationalist rallying point as a demand from Stormont, but a 10,000 strong anti-conscription rally in Belfast in 1941 ended any prospect of conscription.[16] Churchill raised conscription briefly with Roosevelt in 1943, but the president did not care and would neither intercede against it nor endorse it, telling Churchill: 'I frankly doubt whether it would create much of an issue in this country.'[17] When the Americans arrived, it was no longer in the foreground; however, they momentarily replaced it as the focus for nationalist ire, but it proved difficult to unify outrage around the Americans.

'Irish voters in America will take note': Sumner Welles's phoney war

Amid the international crises of the late 1930s, nationalists on both sides of the border endeavoured to utilize American diplomatic efforts to maintain peace to end partition. They linked German oppression of Czechoslovakia, and later Poland, to the British presence in Northern Ireland, having also compared the nationalist plight to the Sudeten Germans oppressed by the Czechoslovakians. This sometimes led to wild speculation, notably in the spring of 1939 when the *Sunday Times* reported, according to Belfast's US consul Ernest L. Ives, 'that official and semi-official groups in Éire, Northern Ireland, Great Britain and the United States of America are reported to be engaged in important negotiations to end partition', to coincide with a visit to America by de Valera.[18] This would involve the new all-Ireland state maintaining external association with the British Empire, America acquiring Irish ports in wartime and

Irishmen permitted to join the US armed forces. This and other efforts demonstrated the perception that the Irish-American vote offered leverage; however, the *Whig* contemptuously dismissed the notion that America would become involved to 'placate Irish-American extremists' in an election year, and the *Irish News* was highly sceptical, but some nationalists publicly entertained the idea.[19] Roosevelt's failure to link the wider world crisis to partition led the *Irish News* to criticize 'the American superiority complex', after a speech, praised by unionist papers, he made to the Pan-American Union.[20] American involvement in Irish affairs was, of course, entirely without foundation, but the idea of America tying its interests to ending partition became a recurring theme within nationalist discourse.

As the phoney war 'raged' in early 1940, Roosevelt sent Undersecretary of State Sumner Welles as a roving envoy to Europe. Welles, the State Department stressed, 'will, of course, be authorized to make no proposals or commitments in the name of the Government of the United States'.[21] He visited various belligerents and still uninvolved Italy, and rumours soon swirled in Dublin that he might visit Belfast, precipitating a rehearsal for the protest which would greet the Americans two years later. These rumours were embellished in nationalist circles with the addition of (the completely groundless) idea that America was making aid to Britain conditional on its commitment to small nations to include ending partition. As the *Irish News* put it: 'it appears that the American government desires that Britain should show sincerity in the matter of her war aims by insisting at the very least, on the restoration of normal democratic rights to the huge anti-partitionist population of the six County area'.[22] Northern Ireland (the 'Six County Junta') was compared to the Sudetenland, with its oppressed German minority, while 'Irish people both at home and in the United States, are awaiting with eagerness' Welles's visit.[23]

Cahir Healy, the Stormont MP for South Fermanagh, immediately wrote to the Dublin (rather than the Belfast) consulate requesting a meeting with Welles during his imagined trip, to explain the oppression of Catholics in Northern Ireland.[24] Francis Styles, the consul general, refused to indulge Healy and added a typed note on bottom of this request: 'respectfully referred to the American Consulate at Belfast for attention, and writer not informed'.[25] On receiving the memo, the Belfast consul, John Randolph, wrote to Ambassador Joseph Kennedy in London, noting that only the *Irish News* had reported the 'visit' and 'it is apparently to be assumed that there is no basis in fact for the rumors'.[26] Randolph also recognized the rumours as 'a new means of fighting the British government'.[27] In a separate 'Voluntary Political Report', Randolph described an anti-partition meeting in Londonderry which had telegraphed Kennedy to 'urge you immediately to request the president USA to instruct Mr Sumner Welles to visit Ireland before returning home to investigate suppression of minorities and refusal of democratic rights by British government, claiming to fight for liberty and democracy'.[28] Randolph argued that a possible visit would simply exacerbate tensions. He then wrote to Healy informing him that his request had been passed to Welles, but advised that his stay in London would be very brief.[29] At a press conference in London, amid answering many questions about the grave European situation, the famously taciturn Welles was asked if he would be visiting Ireland: his reply was 'No'.[30]

With this confirmed, nationalists now considered dispatching a delegation to London.[31] Reporting to Kennedy, Randolph talked of the 'alleged indignation' of nationalists, including an *Irish News* article which had converted Welles's 'No' into a 'refusal to grant interview'.[32] Healy now blamed Lord Halifax, the Foreign Secretary, for not passing on the message to Welles, even though Randolph had. Halifax's response unintentionally facilitated this interpretation, telling Healy: 'excuse the delay in answering your letter received 7th March. Have now ascertained that owing to short of time at Mr Welles' disposal it has not been possible to arrange interview requested'.[33] Nationalists could claim, therefore, that without Halifax's confessed tardiness, Welles might have been able to meet this delegation, when in reality it made not the slightest difference. Indeed, Éire's Department of External Affairs had already told Healy: 'Welles is not coming to Ireland, and not receiving deputation.'[34]

Patrick Maxwell, Nationalist MP at Stormont for Foyle, accused the British of creating a five-day delay to prevent the delegation from seeing Welles: 'it is quite obvious that at all costs the position of Northern Ireland under British rule must be kept quiet'.[35] Maxwell's self-important insularity was such that he believed Britain's overriding priority was not ending the European war but hiding partition from America. He, Healy and Joseph F. Stewart, the Nationalist MP in Stormont for East Tyrone, now threatened Roosevelt with the wrath of Irish-American voters with Healy, paraphrased by the *Irish News*, declaring: 'Mr Welles did not appear to be treating the large body of Irish people in the United States, who had strong views on this subject, with much consideration'.[36] Stewart warned that 'Irish voters in America' would note this snub, while Maxwell vowed to 'put the Irish in America in full possession of the facts'.[37] The originators of the request to see Welles, the Joint Council of the Irish Union Association and the Anti-Partition Council, sent a message to Roosevelt demanding he send Welles or another representative to 'investigate thoroughly the coercive measures and economic oppression employed against the Irish' in Northern Ireland.[38]

In the minds of Irish nationalists, their ancient (and immediate) dispute with Britain was as urgent for international diplomacy as Western Europe's fate, and if Roosevelt refused to prioritize ending partition, then Irish-American voters, already active in isolationist politics, would punish him in an election year. Nationalists, seeing that Welles was coming to Europe, assumed he would visit Ireland; they then reimagined American foreign policy (and British) by making ending partition an urgent priority, through allying their oppression with those already under the heel of or threatened by the Nazi jackboot. When Welles's non-existent trip to Ireland did not happen, and his fleeting stay in London filled with more pressing questions, this was repurposed as an egregious American snub engineered by the British and held up as another example of the latter's perfidiousness towards Ireland, allied to its hypocrisy about small nations' rights. This brief flurry of activity represented a large degree of fanciful thinking that Welles would either visit Ireland or have any interest in the nationalists' cause, but promoted these as fact, however, when neither came to pass, they professed themselves outraged.

'As welcome as the Germans in Norway': Reactions to the Americans.

The frustrations the American arrival created were particularly evident in Londonderry and featured in a revealing *Derry Journal* editorial. They had been sent 'at the request of the British Premier, without any reference to the Irish government', which, for reasons unclear, was the antithesis of American principles and propped up 'Orange rule in this unnatural enclave'. 'Age-long aspirations of National Sovereignty have been plainly impugned by the latest development' leaving 'the Irish leader' de Valera with no choice other than to protest.[39] Maxwell went further: '[a]s far as we are concerned the Americans are as welcome in Northern Ireland as the Germans are in Norway'.[40] He 'wholeheartedly' supported De Valera's protest and emphasized:

> [w]e shall ignore the American forces as far as possible, but there is no discourtesy intended. There is nothing physically we can do to throw them out or we would do so. We consider the landings of the Americans is an aggression against the Irish nation. The closest analogy would be if the Japanese landed in Occupied France to help the Germans.[41]

The Americans then would be ejected given the chance; their presence was aggression against Ireland; and, as if the Norway analogy was insufficiently laboured, the American presence was also compared to the subjugation of France for good measure. Maxwell's fatuousness makes it difficult to take the sincerity of his outrage seriously; nonetheless, his comments were widely reported, including a brief reference in the *New York Times*, which perhaps reveals that this hyperbole was largely for effect.[42] Stewart avoided dubious analogies while expressing a similar view: 'Mr de Valera's declaration is shared by all Nationalists in the six counties . . . the people of Ireland should have been consulted before the army of another country, however friendly, should have been brought into Irish soil.'[43] The support of Maxwell, Stewart and the *Journal* for de Valera masked nationalism's divisions. Those in Northern Ireland felt that Dublin should aid them; however, the Taoiseach unambiguously told a delegation in 1940 their plight was secondary to neutrality, and he would do nothing regarding partition which would endanger this. The meeting's minutes stated de Valera's view that 'the retention of the 26 county status was considered to be of such value that the loss of it could not be risked in any effort to reintegrate the country'; he would make no imminent effort to end partition and effectively abandoned them.[44] Even without the pretexts of war and neutrality, regardless of his public stance, de Valera never prioritized ending partition, preferring to consolidate his and his party's position in Éire.[45] As Fanning eloquently puts it: 'the careful cultivation of the Irish sense of grievance about partition, moreover, suited de Valera's political purposes: both domestically, inasmuch as it helped keep public opinion united behind his policy, and internationally, in that it provided him with a practical as opposed to a theoretical reason for refusing to become an ally of the United Kingdom'.[46]

Nationalists in Northern Ireland were blind to neither this reality nor the fact that their plight was exploited by politicians in Éire; as Healy reflected ruefully in 1926, '[o]ut of power they would use us. In power, they would find a hundred reasons for leaving us to paddle our own canoe'.[47] In January 1943, Buhrman remarked upon cross-border discord among nationalists just before Éire's general election. He cited an *Irish News* editorial hugely critical of those in Éire who opportunistically used partition for short-term political gain, decrying 'speeches and promises calculated merely to prolong Partition'. The editorial condemned those deliberately creating false hopes and demanded that the 'exploitation of partition for party purposes' in Éire end, along with actions 'not only foredoomed to failure but also calculated to make matters worse' (a criticism which could be equally levelled at the paper's editorial policy).[48] Buhrman believed that 'most all objective observers' agreed with the editorial's message; in a perceptive assessment, however, he also argued that 'the general attitude of the Nationalist (Catholic) Party In Northern Ireland tends to solidify the opposition to any union of Northern Ireland and Éire, rather than, as asserted by them, promoting it', and constant attacks on Stormont 'actually discourages union with Éire'.[49] He regarded, therefore, nationalists on either side of the border as equally culpable for partition's persistence and judged their attitudes as self-defeating and, in Éire, deeply cynical. This was perhaps his best analysis of local politics.[50]

The Ulster Union Club was an outlier within nationalist politics, consisting largely of Ulster Protestants dedicated to ending partition, some of whom (to the horror of colleagues) were jailed for IRA membership during the war.[51] It was formed in February 1941, and led by Great War veteran Captain Denis Ireland, with a mission 'to recapture for Ulster Protestants their true tradition as Irishmen'.[52] It offered similar objections to the Americans as other nationalist groups, but hinted that Ireland should join the war, claiming that American troops had landed '[b]ecause the Northern Government is incapable of defending and the national Government is not allowed to defend the whole country'. The club acknowledged Ulster's contribution to the United States, while lamenting the loss of the virtues which had facilitated this, arguing that '[t]he Protestant tradition of Ulster, before its falsification in the interests of Ascendancy, was one of the moving forces in the establishment of the American Republic'.[53] Celebrating America thus rang rather hollow in contemporary unionist politics. Like other nationalist historical analogies, it linked Lincoln defending the union with its ambition of making Ireland whole. The Ulster Union Club, a fringe organization noteworthy largely for its non-sectarian ethos, showed how unionism and nationalism's American narratives were not necessarily exclusive, while demonstrating that each extracted selective lessons from these links.

To nationalism the war, and everything else, was secondary to partition; moreover, American actions were viewed as explicitly endorsing Ireland's division. Some of the protests inferred that an American appeal to Éire's government (or a hypothetical all-island government) would have been considered generously. This, of course, ran contrary to Éire's neutrality – de Valera's fundamental priority – and his negativity towards the Allies at this point. The protests, nonetheless, were at pains to emphasize traditional America-Irish friendship and that American troops would come to no harm.

The nationalist response dismayed W. S. Moody of Strabane, who offered a shrewd assessment of the American presence and the impossibility of objections to it ending partition. Writing to the *Journal*, Moody saw these protests as utterly counterproductive, bemoaning 'the spectacle of leaders of Irish Nationalism helping to defeat the immediate or near future prospects of an all-Ireland Republic, by alienating and antagonizing American opinion'. The Americans, he noted, had previously given the Irish precious leverage against the British, but 'to gratuitously throw away further potential support and sympathy for the sake of a national hyper-dignity to be recognized by the world to some far distant and remote Utopian era . . . compels admiration for the heart but certainly not the head'. He further argued that de Valera could have outmanoeuvred unionists by assisting the Americans at some level, 'but no, the leaders of Irish Nationalism in their recently acquired dignity and status of neutrality can be relied on to scorn all such base compromise . . . thus helping to assure and perpetuate Partition'. Hiding behind neutrality, nationalist leaders fortified partition: 'the fondness of Irish Nationalist leaders for making such defiant gestures and outbursts exceeds their sincere desire for a united Ireland, otherwise they would not so patently allow their means to defeat their end'.[54] This analysis, more thoughtful and with greater insight than anything proffered by professional commentators and politicians, did not require supporting the war or abandoning aspirations; it merely suggested pragmatism was a better strategy than counter productive and tetchy parochialism.

In Dublin, leader of the opposition Fine Gael party William T. Cosgrave had a similar outlook, saying that, paraphrased by the *Whig*, Éire's best interests were best served by politicians offering 'a sensible and discreet silence on their external relations generally'.[55] This essentially happened. Condemning the American presence only alienated American public opinion, so most nationalist spokesmen held their tongues until the war ended, and after the initial outrage, nationalism outwardly ignored the Americans. Protests against the Americans, therefore, were not ongoing, and only briefly resurfaced from August to October 1942 amid tensions surrounding the execution of an IRA member.

Neutrality was understandably non-negotiable for both de Valera and Éire, yet acknowledging the special circumstances necessitating the American presence, and the suspension of anti-partition agitation for the duration (or at least not making partition an excuse for neutrality), proved beyond the dogged adherence to the idea that partition was simply a British imposition and Ireland's problems would be solved with its removal. To the greater detriment of the nationalist cause, as Duggan contends, 'the inexorable demands of the war extinguished any sympathy for Irish neutrality even among Irish-Americans', beginning a process of disengagement in Irish affairs by Americans.[56] To claw back American goodwill, partition was retrospectively emphasized as the rationale for neutrality, with the insinuation that Éire would have aided the Americans and perhaps even participated in the war without this. This was, of course, completely untrue. The protests' impetuous tenor illustrated sincere convictions about partition, and complaints about Stormont's treatment of Catholics were entirely valid; nevertheless, post-Pearl Harbor, nationalists cannot have reasonably expected their practiced outrage to find a sympathetic audience in the States, beyond the most recalcitrant Irish-Americans.

'My country overrun': Cardinal MacRory and the Americans

The Catholic Church advocated anti-partitionism as steadfastly as any other voice within nationalism and acted as a unifying presence amid political nationalism's various schisms.[57] If nationalist Ireland's political cues came largely from de Valera, then its spiritual and moral leader was Cardinal Joseph MacRory, the Archbishop of Armagh and head of the Catholic Church from 1928 until his death in late 1945. Born in Ballygawley, County Tyrone, in 1861, he was already eighty in 1942. At Northern Ireland's birth in the early 1920s he witnessed the sectarian bloodletting in Belfast, in which the victims were disproportionately Catholics, and became a fierce critic of partition. While this rationalizes his political hostility towards unionists, he was also theologically anti-Protestant, calling the religion a 'cult' rather than a branch of Christianity, infamously declaring in 1932: '[t]he Protestant Church in Ireland – and the same is true of the Protestant Church anywhere – is not only not the rightful representative of the early Irish Church, but it is not even a part of the Church of Christ'.[58] Lee contends that MacRory 'had the knack of fuelling the fire of Protestant resentment at the imperialist pretensions, real and presumed, of Catholic ecclesiastics'.[59] Michael McCabe is no more sympathetic, arguing his 'ghetto mentality' was 'a primary cause of lasting sectarian tension in Northern Ireland' in his refusal, unlike his predecessor Patrick O'Donnell, to engage with the new state, preferring to make partition the focal point of his ministry.[60] The American forces provided a renewed forum for attacks on partition, while paradoxically claiming that the Allies' commitment to protecting small nations should also apply to an undivided Ireland.

MacRory was apathetic about the war's outcome, telling Abercorn in December 1939, after a request that the Catholic Church assist the 'Governor's Fund' for war relief that 'I regret I cannot see my way to do what Your Grace ... suggests. I have not a particle of sympathy with this war. I believe that there have been faults on both sides' and urged negotiations.[61] The war was, therefore, none of the Irish Catholic Church's business. It was possible that unionists wanted to put MacRory and the Catholic Church on record as hostile to the war effort, but nothing was made of MacRory's terseness or the church's implicit attitude to the Allied cause; furthermore, Catholics were unlikely to participate in the governor's scheme and Abercorn was naïve in thinking otherwise.[62] Abercorn may have made his request innocently, yet it is doubtful that any senior Catholic cleric would endorse raising money for British servicemen or a fund involving the Royal family at the request of the monarch's representative in what they regarded as occupied territory.

At times, it seemed that MacRory felt his, and Catholic Ireland's, interests were best served by accommodation with Germany. In June 1940, as France collapsed, Hempel wrote of MacRory's receptiveness to possible German assistance in ending partition and that autumn recorded his perception of the Catholic Church's gathering support for Germany.[63] On 18 May 1941, shortly after the Blitz on Belfast, and fearing further Luftwaffe attacks, MacRory visited Hempel seeking assurances that Armagh, the ecclesiastical capital of Ireland, would be spared.[64] Hempel saw MacRory as a personal friend, but also recognized him as strongly anti-British and a staunch supporter of

Éire's neutrality. Hempel was very sympathetic, partly because Armagh contained little of military value (although this had not spared other historic sites).[65] As an aside, Duggan notes that German attacks on Belfast 'shattered to illusion fondly held by the Irish government that the Germans had been respecting the integrity of the 32 counties in refraining from bombing'.[66] The Germans, like the Americans, therefore, recognized partition's reality and cared little for nationalist aspirations.

From the war's onset, MacRory advocated a negotiated peace, and after making a speech about this in October 1941, he and Gray exchanged letters. Gray wondered how, given Hitler's assurances to countries he subsequently invaded, to guarantee such a peace.[67] MacRory again suggested that the Allies seek a negotiated settlement: '[m]y position is that whatever Hitler may be, you ought to try to make peace with him now, because you may have to do so later on'. 'I don't forget Hitler's breach of Treaties', he continued, 'though I fancy he would have something to say about the circumstances in which they were entered into. . . . I regard his action as unjust. But was there no injustice against him and Germany?'[68] Hitler's actions were, then, a legitimate, or at least understandable, response to the Treaty of Versailles; this opinion was not unusual even as Hitler annexed 'German' territories in the 1930s; it was, nonetheless, much less sustainable after the invasions of Poland and western European democracies. Gray called the speech the 'best and strongest' case for a negotiated peace that he had heard, even if he disagreed with it.[69] At around the same time, MacRory was quoted by Walshe as saying that 'a victory for America and England would be worse for Christianity than a victory for Germany', as German Catholicism was stronger and he was wary of Anglo-American 'materialistic humanitarianism'.[70]

In October 1942, MacRory again advocated a negotiated peace as the only 'hope of peace with justice'.[71] Stalemate was a distinct possibility, and he worried that 'if either side wins there will be a peace not of justice but of vengeance which will but sow the seeds of future wars'.[72] MacRory was wary of repeating the errors of the Great War, now seen as major causes of the current conflict. Buhrman sent this address to the State Department, commenting: '[t]he press of Northern Ireland contrasts the Cardinal Archbishop's statement with the German view that if the war reaches a stalemate or negotiated peace under present conditions it would constitute a German victory and the defeat of Great Britain'.[73] In effect, MacRory's reasonable analysis obliquely, if innocently, advocated the best current outcome for Germany. In his Lenten Pastoral of 1943 he now recognized the impossibility of a negotiated peace and that the war would only end when one side was victorious or both realized the war was deadlocked.[74]

The Cardinal made no public comment on the Americans' arrival, but his attitude became problematic during the IRA's campaign later in 1942. MacRory did not publically support the IRA; yet, knowing that it had threatened the Americans, he further stoked tensions in the aftermath of the execution of the man convicted of murdering a policeman.[75] He used a speech at St Patrick's College, Cavan, in September 1942 to complain about being 'overrun' by Allied troops, linking it to the 'grave injustice' of partition. 'When I read day after day in the press,' he declared, 'that this war is being fought for the liberties of small nations, and then think of my own corner of my country overrun by British and United States soldiers against the will of the nation I confess I sometimes find it exceedingly hard to be patient'.[76] This was either singularly inept timing – a generous interpretation – or wilfully provocative. MacRory would have known that the IRA had threatened Americans and that his words could justify attacks against them, and even given impetus to the terrorists' flagging campaign. Gray's anger about the statement led to a robust yet generally restrained letter, stressing their friendship and expressing concern that nationalist veneration of the dead man would see American troops attacked.[77] MacRory just as robustly rejected these criticisms, restating that America's acceptance of 'England's' invitation condoned partition and predicting, correctly it must be stressed, that no Americans would be harmed during the crisis.[78]

MacRory did not go unrebuked. A letter to the *Whig* asserted that he had 'uttered words that are almost unbelievable' due to 'a narrow political expediency'. The correspondent declared that 'the implied comparison between Ireland and Europe is insulting to adult sense [and] an unspeakable degradation of judgment'. He wondered if MacRory would prefer Germans to Americans: 'it must be one or the other'.[79] A writer to the *News Letter* derided MacRory's 'qualms', his and the Catholic Church's silence after the murder of Constable Patrick Murphy and noted the Germans' treatment of Polish Catholics: '[w]hat a contrast to being protected by the American and British soldiers who "overrun" Northern Ireland'.[80] By contrast, Staunton notes MacRory's refusal to comment on the murders of a policeman and a 'B'-Special in the same week as the execution, with the Cardinal suddenly wary about 'saying too much'.[81] Inevitable condemnation from the unionist press (Stormont ministers said nothing) or even Gray – increasingly unpopular in Dublin – had little effect on MacRory. A backlash in America was another matter. A Catholic New Yorker privately warned him that '[i]f Ireland were offered full freedom by Hitler, it would be nothing but right to reject that freedom, however coveted it is by all freedom loving Irishmen', as it would be tantamount to being 'offered salvation by the Devil'.[82] Without American intervention, Ireland risked other small nations' fates, and now was the wrong time to challenge partition as 'compared to the sufferings, of other countries, Ireland even at the present time must be living in a paradise'.[83]

Bishop Joseph Hurley of Florida, a strong supporter of American interventionism and an opponent of the Vatican's attitude towards the Nazis, was highly critical, asserting that America and Britain fought for everybody's rights, including Ireland's.[84] He condemned 'the slur implicit in the Cardinal's words' and denied that US troops were 'overrunning' Northern Ireland: 'there is no evidence of American soldiers conducting themselves in anything but a gentlemanly manner in their dealings with the populace'. He also stressed that they were invited by the legitimate government and had 'a clear right' to be there. That said, Hurley's sympathies remained with Irish nationalists: 'our desire to see the end of partition must not blind us to the fact that international law and Christian ethics look upon the government as de jure'. MacRory's comments were disingenuous as American troops were protecting Éire and would save him from 'the indignity and violence' suffered by Cardinals in other small countries. He also warned MacRory that soon 'more than neutrality will be expected from Ireland' as Hitler had stated that eventually countries would have to take sides.[85] Hurley told Gray he was 'greatly concerned by the public attitudes taken by Irish statesmen and Irish ecclesiastics', and MacRory's statement was 'incomprehensible' to himself and Americans otherwise sympathetic to Ireland.[86] Kennedy, recalled as ambassador in October 1940 due to his defeatism and unpopularity within the UK government, warned Gray that 'Hurley's prestige is not particularly strong amongst either the Catholics, the Irish or anybody else except a few New Dealers in Washington'.[87] John McQuaid, the Archbishop of Dublin, assured MacRory that Hurley's influence was limited.[88] Hurley's real crimes, to Kennedy and others, were his pre-Pearl Harbor attacks on Catholic isolationists and closeness to the Roosevelt administration.

Some American newspapers picked up the story, connecting it to American resentment about Éire's neutrality, and compared the benign American presence to a Nazi invasion.[89] A *Richmond Times-Dispatch* editorial derided 'A Cardinal's Carping', condemning MacRory's 'ill-timed if not incomprehensible remarks', arguing that Éire was protected by Allied forces; indeed, Northern Ireland would be a 'paradise by comparison with the fate of Irish Catholicism under Nazidom'. 'Cardinal MacRory', it concluded, 'would have rendered a service to the cause of freedom by keeping silent'.[90] Jay Franklin of the *Newark News* wondered if the 'war is being fought for the rights and liberties of small nations, why is not Ireland fighting for those rights and liberties?'[91] He denounced the 'queer mixture of quaking cowardice and injured innocence' of Éire's neutrality, concluding 'his voice is only the voice of one man, and an old man at that, rather than the voice of the people or of God'.[92]

More damaging than regional newspaper reports was *Time* magazine's intervention. Recalling his praise for America in a 1935 visit, *Time* reported that 'the 81-year-old Cardinal addressed Americans in a different fashion', noting sardonically: 'by "my own corner", the Cardinal meant 66% Protestant Ulster, where he was born, lives' and accused MacRory of 'lean[ing] so far backward in his effort to be neutral that his head sometimes seems to be in the Third Reich'.[93] Noteworthy in the aftermath is that, unlike when de Valera condemned the Americans' arrival, no-one within nationalism (Cork's Old IRA association aside) came to his defence; this was not motivated by opposition to his sentiments but, instead, the pragmatic need to avoid further alienating America.[94]

Privately, his views on the war were even more extreme. A few months later, Éire's High Commissioner in London, in effect its ambassador, John W. Dulanty reported to Walshe a conversation between Francis Matthews (the vice-president of the USO and an important figure in American Catholic fraternal organizations), Gray and the Cardinal. A shocked Matthews stated that 'Cardinal McRory voiced to them strong anti-English sentiments, saying that he would prefer to have a peace dictated by Hitler rather than by the British'. Matthews affirmed his own opposition to partition and 'held no brief' for the British but stressed that American Catholics 'held firmly, very opposite views' to the Cardinal on the war. MacRory had no answer, but Matthews thought him 'very sad and perplexed'. Matthews and Gray agreed to treat the conversation in strict confidence, but the former felt it necessary to inform Dulanty and the Archbishop of Dublin.[95]

Unchastened, MacRory continued to call for a negotiated settlement and creatively connecting the Allies' war aims to ending partition, while believing that the latter would also make sense to the Axis powers if they were victorious. In his 1944 Lenten Pastoral, moreover, he declared that 'Éire deserves credit for not having allied herself with the Axis nations and offered them hospitality and assistance' due to Britain's history in

Ireland; Gray warned against Churchill speaking out.⁹⁶ In his diary, Sir Wilfrid Spender, head of Northern Ireland's civil service, believed reconciliation between Catholics and Protestants was practically impossible 'whilst the leading men of the former expressed views of this character'.⁹⁷

There was no softening in MacRory's attitude towards the war or the aspirations of Protestants as the conflict drew to a close. In June 1945, Maffey paraphrased a conversation with the Cardinal to Sir Eric Machtig, Undersecretary of State at the Dominions Office: '[w]hy doesn't England stop encouraging these people in the North? If England left them to their own devices they would soon join the South. And they would be thoroughly well-treated, although they don't believe it'. When asked about Northern Ireland's strategic importance in preventing the allies' defeat, MacRory's response was *Fiat justitia ruat cælum*, a Latin legal phrase meaning 'let justice be done though the heavens fall'. Accordingly, Britain should simply abandon unionists, while the inference persisted that the Allies' defeat would have been a price worth paying to end partition, despite the horrors of Nazism having been fully exposed to the world.⁹⁸ To Machtig, 'Cardinal MacRory's obtuseness is pretty remarkable'; he was 'quite immune of the realities of the situation', mused Undersecretary of State Paul Emrys-Evans.⁹⁹

Upon MacRory's death in October 1945, the *News Letter* recognized 'a brilliant scholar and writer . . . a life-long advocate of Home Rule for Ireland, and an outspoken opponent of Irish partition'. Yet his legacy was tainted as 'during the war he avoided saying anything that would be indicative of moral support for the Allies', described the Americans as an 'occupation force' and claimed that Éire deserved credit for not siding with the Axis powers.¹⁰⁰ This apparent moral ambivalence about an Axis victory, indeed, even hinting that he viewed it positively if it ended partition, adds MacRory to the list of Irish nationalists who inhabited what Staunton calls a 'self-referential moral universe' in their attitudes towards the war, attitudes which ultimately sully their reputations.¹⁰¹

'As wise as the serpent and harmless as the dove': The visits of Frank Matthews and Cardinal Francis Spellman

Not all American guests were as welcome as Mrs Roosevelt or the procession of entertainers who passed through. Francis (Frank) Matthews was the most high-profile American critic of partition to visit, arriving in February 1943 in his USO capacity. He was also the Supreme Knight of the Knights of Columbus, an American Catholic fraternal organization, and, according to *Stars and Stripes*, came 'as a representative of the American Catholic Hierarchy'.¹⁰² He called on MacRory, then, accompanied by Gray and US General Edmund Hill, he visited the Red Cross club in Londonderry; and he was Bishop Farren's guest in the city. At the Red Cross Club in Belfast he praised US forces.¹⁰³ He also visited Éire and would report to Roosevelt upon return to the States.¹⁰⁴ Buhrman noted Matthews' public comments, including the 'vital and living questions facing the Irish people in this cataclysmic war, those of unity and of Ireland's traditional part in the struggle for liberty. I carry away with as a sincere hope that these questions will soon be satisfactorily settled'.[105] Buhrman privately found him more vociferous, giving 'the impression of being a zealous proponent of Irish unity and independence' who hoped that the US Congress would intervene. Buhrman developed an exaggerated fear that Matthews would inject the 'Irish question' into American politics, likely embarrassing America's principal ally, negatively impact the war effort and incite the IRA to destabilize Northern Ireland; he recommended, therefore, that Matthews be discouraged from making anti-partitionist statements.[106] The nationalist press covered Matthews extensively, but he drew neither comment from Stormont nor, it seems, any effort to arrange an official meeting (Figure 5.1).[107]

Much more problematic was the visit, in April 1943, of Francis Spellman, the Catholic Archbishop of New York and the Chaplain General of the American forces.[108] Spellman, the grandson of Irish immigrants, was a powerful political figure in America, numbering Roosevelt and Kennedy among his friends and confidantes, while he was a close personal friend of the Pope and subsequently a strident supporter of both Joseph McCarthy and American involvement in Vietnam. Spellman was appointed Roosevelt's representative to the Vatican in October 1939 to foster closer relations with the Holy See, a not necessarily popular move among nativist American

Figure 5.1 Visit of Francis Matthews (United Services Organization and Knights of Columbus) to Northern Ireland in February 1943. Left to right: Maj. Timothy J. McInerney, Maj. Edward McGuire, Francis Matthews, Joseph Cardinal MacRory, David Gray (US Minister to Éire), Col. Benjamin Bassett and Shane Leslie. Francis P. Matthews Papers, 70-5154, Truman Library/Cardinal Ó Fiaich Memorial Library.

Protestants.[109] When America entered the war, Spellman became a roving ambassador for Roosevelt and the American cause. Spellman, with his unconditional patriotism, tried to dispel whatever taint attached itself to Irish-Americans prior to Pearl Harbor, be it isolationism or perceptions that Catholicism made them less American. As for his diplomatic role, his biographer Cooney explains: 'Spellman would act as a clandestine agent for him [Roosevelt] in the far corners of the world. . . . He would carry messages for the President, present the American point of view – forcefully when necessary- and act as Roosevelt's eyes and ears.'[110] This was true when he visited Dublin.

He was in London during a sixteen-country tour for Roosevelt, when Arthur Hinsley the Archbishop of Westminster died, and stayed for the funeral.[111] He then travelled to Dublin, at MacRory's invitation, before visiting American forces in Northern Ireland.[112] On the one hand, Stormont had to welcome an American dignitary of Spellman's standing, but his Catholicism alone would be sufficient to offend many Protestants. On top of this, Stormont officials assumed that a Catholic clergyman of Irish descent would be instinctively antagonistic, and his motives were questioned on this assumption. Stormont's paranoia was understandable given that its anti-Catholic discrimination was a matter of public record among Irish-Americans, and Spellman would be visiting MacRory. With the competing agendas of unionism and nationalism, the visit had to be handled very carefully by Gray, Spellman and Stormont. Spellman may have wanted to avoid legitimizing Stormont, even if it was an American ally; however, the available records reveal no views on partition. Any perceived slight against Spellman or any anti-Catholic bigotry from officials risked Stormont's strategy of portraying Northern Ireland positively. At the same time, ministers, fronting an increasingly unpopular government, were also aware that their core Protestant support would take a dim view of the remotest friendliness to the Catholic Church.

Stormont was conscious that MacRory would meet Spellman first, in Dublin or Armagh, and that he would offer a thoroughly jaundiced view of the state; Andrews, who had little desire to meet Spellman and contemplated snubbing him completely, had to find a way to cause the minimum offence to the maximum number of people.[113] A memorandum written by William Lowry, the Minister for Home Affairs, to Andrews reflected Stormont's concern, not to mention its general distrust of any Catholic's motivations:

> It occurs to me that you and members of the cabinet may think it necessary to consider carefully what your attitude should be. The Reverend Gentleman will, doubtless, be staying with Cardinal MacRory [who has] consistently ignored the existence of this Government. I am inclined to think that Monseigneur [sic] Spellman's visit has a political significance. It might not be desirable from the standpoint of Northern Ireland to ignore him completely. This might give him an opportunity in his capacity as Chaplain General to go back to America and describe the Government of this country as a pack of benighted bigots. To show him some attention, on the other hand, might raise some unfavourable comment from some of the Government's staunchest supporters. Therefore, I think the question requires deliberate consideration.[114]

It continued:

> [i]f you decided to extend some Government hosp[itality] to him, the strong possibilities are that Cardinal MacRory, who will be his host in Northern Ireland, would not accept your invitation. The Monseigneur consequently would in all likelihood follow the same line, so the government, without running any grave risk, could say that it had made a friendly gesture which was declined.

Lowry's memorandum concluded: 'Spellman's activities, I am sure, are sinister. At the same time this is not a good reason for this Government not being as wise as the serpent and harmless as the dove.'[115] Stormont's unofficial line, then, was that Spellman, in cahoots with MacRory, was determined to make it look bad, and in Lowry's mind, possibly even the sole reason for his visit, but a little tact could avoid this. The cabinet decided 'that the course which would arouse least criticism' would be to invite Spellman, along with Buhrman and the head of American forces for a private lunch with Andrews at Stormont.[116] Spellman, it would seem, was not to be accorded the usual diplomatic niceties and would be largely hidden. If the solution was unsatisfactory, it at least would not spark a diplomatic incident and could avoid negative publicity for Stormont. Spellman, perhaps making the same calculations, was unable, by accident or design, to accept the invitation.[117]

Spellman travelled to London, meeting Churchill, then Dublin, with a remit from Roosevelt, reinforced by Churchill, to pressurize de Valera, according to Cooney, 'to try to ease Ireland's hostility toward England and to help the allied war effort. The job was practically impossible, but Spellman undertook it anyway'.[118] Spellman was extremely well received in Éire and garnered much good press, but his key role was as Roosevelt's emissary.[119] The US Military Intelligence Division warned Spellman that de Valera was 'clever [but] believed incapable of being influenced by practical considerations or requirements'.[120] Spellman's arrival coincided with a particular low point in American-Irish relations, with Gray especially unpopular within government circles. Gray wanted to use Spellman to reinforce his and Roosevelt's 'absent treatment' of Éire, an effort to make neutrality as uncomfortable and, at times, humiliating, as possible, so Gray initially suggested Spellman skip Dublin completely.[121] Unable to use his absence, Gray opted instead to exploit Spellman's presence. Roosevelt told Spellman that Gray wanted him to stay at the legation rather than with the Archbishop of Dublin, but 'I want you to use your discretion'.[122] Spellman was happy to facilitate Dublin's discomfort, and by association that of the Irish church, by pointedly and against friends' advice staying at the legation.[123] Gray informed MacRory that Spellman had requested 'no formal entertainment' as it was the Lenten Season; however, the minister would host a dinner at the legation.[124]

The dinner found de Valera in an uncompromising mood and Spellman's efforts were ultimately fruitless. Afterwards, however, Gray reported having never seen de Valera 'so sour and depressed', annoyed that someone with Irish ancestors refused to see the world through his eyes, and whose allegiance was entirely to America, not his grandparents' country of birth.[125] Spellman reiterated his loyalties in a mass where 'our Archbishop slipped in the American viewpoint continuously but of course the Government through its press has soft-pedalled all this and claims the visit as a compliment paid by America to Ireland'.[126] Gray was triumphant: '[o]f course, Dev knows that we put this over on him and that is one thing that makes him so sour. He considers the support of American Catholics for his Nationalistic policies his RIGHT'.[127]

According to the *Telegraph*, at a mass in Dublin, Spellman recalled spending St Patrick's Day in North Africa a few weeks earlier with Irish soldiers, 'not only men from the South but men from Northern Ireland as well', and stated that he would be visiting 'American troops in Northern Ireland'.[128] De Valera's *Irish Press*, however, quoted the Cardinal as saying 'not only men from the Twenty-Six Counties but men from the Six counties'.[129] The *Irish Independent*, a Fine Gael supporting Dublin newspaper, paraphrased him as meeting 'men from Southern and Northern Ireland'; the *News Letter* also paraphrased the speech in its report, saying 'he met men from the South and men from the North'.[130] If the *Telegraph*'s transcription was correct, consciously or otherwise, Spellman made a political statement by using 'Northern Ireland' rather than simply the 'North', or more particularly, 'the six counties', as these terms denoted Dublin's explicit refusal to recognize Northern Ireland's existence. This apparently innocuous, if correct, use of nomenclature could, in fact, be seen as highly provocative given the audience and setting, and was guaranteed to raise the heckles of any Irish republican and be perceived as a very public slight against ending partition with American help.[131] Conversely, if the *Irish Press's* version is correct, he had at least rhetorically sided with Irish nationalism.

The *Derry Journal* reported the 'prolonged cheering from 500 people' on Spellman's arrival in Armagh.[132] The unionist press was on its best behaviour, doubtlessly recognizing the importance of portraying Northern Ireland in a good light, and reported the trip positively, with the *Telegraph* also noting the crowd's enthusiasm.[133] The *News Letter* was equally fulsome, reporting that American troops from across Northern Ireland attended the benediction, the Chaplain General's charity work in Dublin and even that a child in Armagh had been named after him.[134] Éire's newspapers, ironically, with the exception of the de Valera supporting the *Irish Press*, avoided mentioning that he was visiting American forces.[135] Gray drove with Spellman to Cardinal MacRory's official residence in Armagh. MacRory was not at the dinner in Dublin; he and Gray had fallen out after the latter leaked a private response to MacRory's criticism of the American forces, and the minister did not stay for lunch.[136] The spat with Gray led to MacRory being rude to Spellman, for which he later apologized.[137] Spellman was wary of MacRory, characterized by American military intelligence after the trip as 'extremely dangerous' because of his willingness to stir-up anti-Britishness.[138] Spellman, as Chaplain General, may have also taken exception to MacRory's criticism of American troops.

The two clerics did not issue any statement, but in its absence, and perhaps reflecting his irritation at Spellman, MacRory made his own. He tried to expose the apparent hypocrisy of the Allies regarding small nations and interpreted Allied war aims as advocating the end of partition. He again complained about the 'arbitrary political division unjustly imposed upon our people' and wanted 'Catholics and non-Catholics' to come together as 'brother Irishmen'. He then claimed that the Atlantic Charter of

1941, outlining Allied war aims, was 'a sign of repentance' regarding partition which 'gives a solemn undertaking which in case the Allies win the war should be certain to bring Partition in Ireland to a speedy end'.[139] MacRory set up nationalists for further disappointment if, and this seems implausible, he genuinely saw the Atlantic Charter even remotely as 'a sign of repentance' over partition. He also appeared to be positioning himself for further outrage when, inevitably, the fulfilment of Allied war aims had no bearing on partition. As for '[w]hat would happen to us in the event of an Axis victory I cannot, of course, say, but I have a hope that they would see the folly and absurdity of dividing or partitioning a small island like ours, made one by God'.[140] Even as late as 1943, therefore, MacRory either still believed that a positive side-effect of a German victory might be the end of partition or, and only a moderately more charitable explanation, was prepared to cynically use this hypothetical scenario to vent his own political frustrations while fostering future resentment when an unmade promise was broken.

Spellman was apparently too busy to see either Andrews or Abercorn at Stormont.[141] He restricted his engagements to the US military; although this seems unlikely to have been designed as a slight on the government (as noted, not all American dignitaries met ministers), it was certainly taken as such. His one official engagement with Abercorn was cancelled when the duke, perhaps conveniently, developed a 'lame ankle'.[142] There was confusion between American representatives in Belfast, London and Dublin over the visit. Buhrman reported that initially Spellman had indicated that he 'would be very pleased to accept the Prime Minister's kind invitation', if his schedule allowed, though ministers declared themselves 'not particularly pleased' upon discovering his acceptance of MacRory's invitation, but not theirs.[143] Gray explained that Spellman was in Éire 'in no official capacity' – which was not quite true – and understood that the US embassy in London had passed his apologies onto Andrews. As a postscript, Gray informed Buhrman that 'by compressing his schedule', Spellman could call upon Abercorn in Hillsborough, after all.[144] Buhrman was not entirely satisfied with this explanation: '[i]t is rather unfortunate that he could not accept one or other of the invitations that were given to him here. . . . His failure to do so has caused some embarrassment and some hesitation on the part of members of the Government in accepting an invitation to the reception being given by General Hill'.[145] This, of course, could have been a convenient excuse for Stormont ministers not to meet Spellman.

Gray claimed that the embassy was responsible for the mix-up and maintained that the Dublin visit could not be shortened to lengthen his stay in Northern Ireland.[146] Buhrman shifted the blame for these misunderstandings to the embassy and maintained that Spellman turned down Stormont's invitations, embarrassing Hill in the process: '[i]t seems that somebody in London had suggested that he would like to meet members of the Government. However, after the Archbishop had declined both the invitations of the Prime Minister and the Governor it placed General Hill in a rather difficult position to invite them all out to meet him'.[147] That said, despite the confusion, Andrews and two of his ministers attended the function which 'went off very nicely indeed'.[148] In the midst of these discussions, Buhrman complained to the Secretary of State that Spellman 'did not make a very good impression. . . . [He] declined these two invitations on the pretext that his appointments were such and his time so limited that he could not accept them'.[149] From the perspective of Andrews, and to the satisfaction of his paranoia, no slight could be claimed by, or on behalf of, Spellman as he had gone out of his way to accommodate the Archbishop and had met him when the opportunity had arisen.

Irish nationalists sought Spellman's support against 'The Partition Crime'. The elected representatives of 'the Catholics of North East Ulster' wished to discuss 'the conditions under which we live' and, unable to secure a meeting due to 'the circumstances of your hurried visit', telegraphed Spellman. Partition was 'the greatest crime ever perpetrated on our people', committed 'by a big powerful Empire in the interests of a few of its colonists against the native inhabitants of an old and cultured race', and urged the Americans not to ignore 'the dismemberment of our Country'. They then cited Lincoln's determination to maintain the union and also hoped that the justice an Allied victory promised for small nations 'shall also be meted out to us, and Ireland returned to her original dignity as a self-governing unit among the peoples of the world. The restoration of her territorial integrity and the withdrawal of foreign armies of occupation will be the real test of international good faith'.[150] This diatribe at least supported an eventual allied victory, or at least the illusion it would serve their interests, despite their complete lack of a contribution to it. Shortly beforehand, the *Irish Press* had weighed in with the judgement that '[t]here is no kind of oppression visited on any minority in Europe which the Six County nationalists have not also endured'.[151] The Irish-American press was even more vitriolic; the *Irish World* claimed that Catholics confronted a 'tyranny just as ruthless as that which we condemn so vigorously in other parts of the world'.[152]

A reasoned plea came from Tipperary's *Nenagh Guardian*, which wanted Spellman to 'tell of our political hopes in high places' upon his return to America. 'Though Dr Spellman's visit is politically unofficial', it argued, 'many hearts in the North will beat a little faster if this straight speaking prelate' reminded America that his to visit Cardinal MacRory required crossing a border.[153] The reliably unionist *Telegraph* reflected positively upon the visit, noting that Spellman 'had nothing to fear' from coming to Northern Ireland as 'every friend of the United Nations was glad to see him, and to know that he was bringing a message of cheer to the men of his own faith in their war effort'. It also recognized that his purpose was to pressurize Éire and felt that MacRory's most recent remarks about 'wrongs' against Ireland, demonstrated that, to the Cardinal, partition 'count[s] for more than the stern realities of the present, world-situation', an attitude unlikely to win many friends in Washington.[154]

The self-importance of nationalists and the defensive paranoia of unionists regarding Spellman starkly illustrated their highly circumscribed world views and parochialism and their misreading of his priorities. Spellman was an American patriot first and foremost, an attitude heightened by the war; he was, as McNamara asserts, 'the face of American Catholic patriotism'.[155] It would seem that unionists had little to fear from Spellman, while nationalists found no champion in him. His apparent snubbing of the unionist government, if this was the case, was not accompanied by any public (or traceable private) declarations against its treatment of Catholics, and even his courtesy call on MacRory could not be exploited to this end. Northern Ireland was a mere footnote in Spellman's mission, demonstrated by the lack of engagement with the local American consul, and he was evidently disinclined to involve himself in its internal squabbles when far more important matters demanded his attention. His mission demonstrated the inseparability of his Catholicism and his Americanism, and, as with many ethnic Americans, including most Irish-Americans, fidelity to their 'new' country far outweighed any sentimental commitment to the lands of their ancestors. Spellman's visit to Éire also reinforced Gray's desire that America would not be 'pressure grouped' by any hyphenated Americans. Stormont's inability to see a Catholic cleric's motivation as anything other than sinister, notwithstanding positive coverage in unionist papers, cut them off from someone unlikely to be an ally yet, with a little courtesy, could have offered a useful counterpoint to their portrayal in Irish-America.

'The Boston air party': Nascent post-war anti-partitionism

In 1943, a writer from Lurgan condemned Americans arrogantly believing that Northern Ireland had 'been given over to them lease lend style' but saw an irony as 'the nationalists are very indignant to think that their country has been given to America for they have been fighting and quarrelling for years and couldn't get it'.[156] The zealousness of Irish nationalist protests was inversely proportionate to their likelihood of success and motivated as much by frustration and an opportunity to advertise the injustice of partition as genuine anger. These protests, moreover, betrayed the broader problems the war exposed for nationalists marooned in Northern Ireland and effectively abandoned by Éire. The American presence also shattered the illusion of American partiality towards Irish nationalism in its quarrel with Britain and delayed partition's end, highly unlikely with or without American aid, with or without the war, indefinitely. It also illustrated nationalism's powerlessness, regardless of territorial claims or invocations to restore 'a nation made one by God', in the face of wartime realities and the Allies' practical strategic needs.

Even before the war's conclusion, however, Éire was gearing up for a renewed anti-partition drive in the United States, hoping that America's memory was as short as Ireland's was long and that four years of American cooperation with Northern Ireland would be offset by mobilizing Irish-America. The massaging of neutrality by Irish-Americans began with the first transatlantic flight from Boston to Shannon airport in Éire in October 1945. The delegation, including Governor M. J. Tobin of Massachusetts, John J. Barry, the foreign editor of the *Boston Globe* and other members of the city's Irish-American community, had barely touched the tarmac before Éire and Northern Ireland's contributions to the war were reassessed. Tobin claimed that Éire 'was neutral on our side', while Barry dismissed the idea that the lack of Éire's bases cost American lives as 'British propaganda'. It was now recognized, by Irish-Americans at any rate, that de Valera's protest was not against America but against partition. The *Telegraph* asserted that claiming Éire's neutrality did not impede the Allies was 'clear evidence that all Americans have not good memories' and argued that Northern Ireland helped save America lives. This 'Boston air party', it predicted, 'is probably the forerunner of similar missions who will attempt to retrieve the past by reviving the artificial issue of Partition... The present prospect is that there will be a good many tea parties in Boston's Irish clubs before Partition is ended, but this mission is a sure sign that the pressure has begun again'.[157] The *News Letter's* attitude was identical, declaring that 'vigorous propagandist work has begun' to rewrite the war's history and politicize partition again. Both Tobin and Barry, 'it seems, are of South of Ireland extraction', but 'to give their utterances a wider importance, however, would be to credit the people of the United States with either little intelligence or very short memories'.[158]

The American presence illuminated Stormont's hypocrisy in demanding freedoms for other people denied to a chunk of its own, yet wartime exigencies and nationalism's inflexibility made it unable to exploit these double standards. Nationalism's external focus was more on the fact of partition, rather than the daily injustice faced by Catholics (this was stridently illustrated, however, in the *Orange Terror* pamphlet), but its refusal to recognize and engage at some level with the realities of partition and the war, or attempt to find some accommodation with unionism, pushed its ultimate goal far beyond the horizon. It is hard not to conclude that attacking partition was more useful politically for Éire than ending it, especially for de Valera. Catholic resentment was utterly genuine and justified, if at times overstated, but simply decrying partition without a realistic alternative would never bring about its demise. The 'hyper-dignity' bemoaned by W.S. Moody, decreed that partition should cease without any compromise, because its immorality and wrongness was so patently obvious, and the need to correct this historic wrong so urgent, that no compromise, regardless of the world situation, was necessary. Yet this only prolonged the problem it sought to solve. The status quo suited both de Valera and unionists, if for different reasons, and Stormont could, and would, use belligerent nationalist rhetoric to strengthen unionist hegemony and as an excuse not to ameliorate conditions for Catholics. For their part, American officials avoided disrupting the existing social order, keeping Northern Ireland's internal problems at arm's length.

6

'To clear this territory of such forces'

The IRA and the Americans

After the execution of an IRA member for murdering a Belfast policeman in September 1942, US Consul General Parker Buhrman reported to the embassy in London that '[t]he Catholic press' glorified the dead man 'as a martyr to the cause of Irish freedom'.[1] The upshot was that Belfast was on high alert, with 'a number of riotous movements in the city. Nationalist (Catholic) partisans marched through the streets giving the Nazi salute, crying out "Up Hitler"'.[2] Believing that the condemned man was guilty, had received a fair trial, a just sentence and was undeserving of sympathy, Buhrman was astounded by his support in the nationalist population and press. 'The leading Catholic paper', he said, had declared that 'the whole of Ireland was in a state of mourning for a man who been found guilty of firing upon a police patrol and of murdering outright a policeman. The fact that he is a murderer and traitor seems to have no bearing on the situation'. The nationalist press 'never condemns these outrages', he complained, and he wondered if the IRA was 'supported and encouraged by the church in Ireland'. If so, it rendered 'the Irish question in its true light as fundamentally a religious question'.[3]

Buhrman's detailed reports demonstrated his intolerance of the IRA and its goals, yet his terminology and analysis revealed sometimes limited understanding of both. In July 1942, for example, he mentioned the 'necessity of interning some 300 disloyal persons'.[4] Referring to the IRA and its sympathizers as 'disloyal' and later as 'traitors' shows a fundamental misunderstanding of their motivation and its context; although technically legally accurate, they did not regard themselves as 'disloyal' as they did not recognize the state; traitors, at some level, acknowledge the legitimacy of the state they are betraying, whereas the IRA believed itself to be fighting a foreign oppressor. Despite this, his outsider's eye offers an interesting perspective, attempting to comprehend this extreme form of nationalism, Irish republican violence and the Catholic Church's apparent ambivalence towards the latter. His use of 'Catholic' rather than 'nationalist' is instructive, demonstrating that he viewed the situation through the prism of religion rather than competing nationalisms. As he tried to make sense of events, Buhrman's response, and that of Gray in Dublin, also demonstrated that IRA violence was perceived as an immediate threat to American servicemen, a perception the unionist establishment happily encouraged, and a more general threat to the war effort, making it an American problem.

Both the American and the British authorities considered the potential for American embroilment in sectarian street politics, with the latter considering the possibility that US forces could intervene if police were overwhelmed. This ordinarily fell to the British garrison, but as this was greatly reduced when the Americans arrived, contingency plans were discussed. As noted, in early January 1942, Andrews went to London to discuss responses to any disturbances. The Home Office stated that it was 'preferable' if remaining British forces maintained order, implying that Americans could be deployed.[5] Alan Brooke, Chief of the Imperial General Staff, confirmed that some British troops would stay 'for liaison and internal security purposes'; therefore, British thinking included the prospect of sectarian tensions turning violent.[6] Oscar Henderson, perhaps oblivious to these discussions, came to the same conclusions, writing to Gransden on the eve of the American arrival, urging the War Cabinet to retain at least two British brigades for defence 'and particularly to assist the civil power should anything of an untoward nature occur in the near future.'[7] The agreed subtext was that violent Irish republicanism, as in 1916, would use a global crisis to pursue its goals.

The remaining British forces allowed the Americans to stay on the side-lines if there was trouble, even if potentially calling for their assistance was implied. Yet it is difficult to envisage a situation, unless directly attacked, where the Americans would have willingly aided internal security.[8] The Americans do not seem to have been consulted about this possibility but were certainly well aware of the IRA's existence reflecting, in 1944, that it was 'a fanatical anti-British and hence pro-German group', which made the border difficult to police and sabotage a possibility. This had made the British keen at the American, British, Canadian (ABC) discussions from late January to late March 1941 for the Americans to garrison Northern Ireland.[9]

The Americans initiated their own action through the Office of the Assistant Chief of Staff (G-2 section) of SPOBS, created to deal with, among other things, security, the press and censorship and 'Nazi agents working from the German legation in Dublin and the threat of the IRA'.[10] Shortly after the initial American deployment, and resultant efforts by unionist newspapers to have them take sides, General Chaney, head of the SPOBS, recommended that 'personnel should be warned against making comments on the Irish question or Mr de Valera, of the expected activities of Axis spies and of the IRA and against discussing politics and religion. They should be warned that they must safeguard their weapons very carefully'.[11] Hartle acted immediately, ordering subordinates to spend the first days after disembarkation creating directives warning soldiers of the IRA's 'menace' and the prospect of it stealing arms.[12] The Americans believed that the IRA would commit sabotage, pass intelligence onto the Germans and attempt to incite 'dislike and suspicion between British and American forces and the civilian population', with particular warnings to enlisted men about the latter.[13] The Americans had no desire to police local tribalism. Realizing they could become embroiled, an American commander reportedly contacted the IRA privately, through the US forces' head Catholic Chaplain, stating that they would remain aloof if violence occurred.[14] The IRA ignored this and directly linked the renewal of its terrorist campaign in April 1942 to the Americans; in fact, according to O'Neill's chronology of the group in Belfast, it 'obsessed about the arrival of US troops'.[15]

Due to the threat, the Falls Road and other nationalist areas were placed off-limits to US personnel.

'The enemies of England are the friends of Ireland': Declaring war on Britain

During 1939 and 1940, the IRA launched attacks on mainland Britain.[16] A self-important ultimatum was issued on 12 January 1940 demanding Britain's withdrawal from Northern Ireland and generously granting 'a period of four days' as 'sufficient for your government to signify its intention in the matter of military evacuation'.[17] A manifesto then declared war on Britain, baffling even the people of West Belfast when it was posted on walls there.[18] John Cudahy, the US minister in Dublin, received a copy of the ultimatum and informed the State Department that he 'been advised from a reliable source that the number of these violent obstructionists is inconsiderable, probably between 500 and 600'.[19] In another statement the group said that 'the enemies of England are, by that fact, the friends of Ireland. We are no more Nazi or Fascist than Connolly and Pearse were Imperialistic in seeking the aid of Imperialistic Germany in 1916'.[20] The group's claim that its alliance with Nazi Germany was essentially pragmatic was, however, undermined by those within it as either receptive to fascist ideology or harbouring latent anti-Semitism.

Many in the IRA suffered from what Wood calls a 'moral myopia' about the war and the consequences of a German victory, particularly for Ireland's Jews. The organization's *War News*, published in Belfast, for example, was replete with both blatant and unsubtly coded anti-Semitism.[21] Bew asserts that support for Nazi Germany was 'no secret: wartime IRA internees in Belfast plotted the advance of Hitler's armies, first with delight and then despair'.[22] English concludes that there 'is some irony – and a little disgrace' in IRA collusion with the Nazis.[23] There were those, recalled one IRA member, who 'while not pro-German, hoped nonetheless that England would be trounced. We were ignorant of the Nazi philosophy as, indeed was everyone, until the war had ended'.[24] This self-serving equivocation rings hollow. There could be little doubt about what the Nazis represented, yet this was secondary to Ireland's 700-year war with Britain, and England's difficulty was again Ireland's opportunity. In July 1940, the IRA announced that German invaders would be welcomed as 'friends and liberators of the Irish people'.[25] One of its leaders Sean Russell enjoyed German hospitality in Berlin at the war's outset, simultaneously claiming no sympathy with Nazi ideology; in August 1940, he died on a U-boat when returning to Ireland to stir up a revolt with German assistance.[26] Russell's German links probably predated the war, and he may have met German representatives while in America in 1937; indeed, a leading IRA member claimed that the German-American Bund actively funded the group's British campaign.[27] Some members were uncomfortable with such callous pragmatism; one declared: 'if Ireland were to obtain its liberty at the expense of other peoples it would deserve all the execration she herself poured on tyranny throughout the ages'.[28]

The British campaign ultimately left seven people dead, two terrorists executed and the group suppressed.²⁹ Activities in Éire were no more successful. The group, claims Cole, 'was as anti-de Valera as it was anti-British' but was more brutally put down in Éire, with more suspected members interned, six executed and a further three dying on hunger strike during the war.³⁰ Many in the IRA claimed not to understand why de Valera was, in effect, helping Stormont, further enhancing their bitterness towards him.³¹ From de Valera's perspective, beyond hypothetical collaboration with German invaders, the group risked destabilizing Éire politically; its German links endangered neutrality and could even pull the country into the war.³²

After its mainland campaign had fizzled out, in March 1942 the IRA decided to attack the police in Northern Ireland with its leadership unanimously resolving to aid Germany should it invade Ireland with their consent. If the Germans bombed Belfast again (rumours persist that the group aided the Luftwaffe raids on Belfast in 1941), the organization vowed to attack the police and fire brigade, water tanks and the city's electricity supplies.³³ Bizarrely, the gas supply would be spared in 'an effort to avoid undue strain and distress on the civilian population', a magnanimous gesture for which Belfast's people would have doubtlessly been eternally grateful amid the devastation of another blitz.³⁴ In October 1941, evidence emerged that the IRA was actively soliciting another German attack. Police in Éire captured an IRA member carrying a report on the Blitz, a map identifying targets and a request to the Germans to avoid bombing the Falls Road (helpfully colour-coded on the map) and jails housing republican prisoners.³⁵ The Germans were not especially serious about co-operating with the IRA; nevertheless, it developed plans in 1940, codenamed 'Plan Kathleen', to assist a German invasion of Northern Ireland.³⁶ Hempel advocated offering some encouragement to the IRA and had a conduit to the group in Belfast, strongly believed to be former IRA leader Sean MacBride.³⁷ Stormont and unionist newspapers had a vested interest in emphasizing, publicizing and exaggerating these links, reminding the Americans that the IRA's siding with their enemy made it a threat to them. The enemies of Britain may have been the friends of Ireland, but by the same logic, the enemies of Britain were also the enemies of America.

An early indication that the new campaign would attempt to entangle the Americans came in March 1942. Henry Lundborg was arrested on a cross-border train carrying two letters purportedly from the IRA in Dublin asking about American troop strength and the possibility of finding contacts within the US forces. The first letter wanted to know 'what is the reaction in national[ist] circles to the arrival of the American forces in the North? Let me have an immediate report on this, giving the present location and number of these forces to date'.³⁸ The writer also wondered about 'getting publicity from the 'Irish News' for our statement on the American invasion?'³⁹ The second letter was again 'anxious for an immediate report' on the number of Americans but additionally asked about 'the prospect of making friendly contact among them and the strength of the British forces'.⁴⁰ Rather than attacking US forces, therefore, the IRA would attempt to recruit sympathetic Americans against the British. Lundborg, a British veteran of the Great War, claimed no knowledge of the letters' contents and denied any connection with the IRA but was found guilty and sentenced to two years in prison with the magistrate declaring him lucky to avoid the death penalty.⁴¹ The IRA did not abandon distributing propaganda among American troops; in June 1942, its leader in Dublin stated, 'I have given it a good deal of thought and think it is worth trying', and promised a handbill on the subject. His lack of reference to Lundborg infers that this was a new idea.[42]

Gray and Buhrman shared concerns about the explicit link to the US forces and sought additional information on Lundborg. Buhrman reported that IRA activities were limited but had 'dangerous potentialities'; 300 alleged members had been interned in Northern Ireland, and the authorities were 'exceedingly anxious to destroy the movement'. He believed that the Germans distrusted the organization, believing it would prove an ineffective fifth column, though they used it to gather intelligence.[43] Viewing the IRA as a British concern, Buhrman recognized, however, its potential impact upon America's war effort. He also argued that London and Stormont wanted the Americans to 'force the issue' by publishing IRA documents about their forces as they were 'anxious to convince us of the dangers to our troops'.[44] Consequently, the British wanted to secure American assistance against the IRA by publicizing evidence that the group was targeting US troops.

'An affront to the Irish race at home and abroad': The Williams execution

Shortly after Lundborg's arrest, the IRA had decided to renew its campaign specifically in Northern Ireland, and the Americans provided a convenient pretext for the group, hoping to capitalize on nationalist resentment about US forces. On 4 April, Constable Thomas Forbes, a father of ten, was killed in a bomb attack on Dungannon's police station.[45] The following day Constable Murphy, a father of nine, was murdered in a botched attack supposedly to distract police from an illegal parade commemorating the 1916 Easter Rising in West Belfast (where Murphy, one of the force's few Catholics, was from).[46] In May, two men were charged with treason after distributing leaflets calling on Americans to 'join their brothers in Ireland in a fight for freedom from England', although without a direct IRA link.[47] It would not be until August, however, when a manifesto was found at an arms dump that the campaign was again directly connected to the Americans.[48]

Six young men were arrested and all charged with Murphy's murder; in August 1942, in a judicial overreaction, a jury deemed all guilty, and they were consequently sentenced to death.[49] The disproportionality of the punishment alarmed officialdom in London, Washington and Dublin and caused unease at Stormont; the accused were certainly accessories, and Murphy was shot by at least two assailants, but in the absence of evidence identifying who had fired the fatal shots, all six were condemned.[50] The authorities were seemingly ignorant of the lessons of history as six executions could have provided Irish republicans with the catalyst which executing the 1916 Easter Rising's leaders granted their predecessors. Nationalist senators and MPs elected to Stormont appealed to Abercorn and requested to meet Andrews, while petitions for mercy attracted tens of thousands of signatures.[51] Five were eventually reprieved;

nonetheless, Abercorn upheld the death sentence for the sixth, the teenaged ringleader Thomas Williams, even though it was absolutely clear from forensic evidence and known to the public that, although he had shot Constable Murphy, the fatal bullet was fired by one of two of his accomplices.[52]

Supporters appealed to the United States. A reprieve committee, for example, telegraphed Roosevelt urging his intervention, declaring that 'the execution of any of them would be an outrage on justice and an affront to the Irish race at home and abroad', inferring domestic political consequences for Roosevelt if he did not intervene.[53] Paranoia about others' intentions was not the sole preserve of unionists. Éire's minister to Washington, Robert Brennan, accused the Americans of encouraging the IRA as a means of destabilizing Éire's government and undermining its neutrality – an allegation which, as Cole notes, 'was dismissed as nonsense by virtually everyone, including President Roosevelt'.[54] Brennan also argued, and here he had a point, that incidents involving the Americans were 'grossly exaggerated'. This was undermined by his innate sense of grievance when he declared that this was done 'probably by those who are jealous of the good feelings which have always existed between the peoples of Ireland and America' and was, therefore, designed to help 'Orangemen' consolidate partition.[55] Brennan's reputation in the States for parochial sanctimony meant that whatever the validity of his observations, it was lost amid the predictable white noise of Irish-American outrage.

Buhrman seemed more anxious than Stormont about the IRA campaign and the mooted executions entangling the Americans and reported extensively on incidents in August and September 1942. Even minor attacks on individual Americans had the potential to magnify his own fears about the IRA while also, he believed, increasing resentment about Éire's neutrality in the United States. As tensions rose during the late summer of 1942, so too did Buhrman's concerns about the potential to involve Americans and even generate antagonism between British and American troops.[56] Americans were threatened by people claiming to be from the IRA, and '[q]uite a number of them have been brutally assaulted under the cover of darkness'. The IRA, he asserted, tried to attribute these attacks to British troops and may even have been instigated by members who had infiltrated British forces.[57] Moreover, Irish republican sentiment was already apparent in the US forces as '[t]he disposition of the Irish Americans in the American army [is] to respond to the influences of the Nationalist movement in Ireland. One cannot but notice the anti-British sentiments of Irish American soldiers'.[58] The extent of this is impossible to measure; no Americans faced court-martial, for example, for stealing munitions destined for the group, but the possibility that sympathy could become collaboration made Buhrman's job more difficult, while press revelations and police reports undoubtedly fuelled his anxiety.

'Unjustifiable occupation': Targeting the Americans

The weaponry found at two IRA arms dumps in early September 1942 demonstrated that the campaign was planned long before the Americans arrived.[59] A manifesto found at one dump 'proposed to cause ill-feeling if not actual hostility between British and

American forces here', according to the *Whig*.⁶⁰ The police stated: '[t]he terms of the manifesto make it clear that this illegal organization has been preparing for attacks on the armed forces of the Crown, the police, and the United States forces'.⁶¹ The manifesto appropriated the language of earlier nationalist protests by refusing to 'recognize the right of England or any other power to maintain her forces in, or base them on Irish territory without the free consent of the Irish people'. The group also vowed 'to clear this territory of such forces', planning to 'avail itself of the darkest moment in England's history to strike'.⁶² It referred to past help 'from their exiled brethren in America' and stressed that '[t]he Irish people have no quarrel with the citizens of the United States of America, but strongly resent the unjustifiable occupation of a part of Ireland by American armed forces'.⁶³ The British, it claimed, would try to 'provoke conflict' between the IRA and the Americans: '[i]f, in the event of the resumption of hostilities between Great Britain and the Irish Republic, the American troops are drawn into conflict with Irish soldiers, the responsibility must rest with those who presumed to use North-East Ireland as a military base without the free consent of the Irish people'.⁶⁴ This declaration represents a prime example of what Wood refers to as the IRA's 'suffocating self-righteousness'.⁶⁵ The IRA had no hope of expelling the Americans, and its actions against them consisted of beating up GIs or claiming responsibility for these assaults. This overblown rhetoric, therefore, camouflaged that the IRA was never more than an irritant for (off-duty) Americans and it attacked no US installations; if the intention was to generate propaganda, rather than any realistic prospect of military success, however, it served a purpose.

The British and American press often reported German-IRA links, alongside threats against US forces which, notes Cole, 'made many American readers conclude that Éire neutrality encouraged fifth column activities'.⁶⁶ These links were both very real and entirely imagined. The *Whig* was especially keen to connect the IRA to Germany and show that as this was potentially harmful to the war effort, it was also an American problem; therefore, as Brennan had claimed, it was a way of discrediting Irish nationalism in America. For example, a *Whig* headline in late September declared that 'US Forces out to break IRA spy ring: Women Fifth Columnists', whereby the IRA was allegedly spying on the Americans for Germany.⁶⁷ The *Whig* quoted an American source: '[w]e are out to catch the spies, mainly women from across the Border, and certain places in the towns and cities are out of bounds to our men. . . . Generally speaking, the men are security minded, but liquor, especially Irish whiskey, loosens their tongues'.⁶⁸ Thus, with the heightened suspicions of the times, indigenous alcoholic beverages and seductive colleens from Éire were identified as potential security risks. The *Whig* explained that the Americans received 'a strict lecture' about the IRA and were 'disillusioned of the idea that members of the IRA are fighting English oppression', when it was actually 'the enemy's agent'. Americans, it continued, were uninterested in local problems, which the IRA used 'to cause friction between the British people and the American forces' and were 'warned not to discuss politics or religion with the Irish'.⁶⁹ The *Whig*'s sensationalism, it should be noted, had recently included rumours that the IRA was even infiltrating Irish dancing and language classes.⁷⁰

Gray had little sympathy for the condemned men, but he recognized the pragmatism of five reprieves, telling US ambassador to London John G. Winant that 'to take six lives for one may arouse real trouble'.[71] Gray and Buhrman corresponded on the tensions, sharing similar fears that somehow Americans would be drawn in. Both were appalled by nationalism's treatment of the executed man, and another killed by police at the arms dump where the manifesto was found, as martyrs and heroes.[72] Gray complained to de Valera and Roosevelt that clemency demands in Éire's papers 'were exciting animosity against our ally and against our interests in Ulster', whereas criticism of the Axis was forbidden. He saw the reprieves and single execution as 'a very sound solution'. One response in Dublin was the ritual burning of the Union Jack; while Maffey was phlegmatic about this, Gray was not: 'if they did this to the American flag I should have a formal apology before night or leave the country'. To Gray's considerable irritation, de Valera's *Irish Press* printed the IRA manifesto 'and plays up in blackface the paragraph denouncing us for being in Northern Ireland without Irish permission'.[73]

On 8 September, Gray wrote a lengthy memorandum outlining concerns that American troops would be attacked and the consequences of this. Gray reported that the situation throughout Ireland 'cannot be regarded as satisfactory' as 'repeated acts of violence have been committed in Ulster by Irish Republican Army terrorists', including the recent murders of a policeman and a 'B'-Special. Demonstrations had been made against Americans in Belfast, and 'we must be prepared to be confronted with some incident involving American lives. We should be prepared also for the situation which would arise if American soldiers took the law into their own hands and avenged the death of a companion'. Stormont, he argued, was naïve in allowing the publication of the IRA's manifesto, which when reprinted in Éire gave the organization greater publicity than it would have achieved otherwise.[74]

This analysis mirrored Buhrman's, yet to Gray, the primary responsibility lay in Dublin and, inevitably, at the feet of de Valera and his earlier protest. This, Gray believed, worsened the situation, alongside the relaxation of censorship in Éire allowing the reporting of demands for reprieves. De Valera, he said, rationalized the murder of Murphy as 'inspired by a patriotic motive'; while he privately condemned it, he 'is always able to sympathetically understand what motivated the murderers'.[75] Despite creating what Gray felt was 'anti-American feeling which may express itself in murder', de Valera refused to modify his position on the American presence.[76] Gray concluded that de Valera acted because of 'internal political considerations' and contrasted this with his silence after the Germans bombed Belfast. Protests against the Americans would 'incite nationalist feeling against both us and the British . . . to act on the old principle that Britain's extremity is Ireland's opportunity', something he believed easing censorship encouraged.[77]

Gray challenged de Valera about banning anti-German material but not information 'likely to inflame anti-British and anti-American feeling [which] was not my idea of the benevolent neutrality'. He warned of 'serious consequences' should American soldiers be attacked. De Valera replied that '[w]e would be fools to allow the printing of anything against the Germans' and 'the Irish are neutral in fact, but not in feeling as long as the enemy, Britain, remains on our soil', and he would not have prevented the publication of reprieve demands even if he could have. Gray speculated, without evidence, that the Germans might precipitate a rebellion akin to 1916, undoubtedly involving American forces, but British and Canadian representatives felt that he was exaggerating the danger.[78] Whatever Gray's genuine, if hyperbolic, concerns, it unquestionably presented a convenient new channel for haranguing de Valera.

When the initial appeals were rejected, Buhrman reported, '[t]he evidence was clear cut and there is not the slightest doubt in the minds of the police and the court as to the guilt of the men'. He had previously held long discussions with the Ministry of Home Affairs and a senior police officer, who argued that murder would be regarded as treason in most countries and subject to the death penalty.[79] Yet they anticipated that guilty verdicts would enable nationalists 'to stir up as much trouble as possible, with the charges of miscarriage of justice and persecution.... [And] used to foster agitation'. The authorities predicted this, and it had now been followed by petitions 'circulated by the catholic clergy in most of the catholic communities' demanding clemency.[80]

'In essence, the men do not deny their guilt', he continued, '[i]t is a case where religious prejudice becomes political expediency.... There does not appear to be any reasonable grounds for this agitation except political expediency'.[81] Those demanding clemency recognized the condemned men's guilt but exploited it politically. Buhrman believed that reprieves would weaken Stormont and exacerbate sectarian tensions, encourage further terrorism and make the police's job more difficult.[82] When the five were reprieved, demands for clemency, in Buhrman's view 'mostly in Éire', for the remaining condemned men continued, but he saw little prospect of Stormont, which he maintained had shown 'leniency', agreeing.[83] Indeed, he again argued that by granting reprieves Stormont had acted due to 'political expediency as distinguished from justice under the law' and was in a quandary with police officers rumoured to have threatened to resign.[84] That said, the discovery of the weapons caches in early September had strengthened the government's refusal to make further concessions as 'experience has taught that yielding to political pressure tends to aggravate the Irish question'.[85]

After the execution, Buhrman reported, '[h]e is all but eulogized by the Nationalist press', the police were on high alert and tensions rose further with the IRA manifesto now public.[86] Buhrman quoted the document's threats against the Americans at length, concluding that the IRA and nationalists more generally were inciting anti-British feeling among Irish-American troops.[87] He soon reported 'considerable resentment' among Americans over threats and assaults from the IRA during the blackout, notably in Londonderry, assaults they had tried to blame on British troops. He had even heard rumours that these were 'instigated by IRA partisans in the British army'; just as worryingly, 'Irish American soldiers also lend ready ear to IRA trouble makers'.[88] His contention that the IRA had infiltrated British forces seems unlikely, though it was obvious why it might want to exacerbate shaky relations between British and the American troops.

The 'grave tendency' of nationalists 'to eulogize the Irish Republican Army partisans' continued through the first week of September, when nationalists turned out 'almost en masse' for the funeral of the IRA member killed at the arms dump. This was, he said, a spectacle that reminded one reporter of 'Chicago gangster funerals in the days of prohibition'.[89] Yet a number of priests also warned young men against joining the IRA and attacking the police.[90] IRA violence had 'produced a rather tense and grim situation' which was 'regarded as particularly despicable' due to the war.[91] Echoing Gray, he worried about further escalation: '[i]t is a short step from shooting Northern

Ireland policemen to shooting British and American soldiers'.[92] The intervention of some priests aside, Buhrman could find no unambiguous condemnation of the IRA from Catholic clergyman; unionist papers appealed to Cardinal MacRory and Bishop Daniel Mageean to denounce the IRA, but both declined, the former worried that he might say too much. 'In other words', Buhrman concluded, 'there is apparently no disposition on the part of the Catholic clergy of Northern Ireland to condemn outright Irish Republican Army activities'.[93]

Events grew more sinister in early October with the prosecution of a man for possession of IRA literature that specifically targeted British and American troops, in contrast to earlier statements ostensibly seeking to avoid conflict with the Americans.[94] There was a further spike in IRA attacks in October, although the authorities were not overly concerned, even if the perpetrators could avoid detection due to the blackout.[95] Notwithstanding Buhrman's pessimism, by mid-October he announced that the IRA campaign was petering out due to arrests, the discovery of arms dumps and a curfew in West Belfast.[96] This, he asserted, meant that the IRA had 'received its most severe blow [and] is thoroughly demoralized for the time being and no longer an organized danger'.[97]

'Nazi-style salutes and jeering comment': The realities of the IRA campaign

The impact of the execution on 2 September upon Americans was, despite Buhrman and Gray's concerns, rather limited but disproportionately well publicized. After the manifesto's publication, Americans were ordered to stay out of Belfast for forty-eight hours on the day of the execution, as the police warned that 'this illegal organization has been preparing for attacks' on British and American forces.[98] Not all heeded this advice, and nationalists stoned an American officer's car; however, he and his driver escaped unharmed.[99] Why the two were in Belfast was not immediately clear, and according to the American press, they 'were greeted with stiff-armed Nazi-style salutes and jeering comment' by a crowd which had also been singing Irish republican songs.[100] Other American troops at Belfast City Hall, where hundreds of nationalists ('mainly young girls') gathered, also received barracking and Nazi salutes, before the situation was 'handled firmly but tactfully by the police'; two women shouted at Americans and gave the Nazi salute at the YMCA in Belfast.[101] There was an added worry because many Americans were expected in the city that weekend for performances by visiting American actors, but no trouble was reported.[102]

The Americans were otherwise bystanders, yet their minor involvement made international news. The execution and subsequent protests were covered by numerous regional American papers, with the stories, based upon an AP report, sometimes making front-page news.[103] The *Washington Evening Star* used the opportunity to explain Northern Ireland's constitutional position and the differences between it and Éire, while describing the IRA as 'waging what amounts to a continuous civil war'. It also asserted that 'there can be scant doubt that the IRA is in close touch with German agents'.[104] The press covered basic verifiable facts, notably the Nazi salutes and the shouts of 'why don't you stay at home?' directed at Americans who strayed into Belfast. They also emphasized that the IRA manifesto was evidence that the arms discovered were for use against the Americans. Rumours of German involvement were also repeated, notably the allegation that Nazi agents traversed the border freely, with the caveat that officials stressed that none of the weapons uncovered were German.[105] The AP stated that the appearance of Americans triggered only a 'mild demonstration', a fact not always reported, and that despite the execution Belfast remained quiet.[106] The coverage was widespread, but also brief, with the *New York Daily News* (its headline declared: 'Irish salute yanks – the Nazi way') one of the few newspapers continuing reports in the days after the execution.[107]

Reflecting upon the situation in November, AP journalist William B. King noted American sympathy to Irish independence yet now 'find themselves on the other side of the fence when the IRA made the presence of the United States troops in the northern counties a major point in its brief for Irish liberty'. The 'sentimental Irish love a martyr', he observed, describing Constable Murphy's murder as having 'no point other than grim celebration' of the Easter Rising, with the IRA's hope that six executions would cause a new uprising, undermined by the five reprieves. Regarding the current IRA, he believed that 'moderate Irishmen – if there is such a thing – insist that there is no linear connection between the present illegal IRA and the old organisation' and that de Valera's successful suppression of it in Éire had rendered ineffective in Northern Ireland.[108]

The IRA was ultimately suppressed relatively straightforwardly by the separate efforts of Éire and Northern Ireland. De Valera's motivation was partly born of a fear that trouble could spill over the border and destabilize Éire, and ultimately Éire interned more IRA suspects and dealt with them more harshly, and these measures helped subdue it across the border.[109] In fact, in Northern Ireland, Catholic assistance often undid the group.[110] One result, however, was generating publicity and sympathy in Éire and the United States. The IRA campaign had the potential to make negative headlines for Stormont both in the UK and the States, particularly if the response to it was perceived as draconian, demonstrated by six death sentences for one murder. In the end, the single execution denied the IRA the Easter 1916 showpiece it desired; nonetheless, the death saw an outpouring of emotion in nationalist Ireland and briefly threatened to galvanize the various shades of Irish nationalist opinion and became worrisome for both Gray and Buhrman. While Buhrman was guiltier of naivety than scaremongering, recording his perceptions of an unfamiliar situation, he and Gray did greatly overstate the threat to the Americans (conveniently affording Gray another avenue for berating de Valera). Ultimately, attacks on Americans amounted to a couple of stones, some assaults and a few Nazi salutes; indeed, despite the tension, Farrell claims that there was no violence in Catholic areas after the execution.[111]

The threat of IRA violence periodically reappeared. The end of the curfew in West Belfast in January 1943, for example, led to 'a slight revival', and two of its members were injured in gun battle with police, both were under 20 years old, and Buhrman believed they had 'been misled to believe that they are acting in the interest of Irish Independence', but the situation was 'fairly well under control'.[112] The escape of IRA leader Hugh McAteer from Belfast's Crumlin Road prison threatened to increase tensions.¹¹³ He appeared in a cinema in April where another escapee read a statement, but Buhrman reported that 'practically the entire audience of the theater was children who were witnessing a Holy Week program'.¹¹⁴ The statement declared, among other things, that 'Partition is also responsible for the presence on Irish soil of a large number of American troops' and referred to and reiterated the previous year's warning that the 'resumption of hostilities . . . will most inevitably mean that the American troops will also become involved, and that America, the champion of democracy and co-sponsor of the Atlantic Charter, will find herself engaged with Britain in waging a war of imperial aggression and conquest against the Irish people'. The men left after fifteen minutes.¹¹⁵ 'It is interesting to note', Buhrman continued, 'that the Berlin Radio broadcast the substance of his address the following midday before it was published in Northern Ireland', inferring that the statement had been pre-circulated to the Germans. Despite this publicity stunt, the 'IRA movement is losing ground for the time being'.¹¹⁶ The truth was that the IRA was pretty weak when it began its 1942 campaign, and its failure exacerbated this to the extent that its members, reflecting upon it in 1943 either within prison walls or cooped up in safe houses, contemplated either abandoning violence in favour of political activism or potentially combining the two.¹¹⁷

The OSS contextualized IRA activity as a direct response to Stormont's attitude towards Catholics. It reported from Dublin in early 1943 that the 'somewhat repressive attitude of the government of Northern Ireland towards its large nationalist Roman Catholic minority, seems to have strengthened the hand and of all the more radical elements there, and probably has accounted for an increase both in numbers and activity of the IRA within the last 3 years'.¹¹⁸ This recognized, therefore, that regardless of legitimacy or justification, the IRA's actions had a clear political context. By the spring of 1943, the American military attaché in Dublin, Lt. Col. J. L. Hathaway, who characterized the IRA as 'patriotic fanatics', reported that it had 'failed completely in enlisting sympathy' in Éire and was 'under the complete control the government'. It was also viewed as dormant in Northern Ireland (or at least its activities were no longer reported in Éire's newspapers), and there had been a 'complete rupture' between IRA and de Valera's Fianna Fáil party. There remained, however, a residual fear among the Americans that it could still pose a threat in the (highly unlikely) event of Éire using force after the war to end partition.¹¹⁹

The US forces' history of their time in Northern Ireland described the IRA as 'fanatically pro-Irish and as fanatically anti-British', and 'pro-Nazi chiefly because Germany was an enemy of Britain', but doubted if it received much German assistance. The group's existence required troops 'to exercise the utmost precautions in the safeguarding of small arms, ammunition, explosives, and equipment' due to the possibility of sabotage. It also noted that the group 'was expected to employ propaganda rumors, and lies to promote friction among American troops, British troops, Irish civilians', ultimately failing in this endeavour.¹²⁰ This represents a fairly calm and measured assessment of the limited IRA threat, albeit with a measure of hindsight unavailable to Gray and Buhrman. It is worth stressing, however, that because it was either unable practically or unwilling politically, the group carried out no recorded attacks or sabotage against American bases or GIs on duty.

7

'Developments in Northern Ireland'

The Belfast consulate and the war

Shortly before departing as consul in late 1941, John Randolph sent the Secretary of State a memorandum concerning allowances for entertaining local functionaries, explaining: 'Belfast is a semi-diplomatic post: from the point of view of the American consular representative in Northern Ireland this post is in actuality a diplomatic or semi-diplomatic as well as a consular post.' The consulate, though not a diplomatic post, hosted 'multiple dignitaries', including the governor general, the prime minister and other ministers, and senior military figures.[1] In effect, local circumstances meant that the Belfast consulate had to act like a small embassy or legation, thus differentiating it from other regional consulates, but it did so with a tiny staff, numbering one consul, two vice-consuls, four clerks, a messenger and a caretaker.[2] Randolph might have mentioned, too, that it was also a belligerent, bordering a neutral state and with internal frictions which could, in extremis, hamper the war effort and even skew domestic American politics.

Belfast's diplomatic (or semi-diplomatic) links with the United States were almost as old as the republic, as it had hosted a US consulate since 1796; only the second opened after American independence.[3] Prior to the Second World War it dealt primarily with routine consular matters, mainly visas, while also reporting regularly to the US ambassador in London and the Secretary of State in Washington, and was sufficiently important to be elevated to the status of Consulate General in 1924.[4] As European tensions grew, the consulate reported their local impact alongside more parochial considerations, with the rekindling of the IRA's campaign, efforts on both sides of the border to suppress it and the controversy over conscription, all regularly discussed in 1939 and 1940.[5] With Britain's declaration of war on Germany in September 1939, Northern Ireland joined the conflict and became a disembarkation point for supplies from North America. When Ernest L. Ives departed as consul general in June 1939, he was not immediately replaced, leaving Randolph in charge as consul.[6] Pearl Harbor meant that Northern Ireland became an ally and then the destination for American forces. The consulate, initially without a consul general in situ, now acquired a hitherto absent strategic importance for American foreign policy planners.

The consulate was based at the Scottish Provident Building close to Belfast City Hall, and many buildings around it were destroyed or badly damaged in the Blitz of April and

May 1941.⁷ It escaped serious damage but was evacuated due to an unexploded bomb next door, and for two weeks after the May attack its functions were conducted from Randolph's room at the Grand Central Hotel (where he had lived since his arrival in 1939).⁸ Randolph realized the danger of storing all consular material under one roof, so some equipment and paperwork were dispersed to two vice-consuls' homes elsewhere in the city.⁹ He reported the Blitz's impact on civilian morale, including criticizing Stormont's preparedness and the population's abandonment of Belfast at night as many chose to sleep in the open air on its outskirts, yet he regarded the will to win the war as undiminished.¹⁰ In June, he noted local approval for America's occupation of Iceland, quickly followed by support for a rumoured American base in Northern Ireland.¹¹ By September he reported 'many different expressions of appreciation for the help and friendship now being given by the United States to Great Britain', as the base was established and any pretence of secrecy disappeared.¹²

The consulate's significance was enhanced considerably when American troops appeared. It fell upon new consul Parker Buhrman, arriving just ahead of US forces on 6 January 1942, to update the State Department and embassy. Buhrman was the American authorities' eyes and ears during the next year, sending frequent reports entitled 'Developments in Northern Ireland'. Consular correspondence prior to Pearl Harbor provided Buhrman with a useful template. Ives, had written detailed reports to Joseph Kennedy, then US ambassador to London, while Randolph, as discussed in Chapter 5, sent 'Voluntary Political Reports' regarding nationalist demands to meet Sumner Welles in early 1940. Buhrman was a former teacher and lawyer and a highly experienced consular official whose career began as consul in 1918 in Sweden, before stints in Finland (1919–20), Honduras (1920–1), the Dutch East Indies (1921–3), Syria (1923–5), Germany (Berlin, 1928–9, and Cologne, 1935) and Morocco (1930–4), before becoming consul general in Lisbon in 1935 and then in Sydney in 1938.¹³ Buhrman's posting immediately before Belfast was in Glasgow, so he had some knowledge of the UK (and doubtless, sectarianism) and expected a fairly quiet life.

Technically a civil servant rather than a diplomat, Buhrman was a comparatively low-level official, even if, as Randolph noted, the line blurred in Belfast. Moreover, he was not necessarily very well informed by his superiors. He was aware that American technicians had arrived the previous summer but was so far down the State Department's chain of command that he learned of the American forces' arrival at about the same time as everyone else.¹⁴ While there were undoubtedly similarities with Glasgow, Buhrman quickly became aware of the differences, and his naivety is evident as he attempted to comprehend Northern Ireland's sectarian divisions and local political idiosyncrasies. Despite his experience, once ensconced, his dispatches reveal that he was not always especially perceptive, leading to sometimes quite credulous analysis and rather speculative assessments; he also reported rumours and anecdotes alongside fact and detail. That said, his outsider's view is perhaps the strongest aspect of his commentaries.

Like his predecessors, he was well briefed by Stormont, but also carefully read Belfast's four newspapers and referred to nameless contacts, and enjoyed warm personal relationships with officials and journalists. A good indication of consuls' closeness to local government officials came from Randolph, who wrote to Ives in February 1940: 'I understand that one of your great friends in Belfast was and is Sir Basil Brooke.... I might add that I have found Sir Basil and Lady Brooke and many of your other local friends very pleasant and agreeable to know'.[15] Upon leaving, Randolph fulsomely praised Andrews, Craig and the population, thanking everyone for 'a very happy tour of duty', which had made him feel 'as almost a Northern Irelander myself'.[16] Buhrman and his own successor, Quincy Roberts, would also enjoy happy tours in Belfast. Upon his departure in 1948, Roberts told Brooke he was leaving 'with deep regret' what as 'the best post in my long career'.[17] Brooke replied that no 'foreign representative has been held in such high esteem here as yourself, and certainly none has left such a general feeling of regret behind him. I find, indeed, an odd incongruity in the description "foreign representative"'.[18] Consular officials were, therefore, thoroughly welcomed and integrated into unionist political life.

Recurrent issues in Buhrman's reports included strikes, conscription, sectarian tensions, terrorism, Éire's neutrality, local politics, the conduct and reception of American troops and civilian morale. He dealt with everything confronting him generally dispassionately, although he tended towards gloomy prognoses, with a particular oversensitivity about the Americans' behaviour and potential trouble between them and civilians or British troops. As noted, he was utterly unsympathetic to IRA terrorism and did not rationalize it as a legitimate response to partition, but he exaggerated its influence and ability to cause trouble for the Americans. Equally, he was routinely critical of Stormont and supposedly loyal Protestants, the latter frequently found striking or skiving and whose loyalty did not extend to enlisting in great numbers.

Reflecting its enhanced status, Belfast became a Consulate General again in April 1942 and Buhrman consul general.[19] He initially sent reports to the embassy in London, and these were forwarded to the Secretary of State in Washington, but updating the mission in Dublin proved vital, so from October 1942 the reports were also sent directly to Gray.[20] Gray, for reasons of geography and antagonism towards de Valera, took a greater interest in Northern Ireland than either the embassy or the State Department, and he and Buhrman had already corresponded regularly prior to him officially receiving reports. Gray periodically asked for Buhrman's impressions of Northern Ireland as he responded to Éire's neutrality or required a pretext to fuel his feud with de Valera.

'The alleged arrival': Buhrman and the American military presence

Buhrman's first major issue was the impending arrival of American troops. He thought the prospect far-fetched, and barely a week before they disembarked, he still talked of their 'alleged arrival'.[21] He was similarly dismissive of later reports that African American troops were en route and, for reasons unexplained, inferred that this was a bad idea.[22] He saw an obvious strategic value in sending US troops, and like Gray, but without his vindictiveness, also viewed it as a way of pressurizing Éire over the Treaty ports.[23] When the troops arrived, Buhrman noted the contrasting reports in local papers. The nationalist *Irish News* was 'conspicuous by the absence of any editorial comment', whereas the unionist press was heartily supportive.[24] Gray was keen to gauge the local reaction and Buhrman reported that it was excellent, indeed almost excessive, from both communities, and despite the nationalist press, nationalists welcomed the troops as enthusiastically as unionists.[25]

Buhrman shared the American military's concerns about Yanks becoming involved in local problems, the antagonism between British and American troops and the possibility of attacks by the IRA. Buhrman and Gray worried particularly about the last point. As discussed in Chapter 6, these threats were largely rhetorical and overstated, but Buhrman remained apprehensive. Anti-British sentiment among Irish-American troops concerned him, and this went beyond the rank and file; the senior Catholic US chaplain openly declared that the British should quit Northern Ireland. 'In other words,' concluded Buhrman, 'there is disposition on the part of those who have religious and kinship ties with the Catholic population of Ireland to espouse the so-called Irish point of view, which in itself presupposes a positive anti-British attitude'. This, in turn, made them 'susceptible to Irish Republican Army influences'.[26] He feared that the military's measures to ensure soldiers refrained from political discussions would be ineffective as they were not 'aware of the religious implications of the situation'.[27] This bothered Buhrman until the tensions eased when the IRA's campaign ground to a halt by the end of 1942.

Americans continued arriving and the nationalist press, 'apparently taking its cue from Dublin', particularly de Valera's earlier protest, continued ignoring them. 'It was of course inevitable', Buhrman asserted, 'that the Government of Éire should attempt to use the arrival of American troops in furthering the political aims and aspirations of Éire'. He reported Stormont's resentment about statements emanating from Éire and personally saw them as 'prompted by political expediency as distinguished from expressing the sentiment of the Irish people'. He contended that de Valera's attitude was not shared by nationalists north of the border, who welcomed the Americans and, in fact, young nationalists, perhaps reluctant to serve King and Country, were reportedly trying to join the American forces.[28]

Given Buhrman's sensitivities about Americans becoming drawn into local animosities, and bad behaviour generally, he was surprisingly untroubled by Anglo-American hostility. In September 1942 the killing of a Scottish soldier by an American in a brawl saw the American court-martialled and imprisoned, although it seemed that British personnel were to blame. Nevertheless, while relations had deteriorated, it was 'no cause for any special alarm'.[29] The tensions were attributed to national rivalry, pay, Americans inflating prices via the black market and presumably competition for local women. There was little fraternization, and Americans were bored, which fostered ill-discipline.[30] These problems occurred elsewhere in the United Kingdom, but Buhrman recognized that anti-British grievances among Irish-American troops had an obvious outlet in Northern Ireland.

A major, if occasional, source of resentment between locals and Americans were killings by the latter, and Buhrman worried that the IRA could exploit this.

He believed, for example, that the priest at the funeral of Edward Clenaghan, killed by two drunken Americans in September 1942, was trying to inflame matters: '[i]t unfortunately appears that this funeral oration is designed to stir up feelings against American soldiers'.[31] Clenaghan's death (discussed in Chapter 3) came shortly after the execution of an IRA member, and coincided with Cardinal MacRory accusing British and American soldiers of 'overrunning' Northern Ireland, and shortly afterwards a drunken American killed Minnie Martin. These killings were the most extreme manifestation of routinely bad behaviour, and after Martin's death, he reported ruefully: '[t]his is the fourth court martial of American soldiers in Northern Ireland for the murder of British subjects. This apparent lack of discipline . . . is creating a bad impression'.[32] Buhrman's concerns, if sometimes overstated, were not groundless.

Buhrman believed that the absence of conscription and the presence of many able-bodied men of military age not in uniform created resentment among American conscripts: '[o]ne need only look around here to see that the potential man-power of Northern Ireland has not enlisted in the military service'.[33] Gray suggested that conscription could be introduced, but Catholics could claim exclusion on religious grounds.[34] Buhrman believed this unworkable as unionists who enlisted in the Great War apparently returned to find their jobs taken 'by Nationalists who had no sympathy for the British Empire' and were determined 'that no such situation shall be permitted to arise this time', a view probably informed by conversations with government officials rather than reflecting reality.[35] War workers arriving from Éire complicated matters. He estimated in October 1942, amid industrial unrest, that between 5,000 and 6,000 people from Éire were working on projects involving American technicians, a practice supposed to be actively discouraged by his Dublin counterpart, Francis Styles.[36] Styles had received so many enquiries about employment at American bases that he believed the Germans were trying to create a network of agents.[37] This generated potential security headaches plus, Buhrman suggested, anxiety among Protestant workers contemplating joining the armed forces and worried about having no jobs to return to. He reiterated his earlier view that this mirrored 1918 and 'the fear of permanent loss of their positions has prevented many men from volunteering for military service', but this seems purely anecdotal.[38]

These are, of course, highly speculative conclusions, and the lack of unionist recruitment could be attributed to the huge casualties of the Great War, not least on the Somme, or altogether more prosaic: safety and decent wages at home. The twin fears of unionist workers being replaced by nationalists and labour coming from Éire, nevertheless, were constant sources of unionist paranoia. Andrews, for example, obsessed about 'Free Staters' infiltrating Northern Ireland, and Buhrman's source may have been the prime minister or other figures within Stormont.[39] This narrative was, however, hugely convenient for unionism. It was, unmentioned or unrealized by Buhrman, a cynical way of maintaining the sectarian status quo by accusing supposedly disloyal Catholics of supplanting Protestant workers, thereby creating an existential threat to the state and the union, which, in turn, provided cover for discriminatory hiring practices. It was a narrative mostly unquestioned by Buhrman.

'A great deal of loafing': Buhrman and the war effort

Buhrman was unimpressed with Northern Ireland's less than vigorous prosecution of the war and generally doing its bit, a trend he had also noted in Glasgow: 'the average person does not realize at all the life and death struggle in which the British Empire is engaged. They are apathetic and careless of the outcome of the war. Most people are concerned with how much they can make out of the war as distinguished from how much they can do to win the war'.[40] This apathy was reflected in vital war industries: 'there is a great deal of loafing or soldiering on the job in shipyards, the men spend an unusual amount of time smoking and drinking at all hours of the day'.[41] Worse still was the impression that industries were more concerned with their post-war positions. 'It is common gossip in local circles', he reported, 'that the policy of local shipyards . . . is to conserve materials to build up the shipyards for after the war competition as opposed to wartime production'.[42] He attributed this to news about American production, which rendered work in Belfast largely irrelevant to the war's outcome. When future UK Prime Minister Harold Wilson had visited Belfast in 1940, as a civil servant in the Imperial Manpower Requirements Committee, he had been similarly shocked at the lack of productivity.[43] Evidently, little had changed.

While other regions experienced industrial action, Northern Ireland, which had the least pre-war labour unrest, was the most plagued by strikes, with an estimated 260 during the conflict.[44] This was partly because increasing employment due to more war contracts also gave labour greater bargaining power, which coincided with deteriorating relationships with management.[45] Buhrman, in March 1942, reported five different strikes in Belfast over the previous two months and had difficulty in understanding workers' attitudes.[46] Later in the year and perhaps due to renewed strike action intersecting with IRA threats, he naively speculated that either the IRA or the Germans were behind it, and blamed a 'lack of patriotism and failure of union leadership and industrial management, as well as political leadership'.[47] The cause of a strike at Harland Shorts about Sunday working was clear; however, as Sunday working was paid double, 'the workers tended to show up one hundred per cent on Sundays, yet would be absent on the average of one day during the week'.[48] He now noted, in contrast to his earlier speculation about IRA involvement, no sectarian aspect to the strikes but recognized that this was because, actively discriminated against by industries, only 5 per cent of employees were Catholics.[49]

By the end of October, Buhrman reported that the strikes, like those elsewhere in the UK, were 'influenced by subversive activities' even if the instigators remained unclear, with Germans, Italians, Catholics and communists all held responsible, rather than the more mundane explanation of disgruntled workers wanting improved pay and conditions.[50] The authorities shared some of these suspicions thus, while there was demonstrably more industrial unrest in Northern Ireland, there was also a much higher prosecution rate for strike action due to official fears of Communist Party involvement.[51] An additional factor on the mainland was that militant workers could be conscripted, a deterrent absent in Northern Ireland. The truth was neither sectarian nor ideological; it was, as Wood contends, 'a product of antagonistic relations between often authoritarian managements and workers with fresh and bitter memories of pre-war hardship and victimisation' which intensified as the war dragged on.⁵²

The situation was sufficiently serious that Vice-consul John C. Fuess prepared 'Labor in Northern Ireland' an extensive report – some thirty-one pages – which concluded that there 'seems little question' that there was no IRA involvement.⁵³ He believed that all parties, government, unions and industry were 'out of selfish interest, desperately anxious to keep the religious question out of industrial relations and are consequently loath to give their true feelings on this matter'. While the 'great majority of Catholics', he continued, would not disrupt production, the church itself, particularly MacRory and assisted by Éire's government, 'is distinctly antagonistic to Great Britain and her war effort'. Few nationalists would 'actively sabotage the war effort, [but] this element still offers a fertile ground for the sowing of seeds of discontent by subversive agents whose purpose is an intangible retarding of war production'.⁵⁴ The police were not keen to make 'any official conjecture', but Fuess believed that there was a subversive element and, in common with Buhrman, raised the possibility that 'this undercurrent may be German in origin'.⁵⁵

'Fundamental Catholic complaints': (Mis)understanding Northern Ireland

Buhrman accepted the legitimacy of status quo in Northern Ireland, co-operated with it and reported upon it accordingly; moreover, his reports were very Belfast-centric, with few references to Londonderry or anywhere else. He periodically discussed domestic politics, and many reports demonstrated his efforts to understand his posting; as early as February 1942, a month after reaching Belfast, he told Gray: '[w]e may put it this way – the points of view of the Nationalists and Unionists are quite irreconcilable'. This was hardly a revelation, but his need to report it demonstrated how little prior knowledge Buhrman possessed, although he had quickly concluded that Northern Ireland's problems were intractable. He also noted that month the election of Harold Midgley as a Labour candidate in East Belfast reflected Stormont's unpopularity, even among Protestants.⁵⁶ This was not, however, a fundamental change as '[s]trictly speaking, there is only one Party in Northern Ireland, that is, the Protestant Unionist Party. There is no party quarrel or domestic question which is not subordinated to Unionism against Irish Nationalism', and the general political inertia was reflected 'in the fact that the members of the Cabinet when appointed hold office almost for life'.⁵⁷ The government faced increasing criticism for not securing sufficient war work when unemployment remained high; voluntary recruitment to the armed forces remained low and religious discrimination was rife.⁵⁸

A lengthy dispatch in September 1942 about gerrymandering in Londonderry showed that Buhrman was not blind to anti-Catholic discrimination. He described gerrymandering as 'the political sharp practice in the redistricting of the city [so] that the Unionist party is able to gain the majority of the seats'. He recognized that this happened in America but without 'the religious implication and consequently does not stir up the bitterness and resentment which is found in Northern Ireland'.[59] Interestingly, despite, or perhaps because of, being a white Virginian, he made no link between gerrymandering and the racist 'Jim Crow' system which prevented black voting in the American South. Randolph had also been guilty of downplaying discrimination, commenting in March 1940: 'the nationalists and Catholics are perhaps no worse off as regards jobs in Northern Ireland than are the Republicans in the United States when the Democrats are in office or than for the Democrats when the Republicans are in office'.[60] The questionable analogies of Randolph and Buhrman, implying that discrimination resulted from partisan politics rather than officially sanctioned religious intolerance, misunderstood the sectarian nature of unionist rule and revealed their closeness to Stormont.

Buhrman nevertheless identified 'three fundamental Catholic complaints'. The first was the lack of Catholics appointed to government positions 'as long as they as a group express such a disloyal attitude', a judgement effectively condoning the practice. The second was gerrymandering, with the caveat that elected nationalists refused to attend Stormont, which, as with government jobs, shunted the blame back onto Catholics. Finally was the failure of the state to fund Catholic schools.[61] All were underpinned by nationalist opposition to partition, which was blamed on the British, and engendered 'a bitter anti-British attitude'.[62] Buhrman, despite recognizing the reality of discrimination, even while rationalizing elements of it, became increasingly critical of the Catholic Church as the IRA threat escalated. Both he and Gray were appalled by Irish nationalism's veneration of dead IRA members as martyrs and heroes, and the refusal of nationalists or the Catholic Church to condemn the group coloured his view.[63] In December 1942, he reported Stormont's opinion, if not necessarily his own, that nationalists 'are generally regarded as thoroughly anti-British, and in most cases disloyal'.[64] He also referred to the IRA as 'traitors' matter-of-factly, which fundamentally misread their mind-set, even if did reflect that they were charged with 'treason-felony' when brought before the courts.

At the start of 1943, the consul devoted several reports to the changing political climate, including a perceptive assessment of the schisms within nationalism (discussed in Chapter 5) as a general election approached in Éire.[65] Buhrman also evaluated the Labour Party taking a Stormont seat in West Belfast. He believed this was because 'a great many of the Unionist supporters were away in the services or engaged in war work and were absent from the polls', while an independent unionist candidate split the vote; nevertheless, the result revealed growing dissatisfaction with the government. The government, in office since 1921, 'has accumulated the same burdens of office and accusations of dishonesty and wrong-doing that any one party government would accumulate during such a long incumbency'. The campaign concerned local issues, and the winning candidate Jack Beattie opposed partition and promised to try to release republican internees. This, Buhrman argued, meant that Catholics voted tactically and not solely on religious grounds, but 'it does not represent a break from religious party lines'.[66] Beattie's election, he noted, marked the beginning of the end for Andrews with Brooke identified as the likely successor, but Andrews proved reluctant to go quietly.[67] Buhrman followed the manoeuvring which led to his eventual ousting, believing that the Unionist Party's problems were 'greatly exaggerated' by nationalist and British newspapers and would remain in power regardless of its leader.[68] In late April, after Brooke and others resigned from the cabinet, however, Andrews stood down to be replaced by Brooke.[69] The removal of Andrews, Buhrman argued, reflected Unionist Party schisms and its need to reassert its grip on power, rather than any desire for political reform. He believed, however, that the main change would be the impetus and energy Brooke would bring.[70]

An example that his attitudes coincided with those of unionists was his understanding of the Irish language. In September 1942, he argued that 'the practical aspects of the situation are that no second compulsory language is needed in Northern Ireland and the criticism here is that it is also not needed in Éire'.[71] Buhrman reported that Padraig MacNamee, not identified as the president of the Gaelic Athletic Association, Ireland's most important cultural organization, 'urged the study of Irish history to enable them to see the necessity of the Irish language in binding people together and separating them', in MacNamee's words, 'from all other peoples'.[72] Buhrman saw the language and its advocates as parochial and its promotion through the lens of Anglo-American foreign policy, believing its proponents were using it 'to emphasise their isolation' (which certainly tallied with de Valera's attitude to the language).[73] This suggested that 'the attitude of the Irish people at the present time indicates that they are almost totally lacking in an understanding or appreciation of present world conditions. The language agitation is merely one indication of this intransigent attitude'.[74] To Buhrman, therefore, the Irish language was a manifestation of Irish nationalism's insularity and shallowness when Western democracies were locked in a mortal struggle against fascism.

The State Department could end consular postings abruptly. In December 1941, Randolph was summarily redeployed to Washington, with the American consul in London telling him that 'this transfer not made at his request nor for his convenience'.[75] Buhrman was similarly suddenly summoned home in May 1943, but not before a grand send-off from ministers and unionist editors, demonstrating his popularity and familiarity with the unionist establishment. A farewell dinner at the Grand Central Hotel saw the *Telegraph's* Managing Director William Baird and Managing Editor R. M. Sayers sing his praises, as did ministers Lowry and MacDermott who 'testified to his helpful co-operation in official matters affecting the interests of both countries'.[76] For his part, Buhrman emphasized Ulster-Scots' role in creating the United States and mentioned that the surnames he encountered were also to be found all over his native Virginia. Buhrman was presented with the badge of the 'Poor Richard Club' of Philadelphia, created in 1926 in honour of Baird's father Sir Robert, for those who fostered good relations between Britain and America.[77]

After the Americans' deployment to North Africa, there was much less for the consulate to report, and this remained the case even when they returned in late 1943. Roberts, the new (acting) consul general, had arrived in Belfast in October 1942.[78] A Texan, he was another vastly experienced consular official, having begun his career in Europe during the Great War and was detained by the invading Japanese when stationed in China.[79] Roberts' reports were much less detailed and lacked his predecessor's insights into local life and were sent only monthly by 1945, but continued to discuss political issues relating to the war and partition, but with America very much as an observer, rather than a potential participant.[80] There was little to add to the wealth of detail Buhrman provided – much of it voluntarily offered – but Roberts inherited political stability and a favourable wartime situation; indeed, he had to be reminded to send his reports to the London embassy and Dublin legation.[81] Northern Ireland was calmer during the rest of the war, there was little IRA activity of note, the initial novelty of the Americans, necessitating Buhrman's comprehensive reports, had worn off and their presence was very much normalized. The consulate reverted to its routine functions; for example, one of the consul general's roles was to administer the oath of allegiance, required by new American citizens, to foreign-born members of the US forces (including several born in Northern Ireland).[82] It also dealt with requests from Americans living in Éire wishing to cross the border to enlist in the US forces.

The war's end, however, brought renewed anti-partition agitation and communal tensions. Vice-consul William F. Ayer reported in August 1945 that since VE Day the border 'although by no means ablaze, was beginning to smoulder', which included an attack on an Orange Parade in Tyrone marking VJ Day and a meeting of nationalists in Londonderry which, among other things, advocated harnessing the power of the Irish-American lobby against Stormont. According to 'competent observers', this, together with the election of a Labour government in the UK, put unionists 'in the precarious position of losing its hard won place in the United Kingdom'. Nationalists, he also noted, had finally taken their seats in Stormont.[83] The most noteworthy wartime hangover Roberts faced came in January 1946, when the consulate was invaded by irate war brides demanding transportation to America, which he eventuality facilitated.[84] Other post-war matters included warnings to be on the lookout for looted art and Nazis fleeing on neutral passports.[85] With the upheaval of the war behind them, Roberts began scoping sites for relocating the consulate, eventually settling on a property in the Malone Road area, where it still resides today.

8

'Johnny Doughboy Found a Rose in Ireland'

Women and the Americans

The *Pocket Guide to Northern Ireland* offered belated and limited courtship advice, noting that 'a woman's place was, to a considerable extent, still in the home'.[1] It also warned that 'Irish girls are friendly. They will stop on the country road and pass the time of day. Don't think on that account that they are falling for you in a big way. Quite probably the young lady you're interested in must ask her family's permission before she can go out with you'.[2] The sudden influx of thousands of young men would pose problems for any society and local conditions again came to the fore when managing relationships between US forces and women. These problems generally transcended sectarian loyalties as Northern Ireland was a religiously conservative (and largely rural) society regardless of denomination, and the Catholic and Protestant churches' policing of sex and particularly female sexuality was a rare example of cross-community consensus (if not cooperation). They agreed, for example, on celibacy outside of marriage and formally and informally monitored such religious strictures. While this conservatism was evident in the rest of the UK, it was altogether more pronounced in Northern Ireland with its higher church attendance and religious adherence, but similar patterns emerge, not least blaming women for men's behaviour and the paradox of women being held up as both models of purity and those most liable to threaten public morality. Yet there remained a sectarian subtext, with Catholic girls targeted within their own community for 'collaborating' with the Americans and the intersection of religion and class with, on one occasion, Catholic girls also dubbed 'of the lowest type' by a unionist politician specifically in relation to interracial sex.[3] In addition, they were viewed as potential fifth columnists, purportedly seducing and corrupting American soldiers for the IRA. There were then, as McCormick asserts, political implications to women's behaviour absent elsewhere.[4]

Women's attitudes towards sex were evolving, perhaps more quickly than across the border, but more slowly than on the UK mainland. The American presence accelerated this, but it was not simply about handsome, jitterbugging GIs sweeping Ulster's women off their feet, but also growing opportunities to work, earn an independent living and, crucially, the ability to do so beyond constricted kinship and religious networks. Added to this was the excitement of being young in wartime and the freedom and live-for-today attitude which this brought. The *Irish News*, for instance, reported a possible ban on alcohol sales to women in Belfast in October 1942 due to increasing drunkenness linked to the Americans, 'and it is not a rare sight to see girls of tender years under the influence of drink. Many city centre bars already refused to sell to girls, while spirit and wine sales to British and American soldiers were banned.[5] That the Americans were often the outlet for this sense of liberation can be attributed to everything from their exoticism (they appeared to have stepped off the silver screen), their politeness (showing up local men's lack of manners), their uniforms (much smarter than British) and the excitement they brought to grey wartime. The MOI observed in mid-1942 that '[m]ost of the women like Americans, and this in itself, coupled with the amounts of money they have to spend on girlfriends, is bound to upset some of the native men'.[6] Of course, there were negative consequences which go beyond mere generalizations about the Americans being 'overpaid, oversexed and over here'; they brought with them drunkenness, brawling, persistent harassment of women, venereal diseases and sexual violence, all underplayed by the police and newspapers but appearing periodically in morale and censorship reports.

A key, though not universal, exception to the positive welcome given the Americans, therefore, arose when sex was involved. Many Protestants objected as much as Catholics to their womenfolk dating GIs, and women in both communities risked being shunned or worse for consorting with Americans. Evelyn Magee, a child in Belfast, recalled: '[g]irls who fraternised with the Americans were considered very fast and not 'nice' girls'.[7] While Protestant girls could be ostracized, the consequences for Catholic girls were potentially more severe, with one Falls Road resident recollecting that 'girls who had gone out with them [Americans] were likely to get their hair cut off. It was a common occurrence'.[8] Brawling between local men and American troops, both black and white, British troops and the various foreign soldiers stationed in Northern Ireland was routine. John Campbell remembers 'a murdering match' in a Belfast dance hall every Saturday night, 'as men wearing the uniforms of almost every country except the Axis forces would battle with the local men, or each other, over the women'.[9]

Additional anxieties concerned interracial sex and specifically what were euphemistically known as 'Brown Babies'; indeed, this was a prime worry for British authorities on discovering that African American troops were arriving. On the mainland this was aligned to fears that working-class girls would be particularly susceptible to relationships with African American soldiers, and in Northern Ireland similar concerns were occasionally interwoven with sectarian narratives. Stormont MP Dehra Parker reported that in Tyrone, 'the whole situation is bad. Our people do not understand and seem to prefer the black to the white. I am told that this applies particularly to the R.C. [Roman Catholic] population and of course the lowest class of white girl'.[10] Parker not only implied that local women should not mix with African American soldiers but also largely blamed Catholic girls, a point she soon re-emphasized: '[t]he girls who are dancing with the coloured men in Maghera and elsewhere- are mostly the lowest type and belong to our minority – the coloured men are notoriously "talkative." And I think it's all very dangerous'.[11] Parker saw the involvement of Catholic girls with African American troops as doubly unwelcome, therefore, because the former were 'disloyal' and the latter, to quote Parker, were 'talkative' and together they represented a security risk, and an affront to perceived sexual, racial and religious norms.

'The excitement must be intense': Interracial romance

If American troops were glamorous, then black soldiers enjoyed additional exoticness, which both they and the white Americans believed advantaged them when competing for female affection, and consequently exacerbated existing racial tensions within the US military. Anticipating this problem, Isobel Kennedy, a Belfast woman previously resident in the States and now a wartime Red Cross volunteer, alerted Eleanor Roosevelt, the president's wife and an unstinting champion of civil rights:

> The excitement must be intense in these little places when Negro troops,- people they have for the most part never laid eyes on! – arrive in their midst. I am afraid that there may be trouble ahead, – for the young girls will undoubtedly walk out with these strangers in a way which will not surprise the local inhabitants who will wish to be friendly, but they will infuriate your <u>own</u> troops.[12]

Mrs Roosevelt concurred and hoped that Southern white soldiers could be educated but failed to convince the military to take action.[13] Many African American soldiers revelled in this popularity, with some claiming to be Native Americans to further enhance their curiosity value (Native Americans did sometimes join black regiments). White Americans were bemused by women's interest in black troops and infuriated by what they saw as provocative behaviour by their African American comrades, leading to numerous fights.[14] Colonel Arter, the US forces' PRO, explained to Belfast's unionist newspaper editors, the MOI and British military figures 'that in the opinion of the American soldier any white girl who associated with a coloured man was beneath the lowest rung of the social scale'.[15] Beyond trying to implement Jim Crow racism, therefore, the American military also imposed sexual segregation upon black troops, policing interracial sex wherever it could. In its most extreme manifestation this included the death penalty for rape, although this was never exercised in Northern Ireland.[16]

That local girls associating with African Americans could expect to be shunned by white soldiers was amply demonstrated by the latter's correspondence, where hostility towards interracial dating was common. It was used to reassure girlfriends and wives back home: '[h]oney please don't worry about these roses out here. There [sic] only a bunch of thorns, an' we men don't go for any gal who craves more for a negroe [sic] than a white boy and that's how we rate them out here'.[17] More general was fury at African American troops and contempt for their girlfriends. A sergeant wrote that 'Belfast is overrun with girls, but what kind are they. I would not be caught at a dog fight with any of them. They will go out with a Negro just as quick as they will with a white man'.[18] Another reported that he had 'seen nice looking white girls going out with a coon. They think they are hot stuff. The girls are so dumb it is pitiful'.[19] Letters included threats of retribution, specifically lynching, against African American soldiers in the States once the war was over.

The intersection of race, sex and sectarianism provides a potentially distinctive aspect of the American presence and corresponds with disquiet in England about the 'sort' of girl, in other words working class, who associated with black GIs, transposed to

Catholic girls in Northern Ireland.[20] This idea could easily be exaggerated in a society infested with sectarian stereotypes, where bracketing certain kinds of girls, Catholics, with certain sorts of troops, African Americans, could be conveniently fashioned to reinforce existing prejudices. Yet the correlation is imprecise and problematic. Determining how analogous Northern Ireland and England were in this regard is tricky, as interracial relationships were not discussed in sectarian terms by Stormont or the American military nor was this connotation reported in local newspapers. Indeed, Parker's observations are the only even semi-official source to make the connection, and she could have been projecting her own religious and racial views, in addition to her inference that some Protestant girls also engaged in this supposedly transgressive behaviour. Catholic girls were, therefore, no more likely to date African American soldiers than Protestant. Regardless of the sectarian element, as Rose asserts, girls seen with African American servicemen were judged to be 'especially immoral or degraded'; in fact, some whites regarded interracial sex as deviant sexual behaviour.[21]

There appear to be no records of births of mixed-race children in Stormont's archives, although some definitely occurred. A correspondent from Belfast, for example, reported in late 1943: 'I hear that there are already one or two coloured kids in the town already'.[22] The numbers of children born to African American fathers in the UK generally tended to be overstated during the war, but the most realistic estimate is about 2,000.[23] African American troops, except those who married women from the historic black community of Cardiff's Tiger Bay, were in effect forbidden from marrying their British girlfriends and often were deliberately separated from their sweethearts by US military authorities.[24] The Belfast consulate reckoned in July 1945, however, that three local women had married African American servicemen, but as there was no requirement to list race on marriage licences the figure would likely have been higher.[25] There was an especial concern over what the US military termed 'miscegenous unions' if African American soldiers attempted to bring wives home. The US army tried to explain 'to prospective brides and their families the prejudicial treatment in store for them', not least the illegality of such unions in some thirty states, 'regardless of whether the marriage was valid where contracted' which could have resulted in wives and children 'becoming public charges'.[26] This, it must be re-emphasized, was when many whites viewed interracial sex as abnormal, while in the most extreme manifestation of American sexual racism, sex between a black man and a white woman was considered non-consensual by definition.[27] In short, the need to police relationships officially and unofficially by Stormont and the Americans was amplified by race.

'Disorderly or indecent conduct': Prostitution, venereal disease and harassment

Soldiers' willingness to pay for sex added inevitable complexities to the overarching dilemma of managing liaisons between women and the Americans. The Foreign Office worried that British women's behaviour and growing numbers of prostitutes visibly 'haunting the vicinity' of Red Cross hostels could damage Anglo-American relations, particularly if American soldiers contracted venereal disease. Soldiers infected, especially married ones, 'may become involved in many personal difficulties. He will blame this, not on himself, but on the British system which allows temptation to thrust itself so obtrusively on him'.[28] Thus, responsibility lay with British women, rather than the American soldiers, despite them either actively seeking prostitutes or responding to solicitation and then failing to use prophylactics. This situation was predictably replicated in Northern Ireland and resulted in numerous convictions for soliciting and keeping 'disorderly houses', notably in Londonderry.[29] Amelia Street, the closest Belfast had to a red light district and yards from American Red Cross accommodation, was declared out of bounds, while prosecutions and convictions for prostitution and brothel keeping rose markedly.[30]

Self-appointed and quasi-official moral guardians came in many forms, from matronly vigilantism, to the blackthorn-wielding parish priest of Toome, to Home Guard units keeping an eye on dances.[31] All fretted about the liberalization of women's sexuality and mainly blamed the Americans. Mrs Toner, a retired missionary, led a group monitoring Belfast City Hall at night, shining torches on canoodling couples; this moral vigilantism ended when a soldier struck her.[32] The *Mid-Ulster Mail* reported the conviction of two teenage sisters in Dungannon for 'running after' Americans, and 'disorderly or indecent conduct', with the police deeming their behaviour 'scandalous'. The solicitor of another woman convicted of public indecency with an American attempted to shunt responsibility onto the Americans, arguing that Northern Ireland was 'more or less under the influence of transatlantic ideas and probably these were a bit more broadminded. In America they were not as stringent in their ideas on these matters as people of this country'. Unmoved the judge condemned the couple's 'disgraceful conduct'.[33] Such was the desire to maintain public virtue that merely speaking to an American could lead to arrest.[34] The local authorities took some action, inaugurating a Women's Patrol in Belfast in September 1943, a clampdown in Londonderry on women suspected of immoral behaviour and the recruitment of female police officers, beginning in 1943.[35]

In 1943 the medical superintendent for Belfast professed disappointment in combatting venereal disease and advocated 'compulsory notification' to control it.[36] He blamed the spread on 'amateur' rather than 'professional' prostitutes, but once again responsibility lay with women rather than men.[37] The US military contradicted this assessment, stating that its troops' infection rates were lower than elsewhere in the UK, something it attributed to local morality and the absence of established red light districts.[38] This was, nevertheless, at odds with infection rates among British and Canadian troops in Northern Ireland, and, as McCormick suggests, American reports may have been understated for diplomatic reasons and to maintain goodwill between their troops and the population.[39] Yet, according to a British military source, Northern Ireland's VD rates were the UK's highest, with forty to fifty new cases per week, two-thirds of which were soldiers. The report blamed this partly on the lack of entertainment.[40] Preventing the spread of venereal diseases was also hampered by local objections to contraception, including the distribution of prophylactics at Red Cross Clubs; this was circumvented by giving them out via euphemistic 'Aid Stations' in the clubs.[41] The need for contraception, and its successful use, was demonstrated in

Armagh, where US soldiers were deployed to reap a harvest of condoms with spiked sticks from the city's parks.[42]

Many fears about female sexuality, the amateur prostitute, interracial sex and concerns about violence between Americans and locals were encapsulated in the Wiley Harris case. Harris, an African American soldier, killed Henry Coogan in a drunken dispute over payment to a prostitute, Eileen Megaw, outside an air-raid shelter in north Belfast in March 1944. Megaw was a so-called amateur, telling Harris's court-martial that she was a clerk who had 'been earning my living on the streets' for almost a year, soliciting both black and white Americans.[43] Belfast's newspapers tacitly acknowledged the delicacy of the trial, skirting Megaw's prostitution, Harris's readiness to pay her for sex and that Coogan was, essentially, a pimp. All of these factors were alluded to: the *Telegraph* reported that Megaw and Harris went to the shelter without explaining why, before the story jumps to Coogan warning them of approaching police.[44] The coroner in the case, Dr Herbert P. Lowe, finding that Harris had acted without premeditation, blamed 'a definite lack of parental control in Belfast' as some parents were 'humbugging' themselves if they thought '"Oh my Joan or Jean is a wise girl and can watch herself"'.[45] 'If fathers and mothers became 'pals' of their children and advised them in important matters', he continued, 'there might not be so much street-running by these young girls'.[46] Yet 'street-running' girls, not drunken Americans willing to pay for sex, were to blame, and, as Rose argues about the UK generally, the Americans created the impression that 'a wave of "moral laxity" was engulfing the country'.[47]

Women complained frequently about being accosted by Americans; although this harassment may not have developed into sexual assault, it remained common, rationalized by too much alcohol and too little to do.[48] Official records, censorship reports and newspapers were squeamish about reporting sexual violence, but it is implied. In June 1942, for example, the MOI, while acknowledging that many stories about the Americans were exaggerated, untrue or Axis propaganda, reported: '[o]ne of the rumours about Americans, widely circulated, relates to their pathologically sadistic tendencies with women'.[49] One correspondent, quoted in a postal censorship report, wrote in 1943 that '[i]t was by no means safe to be out in the darkness while they were around' and another said that 'they're certainly leaving the trail behind them!! It used to be a respectable place to live in but now I have me [*sic*] doubts'.[50] Women were advised to carry pepper pots and whistles during the blackout to fend off assailants.[51] Local newspapers did not report sex crimes, and they rarely feature in available official records with only one rape, in June 1944, and one sexual assault appearing in police reports to the government.[52] Court-martial convictions for rape and sexual assault in Northern Ireland were negligible, with the Board of Review confirming one sentence for attempted rape in May 1944 and an execution in November 1944 for the rape and murder of a seven-year-old girl.[53] One other American, as discussed in Chapter 3, was convicted of the manslaughter of a deaf-mute woman, and known prostitute, in Castlewellan in October 1942, but his court-martial found no signs of rape, declaring that intercourse had been consensual.[54] A woman admitted to the Mater Dei home, a mother and baby home run by the Catholic Church, 'thought she was doped' by an American before sex, while the notes on another young mother simply stated that she 'met two Americans and was raped. Does not know them'.[55] This scant evidence no doubt hides much greater problems with women feeling stigmatized for being victims of sexual assault, the further stigmatization of reporting it and the notorious difficulty in securing convictions, resulting in so few recorded cases and prosecutions. Moreover, those women who ventured to bring charges against Americans were often ignored or their characters questioned, especially if their reputations could be impugned or they were working class.[56]

'The girl said "yes", but the general didn't': Marriage and military bureaucracy

The Americans were given a range of advice on courting and local women. *Stars and Stripes* suggested that women were not entirely passive in the face of the Americans' attentions, with a cartoon featuring a heavily bandaged GI outside a US Army hospital telling a comrade: 'it was an Irish girl I met in the blackout!'[57] Publicizing the publication of the *Pocket Guide* in October 1942, the *Stars and Stripes* warned GIs not to 'get Irish girls wrong'.[58] An American soldier, perhaps only half-jokingly, observed that 'if you go out with an Irish girl more than three times you're practically engaged'.[59] A County Tyrone native recalled parents' efforts to maintain their daughters' good characters, seeing them walking arm-in-arm several paces behind their daughters and their sweethearts on dates.[60] The American Red Cross, in charge of off-base welfare, also policed sexual morality and vetted the 'sort' of girl associating with the Americans. Mary Anderson, the assistant programme director at the Red Cross in Belfast, assessed the girls coming to events. The *Washington Evening Star* reported that she 'helps the doughboys by picking their dance partners'. She was, it explained, 'young, cheery, efficient, endowed with a sense of humor, gifted in the art of summing up her neighbors', and exercised a veto over who could attend dances: '[n]o invitation is issued to any one whom Miss Anderson has not met'.[61] Stormont was keen to assist, with the press officer, F.M. Adams (also the MOI's Regional Information Officer), requesting that local hospitality committees create lists of 'suitable partners' at dances and 'exclude undesirables' (Figure 8.1).[62]

Romance frequently blossomed, and many Johnny Doughboys did indeed find their Irish Roses, but this was not without its complications as the War Department discouraged marriages and warned couples of the potential pitfalls of tying the knot.[63] The American military had various concerns regarding troops marrying while stationed abroad. It anticipated larger problems than during the Great War due to more men being deployed for much longer, proportionately more of them being single, and so many British men in uniform and overseas. They also feared bigamists within their own ranks and gold-diggers, attracted by the Yanks' better wages, among potential wives.[64] American military law did not forbid soldiers from marrying without their commander's permission while abroad, and they had been told as much before departing, but this was something that Hartle endeavoured to change. He wrote to the War Department in March 1942, prior to the first wedding, to 'strongly recommend ... exempting Northern Ireland' from the rule allowing soldiers to marry. He warned that

Figure 8.1 'American soldiers and sailors and their invited guests enjoy a dance during a party at an 8th Air Force station at Nyack [US Army Air Force Composite Command Station 231 at Kircassock House, Magheralin, County Armagh], Northern Ireland on 25 April 1943'. (NARA). Image courtesy of Clive Moore.

'local marriages will become quite a problem', not least among men with wives back in the States.[65] The Judge Advocate pointed out that a commander had no right to prohibit marriage; in fact, he told Hartle, as marriage had been traditionally encouraged he was reluctant to stop it.[66]

The first marriage took place within three months, between Belfast woman Thelma Smith and Private Herbert Cooke of Cleveland, Ohio.[67] Smith and Cooke were conscious of the army's likely hostility, stating after their engagement 'the only thing that was worrying us now is all the talk about the American authorities putting a ban on such marriages, that is why we're hurrying up the wedding'.[68] 'The girl said "yes," but the general didn't' was the Associated Press's view with the wedding initially postponed because Hartle had not granted permission.[69] Undeterred, the couple married in secret on 13 April 1942 at College Square Presbyterian Church in Belfast, with Cooke risking the military's ire.[70] Smith's father was late and missed the ceremony which, according to an American news report, 'was conducted with such secrecy that only four persons, including the sexton, were witnesses'.[71] According to the Americans' base history, '[t]he clergyman took the position that as long as the license to marry was in order, he was not obliged to secure permission from the prospective groom's commanding officer'.[72] Any disciplinary consequences for

Cooke were not reported; in fact, the amount of publicity likely saved him from punishment.[73]

As McCormick observes, there were many reasons for discouraging marriages, from the morale of unmarried soldiers to Anglo-American relations, so securing permission was made as bureaucratic as possible.[74] Due to the Cooke-Smith and other marriages, in June the War Department introduced new regulations, Circular 179, barring marriage without a commanding officer's approval.[75] Some restrictions were soon relaxed; Circular 20 lifted the nominal ban by requiring soldiers to apply for permission in writing three months in advance, 'accompanied by a letter of acquiescence from the intended mate'. A commander could, however, reject the application if it would have 'injurious effect upon the character of either party', and there were no widows' pensions.[76] The waiting period was reduced to two months in October, but relaxed where the husband was about to be deployed or in cases of 'illegitimacy and pregnancy', to avoid scandal.[77] Lieutenant General Frank M. Andrews, who briefly commanded American forces in the ETO from January 1943 until his death in an air-crash that May, concluded that the regulations were 'basically sound and accomplished the requisite restraint on hasty marriage', with flexibility in 'special cases'.[78] All the advice stressed that wives did not automatically become American citizens, husbands had no special privileges, for example, married quarters, and the American authorities would not cover the wife's passage to the States.[79] The military regularly reaffirmed that no special privileges would be bestowed upon couples; moreover, the US Immigration and Naturalization Bureau stated in April 1944 that wives would remain 'non-quota immigrants'.[80]

In response to an enquiry from the Catholic Church, the June 1942 guidelines were confirmed by the Judge Advocate General Department (JAGD), the US military's legal arm. This also emphasized that wives had to wait three years (it was usually five) before they could become citizens, warned that married men could be deployed without warning and that widows were not entitled to a pension or compensation if their husbands were killed.[81] This message was conveyed to Mass-goers in the diocese of Down and Connor (counties Antrim and Down) by order of Bishop Daniel Mageean.[82] There were some caveats, for example, the *Telegraph* reported that women marrying officers became citizens immediately.[83] In August 1943, *Stars and Stripes* cautioned wives that citizenship was not guaranteed even after the war; moreover, although not subject to quota restrictions, they would enter the United States as aliens, and, as immigrants they had to demonstrate that they could support themselves or had support in place. It also noted that the UK government required emigrants to have an exit permit, yet another hurdle to overcome.[84]

The prospective bride underwent various security and medical checks, whereas grooms did not. The American Red Cross even employed a local woman to vet would-be brides, and the police were on the lookout for those with subversive connections.[85] Maureen Mathes, who worked at the Londonderry naval base, for example, came home to find that a policeman had visited because her sailor boyfriend asked for his commander's permission to marry. It was the first her parents had heard of the couple's intentions.[86] By making its consent compulsory and imposing seemingly endless delays, the military exercised some control over marriages and ultimately hoped to deter couples.[87] Would-be husbands, white ones at any rate, had it much easier, by simply demonstrating they were not already married. Some sweethearts took an innovative approach. A couple inconvenienced by the Atlantic when an American was redeployed to the States apparently 'married' by conducting the ceremony via a military radio. As the military's legal journal reported in December 1944, 'the little lady procured a Justice of the Peace (reason unknown, except it was an attempt to inject some legality into it) and took him along while she wired her acceptance'. Then, alluding to fears about gold-diggers, it sardonically noted that this and other marriages 'are all followed by the filing of an application for a family allowance'.[88]

Some problems reflected local divisions. An unexplored aspect of these transatlantic love affairs, and sadly beyond the scope of this work, is responses to marriages between women and Americans of the 'other' religion. Muriel Mitchell's parents, for instance, objected to her marriage to Ray Friscia less because he was American than because in their experience a so-called mixed marriage (Muriel was a Protestant, Ray a Catholic) was doomed to failure. Their attitude, therefore, was driven not by innate prejudice against her beau's faith but merely by their perception of the fate of such 'mixed' marriages; however, it is easy to speculate that other parents may not have been quite as understanding.[89] On the whole, however, parents, but mothers more so, appear largely supportive of their daughters' choice of husbands, and one American wrote home that '[m]others and grandmothers seem especially happy if an American soldier pays attention to an unmarried daughter'.[90] This far from precluded the more generalized hostility directed at these relationships, mainly from men, which transcended tribal loyalties. Despite all of these obstacles, couples persisted, and around 1,800 women from Northern Ireland married Americans, with some 600 children born to American fathers before the war's end.[91]

In January 1944, General Collins issued instructions regarding 'children born in Northern Ireland whose fathers are US citizens'. Births had to be reported immediately to the consulate; enlisted fathers needed to provide proof of citizenship, whereas officers did not. Once verified by the consulate, the child was recognized as a US citizen until the age of eighteen, provided the father had lived in the States for ten years, five over the age of sixteen.[92] Then there were illegitimate children. In October 1944, Stormont officials reported ongoing negotiations between the Home Office and the Americans regarding allowances payable to the illegitimate children of US servicemen. Interestingly, it was not clear if the outcome of these negotiations would apply to Northern Ireland, but the unofficial American view was that they should, and Stormont officials wanted to establish how many cases they were dealing with.[93] The consulate was called upon to help unmarried mothers trace their children's fathers, alongside the sadder task of aiding women whose husbands were killed in action.[94] If fathers could not be found, then women were faced with the choices of raising a child alone, an especially daunting task in the 1940s, or within the family (some were raised by grandparents as their mothers' siblings, discovering the truth years later), or by an unsuspecting or forgiving husband, or by giving it up for adoption.[95] Some women and their children had the misfortune to end up in notorious 'mother and baby' homes and 'Magdalene Laundries', run by both the Protestant and Catholic churches.[96]

'Your husbands want you and you want your husbands': Reaching America

Assuming that a couple had gained a commanding officer's permission, passed all of the security and medical checks, had a ceremony before the husband-to-be was sent to the front, overcome both local prejudice about Americans carting off their womenfolk and American fears about gold-diggers ensnaring their sons, the couple still somehow had to be reunited in the States.[97] As noted, the US military's original attitude was that brides travel at their own expense, but by the end of the war, facing growing pressure from couples and a more sympathetic American press, the authorities relented and covered the costs of bringing brides home. Yet, as with everything else involved in transatlantic marriage, this was tedious, frustrating, endlessly bureaucratic, with the added perception among Ulster brides that those from England and Europe were being prioritized, meaning that some couples were not finally reunited until late 1946. While they waited, war brides were prepared for what lay ahead. Marcia Mackie, at the American Red Cross in Belfast, organized ten classes in July 1944 upon which 120 brides enrolled, and these covered practical aspects of life in the States, such as education, clothing, customs, cooking and 'interior decoration', as well as politics – for example, Anglo-American relations and post-war international cooperation. The first class handled 'Americans in the eyes of an Ulsterwoman', and Quincy Roberts was later on hand to take questions on naturalization.[98]

The first local bride to officially arrive in the States did not actually marry a serving member of the American forces. Memmi Little, the daughter of unionist MP Reverend James Little, met Clair M. Waterbury, an American in the RAF, at a dance in Antrim, and the couple married in September 1942.[99] Shortly afterwards, he transferred to the US Naval Air Service and the pair moved to the States, and she apparently became the first war bride from Northern Ireland to do so. The now Mrs Waterbury caused quite a stir upon her arrival, making the front pages of American newspapers. The couple returned briefly to Belfast in February 1945 when Lieutenant Waterbury was posted to England, and she was again in the papers with the *Telegraph* declaring her the first bride also to make the reverse trip.[100] The Waterburys made headlines, but their positive experience of negotiating American military bureaucracy was very much the exception. Muriel Mitchell fretted constantly in letters to Ray Friscia. She worried that Ray would not get his old job back after the war and that she could not afford passage to the States. She asked him to see if the US government paid for wives to go and 'if so we'll get married by proxy'.[101] By this stage, October 1944, the couple had been apart for fifteen months, and it was almost another year before they finally married in Belfast.[102] Husbands resented the American authorities' actions and questions about their wives' motivations. Sergeant Frederick S. Deleo, stationed in Northern Ireland, reacted angrily in the *Yank* to an official's criticism of marriages, arguing that the labyrinthine process of marrying was ample evidence that these unions were far from hasty.[103] 'After going to all this trouble', he complained, 'with the usual amount of red tape, and finally getting married, a soldier has to put up with the likes of this man.... Did it ever occur to you, sir, that we who have married over here could be in love with our wives?'[104]

Amid growing pressure from husbands and wives alike, the military overturned its prior obstructions and eventually facilitated their desire to be reunited.[105] Yet there was also hostility in the American press to contend with, where, as Friedman demonstrates, war brides were 'framed as predators' even by the *New York Times*.[106] The *Washington Evening Star* joked in March 1943 that 'there's talk of organizing here a club of war brides of United States soldiers. Sponsors say it would have a surprisingly large membership, for American soldiers continue to wed Ulster brides'.[107] Some Americans resented using precious transportation for war brides arguing for the prioritization of veterans (some of whom had been gone for several years), former POWs and the wounded and viewing war brides' demands as selfish.[108] Press attitudes softened during 1944 as did officialdom when Congress passed the War Brides Act of 1945 and the Alien Fiancées and Fiancés Act of 1946 essentially giving wives and fiancées the right to go to America.[109]

The first contingent from Northern Ireland, among some 'sixty young attractive war brides', according to the *New York Times*, arrived with a great deal of fanfare in September 1944.[110] They had married sailors and marines stationed in Londonderry, including the three Jack sisters from the city.[111] Maureen Mathes was chosen as the first bride to disembark and had her very own Milburn Henke celebrity moment as she was greeted with a fusillade of photographers' flashbulbs.[112] Yet these brides were very much the lucky ones; even after the war had ended, making the journey remained enormously difficult, with most wives still marooned in Northern Ireland at the end of 1945.[113] The problem came to a head in January 1946 when around 100 women took matters into their own hands and occupied the consulate, responsible for granting visas and organizing transport, demanding to go to the States. Roberts assured them that he was doing everything possible, including pressing the military to send a ship. He told the group: 'I am using every bit of influence I have to get you away. Your husbands want you and you want your husbands, and, believe me, we don't want to detain you here one moment longer than necessary.'[114] To his credit, Roberts prioritized transportation arrangements, delaying his regular political reports to the embassy and taking his staff off all but the most urgent tasks to facilitate this.[115] Roberts perhaps understood their situation better than most as in September 1945 he became the latest American to marry a local woman.[116] How the women found each other is uncertain (it may have been via Red Cross classes the previous summer), but it undoubtedly took a degree of organizing to mobilize such a large group.[117] The women, representing around 1,200 wives, some as young as seventeen, and around 400 children, believed that they had been forgotten in favour of brides elsewhere and threatened to protest at Stormont and even embarkation points in England if necessary. Their spokesperson, Mrs Jean Daly, complained that many had been married longer than their counterparts in England and Europe, with one married for four years. They also emphasized the emotional strains of separation, as some husbands had not yet met their children, alongside the financial problems it brought.[118] Muriel Friscia, for instance, wrote to an impatient Ray of going to consulate several times and now making an appointment to see an Immigration Inspector who had been sent 'to interview each and every one of the 1,200 Irish brides' before they could depart.[119]

The protesters were not entirely satisfied with Roberts' response, but within a few days the women received questionnaires regarding arrangements, although without guarantees that they could depart from Belfast.[120] The American authorities, nevertheless, finally took action. In March, 314 war brides accompanied by 140 children left Belfast on the SS *Henry Gibbins*, the first of three sailings over the next six weeks.[121] The converted troopship had been specifically fitted out to accommodate the women and their children, with nurseries, play areas, a cinema and a library, while they were given dollars to spend, assistance from Red Cross workers and talks on what to expect in their new homeland.[122] According to the captain, the women learned *The Star-Spangled Banner* and sang it as they passed the Statue of Liberty on their way into New York.[123] In early April a further 450, including Muriel Friscia, departed on the *Gibbins* with their children, but some 600 brides remained.[124] The final ship to depart Belfast was the slightly more luxurious SS *James Parker*, in late April, which had 152 women and 44 children on board, with some joining the voyage at very short notice due to others having to drop out.[125] This meant that those left would have to travel to Southampton before finally making the trip.[126] After an eight-day voyage, some were met by their husbands in New York, but many had journeys as far as California, as they were scattered across the country.[127] Some brides already had family in the States, while one looked forward to bringing her parents and siblings over.[128]

At Stormont, Adams liaised with US public relations officer Lieutenant J. O. Mays in organizing press for the brides' departure, and unionist newspapers obliged with plenty of coverage.[129] The *Telegraph* conveyed the emotion of the occasion for those departing and those they were leaving behind. Women on the *Gibbins*' first trip passed notes to their families, wore brightly coloured scarves and waved handkerchiefs, which were soon 'held to their streaming eyes' as the ship pulled out. One grandmother clutched a single shoe as a final memento of her granddaughter. Those on board and those watching from the quayside sang 'When Irish Eyes Are Smiling', before dockers started singing more upbeat tunes.[130] Not everyone could make the journey, some for the most heartbreaking of reasons: eight-month-old Essa Anne McDaniel died of pneumonia the day before she was due to leave, and three-month-old Desmond Hoover, also with pneumonia, had to go to hospital. His mother had no family in Belfast, but was invited to stay with Mrs McDaniel's parents.[131] Eleanor Meeks, already a widow after her husband was killed in France, decided that she and her seventeen-month-old daughter would stay for the moment rather than leave on the *Parker* to join her late husband's family in Illinois.[132] Two-and-a-half-year-old Anna Bourgeois left to be with her father, one of the first technicians in Londonderry, having lost her mother, formerly Jane McIntyre, when she was a month old. She had been raised by her aunts but travelled to America in the care of one of the other war brides.[133] Reflecting upon the torturous process of joining their husbands, shortly before embarking, one of the women pointedly declared: '[w]e had to fight our own battles'.[134]

The extent to which the war was transformative for Northern Ireland's women is debatable. Many women were able to exercise a degree of economic and sexual independence, and while the former was encouraged by the immediate needs of the war, it also had a sense of impermanence; the latter, however, was resisted by the forces of religious conservatism. The visibility of women expressing their sexuality and the perception of widespread immorality posed a threat to previously accepted social norms and to the moral well-being of American servicemen, and therefore had to be policed. The war led to greater efforts to monitor and restrain female, particularly working-class, sexuality, and in this regard, McCormick's argument that class trumped religion has merit.[135] The Americans were the most visible evidence of this challenge to accepted social norms, both in terms of sex and in more prosaic matters of courtship and manners, offering a glamorous and adventurous alternative to local men. In this regard, certainly for war brides, the Americans broadened the horizons of Northern Ireland's women.

9

'The Dusky Doughboys'

Jim Crow racism in Northern Ireland

It was a long way from the Deep South to the Bessbrook, County Armagh, and for African American GIs, the culture-shock of an entirely white society was exacerbated by the weather, strange accents and stranger customs. The locals, however, proved hospitable, apparently confirmed when some delighted African American soldiers discovered a dance advertised in the village for the 'blackmen'. Showing up at the appointed hour, the soldiers were refused entry, despite a sign clearly stating that the dance was for blackmen. It momentarily seemed that America's 'Jim Crow' segregation had pursued them across the Atlantic, but what appeared to be a brush with racism was actually the troops' first encounter with Northern Ireland's idiosyncrasies, as the dance was for the Royal Black Institution, a Protestant loyal order known as the 'blackmen'.[1] Most people, outside Belfast and Londonderry's ports, had never seen a black person before, so they were certainly a novelty, yet when announced in May 1942 that the latest wave would include black GIs, as part of a larger force making up the third phase of *Magnet*, press interest focused more on the (white) armoured division also arriving. What comment there was on the unfamiliar new arrivals, while pandering to some racial stereotypes, did not include fears about the potential importation of Jim Crow racism. The experience of African Americans troops in Northern Ireland was generally, though not entirely, positive, while the local response was mostly friendly and, for all of their apparent exoticism, they were often defined more by their nationality and their contribution to the war effort than the colour of their skin.

African American troops were sent to the UK in 1942 over London's objections. The British were concerned about their impact, and especially the so-called brown babies they would undoubtedly leave behind; London, therefore, specifically requested that America send only white troops. General Chaney agreed, emphatically telling the War Department: 'Colored units should not, repeat should not, be sent to the British Isles'.[2] American officials refused, declaring that as their troops were coming at British request, they had no say in the matter. As Secretary of War Henry Stimson informed General Marshall, 'Colored troops will not be utilized in a country against the will of that country's government, when the United States government is the petitioner'; however, as the UK had requested military assistance, it had no say on what forces were sent.³ As an aside, this meant, in theory, that if had it been Roosevelt's idea to dispatch forces to the UK, rather than Churchill's, the British could have rejected African American troops. The British government and military then fretted about enforcing a 'colour bar', in other words, adherence to American-style segregation. The government worried that this was against the British sense of fair play but, more importantly, would be unpopular in the Empire, notably India. The British had long debates, with some opinions not flattered by posterity, and having lost the argument with the Americans, it became a question of how to negotiate American race relations. Different government departments took very different perspectives. The Colonial Office was acutely aware that embracing segregation would be poisonous in the Empire; the War Office and some senior military figures were ambivalent towards racism and black people; indeed, some had views familiar in the Deep South. Secretary of State for War, Sir James Grigg, advocated allowing the Americans to impose segregation, but not to endorse this officially, even while 'educating' British troops about American race relations. General Arthur Dowler wrote an infamous memorandum, 'Notes on Relations with Coloured Troops', in November 1942 detailing American racial etiquette and providing 'practical advice' on the matter.⁴ The cabinet eventually decided neither to impose nor enforce Jim Crow, and would not police it on the Americans' behalf. Equally, blatant American racism would go unchallenged when encountered; if the Americans imposed informal segregation, then that was their business.⁵

One indication of the American perspective came in the summer of 1942. James Warburg, Overseas Branch deputy director of the Office of War Information (OWI), reported a conversation on the race question in the UK to his boss in Washington, Elmer Davis. Warburg attended a meeting in London with Admiral Harold L. Stark, US naval commander in Europe, Commander R. E. Vining, who was familiar with Northern Ireland, British liaison officer Vice-Admiral Geoffrey Blake and Arthur Hays Sulzberger, the publisher of the *New York Times*. Sulzberger had very clear ideas on race, including stationing African American troops in cities as rural populations 'have no experience with foreigners, let alone colored people, particularly the girls, do not know how to take the negroes and, as a matter of fact, are very much attracted to them'. Sulzberger conceded, Warburg noted, that that the 'universal opinion seems to be that they are much quieter and gentler than the white American troops', yet argued that it would be better to station them in ports which were used to hosting foreigners. If not, then 'nine months from now there will be very serious problems'. Warburg was not entirely convinced by this analysis, but was wary of 'transplant[ing] into this country a problem which we have been unable to solve at home'. He also fell back upon dubious arguments that African American troops were better suited to sunnier climes and would struggle with the winter. Warburg's view was that 'as a matter of principle, we should draw no color distinctions whatsoever, but as a practical matter I do foresee trouble if we don't use some discretion in where we use our colored troops'. By way of postscript, he argued that 'people here are so completely without prejudice, and treat the colored troops so well', but this would quickly turn to prejudice in the event of negative interactions with African American troops; but equally, good treatment would make African Americans unwilling to accept Jim Crow when they returned home.[6]

'We all think alike on the Coloured question': policing Jim Crow

In May 1942 Buhrman reported rumours about the imminent arrival of African Americans troops to Gray:

> [t]his created a little stir in official circles. There are various reasons why they would not want American Negroes stationed in Northern Ireland. From my own standpoint it would seem to me to be wise policy. I have inquired of our army authorities as to whether there is any truth in these rumors and I am informed by them that they are without foundation; that it has not been contemplated at any time sending a contingent of Negro troops to Northern Ireland.[7]

Two weeks earlier, however, War Department instructions on African American troops specifically included Northern Ireland, and they duly arrived the following month.[8] It is difficult to determine from Buhrman's language whether Stormont was opposed, or if this was simply his view, as he does not explicitly state that officials objected, or which element was 'wise policy'. The inference, in so far as one can be drawn, is that Stormont, in line with London, did not want black troops. The US military's emphatic denial of the rumours, to be almost immediately contradicted, demonstrates either that the military did not wish to divulge this information to Buhrman, or his contacts just did not know. It also illustrated that the local rumour-mill was sometimes better informed than the American consul.

Stormont was not part of the London discussions, but it was granted a degree of latitude in implementing policy, within Brooke's overall remit for managing the Americans, and within the constraints created by the British and the Americans. It would not enforce segregation; like London however, it periodically turned a blind eye to discrimination. The first African American troops arrived in June, yet it was not until August and September, when interracial tensions within the American forces were becoming problematic in England (friction was already evident in Northern Ireland), that attempts were made to formulate at least a semi-formal policy. Brooke devoted a good deal of time to this and was troubled by any suggestion of a colour bar. In common with London officials, Brooke was often vague, even in the privacy of his diary, about the 'problems' presented by African American soldiers; however, he refused to countenance American segregation. In July he met privately with Colonel Arter, the Americans' Public Relations Officer, who offered 'the USA viewpoint on the various problems that confront us'.[9] He discussed race at length with a British officer, Colonel Turnham, who explained that the British military was using lectures to educate its troops, and he wanted, Brooke wrote, 'to make our people aware of the dangers, which seems difficult as it would be said that we are discriminating against American citizens'.[10] This insinuated that segregation was being considered, but avoiding a written record through lectures, rather than, say, a booklet, gave the British plausible deniability. Brooke was equally vague after an informal meeting with two of the Americans' Headquarters Staff, concluding that 'their unofficial view is that we should take drastic action. Officially there is no difference', again implying segregation.[11] Brooke, even within his diary's confines, never properly articulated what the policy actually was, beyond telling Andrews that it reflected 'the difficulties we were up against with the Coloured question'.[12] In August, at a briefing for unionist newspaper editors, not attended by Brooke, Turnham suggested 'a measure of segregation', while Arter warned of white Americans' hostility towards interracial sex.[13] This hinted that both militaries' preference was for some segregation in order to avoid trouble, while acknowledging that white Americans were its likely instigators.

Brooke took up the matter with the MOI in London in September and obtained reassurance that 'we all think alike on the Coloured question' and 'we are in complete agreement'.[14] What they were in complete agreement about was again vague, but Brooke secured some leeway to work largely independently within London's guidelines without Stormont having to officially outline its response. Written Home Office guidance quickly followed, focusing on African Americans' interactions with other troops and local women. This stressed that segregation was an American matter and that the police were not 'in any way responsible for enforcement'.[15] Brooke agreed with this approach. Gransden also dedicated much time to this, referring to 'our many talks' in correspondence with Turnham (none of which were written up).[16] As in the rest of the UK, Northern Ireland would make African American soldiers welcome, but would limit their contact with the population where possible. The number of black troops who served in Northern Ireland is difficult to determine accurately, but based on the thirty-five companies and four detachments from 'Colored' units which spent some time there, this would put the figure somewhere between 4,000 and 12,000 men. Given that 300,000 Americans passed through Northern Ireland, this suggests a proportionately lower figure than the 10 per cent of the armed forces which they made up overall, and a lower proportion than sent to England.[17]

London discouraged physical intimacy between African American troops and civilians, for example, not billeting or entertaining them in private homes, in contrast to securing invitations to tea for homesick white soldiers, or to spend Christmas with families. The Moneymore hospitality committee tried to negotiate this, reporting that 'owing to the difficulty of providing private entertainment for negroes, the committee run social evenings for these men, who appreciate the form of amusement'.[18] The manner of the 'difficulty' is implicit, but at least the men's needs were not ignored. In Cookstown, by contrast, '[a] number of American coloured troops were entertained in private homes', while Colored Welfare Officers from Belfast kitted out a hall for African American troops.[19] These local arrangements seemed to be effective, and strayed beyond the parameters set by London.[20] In fact, the Foreign Office and the MOI received fewer reports of racial problems from Northern Ireland than from any other region, for example, one Foreign Office memo from early 1944 noted that 'the colour question has produced no comments of interest and it would seem that the topic has not come up'.²¹ It should be remembered, however, that the MOI was in effect run by Stormont, and it had a vested interest in demonstrating that it was coping well and may have underplayed problems.

'We sho like it here': Reactions to African American troops

The press occasionally reported on the newcomers and though guilty of perpetuating stereotypes, it did not engage in racist scaremongering.²² Upon their arrival, the *Down Recorder* noted that '[t]here are a number of negroes for the supply services'.²³ The *Mid Ulster Mail* remarked that '[t]hey are a combat force, and are fully armed and equipped .... [but] part of their duties will consist of the maintenance and construction of military establishments' and were led largely by white officers. It also stated that not all were from the 'Sunny South'.²⁴ The *Dungannon Observer* commented that 'their presence in Northern Ireland has created the utmost interest. They strike observers as being exceedingly competent'.²⁵ Locals were also apparently surprised that some had Irish or Scottish surnames.²⁶ The *Telegraph* was the most active and its stories, though well-meaning, relied upon stereotypes about African Americans being superstitious, childlike, loyal and musical, and even quoted them in their apparent dialect. It reported in July 1942 that 'the dusky doughboys have been winning all hearts by their cheery ways. As for the men themselves, their unanimous verdict seems to be: "We sho like it here"'.²⁷ It later reported an all-black choir making its first public appearance in Northern Ireland: '[i]t is said that if you pick up four coloured men in any part of the United States, in 90 cases out of a hundred you have a singing quartet ... (not every negro is a Paul Robeson) but they are never discordant and they blend beautifully'.²⁸ The *Mid-Ulster Mail* felt the need to 'explain' the troops' different skin tones noting that '[s]ome are so light in the complexion as to pass for Indians or Latins, but others are full-blooded Negroes'.²⁹ The press tried to portray African American troops positively, but, in avoiding the crassest of negative stereotypes, succeeded in reinforcing many others. It is worth noting that press curiosity was largely absent during the much larger American deployment from late 1943.

The African American press enthusiastically covered the arrival of these servicemen, as the first such troops in Europe since the Great War and a sign of the black community's full participation in the war effort, but made no particular comment on where they were.³⁰ In August the *Chicago Defender*, one of the most important black newspapers, included a picture of recently disembarked troops with the headline 'more fighting boys for Ireland', noting their high morale.³¹ The African American press provided plenty of coverage of racial problems in the US military but never specifically about Northern Ireland. In the white press, even the *New York Times* quoted African American soldiers in their supposed dialect.³² Quentin Reynolds, of the progressive *Collier's* magazine, reported a conversation with 'one big lad from South Carolina [who] drawled': 'People here jes' like our officers, no one ever yells to us "Hey Niggah"'. Reynolds, trying to report on the positive experience of African American troops, did not quote a white Texan officer in dialect and made no comment that not referring to them as 'niggers' was hardly evidence of the liberalization of racist attitudes in the military.³³ Their presence was not lost on Axis propagandists, German radio declared: '[f]urther detachments of Roosevelt's Upholders of Culture in the form of nigger troops have landed in Northern Ireland, which is still oppressed by Britain', simultaneously managing to be racist, and make a dig about partition.³⁴ The Italians also took a twofold approach, asserting that '[t]he Anglo-Saxons observe the principle of race equality only when it is a question of sacrificing the lives of Negroes', while exhibiting their own racism with the declaration that '[t]o send Negroes to invade Europe is an insult to us' (Figure 9.1).³⁵

Most of the troops thoroughly enjoyed their newfound celebrity, reporting how well received they were and how much the locals loved them. One declared that '[t]he Irish treat us as if we were one of them', and they 'never hear of discrimination and stuff like that'.³⁶ Some even accentuated their exoticism by claiming to be Native Americans.³⁷ Many letters, morale reports, and official documents confirm the popularity of African American soldiers. 'The morale of the men is very high as they are well pleased with the hospitality accorded them by the Irish people', wrote one soldier. 'They know nothing of race and we are treated royally', he continued, '[i]n fact they lean toward the American colored soldier with high respect'.³⁸ This suggested that black troops, noted for their good manners, were actually more popular than white, as one oft-quoted English observer noted: 'I don't mind the Yanks, but I can't say I care for those white chaps they've brought with them'.³⁹ Despite this, racism was far from absent, particularly where sex and the attendant concern about 'brown babies' were involved; a correspondent from Belfast reported disapprovingly in late 1943 of rumours of mixed-race babies.⁴⁰ Vital to the African American experience in Northern

Figure 9.1 This picture appeared in the *Chicago Defender* on 8 August 1942 with the headline: 'More fighting men for Ireland'. Getty/Acme.

Ireland (and elsewhere) was decent treatment from a white population which did not impose a formal colour bar, and this was not easily forgotten on returning to the segregated United States.[41]

A positive experience was not universal. A soldier, stationed in Carrickfergus, complained directly, but anonymously, to Stormont about racism and segregation: '[w]e hate to walk the streets of Belfast, merely because, we are insulted, they use the words, Nigger and Darky, these are two words that we hate. Those words were brought here by the American whites'.[42] The last point is instructive: the questionable claim that racism was an American import, rather than already present. He concluded: 'Carrickfergus is the only town in Northern Ireland that we like, because when we visit there we are treated like human'.[43] African American troops were reminded constantly of their oppression, however, there is little to suggest that they felt any affinity with Catholics, another oppressed group, or had an interest in local politics. When asked by a priest if he was a Catholic, for example, a soldier replied, 'Holy snakes, no, it's bad enough being a Negro in Northern Ireland'.[44] For Catholics, black troops represented American recognition of partition, and this made them at least rhetorically unwelcome; indeed, as some nationalists resorted to Nazi salutes and taunting Americans over military defeats, racist abuse of African Americans could have been another avenue to express resentment at the American presence.

Their cruellest treatment was from their white colleagues. 'I would like to get away from this place. It gets worse everyday', reported a black GI, continuing, 'I am not going to town at night. It is too dangerous. Our white soldiers make our life miserable and I do not want to come into a fight'.[45] Another wondered whether he had been sent to fight white Americans or Nazis.[46] White Americans not only resented their black comrades but also friendly civilians, with one declaring that that it was 'necessary to lay down the law to the Irish and the coons'.[47] Many white Americans hated what they perceived as provocative behaviour by African Americans, especially with women, their refusal to be submissive and the population's rejection of Jim Crow. Furthermore, the police reported in September 1942 that good relations between British and African American troops were another source of friction, exacerbating tensions between British and white American troops, as well as highlighting racial problems within the US military.[48] Interracial sex, the ultimate white Southern taboo, was the prime source of resentment, and the anger in white correspondence is tangible. A white officer warned that he was 'tired of hearing that the men were getting into fights with the black soldiers ... because they were squiring white girls'.[49] As discussed in Chapter 8, that some women liked African American troops was actually used to reassure girlfriends and wives back home, but the overriding sentiment was that African Americans were 'making hay while the sun shines'.[50] This resentment would outlast the war with one white soldier warning: '[w]ait'til Georgia gets those *educated* Negroes back there', an implicit threat to repeat the lynching of black veterans which followed the Great War.[51] Hostility extended to African American women with several white GIs threatening to beat up J. Clarice Brooks, working alone one evening at the 'colored' Red Cross in Belfast, only for a white officer to intervene. She tried to press charges, but nothing ever came of it.[52]

The Americans were certainly conscious of the racism in their ranks and the damage it could do, and tried to keep it from the public. In June 1942, for instance, Admiral

Stark personally censored an article written by Frederick R. Kuh of the *Chicago Sun* about race relations among American personnel in Londonderry, which quoted a white sailor telling an African American comrade that 'for me you're just a nigger and will always be a nigger'.[53] The American military officially frowned upon discrimination, while informally implementing it everywhere in army life, and ordinary white soldiers were determined to enforce Jim Crow regardless of policy. The military publically condemned racist violence, but refused to confront white responsibility for it, preferring to make segregation more efficient, rather than eliminate it. One early effort was a 'Good Conduct Committee' set up by Hartle in August 1942, involving liaison between black and white NCOs. This committee developed 'rules of conduct for military personnel in all cases where because of location or station troops of more than one race are involved'.[54] In practical terms, these rules endorsed and enforced segregation, but recognized that the two races would unavoidably come into contact, for example, in Red Cross Clubs and at dances hosted by civilians (Figure 9.2). If this happened then 'the races should avoid intermingling such as sitting at same tables etc'.[55] If invitations from local girls were to both races, the soldiers were to 'emphatically inform the girls that mixing of races at parties is not advisable and all soldiers should discourage invitations which lead to mixed parties. One race must not attend dances given for the other race. Dances

Figure 9.2 'Miss Mary L. Divers, Handley, West Virginia, ARC, addresses the dancers at the American Red Cross dance held at Cookstown, Northern Ireland. On her right are S/Sgt. Clarence M. Patterson, Dayton, Ohio and S/Sgt. Augustus M. Grant, Charleston, South Carolina. 30 Oct. 1942'. NARA. Image courtesy of Clive Moore.

must not be "crashed"'.[56] It was also stressed that 'neither race must interfere with or 'cut in on' soldiers of the other race in the company of girls'.[57] While well intentioned, the guidance delegated the problem to ordinary soldiers, absolving officers at every level from responsibility, and ultimately failed to lessen racial tensions.[58]

Racial friction culminated in the killing of Private William Jenkins by Military Police in Antrim in September 1942, which had the hallmarks of a lynching. Bob Fawcett, a teenager at the time, recalled the incident in vivid detail, hearing running feet and three shots, before local men ventured outside to find Jenkins 'in a pool of blood and handcuffed to the railings and obviously dead'. Jenkins' comrades also arrived; soon the local police ordered people to stay indoors as armed African American troops descended on the town to exact revenge on any white soldiers they found. Fawcett again heard running and more gunfire as a white soldier, walking his girlfriend home and unconnected with the incident, was hit by two shots. He was taken to a nearby house where Fawcett's mother, a nurse, attended him until a medic and ambulance arrived.[59] No one was ever charged in connection to Jenkins' death. Such incidents were common wherever Americans were stationed, for example, Bamber Bridge, Launceston and Bristol.[60] The problem was so bad in Northern Ireland, however, that Smith claims that American racism became a worse problem than sectarianism.[61]

Fawcett, who befriended and ran errands for black troops, recalls an earlier episode which illustrated African American soldiers' anxieties, but with somewhat comedic consequences. Awoken by breaking glass, his family found a black GI in their living room; avoiding an MP, in the blackout he mistook the low front window for an alley and careered through it. The soldier came back the following day, to pay for the window and present Fawcett's father with a bottle of whiskey as compensation.[62] Responses to Jim Crow varied. Signs at the Ulster Hall in Belfast, and in Omagh and Antrim, declared 'whites only', yet the motivations for informal segregation are potentially complex.[63] White Americans often forced landlords to display these signs and sometimes wrecked places that refused; moreover, 90 per cent of troops were white, therefore, the economics favoured segregation.[64] Yet there was local antipathy to African American soldiers, for instance, in the York Road area of North Belfast, John Campbell, a boy at the time, recalls locals avoiding and being wary of black troops due to a couple of unpleasant incidents (including the Coogan killing): 'most of the locals were frightened of the black soldiers who moved about in groups. When they came down our street the women who would be chatting to each other would hastily go inside and close the door'.[65] One reason for their tendency to congregate in groups was that individual African American soldiers were easy targets for white GIs. Their white comrades, on the other hand, were popular and conformed to the 'any gum chum?' archetype according to Campbell.

A March 1943 incident demonstrated that some locals did not share the American fixation with race. Three African American soldiers left a dance in Belfast, where police said their 'conduct was exemplary', but soon got into a fight with local men.[66] The American military paid compensation to these men and the soldiers' commander apologized for the fracas to the Lord Mayor, as it involved 'coloured soldiers of this command', and stressing that 'the coloured soldiers concerned have been tried by courts martial'.[67] The American officer emphasized race, however, the Lord Mayor responded without any reference to it, merely stating that he was 'quite satisfied that any offences committed by American troops are frowned upon by your authorities'.⁶⁸ Locals used racist terminology, reflecting existing racist ideas created by Britain's empire and exposure to American popular culture, but this was not the adoption of ideological and systemic American racism. In fact, many ordinary Britons saw themselves as much more tolerant than Americans, and viewed the Empire and its paternalistic racism as progressive, certainly in comparison to Jim Crow America.⁶⁹ Residential, educational and social segregation along religious lines was all too familiar in Northern Ireland and, in effect, accepted by both Protestants and Catholics (as opposed to discrimination, especially in employment, which Protestants defended and Catholics challenged); however, racial segregation felt alien and people generally rejected American attempts to impose it.

The most serious incident involving an African American soldier came in March 1944 when Private Wiley Harris murdered a pimp named Henry Coogan in a drunken row about money. Harris was found guilty and sentenced to death by a court-martial, a trial which was open to and well attended by the public, but it is worth noting that the press and local witnesses highlighted Harris's nationality more than his race, whereas the American military, including his defence counsel and the review board which confirmed the death sentence, emphasized race.⁷⁰ The review of his sentence pandered to stereotypes about over-sexualized black men preying on white women, and reflected institutional racism within American military justice.⁷¹ To most in Belfast, however, he was the 'American', the 'coloured soldier' or simply 'the soldier'.⁷² The coroner at Coogan's inquest specifically warned the jury to ignore the race of the perpetrator, with the *Irish News* reporting his instructions that 'a white man had been stabbed by a coloured man, but this fact should be swept away from their minds'.⁷³ When the death sentence was announced, petitions for clemency included concerns that Harris's race condemned him, with a 'Loyal and Law-Abiding Citizen' rhetorically asking Brooke 'whether such a severe sentence would have been imposed on a white U.S. soldier in similar circumstances, possibly the answer is "Yes" but still the doubt remains'.⁷⁴ Labour unions and Protestant churches urged the Americans to commute the death sentence, and pressed Brooke to do likewise.⁷⁵ Brooke privately conceded to the cabinet and Abercorn that Harris would have probably been spared by a local court, however, as the Americans had jurisdiction over their personnel, there was nothing he or the Northern Ireland government could do to save Harris's life.⁷⁶ Despite calls for a reprieve there was, as noted, evidence of racially specific resentment in North Belfast after Coogan's death, as locals became suspicious of African American troops while maintaining good relations with white Americans.⁷⁷

'The posting of certain troops': Second deployment

Jim Crow returned with the Americans in late 1943. Still adhering to London's policies, but with the benefit of Brooke's creation of hospitality committees, Northern Ireland was much better prepared. The new American commander, General Collins, acknowledged that '[t]here is no blinking the fact that there is a problem, but it can be and is being handled', but stressed that '[t]here will be very few coloured troops here'.⁷⁸ Gransden emphasized Brooke's determination that there would be no difference to elsewhere in the UK 'in connection with the posting of certain troops here' to newly-arrived British general G. S. Brunskill.[79] When, however, the Castledawson hospitality committee sought advice on entertaining African American troops, Brooke suggested that it 'should first consult the nearest American commander', which, of course, invited segregation.[80] Brunskill advised organizers not to invite both black and white troops as 'mixing led to trouble'; Collins concurred.[81] Brooke and Brunskill essentially deferred to the Americans, accommodating segregation without officially sanctioning it. Recognizing that Jim Crow would not be overturned, Brooke had to manage it efficiently, which meant seeking American approval before offering hospitality to black personnel.

One vital way, suggested by General Devers, that the Americans tried to prevent violence among their troops was to designate particular towns and villages, or nights of the week, to troops according to race. This, it was hoped, would also lessen white resentment to African Americans associating with local women, partly because they would not witness it.[82] These measures were often reactive, usually enacted after disorder, and shifted rather than solved the problem. They also tended not to involve consultation with Stormont, making it something of a spectator as informal segregation was implemented. Local officials certainly knew the extent of the problem, and its underlying reasons, particularly following serious incidents in Magherfelt and Londonderry in late 1943 and early 1944.[83] This was especially worrying as the Americans had just returned and was an ominous portent for the months ahead (Figures 9.3 and 9.4).

Gransden and Brunskill engaged in their own investigation. Dehra Parker inferred that the Americans were not updating Stormont on their policies, telling Gransden that Cookstown was 'out of bounds the coloured men', but with the possibility of them

Figures 9.3 and 9.4 Soldiers from the 2nd Battalion, 28th Quartermaster Regiment passing in review on James Street, Cookstown; October 1942. (NARA). Images courtesy of Clive Moore. Note that the officer on the right (obscured by his salute) in the first image is African American. Black units were led largely by white officers, especially at this point in the war, while most African American officers were chaplains.

visiting the town a couple of times a week, but '[t]here is no official agreement – it can only be done by an "understanding" between the units concerned'.[84] Following the 'very serious trouble' in Magherafelt, she reported that 'an "arrangement" was made for <u>alternate nights</u> weekly – white and black – (presumably the officers of the black troops were not agreeable to a more equitable arrangement)'.[85] Interestingly, this could suggest that African American troops had more favourable treatment; either way, Devers' policy of separate nights clearly had been implemented. This was useful, but Brunskill decided to visit bases in Derrymore, County Antrim, and Bessbrook for first-hand information.[86] The commander at Derrymore told him of Devers' orders: 'the general line was that if a row took place everybody concerned was courtmartialled and punishment doled out all round'.[87] He also informed Brunskill that the African American troops were mostly from 'the extreme South, are very poor, are not accustomed to mixing with white people, and on the whole are very docile'.[88] They preferred to spend their leave locally, rather than in Belfast, as some of the pubs welcomed them and there were 'even a few girls to dance with'.[89] Brunskill was sceptical about the apparent docility of the troops, noting that 'before they were allowed out they were searched to see that they carried no knives or knuckle dusters'.[90] All Americans were supposed to be searched before leaving base, but African Americans carrying weapons (and moving in groups) reflected their need for means of self-defence, and their refusal to be the passive victims of white violence.

Much recent historiography on Jim Crow in wartime Britain argues that, certainly towards the war's end, the British were starting to mimic American racism and that segregation was informally sanctioned. Lilly and Thomson, for example, state: 'Jim Crow was operational in Britain. Instead of British open-mindedness influencing the [US] military, just the opposite occurred.'[91] There is no reason to suspect that Northern Ireland was more progressive than anywhere else, but Brooke deserves recognition for his handling of American racism, rejecting a colour bar, even if he was pragmatic about informal American segregation. Like London, Stormont preferred to avoid close contact between civilians, especially women, and African American troops, which led to a sometimes uncomfortable accommodation with racist American policies. Where he tolerated Jim Crow, Brooke's deference was out of a perceived need not to jeopardize the wartime alliance, rather than sympathy for systemic racism (demonstrated by his attitude in the Harris case). Fewer reports of racial friction appear in reports from Northern Ireland to London, compared to other regions, which, with the caveat that Stormont closely monitored these, implies that it coped reasonably well.

White American troops had a vested interest maintaining segregation, effectively endorsed by the military; Northern Ireland's population, however, did not. The concept of a racial caste system was alien, despite the de facto religious segregation and anti-Catholic discrimination which plagued Northern Ireland and arguably paralleled American racial problems. Encounters with and responses to racism were, therefore, typical of elsewhere and not exacerbated by Northern Ireland's internal problems. Racism did exist, but it was not the ideological white supremacy imported by many Americans. Northern Ireland nevertheless works as a useful case study in understanding how American racism functioned abroad, how it was resisted (up to a point) by a white population, but equally, how this population's attitude towards people of colour more generally remained unchanged. Regarding this latter point, because Northern Ireland did not experience mass Commonwealth immigration, it acts as an outlier in determining how the war shaped attitudes in the UK; indeed, the province's racism was hidden in the post-war years by endemic sectarianism. The transience of these 'Dusky Doughboys' did not make Northern Ireland any more tolerant. It did not make Protestants and Catholics reassess their attitudes towards each other, and Protestants certainly failed to question their home-grown 'Jim Crow' system; insularity and sectarianism remained as entrenched as ever. As Gardiner correctly argues, moreover, the presence of African American servicemen in the UK was an 'interlude', and they were welcomed because they were allies and would not be staying, meaning that their presence quickly became little more than a memory.[92] This contrasted with mass immigration to the UK mainland with the arrival of the *Empire Windrush* from Jamaica in London in 1948. Northern Ireland's encounter with Jim Crow had little, if any, long-term impact, beyond the few 'brown babies' left behind.

The experience of African American soldiers offered some respite from the systemic racism of their homeland, and the military in which they served, and made many unwilling to accept second-class citizenship quite so readily back in the States. They challenged, consciously and unconsciously, social and sexual racism, emerging with an enhanced self-worth. A tiny percentage served in Northern Ireland, but their experiences would play their small part in a civil rights revolution thousands of miles away, just as Northern Ireland was about to experience one of its own. To illustrate this point, when the USS *Mason*, the first ship with an all-black crew, docked in Belfast in the summer of 1944, it came and went without comment from the local press, but its fleeting stay had a profound impact on the sailors themselves. Its company went ashore with some trepidation, only to be struck by their lack of novelty, and the warmth of their welcome. 'The Irish people didn't look on us as our skin color', one reflected on a returning some fifty years later, '[t]hey looked on us as Americans- American fighting men'.[93] The *Mason's* brief sojourn offers an appropriate epilogue to the experiences of African American servicemen in Northern Ireland.

10

'A testy old gentleman'

David Gray, hyphenated-Americans and partition

In his unpublished manuscript *Behind the Green Curtain*, former US minister to Dublin David Gray predicted that '[s]uch Ulster names as James Craig, Basil Brooke, the Abercorns, J.M. Andrews will pass into our history with the Ulstermen who, two centuries before, stood by George Washington in his darkest days. They, like the comradeship forged during the dangerous years, have become part of our American heritage'.[1] Like their supposed revolutionary forebears, their contribution to American history would be largely forgotten, and Gray believed them overshadowed by those he routinely disparaged, in language flirting with nativism, as 'hyphen-Americans' and those in neutral Éire who he believed hid behind ancient animosities during America's life and death struggle against fascism. Gray represented the United States in Éire for the bulk of the Second World War, appointed as Envoy Extraordinary and Minister Plenipotentiary in February 1940, and taking office in April. Gray was neither a diplomat nor especially diplomatic. He owed his posting to family ties to Franklin Roosevelt and a chance encounter on a transatlantic crossing in August 1939 with the current incumbent, John Cudahy, an old acquaintance of the president who wanted a more glamorous post. Edward J. Flynn, a New Yorker and close associate of Roosevelt, was the initial choice to replace Cudahy, but a family illness prevented this, so, at short notice, the president selected Gray instead.[2] His qualifications consisted of affection for Ireland developed over several visits and his marriage to Eleanor Roosevelt's aunt Maud and this connection secured the position. Gray later acknowledged that 'the appointment was obviously nepotic'.[3] That Roosevelt would appoint a rank amateur could reflect how important he viewed Éire early in the war, but it also showed his need for someone who he trusted entirely to represent his interests and their closeness is demonstrated throughout their correspondence, which Gray usually began with 'Dear Boss'. Gray, seen as guileless and vindictive both by Éire's officials and most of the historiography, remained until 1947, despite persistent demands, from as early as May 1941, for his recall, and he was a visible reminder of official American annoyance at Éire's neutrality.[4] Yet his wartime belligerence was unquestionably at Roosevelt's behest and with his active encouragement, and the president often revelled in the latest slight against de Valera as Gray implemented the 'boss's' policies.[5]

Already seventy in 1940, Gray graduated Harvard in 1892, was the son of a newspaper owner and member of the bar, but after an unsuccessful legal career he was variously a journalist, writer and occasional farmer, and served with distinction in the Great War. Gray's diplomatic impulsiveness and tunnel-visioned view of Éire's neutrality have been detailed in multiple histories, however, with little attention to his assessment of partition and unionism. Both publicly and privately, he challenged many central conceits of Irish republicanism and often received unconvincing replies from its most forceful adherents. He eventually wrote long, unpublished tirades against de Valera based on his experiences, and a polemical reappraisal of Irish independence. He was what Ervin 'Spike' Marlin, an American agent in Éire and nominally Gray's 'special assistant', referred to as 'a testy old gentleman'; Frederick Boland in Éire's Department of External Relations was more forthright, calling him 'an unprincipled old villain'.[6]

As Bew notes, historiography on Gray is largely negative, with Jeffery, for example, describing him as an 'ineffably ill-informed Hibernophobe', when, in fact, he actually loved Ireland.[7] Maurice Walsh calls him 'petulant . . . unhelpful . . . unbalanced', the third these descriptions is perhaps true of later life, and the second entirely subjective; the first is certainly accurate, but born of experience.[8] Fisk notes his 'pushy, forthright, bullying personality', a fair assessment.[9] Tully contends that 'he had no real interest in cultivating an understanding of Irish political culture', but arguably his contrariness developed precisely because he understood its insularities, particularly regarding the war and partition.[10] Dwyer is Gray's harshest critic; in his estimation, Gray was a tactless, ignorant, irrational amateur, untrusted by either his Canadian and British diplomatic peers or American intelligence operatives, tormenting de Valera for Roosevelt's amusement. Moreover, he dismisses Gray's unpublished works as worthless, revealing a 'pathological determination to discredit de Valera by sheer distortion', although Dwyer did borrow the title, *The Green Curtain*, unacknowledged, for one of his own books.[11] There is historiographical agreement that when formulating American policy, he deliberately ignored evidence demonstrating Éire's cooperation with the Allies and even falsified reports to pursue his vendetta against de Valera.[12]

Bew offers nuance, recognizing that Gray initially 'had significant emotional sympathy for Irish nationalism' while perceiving unionists as 'the sole obstacle to Irish unity and, therefore, gaining Éire's support for the anti-Nazi alliance'.[13] Bartlett states that he arrived 'as an enthusiast for things Irish, but had soon turned into a harsh critic of de Valera's conduct of Irish neutrality'.[14] This is shared by Coogan, admittedly one of de Valera's toughest historiographical detractors, who highlights an entirely mutual obsessive loathing between the two.[15] Girvin's assessment is altogether more sympathetic, indeed, it is perhaps overly corrective, but it rightly notes that Gray's attitude developed due de Valera's implacability over neutrality and the inflexibility of those who implemented and defended it, yet he neglects substantive and justifiable criticisms of the minister.

Much of the criticism of Gray, both from historians and contemporary observers, can be rationalized, indeed, justified, particularly over his ill-judged 'American Note' of February 1944 demanding the removal of Dublin's Axis legations, and tendencies to over-react and interfere. In the context of Northern Ireland, this was mirrored in his obsession with a fringe loyalist paper the *Ulster Protestant* and occasionally showing up uninvited across the border for quasi-official visits. Yet despite all of this, his analysis of Éire and the war was far from unreasonable. There remains a lingering sense that his unpopularity stems partly from being the rare individual who confronted Irish republican shibboleths and would stand up to de Valera and his more archaic presumptions about Ireland, the double-standards (exaggerated certainly, but not entirely imagined) of Éire's neutrality and the realities of partition. In addition, to contemporary Irish critics Gray's fault was, in effect, to represent America's interests in Éire, rather than vice versa.[16] That he was often, to use Walsh's term, 'petulant' (something of an act, correspondence with Roosevelt reveals) and has been ridiculed for dabbling with spiritualism, makes him easy to summarily dismiss and enables his critics to evade some uncomfortable truths he exposed about Éire, its leadership and partition. The charges levelled at Gray are, moreover, equally applicable to his foes in Éire's political establishment, particularly Frank Aiken, Joseph Walshe and Robert Brennan, each of whom was guilty of sanctimonious, narrow-minded, asininity, seeing every international crisis as either secondary to 'the crime of partition', or as leverage, especially in the States, to end it, and Gray was not the only American official who wearied of this.[17] Gray was neither an Anglophile nor a Hibernophobe on arrival; in fact, as he reflected in 1945, he was 'a good deal of a Sinn Feiner and a very ardent admirer of Mr de Valera' when he arrived.[18] It was his experiences which turned him not into a Hibernophobe, but rather a de Valeraphobe.

'A great deal of wishful thinking': Gray's early interventions

Éire periodically used the notional American-Irish friendship to try to enlist the States to pressurize the British over partition. In the late 1930s, Éire's new constitution, whereby the Irish Free State became 'Éire' and 'Ireland', and claimed the whole island, marked a renewed if half-hearted, effort to involve America in Irish politics. De Valera wrote to Roosevelt in January 1938 urging him 'to use your influence' to end partition, but Roosevelt demurred.[19] The deteriorating European situation meant that, regardless of some Americans' sentimental attachment to Ireland, European democracies had to be supported. Éire's demands were seen as trivial and selfish amid the rise of fascism, particularly as de Valera opportunistically made any commitment to defence dependent on ending partition.[20] Even without the war, America was unlikely to pressure Britain to end partition, yet Gray assumed that his task was to find a 'solution' to the 'problem' of partition and enthusiastically embraced this. He saw his mission as twofold: urge Éire to join the Allies or allow use of its ports, and mediate an end to partition. Shortly after his appointment, Brennan hosted a dinner for Gray in Washington. Gray said he was visiting the British ambassador the following day and 'intended to impress on him the necessity of ending partition'.[21] He reiterated this to William J. B. Macaulay, Éire's minister to the Holy See, with the addendum that American would be reluctant to aid Britain otherwise, and that Roosevelt 'has instructed him personally to do all he can with the British'.[22] Gray even claimed Roosevelt had appointed him specifically to broker an end to partition.[23] The American position was that Northern Ireland was part of the United Kingdom and, therefore, an internal British matter, making Gray's interest largely personal. Prior to Pearl Harbor he saw ending partition as serving American interests, but he also believed that maintaining it would mean British defeat;

post-Pearl Harbor, however, fortifying Northern Ireland militarily and diplomatically became vital. This initially fervent interventionism demonstrates that something went badly awry for him to become such a bitter foe of Irish unity's most forceful adherent. Gray's hostility increased exponentially as Éire's neutrality appeared more entrenched, its anti-partitionism more intransigent and veiled threats about interfering in American politics more apparent.

Regarding Northern Ireland, Gray's stance evolved beyond a simplistic sense that partition was innately wrong, to understanding the impossibility of creating a single Irish state without unionist consent. His analysis that retaining partition actually benefited de Valera politically (now broadly accepted in historiography) and that Éire's politicians had little interest in engagement with unionists, often viewing them as colonists who either had to accept Irish rule or 'go back' to Britain, was a fair reflection of the political context.[24] Gray soon recognized the absurdity of this and was astounded when senior Irish politicians and Catholic clergy had no idea what to do with Northern Ireland's Protestants if partition ended, with de Valera apparently even suggesting a population exchange with people of Irish descent living in Britain as a workable solution.[25] When Northern Ireland became an ally in December 1941, his attitude towards the semantics of Irish nationalism hardened. Gray was the rare person who challenged the Taoiseach about partition, and offered something beyond the echo-chamber of Éire's establishment. The protests greeting American troops in January 1942 confirmed to Gray that nationalism was governed by parochialism and a self-serving myopia about the international situation, whereby the global fight against fascism was nothing compared to the injustice of partition. Yet his cynicism about nationalism made Gray dismissive of discrimination against Catholics in Northern Ireland, viewing their predicament merely as part of nationalism's capacity for hypersensitivity, rather than accurately reflecting the realities of their everyday lives.[26]

As Bew rightly argues, Gray was 'no cultural relativist' but believed that Britain was defending democracy and incorrectly assumed that de Valera shared this goal and 'was, at heart, a principled anti-Nazi'.[27] If anything, Gray arrived naively pro-Irish, both about Éire's neutrality and partition. His British counterpart Sir John Maffey remarked that he 'does a great deal of wishful thinking in regard to the partition issue' believing that with its end Éire would join the war, and advocating that the British pressurize Craigavon, who he saw as unwilling to make wartime sacrifices, to secure this.[28] His eventual hostility grew out of his many encounters with the duplicitousness, real and perceived, of de Valera and key political voices in Éire. This was compounded by the realization that Éire's neutrality was non-negotiable, partition or not, something unionists were acutely conscious of.[29] That said, his irritation, exacerbated post-war upon the revelation of Éire-German contacts, blinded him to the country's precariousness position, sandwiched between belligerents, reliant on one side economically and desperate not to provoke the other, even at the expense of American goodwill.[30]

He ultimately viewed de Valera as the main obstacle to conciliation between Éire and Northern Ireland; indeed, his conclusion that partition was vital to de Valera's political agenda, serving as a rallying point for his party and a distraction for Éire's people, appeared repeatedly in his correspondence.[31] This realization was linked, but subservient to, what he perceived as de Valera's hypocritical neutrality and 'rancid ingratitude', and made Gray increasingly hostile to both the Taoiseach and his state, and precipitated various wartime crises.[32] It also led Gray to modify his preconceptions about Stormont, becoming more understanding, if not necessarily sympathetic, and encouraging its leaders to challenge American preconceptions of it.[33] His primary motivation was his fear that de Valera would inject partition into American politics, evidenced by agitation prior to Pearl Harbor and a renewed anti-partition campaign in post-war America. Indeed, his infamous 'American Note' was, using security concerns as a pretext, driven by the desire to discredit de Valera in the eyes of American voters and his own refusal to allow America to be pressurized by 'hyphenated Americans'.[34]

Evidence of Gray's initially benign attitude towards Éire, alongside his fundamental naivety about partition was apparent early in his tenure. He asked Churchill if he should meet Craigavon 'to get first hand his side to this tragic triangle'. Churchill arranged this in London, but 'though not emphatically said that Ulster could not be coerced'.[35] Gray believed de Valera 'should convince Ulster of the South's friendliness' (in the absence of evidence of this apparent friendliness).[36] His initial assessment of de Valera was positive about the person, but ambivalent about the leader: 'I like him and admire him but he is not the man for a war'; moreover, his only slogan was 'a united Ireland'.[37] De Valera suggested Northern Ireland join Éire in neutrality and 'in return he would reaffirm publicly their adherence and loyalty to "external association" with the British Commonwealth'. This was fanciful and Gray realized that Britain could not allow the whole island to be neutral and that unionists would instantly reject such a proposal in any case.[38]

Gray first met Stormont representatives in June 1940 around the time when Britain offered ending partition in return for Éire joining the Allies. Maffey, Gray reported, said that Downing Street had given Craigavon 'merry hell all but ordering him to make up with de Valera ... and end partition on the best terms he could'.[39] Craigavon, however, refused to compromise 'blaming the south for this and that just as de Valera keeps blaming the North'.[40] Gray wondered if Craigavon would be a 'crushed statesman' after his London dressing-down, but found him defiant. Craig was 'a red-faced, hard-bitten fellow of 71, with fishy gray-blue eyes set at an angle. He has a pleasant smile for a face cut out of granite rock', but Gray 'liked him from the start'. Paraphrasing Craigavon, he reported: 'the Ulster people were a different race, were part of Britain and were not interested in Southern Ireland which had been disloyal' and 'absolutely refused' to differentiate Northern Ireland from Britain.[41] Gray advised Abercorn, who was 'very charming, though he is not that bright', of the need for the 'closest military co-operation' between Northern Ireland and Éire, and reaffirmed his desire for an all-island state by choice.[42] He told Abercorn that Craigavon must make a 'striking gesture' 'in ... the direction of Geographical Unity for the purpose of island defense [or] the consequences will be grave', in other words, a British defeat.[43] Maffey informed Gray of the deal to end partition, but Gray told Roosevelt that it 'would look like a trap' to Éire as '[t]hey naturally feel very timid these days and wishfully think that by not plumping with England they are going to make their lot easier in the event of a German crushing victory'.[44]

Éire's irredentism over Northern Ireland quickly became apparent. A few weeks later, he asked Sean T. O'Kelly, who would become Éire's finance minister the following year and later its president, what price Éire should pay for ending partition. "'No price at all'", he shot back, "it is ours by right'", yet when pressed, O'Kelly had no idea how to accommodate, in Gray's words, 'eight-hundred thousand black Protestants'.[45] Despite this, Gray, after the furore over the offer to Éire had subsided, remained sympathetic to an all-island state, but now believed the main hindrance was anti-British sentiment in Éire's government.[46] He concluded: '[t]he outlook for ending partition never has been darker than at present. De Valera won't compromise, won't deal. Unless he gets into the war through invasion he will not be a good position at the end in which to ask Churchill to throw out Craigavon. Yet this thing ought to be ended for everybody's sake'. He then suggested that Roosevelt might be able to broker a deal post-war.[47] The idea that Churchill could simply throw Craigavon out, even if Éire joined the war, is a further example of Gray's 'wishful thinking'. Another recurring source of irritation was de Valera's public insistence that Éire was equally threatened by the British and Germans and, in effect, blockaded by both. Gray constantly reminded the Taoiseach that Éire relied on British supplies, and that its censorship kept this from the population.[48]

By mid-1941, months before Pearl Harbor, American engineers in Northern Ireland precipitated another quarrel. Gray described de Valera's response to Americans occupying Londonderry's naval base as 'fatuous', as while 'he recognised the de facto occupation' by Britain, Éire could not waive its sovereignty claim. Gray feigned ignorance about the base but knew it meant that the British and Americans had given up on acquiring the Treaty ports, and would make Northern Ireland 'a fortress'.[49] Adapting Londonderry (and fortifying Lough Erne) served practical and symbolic purposes, demonstrating to Éire 'that we were preparing to get along without their help'.[50] By now, Gray's enmity was growing: '[t]here is no use of you trying to do business with this man', he told Roosevelt. The president shared this frustration: 'people are, frankly, getting pretty fed up with my old friend Dev'.[51] Gray saw not only the base's military importance, but also its political benefits as 'we do not liked to be pressure-grouped by ANY hyphenated minority'; moreover, the bases would exacerbate de Valera's 'anxiety ... alone and unarmed in a jungle world'.[52] Éire's protest was exactly as Gray predicted, with Dublin politely asking for an explanation and Brennan soon warning that 'Irish people everywhere' objected to any recognition of partition. Both were given short shrift by the Americans, who had officially signalled acceptance of the reality and legitimacy of partition.[53]

'A child, entirely unconvinced of his error': Gray, MacRory and American troops

Upon the arrival of American forces, Maffey reported to Gray that de Valera was 'resentful' and had 'never seen him so depressed', but to Maffey's surprise he 'did not fly into a rage'. Gray attributed de Valera's resentment to Éire's territorial claim and internal threats from extremists and, indeed, within his own party. Gray also felt that Dublin had not anticipated America being drawn into hostilities, despite his repeated warnings of this likelihood.[54] De Valera, Gray claimed, believed that a German attack on Éire would simplify things, and allow him to aid the Allies openly. Despite his antipathy towards de Valera and the sense that Éire was shirking, Gray acknowledged that its forces had good, if informal, relations with the British, and he hoped the Americans would enjoy something similar. He was concerned, nevertheless, about conflicts between Americans and civilians in Northern Ireland, specifically Catholics, and worried that nationalist leaders' attitudes made this more likely.[55]

When in October 1942 Cardinal MacRory complained American troops 'overrunning' Northern Ireland, Gray was livid.[56] He told Roosevelt the Cardinal had 'broke loose' and 'plays directly into the hands of the IRA', and it could 'incite the murder of American troops'.[57] He wrote privately and politely to MacRory, recognizing that '[y]our kindly friendliness to me has won my regard, as your courageous honesty and frankness have won my respect. I know where I stand with you and if we disagree, I know that you will be outspoken and not attack from behind'. Gray noted de Valera's criticism of the American landing, but remained silent when German planes bombed Belfast. Gray feared that MacRory's statement could provoke the killing of Americans: 'we have seen recently the tragic results following the execution [of a terrorist] . . . all over Éire shops were forcibly closed during the hour of the execution by IRA groups and their sympathizers'. In fact, the killer 'was invested with some of the sanctity of martyrdom'. Gray also pointed out that he would have been executed had he murdered a police officer in Éire.[58] The Cardinal's response was immediate and forthright: '[t]he USA has condoned the partition of Ireland by sending, at England's invitation, armed forces into Ireland without our nation's consent . . . United States' kindness and manifold beneficence to Ireland I fully and freely acknowledge and most cordially appreciate; but no such considerations affect the essence of the question'. He concluded: 'not a hair of the head of any American soldier will be injured on account of anything I have said. Our people know well that I do not encourage violence'.[59] MacRory, as noted, was certainly borne out on this final point, with only one or two isolated and very minor incidents involving the Americans.

Gray did not intend to publish the letter but, after acquaintances wondered why he had made no public statement about MacRory's comments, he made about a dozen copies. These he forwarded to interested parties, including senior American Catholic clergy and Oscar Henderson.[60] Gray also sent Henderson a copy of Archbishop Hurley of Florida's condemnation of MacRory, suggesting publishing it in local newspapers.[61] In addition, he sent it to O'Kelly (expecting it to land on de Valera's desk), Roosevelt, US military sources, and fellow diplomats.[62] In accompanying letters he described the disagreement as civil and asserted his continued affection for the Cardinal, telling Roosevelt he was 'a dear old man with an understandable obsession about the wrong of Partition. The war means little to him as long as "The nation which God made is divided by man"'.[63] Patronizing references to MacRory as a 'dear old man' litter this correspondence, also describing his attitude as 'childlike', telling Winant of 'talking to him as if he were a naughty child' and General Hartle that he was 'like a child, entirely unconvinced of his error'.[64] He further told Winant that '[a] Cardinal Primate with less love in his heart and more discretion in his head would be less dangerous in the present situation'.[65] Gray had a point about MacRory's parochialism regarding the international situation and his needlessly provocative comments about the domestic, but his attitude still reeked of condescension. For his part, MacRory could not understand Gray's agitation.[66]

The letter was unlikely to remain secret, and it began circulating within Dublin, purportedly through Protestant clergymen and their wives, and eventually Northern Ireland before arriving at the *Daily Mirror* and the Dominions Office in mid-1943.[67] Though there were slightly different versions, the Dominions Office was convinced the letter was genuine, and noted it had been 'suppressed by Éire Press Censorship' and 'is now being copied by various methods and passed from hand to hand with great secrecy'.[68] The *Mirror*'s editor in northern England phoned the American legation in Dublin to establish its veracity and spoke to a member of staff, with Gray quite probably listening in. Gray then spoke directly to the editor to confirm its authenticity, but '[i]t is confidential and not for publication' and he did not know who had circulated the additional copies. At the conversation's end, he again stressed that 'I cannot consent to its publication', the editor agreed, but wanted to 'keep it as a historic document'.[69] This suggests no desire to make the letter public, despite his rash and widespread sharing of it making this almost inevitable, and offers further evidence of his guilelessness. Those circulating it were clearly conscious of its potentially explosive contents; one described it as 'a clever piece of propaganda' which had been deliberately leaked; another sent it to Sir Douglas Savory, urging him to pass it on to his fellow unionist MPs.[70] How each acquired the letter was unclear. MacRory became aware of the letter's distribution and suggested that it and his reply be published together, to which Gray was agreeable. Gray also confessed that he had circulated copies and spoken to a newspaper editor, but stressed to recipients that he and the Cardinal enjoyed a good relationship and that the latter 'entertained no unfriendly sentiments toward my country'. He also assured MacRory he had not authorized its publication.[71] The release of both letters never happened, and Gray's was eventually published Fermanagh's *Impartial Reporter* days before Cardinal MacRory's death in October 1945.[72]

'A back-alley scum sheet': Gray, the *Ulster Protestant* and unionism

Gray encountered Protestant bigotry when the virulently anti-Catholic *Ulster Protestant* came into his possession in the autumn of 1941. The newspaper of Ulster Protestant League, a sectarian and anti-government group which had emerged in the early 1930s, Gray ascribed the publication an importance it simply did not deserve. He feared, however, that it would end up in the States, possibly via Éire's Department of External Affairs, gravely offend millions of American Catholics and revive Anglophobia.[73] He immediately contacted Abercorn about having the paper suppressed. Abercorn, unaware of its existence, declared it 'a poor rag with a very small circulation', but promised to ask Sir Richard Dawson Bates, Minister for Home Affairs, to approach the editor 'whoever he is'. Abercorn felt that if the editor 'is not prepared to take a hint the paper may have to be banned', but worried that this could be counterproductive 'because of the outcry it would make against muzzling the press'.[74] Gray also contacted

MacRory, telling him that Abercorn had been horrified and called it 'a back-alley scum sheet' (which he had not, in writing anyway), but at least registering his and the Duke's outrage to the Cardinal and their desire to suppress the paper.[75]

The minister's ire at MacRory's comments about American troops had barely abated when the bigotry of the *Ulster Protestant* resurfaced.[76] While it remained 'a back alley sheet' it was freely available and Gray was concerned that it 'would cause trouble with our twenty million loyal Catholics', and with the US and Britain now allies and Catholic American troops in Northern Ireland, there was added urgency about silencing it. He immediately contacted Winant in London and Abercorn to this end, warning the latter that he would have to report its free availability to the American government.[77] Gray took the rather far-fetched view that the *Ulster Protestant* 'could only be inspired by German agents. If this could be established, it would be of great assistance'.[78] Vitriolic anti-Catholicism among Protestants, including those in senior government positions, of course, needed no German encouragement.

Gray raised the issue with Prime Minister Andrews when Eleanor Roosevelt visited in November 1942, but was disappointed with official responses. The Home Office in London refused to intervene, regarding it as an internal matter for Stormont, while Maffey believed that little could be done without accusations of censorship. Gray was conscious that his criticism of MacRory required him to be even-handed, yet without any inkling that even the hint of equivalence between the two was problematic. His concern about the publication reaching the United States led him to assure Cardinal Spellman, whose prior knowledge its existence was likely to have been zero, that he had 'taken such unofficial measures as lay open to me to have this thing muzzled and finally suppressed in the interests of decency'.[79] That Catholics had not tried to exploit this was largely because, he told Washington, 'they are so used to this kind of thing', a rare acknowledgement of anti-Catholic prejudice.[80] At the start of 1943, Gray again warned Maffey that it was available to Catholic soldiers and their chaplains, and could be circulated in the States. He wanted the publishers prosecuted and noted that American anti-British sentiment had subsided due to the war and that 'nothing could be more unfortunate than that Northern Ireland, which in a peculiar sense is beneficiary of this attitude, should show lack of appreciation'.[81] Maffey agreed, but also pointedly noted: 'you never hear complaints about such publications from Cardinal MacRory'.[82] Neither Gray nor Maffey were persuaded by Stormont's argument that its small circulation, around 7,000, rendered it largely harmless.[83]

An Irish republican publication expressing comparable sentiments would have likely been banned under Special Powers legislation, but the *Ulster Protestant* proved difficult to suppress.[84] In London, Home Secretary Herbert Morrison felt it would be hard to ban as 'it was profuse in its expressions of loyalty' and the need for 'the utmost possible liberty . . . for expressions of opinion'.[85] Stormont's new minister for Home Affairs William Lowry pressurized the printers, the *Derry Standard* (its owners had no links with the Ulster Protestant League); Brooke exerted pressure on the Orange Order about the paper's 'ardour', and the order's Grand Master, Sir Joseph Davison advocated a ban.[86] Upon returning from a three month visit to the States in September 1943, Gray was again greeted by the *Ulster Protestant* and a headline about trying the Pope as a war criminal. Gray's anxiety about Irish-Americans dividing Britain and America after the war had been heightened by this trip; he told Maffey that if Americans became aware of the paper 'a serious menace to Anglo-American relations might result'. The publication's declarations of loyalty were, he believed, self-defeating, and wondered why it could not suspend its bigotry for the sake of the war effort.[87]

Partly because it was unclear whether it constituted a newspaper, it would have required amending the Special Powers Act to ban the *Ulster Protestant*. The act was eventually expanded in December 1943, but the paper remained legal.[88] The internal dynamics of unionism played a part in the decision. In the mid-1930s, the Ulster Protestant League's vitriolic anti-Catholicism, including precipitating the sectarian riots of 1935, had briefly threatened the government's hegemony over the Protestant community. Banning its newspaper could have revived the group and emboldened the government's Protestant opponents; further alienation of Catholics to prevent this was deemed a worthwhile political risk.[89] That a fringe Protestant newspaper with a tiny circulation could jeopardize the Anglo-American alliance, even if its ravings found their way into the similarly virulently anti-British Irish-American press, was patently absurd, but Gray persisted, magnifying its apparent influence. Alongside his earlier, and frankly ludicrous, hypothesis that Germans funded the paper, in January 1944 he offered Brooke the even more preposterous suggestion that nationalists might be subsidizing it: 'stranger things have come to light'.[90] Gray was unable to offer anything stranger than this particularly bizarre theory. He also emphasized the need to 'get the *Ulster Protestant* muzzled as a war measure' before any hypothetical trip to the States by Brooke could take place.[91]

'The wrongs are difficult to appraise with entire fairness': Gray and sectarianism

Gray's Dublin meddling was occasionally evident in Belfast, over and above his early efforts to end partition and one-man campaign against the *Ulster Protestant*. When he accompanied Francis Matthews, of the USO (and the Knights of Columbus), on a trip to Londonderry and Belfast in 1943, Buhrman reported criticism within Stormont of 'this and other semi-official' visits across the border.[92] This interference was notable again in April 1944, amid the controversy surrounding the 'American Note', when Gray requested information about the IRA from Brooke. Brooke consulted the police Inspector General who was 'strongly against us doing anything of the sort'.[93] Gray was viewed as a potential security liability by Northern Ireland's authorities. Buhrman reported to Gray in January 1943 that the police in Northern Ireland believed someone from the Dublin legation was corresponding with Denis Ireland, of the Ulster Union Club, a largely Protestant group opposed to partition, which had members with IRA links.[94] It turned out to be Gray. Ireland was, warned Buhrman, 'indirectly connected with the IRA, although not a member of that body and himself not a Catholic'. The police, he continued, conceded that Gray's correspondence was none of their business, but warned that Ireland opposed the American presence and was 'entirely devoted to . . . getting the American soldiers out of here'.[95] Gray knew Ireland personally and they lunched when the latter visited Dublin; he was, Gray claimed, 'a crank but, like many of the extremists who oppose governments, has many good qualities'. Gray asserted that he shared nothing sensitive, rather 'I have never written him anything but good advice and a succession of warnings not to be foolish', and on the contrary Ireland was actually a good source. Ireland had reported to Gray that the minister's letters were seized when police raided his house, but Gray was unconcerned, telling Buhrman that they contained nothing controversial.[96] In fairness to Gray, he engaged in lively correspondence with many important cultural, political and intellectual figures, and had numerous acquaintances from all walks of Irish life. He was, for example, scorned by de Valera for having 'ascendancy friends' (Protestants in Éire who identified as British), but included former IRA gunman Dan Breen and future Poet Laureate John Betjemen among his contacts, so his social circle was diverse enough to include Ireland without it being a worse breach of etiquette than some of his other associations.[97]

Gray's jaundiced view of nationalism led him to seriously underplay the treatment of Northern Ireland's Catholics; conditioned to what he saw as hyperbole and self-absorption in Dublin, he assumed that they cynically exaggerated their grievances, which had a modicum of truth, but discrimination was very real.[98] He made the extent of his skewed understanding clear to the State Department in May 1943: '[t]he wrongs of the nationalists in Northern Ireland are difficult to appraise with entire fairness'.[99] As most nationalists refused to attend Stormont or recognize the government, he continued, 'they have only themselves to blame for having no share in the civil service patronage'.[100] He conceded that gerrymandering was 'really very bad and as a beautiful piece of jobbery as anything we have ever achieved in America, but there is absolutely no inequality in civil rights and civil freedom and the discontent is chiefly due to tub-thumping and partisan incitation', which periodically manifested itself in terrorism. Thus, 'it is unavoidable that some peaceful and decent citizens should have their rights invaded', a conclusion rather at odds with his invocation of the Magna Charta and the American Bill of Rights to defend Stormont six months later when trying to engineer a visit to Washington for Brooke.[101] Nationalists, he asserted, were treated no worse than Republicans in Alabama or Georgia, and, in a secret ballot, many with property would vote to stay in the United Kingdom for economic reasons.

Gray's analysis is wrong for all sorts of reasons. Firstly, by using the term 'nationalist' rather than 'Catholic', he completely ignored the religious dimension underpinning unionist rule, reducing sectarian discrimination to mere political choice. He had a point about nationalists' lack of engagement with Stormont, but Craig's declaration that it was a 'Protestant parliament for a Protestant State' was difficult to contest. Every government minister since its inception had been a Protestant, most were also Orangemen and several were Protestant clergymen, and they did nothing to make Catholics feel part of the state. Finally, regarding gerrymandering, the obvious, and inconvenient, comparison (also missed by Buhrman in his analysis the previous year) was to discrimination against African Americans in the South rather than Republicans.[102] Gray's analysis betrayed his attitude towards de Valera and Éire rather than any understanding of the realities of life for Northern Ireland's Catholics.

'The grievance rather than the solution': The American Note

It is not the purpose here to re-examine the 'American Note' of 21 February 1944 at any great length as there are plenty of good accounts of it. It will, however, argue that Gray was motivated much more by the spectre of post-war anti-partition agitation in the States, instigated by Éire, than current historiography suggests, and, in fact, this obsession was absolutely central to exposing de Valera's perceived dishonesty to Americans.[103] Gray and de Valera's relationship had deteriorated completely by 1943, and the American minister wanted Éire's leader 'on record' about his refusal either to aid the Allies or eject the Axis legations from Dublin and to expose his duplicitousness, as Gray defined it, partly to the Irish people, but mainly to the American electorate. In doing so, Gray hoped to thwart de Valera's encouragement of Irish-Americans to pressurize the president over partition in post-war American elections.

Gray's hostility towards Irish-Americans could be construed as straightforward nativism, reflecting Protestant America's residual anti-Catholicism, but he maintained that it was entirely secular as he had quit the Republican Party in 1928 due to anti-Catholic bigotry against Democratic presidential candidate Alfred E. Smith.[104] The negative role of Irish-Americans in politics, especially as it affected Roosevelt, was not a figment of his imagination. Some Irish-American groups sought common cause with Germans, notably the German-American Bund in the 1930s, and were among the country's most ardent isolationists, partly because easing neutrality meant aiding Britain. Yet, to Joseph Kennedy, the notion that Irish-American patriotism was questionable was preposterous and he told Gray so in no uncertain terms: '[t]his idea that any but a few people in this country of the Irish-Americans are Irish first and American after is poppycock pure and simple'.[105] Gray, however, persisted, believing American democracy had to be purged of the malign influence of this group of 'hyphen-Americans'.

In April 1941 Éire's government, in effect, sanctioned harnessing the Irish-American lobby to foster Anglophobia and influence America's foreign policy. At Gray's suggestion – it must be stressed – Éire's defence minister Frank Aiken visited the States to secure arms, but Gray hoped also he would witness increasingly pro-Allied sentiment.[106] Belligerently anti-British, even seen as pro-German by some, many judged Aiken an intellectual lightweight: Maffey described him as 'rather stupid'; Fine Gael's James Dillon said he had 'a mind halfway between that of a child and an ape' and 'the mentality of a boy gang leader'.[107] Aiken proved a poor choice for this delicate mission. In preparation for the visit, Brennan contacted Irish-American congressmen sympathetic to Germany, while Walshe told Aiken to stress Irish-America's political importance.[108] Hempel reported: '[t]he Irish Government apparently believes that if the Irish element in the United States is properly used, it could constitute a powerful influence in our favour, likewise the Irish-American press'.[109] The visit coincided with the German invasion of the Balkans and British reverses in the Middle East, and was, therefore, a low priority to the Americans, even if Aiken and Brennan saw it otherwise. Aiken met Welles, treating him to a 'rather extraordinary diatribe' against Britain; Welles was unimpressed.[110]

Aiken and Brennan then infuriated Roosevelt by suggesting that American weapons supplied to Éire's armed forces might be used against the British. This tetchy encounter did not trigger Roosevelt and Gray's resentment towards de Valera and Éire, but it marked the point where reconciliation became virtually impossible.[111] At about the same time, and in response, Gray (belatedly) criticized de Valera's St Patrick's Day speech to America (which equated the British and Germans) to his face: '[h]alf way through he got red as a beet and shouted out, "this is an impertinence to question the statements of the head of state"'. To Gray, Aiken's mission was another attempt to undermine Anglo-American relations by encouraging anti-British sentiment in the States.[112] Gray had, however, gone too far. Maffey told London that de Valera wanted rid of Gray and viewed him as 'little less than a disaster ... [and] doing definite harm'. Maffey, by contrast, called Gray 'a splendid representative of his great country', warning the State Department and the Foreign Office to be wary of intrigues against him.[113] By the end of the month Gray knew of de Valera's request for his recall.[114]

Aiken, under the auspices of the American Friends of Irish Neutrality (AFIN), an umbrella organization of Anglophobic Irish-American isolationists closely linked to Éire's government, soon embarked upon a rabble-rousing tour of Irish-America, stoking anti-British feeling and promoting isolationism; he also liaised with Charles Lindberg and American First.[115] This cooperation with pro-German groups, it should be noted, took place as Belfast, Ireland's second largest city, was twice blitzed by the Luftwaffe. The Irish-American press, bellicose but not necessarily representative of Irish-American opinion, was also staunchly isolationist, as were many Irish-American politicians.[116] Some were happy share platforms with Lindberg, even as America First rallies, often with large Irish-American contingents in the audience, descended into anti-Semitism and Hitler salutes.[117] Gray's hostility towards the Irish-American lobby was exaggerated and paranoid, but not irrational and its efforts, in league with Dublin, to steer American foreign policy, were clearly demonstrable until Pearl Harbor.

Gray was furious that de Valera would exploit the war for his own narrow political ends, so he wanted Irish-America and Éire neutered before the war's end, preventing de Valera subsequently rewriting Éire's wartime history to create international pressure over partition.[118] While successful prosecution of the war motivated Gray, counteracting anti-partition propaganda was significant in his thinking, as evidenced within his correspondence regarding what became the 'American Note'. Where London, Belfast and the State Department largely ignored or responded with eye-rolling weariness to de Valera's regular denunciations of partition and idle threats about ending it, Gray took them seriously and advocated a hard-line response. This included an embargo if de Valera did not stop interfering in Northern Ireland, which he predicted within three months would see the Taoiseach 'discredited if the responsibility for the withholding of supplies was securely saddled to his back'.[119] Gray wanted a clear and public demonstration of American displeasure, which could not be hidden from Éire's population but in doing so he, in effect, sought the removal of neutral country's democratically mandated government.

In a lengthy memorandum to the State Department in May 1943, Gray asserted that de Valera was preparing a new anti-partition campaign and 'prefers the grievance rather than the solution', in other words, partition was politically useful, ending it, therefore, was not his priority.[120] More worryingly for America was information that Irish-America's campaign had already begun with the Federation of American Societies for Irish Independence passing a resolution demanding Congress make ending partition part of post-war peace negotiations.[121] The question, to Gray's mind, was how to respond, he suggested that economic pressure was the best option, under the guise of only supplying countries assisting the Allied war effort. It was time to act, as if de Valera tried to introduce anti-partition into American elections or stirred up trouble in Northern Ireland then this threatened the post-war Anglo-American alliance. It was vital to discredit de Valera now, therefore, while the war was still on, rather than allow him 'to develop his skilful and mischievous intrigue'.[122] 'Whatever the rights and wrongs of partition', Gray reemphasized, '[t]he grievance is politically of more importance than the solution'.[123]

Gray returned to America in June 1943 for three months. Ostensibly on leave, in reality he gauged the attitudes of key Irish-American figures, mainly Catholic clergymen, about Éire, partition and the war. He also discussed these with Roosevelt and Churchill at Hyde Park on 14 August, with the latter reportedly unmoved by his analysis.[124] During his trip, he wrote another lengthy report, a 'Memorandum on the Irish Situation', outlining his mission's rationale and the responses of those he had spoken too.[125] In Éire's recent general election de Valera had, he claimed, relied on partition 'for domestic political purposes', but still fell short of a majority.[126] Gray told the Taoiseach that partition would remain for the foreseeable future due to Northern Ireland's wartime role, and America would not intervene as it 'had given us bases while Éire denied us bases and even protested our use of the bases in Northern Ireland'. De Valera had apparently suggested a population exchange, which Gray believed 'could only mean the expulsion of the 800,000 Protestants in Northern Ireland and their replacement by an equal number of Catholic Irish in England', which he thought was an appalling idea.[127] Gray also recorded a couple of sources confirming that de Valera expected the Anglo-American relationship to collapse after the war, paraphrasing the Taoiseach as asserting: 'Britain and the United States will quarrel and the United States will see that we have been right'.[128] He seemed to think that de Valera, by even suggesting this, had some mystical power to ensure it happened, enhancing his threat to the alliance.[129] Post-war American politics, Gray concluded, 'is not only the most promising course for Mr de Valera to pursue, but the only course left to him if the Allies win the war'.[130] He believed de Valera would, as MacRory already had in April 1943, invoke the Atlantic Charter to demand the end of partition 'as a major political wrong comparable to the major crimes of the Axis'.[131] When Britain inevitably rejected this, he would appeal to 'England haters' in America and might encourage people to vote for isolationists and prevent post-war cooperation with Britain'.[132] Secretary of State Cordell Hull approved his suggestion that he speak to 'notable leaders of Irish descent', including numerous senior Catholic churchmen, Massachusetts Congressman John McCormack and Kennedy.[133]

The following day, Gray met Sean Nunan, Éire's consul general in Washington, and Nunan reported the substance of their conversation in a lengthy memo to Brennan. Gray sought to bring Éire into the war with the end of partition ('his dearest wish') as its reward. Nunan explained that Éire's people were squarely behind neutrality, but Gray insisted that de Valera could persuade them otherwise. Gray warned that Anglo-American cooperation would continue, and there would be little sympathy in America for Éire's aspirations. Gray revealed his conversations with unnamed archbishops, who wanted Éire in the war, while the US wanted it at the peace conference which would follow the Allied victory. Nunan offered the stock answer that partition was the problem, telling Gray: 'let England abolish Partition which she had set up'. Gray asked about unionists, but Nunan refused to consider any compromise: 'I asked why should we – the majority of the people of Ireland – be always expected to give way, why should not England and the Northern Government. They had nothing to fear from a United Ireland.' Gray urged pragmatism, arguing that there was simply no immediate prospect of Britain ending partition. Gray then raised post-war anti-partition agitation in the States potentially led in person by de Valera: '[f]rom this I gathered that someone was worried lest the "Irish Question" be used in a campaign against America's participation in whatever international post-war arrangement she may have in mind to be a party to'. Throughout Gray emphasized his admiration for de Valera; he also acknowledged his own unpopularity in Dublin and the likelihood that it would cause his removal.[134] What Gray hoped to achieve here is unclear, unless simply to ensure that the conversation reached de Valera via Brennan, as a warning that he too had taken his campaign to Irish-America. The most revealing aspect of the exchange, however, is the subtext that Gray feared another American victory being squandered partly due to the vitriol and insularity of Irish-Americans which recalled their role in preventing America joining the League of Nations after the Great War.[135] Gray's paranoia, if still exaggerated, makes more sense in this context.

As for his mission, Gray reported to Archbishop Edward Mooney of Detroit that those he spoke to '[a]ll hope that American and Irish interests may not come into conflict, all see the need for wise forbearance as well as the danger that Mr de Valera will toss the Partition issue into our lap as soon as the war ceases'.[136] The best possibility for ending partition was for Éire 'to take some limited part in the war' such as leasing facilities and breaking relations with the Axis governments and establish 'such a friendly relation with Northern Ireland as would promote unity'. If Britain emerged victorious it would 'neither be intimidated by de Valera nor coerce Northern Ireland', whereas cooperation would allow Éire a say in the peace.'[137] A Democratic leader of Irish descent in New York State told him that Irish-Americans were 'perplexed' about de Valera's attitude to the war, but suspicious of Britain.[138] None of these meetings, however, produced any constructive suggestions regarding partition.[139] Upon his return to Dublin, Gray reiterated his pre-trip analysis that de Valera would use 'the grievance' of partition and 'the subversive American press will be fed from Éire with a formidable anti-partition, anti-British propaganda as the war ends'.[140] He, therefore, had to make de Valera responsible for any breakdown of American-Irish relations and ruin his credibility in the States.[141]

Gray decided to draft a note to Éire's government demanding the Treaty ports and the removal of Axis legations, and thereby end the Irish question in America 'by securing for Éire a place at the Peace Table' and its cooperation in the post-war world. If rejected, it put Dublin 'on record' for refusing 'a friendly and generous offer'.[142] For that reason, the note, delivered on 21 February, was primarily for American public consumption by very visibly illustrating the schism between the United States and Éire, or rather, between Gray and de Valera.[143] The threat of 'hyphenated' Americans disrupting post-war politics was central to Gray's thinking, thus removing Axis legations in Dublin was a pretext to destroy Éire and de Valera's standing in America, and enable the Anglo-American alliance to prosper. The real or imagined dangers posed by the Axis legations were subservient to the somewhat apocalyptic belief that American democracy needed protection from de Valera and the Irish-American lobby. To borrow Gray's oft-repeated criticism of de Valera, the grievance had become more important than the solution.

British cabinet members had privately raised serious objections to the note, for example, Foreign Secretary Anthony Eden, Gray told Roosevelt, had an understandable 'fear of being embarrassed by the Partition issue'.[144] Maffey saw it as counterproductive, concerned that it would actually embolden Irish-Americans, enable de Valera to raise partition in the States and cost Roosevelt votes in the forthcoming presidential election. Cabinet opponents also worried that even a token gesture by de Valera could be construed as quid pro quo for ending partition after the war, a very poor trade as it betrayed unionists when victory was in sight and the need for Éire's bases long gone.[145] One official reported that Maffey and the Dominions Office 'opposed the move as they thought it better to let Ireland stew in her own juices and discover for herself how she had alienated opinion both here and in the USA'.[146] Churchill, over cabinet objections, now accepted Gray's analysis, and fully endorsed the note.[147] The British then slightly belatedly, on 22 February, offered their own note.[148] Roosevelt and Hull actively encouraged Gray to put de Valera 'on record'; Hull, however, while agreeing with Gray's analysis of Irish-America's threat to the Anglo-American alliance, required convincing of the value of the bases.[149]

As various historians have demonstrated, the row was utterly needless on a security level as the legations posed little danger to the impending invasion of Europe; indeed, the Germans' radio transmitter was already sequestered in a Dublin bank vault.[150] It is also apparent in the historiography, moreover, that Gray probably ignored intelligence cooperation between Éire and America, and peremptorily dismissed evidence of this.[151] Gray quickly dropped any demand for bases, previously a supposedly key area of contention. Churchill had told Gray as early as November 1942 that the Allies no longer needed the ports, while Marshall and the Joint Chiefs felt that they were more trouble than they were worth.[152] This demonstrated that the Allies in reality had no practical strategic need for them, but Gray had persisted. Abandoning the bases, however, now eliminated any potential military cooperation which Éire could later exploit. Instead, the note sought the altogether more coercive and draconian removal of the Axis delegations, on the pretext that their (now removed) radio transmitters threatened the invasion of Europe.[153] The consequences of Éire's failure to acquiesce were uncertain, but this punitive demand was diplomatically impossible for any neutral state to reasonably accede to.

The State Department eventually made the note public on 10 March 1944, amid rumour and speculation and pre-empting the Associated Press breaking the story. This led to weeks of sensationalist, negative coverage of Éire in the American press.[154]

Domestically, however, De Valera skilfully misrepresented the note as an American ultimatum.¹⁵⁵ Whether de Valera actually believed an attack was imminent is moot, and Roosevelt had previously guaranteed Éire's neutrality, but the Taoiseach triggered an invasion scare, allowing him to call a general election in May where, his defiance popular with Éire's electorate, he finally won a majority.¹⁵⁶ Gray's scheme had actually made de Valera more secure than at any point since his initial election in 1932. Yet Gray judged the note a triumph; to his mind, it demonstrated publicly de Valera's hostility to the Allies. On one level the note was a gratuitous and dangerous act of folly, but it presaged, as Gray hoped, post-war American antagonism, for example, meaning that Éire was not invited to the United Nations' inaugural meeting, so it was partially successful.¹⁵⁷ Gray's prediction that de Valera and Irish-Americans would inject partition into post-war American politics proved correct, but even this hardly justified precipitating a distracting international crisis at a crucial point in the war.

Ironically, Gray's belligerence towards de Valera vicariously aided wartime Anglo-Irish relations, and the British arguably even manipulated him to protect the Anglo-American alliance – and thus British interests – from Irish-Americans after the war. Maffey shared Gray's fear of anti-partitionism in the States, and tried to avert this. Seen by Dwyer as an ingénue using Gray to stoke American resentment at Éire's neutrality, in 1943 Maffey told Machtig at the Dominions' Office, that 'it would be ungracious on our part not to recognise how great a debt we owe to Mr David Gray'. Due to American-Irish links, 'the American Minister is expected to say comfortable things'; however, Gray refused, and his initially positive predisposition towards Éire had shifted dramatically.¹⁵⁸ 'Though it may escape the notice of the historian', Maffey declared, 'Mr David Gray's arrival in Dublin was a milestone in Irish history'. He was an American minister who had 'the temerity to make it plain to Irish Nationalists that they were no longer the darling Playboy of the Western World, and to point out that the audience were bored'.¹⁵⁹ This represented, he believed, a transformation in American-Irish relations, and the British 'have been able to coordinate our policies with Mr Gray in every way . . . [which] cannot fail to have decisive consequences in laying the Anglo-Irish spectre'.¹⁶⁰ Maffey was well liked in Dublin, with Fisk noting his 'reputation for political integrity', and a genuine friendship between him and Gray persisted far beyond the war.¹⁶¹ He had good relationships with both de Valera and Gray, perhaps enhanced by their mutual loathing, and had a unique insight into their feuds as each complained about the other, but this suggests Machiavellian tendencies. Maffey recognized that regardless of personal relationships, his sole duty was to serve British interests, which periodically required playing off his host and his ally against each other.

Gray eventually left Dublin in 1947 and his successor was America's first ambassador to Éire when it became a republic two years later. When Gray's letter to MacRory had surfaced at the Dominions Office in mid-1943, Norman E. Riches, a British representative in Dublin, commented: 'Mr Gray appears to be the best propagandist we have ever so far had in Éire'.¹⁶² There is some truth to this, but Gray operated on his own initiative and for his own ends. Unionists saw little point in making their case south of the border; the British avoided provoking Éire over partition, preferring wartime cooperation, and, quite frankly, partition had no bearing on British electoral politics.

Gray's initial sympathy with Éire, borne of 'wishful thinking' about partition and the assumption that de Valera was essentially on the Allied side, quickly dissipated when confronted by de Valera's irredentism. This was compounded by the non-negotiability of neutrality, even with the inducement of ending partition, and the realization that the Taoiseach's overriding priority was fortifying his domestic position. Coupled with this was what Gray saw as the undue deference of Dublin to the Axis powers and its refusal to acknowledge that Éire's neutrality and economy were effectively guaranteed by the Allies.

His fear that de Valera would inject partition into American elections became exaggerated, obsessive and paranoid, but was not groundless. De Valera claimed, after all, to be the leader of Irish people everywhere and this included veiled threats to harness the Irish-American vote to the anti-partition cause, which could have affected Roosevelt's Democratic Party, and potentially America's participation in a post-war international organization. De Valera did attempt this after the war, even if both he and Gray overestimated the importance of the Irish-American bloc in presidential elections. Gray clearly was not the 'Hibernophobe' claimed by some historiography, but, rather spoke truth to power in Éire's political establishment regarding the war and partition. Yet he did so recklessly and tactlessly, incinerating bridge after bridge in the process and, in 1944, delivering to de Valera the majority he had craved for more than a decade. To Gray, de Valera repeatedly demonstrated that his allegiance was primarily to his own dogma rather than any practical remedy to partition. Gray was, however, no unionist, but he did see value in their counter-narrative to attacks on partition and merit in Stormont more generally. This suited his purposes: quite simply, Northern Ireland was an American ally and Éire was not, thus, the principle of 'my enemy's enemy is my friend' applied. He also concluded that partition was perpetuated mainly by anti-British, anti-unionist and anti-Allied attitudes in Dublin, rather than a Bourbon clique in Belfast propped up by Britain. Despite all of this, he still idealistically believed that the solution to the Irish question was ending partition, but based on cross-border conciliation, rather than the coercion of unionists implied by Irish nationalist rhetoric. Unionists certainly appreciated his cooperation, Oscar Henderson wrote to Gray in 1957, to 'thank you for all you have done for the state of Northern Ireland'.[163]

11

'Ulster Had a Hand in the First Independence Day'

Ulster-American revivalism and the Second World War

Hi! Uncle Sam!
When freedom was denied you
And Imperial Might defied you,
Who was it stood beside you
At Quebec and Brandywine?
And dared retreats and dangers,
Red Coats and Hessian strangers,
In the lean, long-rifled Rangers,
And the Pennsylvania Line![1]

In his 1904 study, *The Scotch-Irish in America*, John Walker Dinsmore noted that '[f]or 200 years and more the Scotch-Irish race has been a very potent and beneficent factor in the development of the American Republic'. 'All things considered', Dinsmore, a Presbyterian minister, mused, 'it seems probable that the people of this race have cut deeper into the history of the United States than have the people of any other race', without being 'the most numerous or boastful'. He claimed that '[u]ntil recent years the Scotch-Irish have been mostly silent about their achievements. They have been content to do the work given them and let others take the glory'.[2] Unionism resurrected this seemingly forgotten contribution by a neglected diaspora during the war to assert an earlier link to America than Catholic Ireland; furthermore, the ideas of Dinsmore and his contemporaries were readily and regularly paraded to challenge anti-partition propaganda and claim the essence of the American spirit.[3] In May 1942, for example, the BBC broadcast a talk by historian A. J. Tulip on 'American Presidents of Ulster descent' avowing that at least ten, 'some claim 13 or 14', and nine from 1830 to 1900 had Ulster roots. 'And now', he declared, 'American troops are in Northern Ireland. Remembering Jackson, Polk, Grant, Wilson, and all their fellows, we cannot regard them as strangers. They are a welcome return for the Presidents Ulster has given to America'.[4] Tulip summarized the recurring tropes in unionist coverage of Ulster-American links, namely, that Ulster 'gave' America many presidents and important figures and Americans were 'returning' to an ancestral homeland. This notion would be expanded, particularly by Presbyterians, Northern Ireland's largest Protestant denomination, to proclaim that the gift of these presidents was augmented by a bequest of fundamental traits not only central to the American character but which also shaped revolutionary philosophy and the republic which emerged from it. Harnessing the American presence to propagandize this narrative in order to challenge anti-partition agitation United States, however, proved difficult.

Stories in the unionist press about historic Ulster-American links are confined mainly to 1942. There was, moreover, no specific direction from Stormont about publishing this material, merely that they avoid negative coverage of the Americans. These stories focused on figures of Ulster descent involved in Colonial and Revolutionary America, their influence on American life, emphasizing that they were neither 'Irish' nor Catholic, and arrived decades before the Great Famine.[5] It is not the intention here to detail this historic relationship or the veracity of accounts of it, merely its resurrection and utilization during the war, its nativist roots in late nineteenth-century America and assess these as part of a longer Ulster-American narrative. That said, understanding the historic and historiographic contexts of this revival, or reinvention, is vital. This discussion, therefore, will locate the war within the wider historiography of the Scotch-Irish and the United States as this informed contemporary perceptions which are described here as 'Ulster-American revivalism'. The historiography, whether the uncritical, celebratory accounts of the turn of the twentieth century or more recent debates, agrees that the Scotch-Irish (or 'Scots-Irish' or 'Ulster-Scots') played a crucial, if sometimes exaggerated, part in American history.[6] Absent from modern historiography on the subject, however, is the attempted renewal of Ulster-American connections during the Second World War, a gap which this chapter will fill.

'Taciturn to a fault': The invention of the Scotch-Irish

Until mass and overwhelmingly Catholic immigration of the 1840s, Protestant immigrants of Irish origin classified themselves simply as 'Irish'. The newer Catholic arrivals with their alien, and possibly subversive, religion led America's Protestant Irish to reinvent themselves and disavow some of their Irishness by distinguishing themselves from the newcomers. An essentially American creation, 'Scotch-Irish' came into common usage in the States (and is the term adopted in this chapter) by the mid-nineteenth century, quickly becoming an all-encompassing term for Protestants of Irish descent.[7] This Scotch-Irish revivalism was intertwined with burgeoning anti-Catholic nativism, which saw the Scotch-Irish accentuate their distinctiveness, tying it to Protestant Anglo-Saxonism; to avoid being 'othered' alongside the Irish, the Scotch-Irish had to assert their Anglo-Saxon credentials.

Anglo-Saxonism, an ideology promoting the cultural and racial superiority of 'English-speaking peoples', was associated with Teutonic 'germ theory' (a pseudoscientific combination of biological determinism and nationalism, popular within the American historical profession in the late nineteenth century) and had subsequent connotations with eugenics and Nazism.[8] Scotch-Irish revivalism adopted something of Anglo-Saxonism's more extreme eugenicist or Social Darwinian tendencies, embracing 'scientifically' identifiable racial and national characteristics, fashionable in the late 1800s but subsequently utterly discredited. The Scotch-Irish narrative was part of a broader racialized context in that the multiple contemporary definitions of 'race' could refer to ethnic groups or nationality; regardless of the semantics, Anglo-Saxonism had clearly racist overtones.[9] The Scotch-Irish became a branch of the Anglo-Saxon genetic lineage, whereas the Catholic Irish were an inferior 'other' race. Scotch-Irish history is further tainted regarding supposedly exclusive bloodlines. Dinsmore claimed that 'whatever blood maybe in the veins of the genuine Scotch-Irishman, one thing is certain, and that is that there is not mingled with it one drop of the blood of the old Irish or Kelt [sic]', which was patent nonsense.[10] The Scotch-Irish revival also coincided with and condoned racialized caricatures of Irish Catholics as ape-like and therefore, racially inferior to the Anglo-Saxon.[11] By the Second World War, the less politically loaded – but still problematic – concept of 'English-speaking peoples' was employed by unionists (and the British more generally) to denote shared Anglo-American heritage, and the values of freedom and democracy, while the philosophy of Anglo-Saxonism now felt rather too close to Nazi ideology.

Scotch-Irish revivalism also developed amid the rise of ethnic and national fraternal organizations after the Civil War.[12] The idea of a Scotch-Irish cultural organization was first mooted by the Ulster-born Colonel Thomas T. Wright, a Nashville businessman, with the Scotch-Irish Society of America (SISA) eventually founded in May 1889 in Columbia, Tennessee.[13] Dinsmore was a founder member, and Donegal-born New Yorker Robert Bonner, owner and publisher of the *New York Ledger*, was its first president. The society consciously sought post-Civil War reconciliation between North and South, noting that the Scotch-Irish fought for both Union and Confederacy. Yet it was also a time of increased nativist sentiment often characterized by anti-Catholicism. The SISA was routinely accused of this, despite Bonner's insistence that it was non-sectarian and apolitical.[14] Its first Congress in Columbia had between 6,000 and 10,000 attendees over three days.[15] It had notable delegates during its short life: President Benjamin Harrison attended in 1890, future vice-president Adlai Stevenson in 1891 and William McKinley, then governor of Ohio, in 1893. With decreasing numbers and the deaths of key members, however, the society's final congress was held in 1902. The Pennsylvania Scotch-Irish Society (PSIS), founded 1889, continued to thrive and eventually became the Scotch-Irish Society of the United States of America (Figures 11.1 and 11.2).[16]

Both the Scotch-Irish revivalism in the 1890s and more particularly its Ulster-American equivalent in the 1940s were motivated by resentment that Ulster never received sufficient credit as its role in the founding of the American republic was subsumed into a generalized Irish contribution, rather than an explicitly Ulster (and Protestant) one. To redress this, by the early twentieth century various histories of the Scotch-Irish appeared, establishing their importance in settling the original colonies (notably Pennsylvania), in the revolution, and in formulating the American character. Some made rather dubious claims. Henry Jones Ford, recommended to the PSIS by

THOMAS T. WRIGHT.

Figure 11.1 Thomas T. Wright, founder of the Scotch-Irish Society of America.

no less a personage than President Woodrow Wilson (another president claimed as an Ulsterman), published his history of the Scotch-Irish in 1915, a tome replete with exaggerated tales of these rugged folk, crediting them with, among other things, taming the West, industrialization, the legal system and schools.[17] These histories, however, later provided the template for those using the Second World War to reclaim Ulster's place in America's national story.

The Second World War was not unionists' first attempt to exploit Ulster-American links or draw parallels with United States' history to aid their cause and discredit Irish nationalism. The appeal of unionism in America was limited, but there was hope during the early Home Rule period of the 1880s and 1890s that a transatlantic unionist community could develop to counter Irish nationalism in the States. This was based on shared Protestantism as well as shared history, and, at this point, unionists viewed themselves as Irishmen with partition not contemplated as a solution to the Irish question. It nonetheless marked the start of unionists and the Scotch-Irish questioning their immediate and ancestral Irishness.[18] This also coincided with Anglo-American rapprochement in the 1890s, coalescing around Anglo-Saxonism.[19]

As Flewelling very ably demonstrates, the Home Rule crises in the late nineteenth and early twentieth centuries and the subsequent Irish war of independence saw these connections eagerly, if not necessarily effectively, recalled. Anti-Home Rule unionists emphasized broader themes than those highlighted during the Second World War, but

Figure 11.2 Robert Bonner, first president of the Scotch-Irish Society of America and owner of the New York Ledger newspaper. Hulton Archive/Getty Images.

the basic premises remained much the same. In the earlier period, there was more focus on the Constitution, the concept of unity, as epitomized by the Civil War, transposed to British unity including Ireland (rather than the Irish nationalist notion of unity on the island of Ireland, embracing the Catholic, Protestant, dissenter ethos envisioned by the United Irishmen of 1798). Important parallels were also drawn between unionists and revolutionary-era Americans prepared to fight to maintain their perceived rights.[20] These often abstract ideas, sometimes as sophisticated as they were paradoxical, had faded by the 1940s. Utilization of historic links, however, with their anti-Catholic undercurrents, was merged with contemporary hostility to Éire's neutrality. The earlier broader narrative, encompassing the Constitution or the Civil War, was abandoned in favour of emphasizing the Revolution and the creation of the new republic.

One voice raised in opposition to Irish-America's appropriation of Scotch-Irish achievements was Teddy Roosevelt in his 1891 history of New York. The future president mused that '[i]t is a curious fact that in the Revolutionary War, the Germans and the Catholic Irish should have furnished the bulk of the auxiliaries [mercenaries] to the regular English soldiers, but the fiercest and most ardent Americans of all were the Presbyterian Irish settlers and their descendants.'[21] His life-long friend Owen Wister, a writer of Western novels, most famously *The Virginian*, was much more forthright in 1920, when de Valera was in America drumming up support for independence. In *A*

Straight Deal, an invective about the malevolent influence of Irish-Americans (among others) on American politics after the Great War, Wister declared: 'Americans are being told in these days that they owe a debt of support to Irish independence because the Irish fought with us in our own struggle for independence. Yes, the Irish did, and we do owe them a debt of support. But it was the Orange Irish who fought in our revolution, and not the Green Irish'.[22] Wister presented a polemical assessment of Irish nationalist demands for independence with particular scorn reserved for Sinn Fein and Irish-Americans sympathetic to their cause, and criticism of Irish-American interventions in American politics, in contrast to the stance of Britain during the Civil War and its recent status as an ally.[23] These ideas would be implicitly and explicitly resurrected by Presbyterian ministers in Northern Ireland during the Second World War.

Many of the wartime pieces in unionist newspapers stressed not only Ulstermen in American history but also supposed similarities between Ulster and America and the former's role in shaping the latter. To this end, newspapers gave occasional platforms to prominent Presbyterians to celebrate their transatlantic brethren. The assertion throughout was that the American character evolved from the Ulster-Scot and chiefly the Presbyterian; hence, the traditional stereotype of the dour Ulsterman is positively transformed, without whom America's revolution would have failed and perhaps not even happened. In this reading, pious, sturdy, individualistic yeomen were driven from one land, Ulster, and determined not to lose another, established a new country by securing its freedom, shaping its politics, culture and outlook, and taming its wilderness all through their unique anti-authoritarian (and manifestly Protestant) spirit.

This view was broadly endorsed by both the contemporary historiography and the earlier propagandist tracts. Writing in 1944 about the Ulsterman in colonial Pennsylvania, American historian Wayland Fuller Dunaway described him as follows:

> He was at once venturesome and cautious, taciturn to a fault, but speaking his mind freely when aroused. Serious in his outlook upon life, he nevertheless had a sense of humor, was fond of sports, and was by no means unsocial. Though ordinarily undemonstrative, his rough exterior often covered a great tenderness of feeling, and his love of family was deep, strong, and enduring. Steadfast and loyal, he was as hospitable to his friends as he was unrelenting to his foes ... his nature rebelled against anything that savored of injustice or deceit, nor did he take kindly to restraint of any kind.[24]

This sequence of flattering generalizations – undoubtedly vital frontier qualities but applicable to most immigrants – certainly tallied with the current Presbyterian perspective of the Ulster character and the notional American debt to Ulster.[25] Dunaway, however, ignored the obvious contemporary connection, the Americans in Northern Ireland, illustrating the difficulty of the unionist narrative gaining traction in the United States.

The historiographical hyperbole that accompanied that Scotch-Irish revival did not age well. Writing amid renewed interest in Ulster-American connections during the US bicentennial in 1976, John W. Blake (Northern Ireland's official war historian) argues that these chronicles reflected an 'uncritical and even euphoric and pietistic exaggeration' among their boldest adherents.[26] This cynicism should, however, be tempered. Presbyterianism as especially crucial to the shaping of an American nationalism has some foundation. James G. Leyburn, in his key 1962 study, argues that Presbyterian settlers were the first to identify as specifically 'American' rather than by their colony or country of origin and were 'an augury of Americans-to-be' and 'archetypal' Americans; alongside this, their dispersal throughout the new United States was fundamental to the kind of republic which emerged.[27] Yet this also meant that the Scotch-Irish, despite considerable prejudice against them before the revolution, were generally assimilated by the nineteenth century, rendering them increasingly indistinct as a diaspora.[28]

Many Presbyterians spent a comparatively short time in Ulster, arriving from Scotland at the start of the seventeenth century as part of the Ulster plantation, and their departure to North America represented another stage of a nomadic existence. There is a curious, though far from unique, paradox between a group essentially compelled to leave their native land and the subsequent celebration of their later achievements by this land. Thus, wartime accounts largely ignored the reality that Presbyterians left Ulster due to real and perceived religious persecution, not at the hands of Catholics, but rather the Anglican Church of Ireland. These accounts also neglected the importance of economic necessity, as Presbyterians felt unable to compete with Catholics for land. The most pertinent omission in the wartime context was that some Presbyterians who remained in Ulster later, as the United Irishmen, made common cause with Catholics in the 1798 rebellion against British rule (which certainly tallied with their rebellious reputation in America).[29] The focus on Ulster also ignored Scotland's similar, if slightly more ancient, claim to most if not all of the presidents of Ulster stock.[30]

Despite the paradoxical nature of Ulster-Scots history, it was nevertheless a rare, distinct and legitimate, if periodically dormant, diaspora which the war provided Northern Ireland an opportunity to claim, even if unionists struggled to reconcile its contradictions.[31] The American presence certainly offered an opportunity to resurrect and commemorate these links, both for local consumption and as a way of currying post-war American favour. Absent from the celebration of Ulster-Scots in North America, however, is any sense that their values were anti-British and essentially republican, which represented an uncomfortable counterpoint to contemporary loyalty to the crown. Also ignored was the unpleasant reality that many Scotch-Irish fought brutal frontier wars against Native Americans, some were involved in slavery (even if some Presbyterians were early to denounce it), and they have been accused of formulating white supremacy.[32]

The experiences of Ulster-Scots and later Catholic Irish immigrants in America had evident parallels, for example, taking time to assimilate, a process admittedly more prolonged for the latter. Yet thorough Ulster-Scots assimilation by the nineteenth century and the lack of nostalgia for the old country they voluntarily left mitigated against the development of a diasporic mentality.[33] Irish Catholics, conversely, had little choice in leaving their homeland due to the Famine and were then actively excluded from political life in America, requiring them to forge semi-autonomous political, economic and social lives in places such as New York and Boston. They then developed into a politically powerful ethnic bloc, an outcome predicted and feared by nineteenth-century nativists, and would eventually use this influence within the Democratic Party to agitate against partition. By contrast, the voice and contribution of Ulster-Scots seemed almost entirely mute.[34]

By the Second World War the Ulster diaspora, such as it was, consisted of Orange Order lodges dotted around the United States and some Scotch-Irish cultural organizations such as the Ulster-Irish Society of New York and the Scotch-Irish Society of the United States of America; however, these were small and had limited political influence, especially when compared to Irish-America, with its self-conscious political connections and thriving, militant, press.[35] When links to Ulster were reported in America during the war, it reflected curiosity about where troops had been sent and was explained in broad terms. The only demographic likely to be receptive to challenging Irish-American political power were the descendants of the same anti-Catholic forces which prospered in the nineteenth century. By the 1940s, this meant the nativist Protestant wing of the Republican Party with its residual anti-Catholicism (not to mention isolationism), hypothetical allies likely to do Northern Ireland's cause more harm than good, and never approached by Stormont. Indeed, as discussed in Chapter 5, isolationists found common cause with Irish-Americans prior to Pearl Harbor. Despite demonstrable and important historic links, therefore, Ulster lacked a vocal and visible diaspora willing to take up its cause, embrace its complex history and subvert the thoroughly entrenched Irish-American narrative about Irish history and partition.

And when the days of trial came/ Of which we know the story/ No Erin son of Scotia's blood/ Was ever found a Tory.[36]

As noted, when the Americans arrived, the *Derry Journal* scorned 'the mushroom show of specious regard' that unionists had suddenly discovered for the United States.[37] Yet, to an extent, the inverse was also true. Nationalist Ireland's friendship with the country which was credited, exaggeratedly so, with securing an independent Irish state was hastily shelved with a similarly specious disregard for America in its own hour of need. The nationalist press consequently mostly ignored the Americans, partly to avoid legitimizing, even rhetorically, partition and the hated 'Six County Ascendancy' but primarily to avoid offending American public opinion. There were, however, early and occasional efforts to negate and discredit the developing unionist narrative.

One of the first forays into shared history after the initial publicity about the Americans had subsided came not from Belfast's triumvirate of unionist papers but from the *Irish News* and exposed a darker side to Ulster-American ties. Its columnist Cathal O'Byrne, a singer, poet, writer (best known for his 1946 collection *As I Roved Out: A Book of the North*), former IRA member and one-time resident of the United States, wrote of Belfast merchants' involvement in the 'nefarious and inhuman' slave trade.[38] By contrast, the Catholic Church in Ireland abolished slavery as early as 1170, 'the first country in the civilized world to set that example'.³⁹ He reported an 'Amicable Society of Belfast' resolution in 1780 condemning an advertisement in the *News Letter* offering a reward for an escaped 'Indian black'.⁴⁰ There was regular trade between Belfast, and indeed Dublin, and the West Indies from as early as 1740, although neither city was as implicated as, say, Bristol or Liverpool, both ports benefited indirectly from slavery.⁴¹ O'Byrne stated that in the 1790s, Thomas McCabe, father of United Irishman William Putnam McCabe, opposed the raising of a slave ship crew by Waddell Cunningham, the richest man in Belfast, Caribbean plantation owner and, according to Wolfe Tone, 'a lying old scoundrel'.⁴² Cunningham, O'Byrne pointed out, 'is buried in Newtownbreda Churchyard, where a grand and imposing tombstone is erected over him'.⁴³ McCabe was also friendly with other United Irishmen, Henry Joy McCracken, Thomas Russell and Tone, therefore connecting noble abolitionism to Irish freedom.⁴⁴

That the *Irish News* neglected to highlight the paradox of unionists celebrating early Protestant Irish republicanism's association with the American Revolution perhaps reveals that the paper saw nationalism as essentially Catholic.⁴⁵ The day after Byrne's piece came the tale of an Irishman 'named Brendan' who apparently discovered America in the sixth century, supposedly spending seven years among Native American tribes and inspiring the *Sinbad the Sailor* tales, but this was just about the extent of the *Irish News's* coverage. It did not offer an alternative narrative stressing Irish Catholic links with the United States or exposing discrimination within Northern Ireland, as reporting the American presence effectively condoned it.⁴⁶

In early 1946, O'Byrne provided a diatribe against Ulster-American friendship, by assessing one of the most revered Ulstermen in this narrative, Andrew Jackson. Jackson's family fled Ulster 'for some political reason and to be out of the reach of the English Yeomen', and his mother's stories of their persecution 'early imbibed a deadly hatred of England and the English'.⁴⁷ The army he led to victory over the British at New Orleans in 1815 had, according to gravestones, many Irishmen in it: 'the percentage of Keltic [sic] names is large enough to cause Ireland to feel proud of her share in America's fight for independence'.⁴⁸ The British were apparently 'fresh from the field of Waterloo' – a battle which took place six months later – while Jackson, demonstrating an ecumenism which would no doubt offend modern Protestant Ulstermen, attended mass in New Orleans prior to the battle. Unionists' purposely shallow approach to their relationship with America was also deconstructed: 'much is written from time to time about Ulster giving a certain number of Presidents to the United States, but we never hear a word as to why the fathers and mothers of these Presidents had to fly from Ulster'.⁴⁹ This was a fair point, which together with fighting against the British in the Revolution, those celebrating Ulster-American links never adequately addressed.

Jackson also opposed Southern secession, which O'Byrne transposed onto the partition of Ireland. Stories now circulated that 'delegations representing Unionism and Orangeism' were to go to the States to challenge anti-partition propaganda: 'we wonder what case these "Irishmen" who hate Ireland, these slaves who love their chains, we wonder what case they will attempt to make out for their unholy cause'.⁵⁰ As for America, it 'knows something of the attempted partition of the Secessionists. The Civil War struck its death blow . . . who knows but that the death blow to Ireland's Partition may be struck there'.⁵¹ This outburst, inferring that nationalists did not regard unionists as 'Irishmen', believed unionists deluded themselves in considering themselves British and viewing their cause as entirely illegitimate, was far from atypical amid the increasingly extreme and sectarian politics of Irish nationalist anti-partition rhetoric after the war.[52] With the first of these stories, unionist Ulster's bond with America was tainted by slavery; the second allowed nationalists to assert the earliest American link; and the third savaged the Ulster-American narrative and hoped that America would aid anti-partitionism.[53]

Unionist newspapers promoted an altogether more positive and uncritical narrative, for example, the *Telegraph* recounted the 'epic deeds' of William Johnson 'The Co. Down man who became an Indian Chief'. Dubbed Wariaghejaghe – 'he who is in charge of affairs' – by the Mohawk tribe, Johnson married a chief's daughter, and then 'saved the British Empire in North America' during the Seven Years' War of 1756–63 by persuading tribes to switch sides from the French to the British.[54] Unionist coverage was, however, dominated by Presbyterians determined to make contemporary political points and relying upon Scotch-Irish historians, minus their eugenicist and overtly nativist tendencies, to do so. Two brothers, Presbyterian ministers Reverend Professor Robert Lyons (R. L.) Marshall, of Magee College, Londonderry, and Reverend William Forbes (W. F.) Marshall, drove this narrative. R. L. Marshall used Presbyterianism's tercentenary in Ireland in 1942 to claim American friendship by emphasizing the neglect of Ulster Presbyterians' role in the American Revolution. He underlined Presbyterian Ulster-Scot emigration to North America in 'Ulstermen's Part in War of American Independence' published in the *Whig*, which, like the *News Letter*, had Presbyterian roots.[55] The causes of this mass emigration, including the persecution of Presbyterians by the Church of Ireland, were not mentioned, nor were their shifting allegiances from being among the first Irish republicans in the late eighteenth century to the staunchest of unionists in the twentieth; there was also more than a hint of sectarianism in Marshall's words.

'The welcome presence of American troops in Ulster', Marshall asserted, was a reminder of 'the close connexion of Ulster Presbyterianism with the foundation and growth of the Republic of the West'. Ulster's role in American independence had been usurped by Irish Catholics and their 'genius for propaganda'. 'It is no secret', he continued, that Irish-American Catholics had pressurized America to 'squeeze the North into compliance with Dublin demands'.[56] Roosevelt, he noted, gifted a copy of the Declaration of Independence to de Valera, but this 'might more appropriately' have been presented to Stormont, as 'the War of Independence was won by the dour and dogged fighting spirit of Ulster Presbyterians and their children'.[57] Marshall re-emphasized that Presbyterian immigration predated Catholic, as 'at least half a million souls' left Ulster between 1730 and 1770 and would become stalwarts of the revolution.[58]

Presbyterians carried their grievances with them going 'with hearts burning with indignation' and during the revolution 'were almost to a man on the side of the insurgents'; some of Washington's best troops, including the famous 'Pennsylvania Line', were Ulstermen.[59] That the Pennsylvania Line was fighting British troops was not a cause for comment. 'Our American friends are', asserted Marshall, 'therefore, rightly at home today in Ulster'. He hoped that when home, the Americans would view Northern Ireland sympathetically and 'not suffer themselves or others to be made the unwilling tools of misrepresentation, so often malicious and flatulent'. 'We have surely some small right', he continued, 'for the sake of our fathers' essential part in their country's foundation and development, to claim such sympathy', in some future 'hour of need'. He concluded: '[f]or we and they are of that stock which, when things precious were at stake, were always "the first to start and the last to quit"'.[60]

W. F. Marshall's 1943 book *Ulster Sails West* published with the assistance of the *News Letter* took a similar stance. As well as a Presbyterian minister, Marshall was also a poet, playwright, novelist, expert on Ulster language and dialect and nicknamed the 'Bard of Tyrone'. His work's antecedents are clearly the earlier histories of the Scotch-Irish, and he repeated many of their claims about Ulster's role in America's development. He asserted that chronicling these connections was 'more urgent' as 'few of these welcome friends have heard our story'.[61] He charted Ulstermen in the Revolution, repeatedly referencing the appropriation of their achievements by later Irish Catholic immigrants. By accident or design this undermined Ulstermen's importance by characterizing them as 'Irish' without distinguishing Ulster from the rest of Ireland. Thus, some writers disingenuously used 'Ulsterman' and 'Irishman' interchangeably, crediting the latter for the former's feats. It was vital to 'make clear the part of Ireland the contribution came from. What is most unfair and dishonest is to claim this contribution as Irish, and then use it as the basis of propaganda' against Northern Ireland. 'The best antidote to such poison is the truth', he declared.[62]

Emphasizing Presbyterians' contribution in particular, Marshall contended that the first battle of the revolution was fought not at Lexington but on the Alamance River in North Carolina on 14 May 1771 between 'the Ulster-Irish' and a British force. This now discredited conclusion was then the broadly acknowledged historical orthodoxy.[63] In 1893, for example, future president William McKinley declared the Scotch-Irish 'the first to proclaim for freedom in these United States, even before Lexington, Scotch-Irish blood had been shed on behalf of American freedom'.[64] Accurate or not, Alamance perfectly encapsulated the Presbyterian argument. Marshall also pointed to various pronouncements by Ulstermen prior to the Declaration of Independence; moreover, the Presbyterian synod was the only 'national' colonial body and met in Philadelphia at about the same time as the Continental Congress in 1775 but made more forthright demands for independence.[65] He added seven vice-presidents to the roll-call of presidents and other notables of Ulster descent, alongside the oft-repeated reminders that the Declaration of Independence's first signatory was an Ulsterman, John Hancock, before being transcribed by another, Charles Thomson, and printed by yet another, John Dunlap.[66]

Marshall found it particularly egregious that the Knights of Columbus and Ancient Order of Hibernians, two Irish-American groups, had recently carried a banner of Anthony Wayne, a Revolutionary War general whose grandfather had fought with King William at the Battle of Boyne: 'our laurels are stolen without scruple and without shame'.[67] 'These are the deeds', he asserted, 'of our kindred and not theirs. This is the record of Protestant Ulster'. He stressed, however, that this was about historical accuracy and not bigotry as '[t]o state facts is not to appeal to religious prejudice'; 'Southern Irishmen' did not make a contribution to American freedom as they simply were not there.⁶⁸ In a barbed return to the present, he declared: 'Southern Ireland was no more in that war than it is in this one.'⁶⁹

He was determined that Ulster claimed deserved credit, refusing to let it 'be stolen from those to whom it belongs, and made part and parcel of a tireless propaganda for our political extinction'.⁷⁰ By way of conclusion, Marshall stated that Ulster would not beg for American support, nor would it petition Congress, as '[w]e can fight our own battle. We can still be the last to quit'.⁷¹ He did request, however, that 'American opinion on the Ulster question should be guided by knowledge and understanding rather than by Republican clamour'.⁷² Stormont was alert to *Ulster Sails West*'s potential propaganda value. The Cabinet Publicity Committee, in March 1944, discussed subsidizing the book's distribution in the States and Canada to counter anti-partition propaganda. With the author's consent the matter would be discussed with the MOI and US embassy.⁷³ Sir Ernest Cooper, Director of Information Services at Stormont, was consulted and declared the book 'both interesting and informative'; however, 'its treatment of the subject is such that it might do more harm than good to Ulster in the USA'.⁷⁴ The basis for Cooper's objections was unclear and the plan was dropped.

The celebration of all things American by Stormont and the unionist press meant, as noted in Chapter 4, negotiating the uncomfortable reality of the United States' break from the British Empire as the 4th of July loomed in 1942. The *Telegraph*, for example, published a long article entitled 'Ulster Had a Hand in the First Independence Day'. This declared, among other things, that 'Ulster might aptly be described as America's First Ally', noting that Protestant survivors of the Siege of Derry in 1689 travelled to North America.⁷⁵ Of course, the irony of staunch unionists celebrating America's secession from empire was self-evident, and if it could not be reasonably disregarded, it could be summarily if inelegantly dismissed. 'Into the rights and wrongs of that struggle it is unnecessary now to enter' was the *Telegraph*'s prevarication. It did, however, as would other reports, stress the large-scale emigration from Ulster to America during the eighteenth century, reminding any American readers that the 'Ulster Irish' arrived long before the famine.⁷⁶ The *News Letter* had a particular connection to the United States and the 4th of July, being the first publication outside of North America to report the signing of the Declaration of Independence. The ship carrying a copy of the declaration to England was forced to dock in Londonderry by bad weather, and the document was taken from there to Belfast to be sent on to King George III in London. The *News Letter*'s enterprising editor, however, printed its contents on 23–25 August 1776. As the paper's own history notes, 'being a radical Presbyterian organ, [it] was enthusiastically in support of the colonists, championing their cause for independence'.⁷⁷ Recollection of support for severing British links was, needless to say, absent in 1942.

Another noteworthy episode absent from press coverage involved one of Brooke's ancestors, Colonel Arthur Brooke. In the War of 1812, Colonel Brooke served under General Robert Ross, another Ulsterman, who captured and sacked Washington, DC, in 1814, burning the White House and other key buildings.⁷⁸ Brooke does not appear to have mentioned this during the war, but in North America in 1950, he joked:

> I faced my first engagement on American soil, in the city of Washington, with some trepidation. For the contribution of Ulster people to the history of the United

States has not always been something to boast about. You see, one of my ancestors was in command of the British troops which burned down the White House in the war of 1812.

His American audiences took the story in good spirit, however.[79] The Americans were stationed in Ross's home town of Rostrevor, which one GI reckoned would have the general turning in his grave.[80]

After their initial interest in Northern Ireland which accompanied US forces, American papers became more concerned with Éire's neutrality, resulting in little further coverage of Ulster-American history. As noted, passing columnists fixated on mutual culture-shock rather than mutual history and made little distinction culturally between Northern Ireland and Éire during usually brief visits, stressing merely that the former was at war and the latter neutral. An exception occurred in the summer of 1942 when numerous papers carried a *National Geographic Bulletin* story about Ulster being the 'grandmother' of the revolution, allowing readers from New England to New Mexico to learn about this little told aspect of American history.[81] This coincided with the opening of an Officers' Club in Belfast, and readers were informed that for many American servicemen who were 'a wee bit Scotch-Irish', Northern Ireland was either 'a return to the land of their ancestors' or linked to a president.[82]

American connections to Ulster featured in the *New York Herald Tribune* that November. The *Whig* reprinted this 'recent leading article' by John W. McPherson, secretary of the PSIS, entitled 'Londonderry Air'. In the spirit of the heyday of the SISA, McPherson commented that many Americans were returning to ancestral homes and that immigration from Ulster 'gave the American people one of its most vigorous and influential foundation stocks', noting their independence and 'fighting qualities'. 'Their contribution', he asserted, 'to the composite American character was rich and influential', while 'their names stud and ornament our annals', including numerous presidents.[83] As 'Londonderry receives back after many years many of its sons', he concluded, 'it will find their combativeness and their resourcefulness in good order'.[84] This encapsulated the self-declared role of Presbyterians in creating the American character and demonstrated that this narrative could return across the Atlantic.

Americans in Northern Ireland periodically referenced these links, with Buhrman noting in December 1942 that people 'constantly express their friendship for the United States. They place much store by their long associations with the United States through Scotch/Irish influences'.[85] On the second anniversary of the landing in January 1944 an unnamed American general declared:

> you have not received strangers. When we study history, we realise you belong to us and we belong to you. The honour roll of our Revolutionary War is filled with the names of Ulstermen. The honour roll of our Civil War is filled with the descendants of Ulstermen. Many of the Presidents of the United States have been of Ulster stock, therefore, I flatly refuse to be treated as a stranger.[86]

At the ceremony marking the departure of the Americans in August 1945, a message from General Lee declared that 'countless families, including my own, left Ulster for

America fearlessly seeking the freedoms they were denied', and asserted this was why the Americans got on so well with the locals.[87] The American military, therefore, occasionally embraced the Ulster-American narrative, or at least flattered its hosts by alluding to it.

By way of epilogue, the narrative was briefly reprised in 1976 during America's bicentennial celebrations and amid almost 300 deaths in one of the Troubles' worst years. Reverend Ian Paisley, a vehemently anti-Catholic Free Presbyterian minister, published *America's Debt to Ulster* in the hope that 're-telling of this story will give strength and courage to the much tried and gravely misrepresented loyalists of Ulster'.[88] Paisley, a contributor to the *Ulster Protestant* from as early as 1948, wrote the book with the assistance of Bob Jones III, the grandson of the founder of Bob Jones University, an evangelical Protestant institution with a history of anti-Catholicism (Bob Jones Sr. was intimately involved in the Republican crusade against Catholic Democratic presidential candidate Al Smith in 1928).[89] The book's purpose was very firmly rooted in the present, explicitly reminding Americans, at a moment when Irish-America was funding IRA terrorism, of their historic connections to Ulster. In his foreword, Jones declared that 'Southern Ireland has received more favourable propaganda than is warranted, to say nothing of contraband weapons for the Irish Republican Army. Until this book, the truth about, to which Ireland, America owes her gratitude has been perverted'.[90] Paisley then revisited the work of the Marshalls to make essentially the same case, but within an altogether more fraught political context, before closing with W.F. Marshall's determination not to plead for American aid.[91] If America did owe a debt to Ulster, then Paisley was a poor choice of debt collector.

Stories about the Americans in the unionist press served an important purpose in fortifying support for the war effort and projecting a harmonious relationship with these visitors. Whether nationalists paid attention was moot, so the main audience was unionists, who already supported the war, and this reminded them of the importance of the Americans to the war effort and, by association, also emphasized Northern Ireland's vital role. There was also the perception that an imprecise American hostility to Northern Ireland needed to be challenged, hence stories referring to historic links and ad nauseam references to presidents of Ulster stock. Yet without effective publicity and newspaper coverage in the States, all of this effort operated, ultimately, in both an echo chamber and a vacuum.

12

'Letters from Ulster'

Propaganda, memory and the Americans

Daniel Cunningham, a Coleraine Justice of the Peace, contacted Andrews in June 1942, enclosing the piece by Reverend R. L. Marshall in the *Whig* on Ulstermen in the American Revolution, and urged the prime minister to capitalize on the American presence. He had a map of Ulster in his shop window which the Americans found interesting but, in his view, were entirely ignorant of history, knowing 'little of the truth about Ireland and are prepared to swallow and believe anything' spread by Irish nationalist propagandists. 'I feel', he declared, 'that "now is the day and now the hour", when the Americans are in Ulster, is for us a critical and historical period and that NOW is OUR opportunity! I need not presume to say to a Protestant Cabinet what to do'.[1] Andrews fully agreed and certainly did not dispute leading a 'Protestant Cabinet'. 'We should do everything possible to make the Americans understand the position here', he replied, and was, in fact, already acting, meeting generals and officers whenever possible and 'making speeches from time to time pointing out Ulster's position'. He nevertheless asked Cunningham for suggestions; a prime minister soliciting advice from a random citizen on a vital matter was distinctly un-statesmanlike and also implied that he had given the matter little thought.[2]

'Codename Rover': Eleanor Roosevelt's visit

Many civilian and military VIPs and Hollywood stars visited Northern Ireland during the war, and the most significant civilian visitor was Eleanor Roosevelt, who arrived in November 1942. As he was unable to walk unaided due to polio, Mrs Roosevelt was her husband's roving ambassador throughout his presidency, and this assumed an international dimension with the war. The unionist press could barely contain its excitement, covering her visit with a degree of sycophancy usually reserved for royalty. A *Telegraph* editorial declared her 'thrice welcomed': as the first lady, as the 'wife of a great man who has already left an indelible mark on world history' and as 'an outstanding public personality in her own name.' She would, it asserted, 'see plenty of evidence of a steadily growing friendship' between Northern Ireland and America, while 'her visit as an ambassador of goodwill will be another link in the impressive chain which stretches between Ulster and the White House'.[3]

Given the codename 'Rover', to her great delight, she arrived at Langford Lodge from Manchester on 10 November.[4] Her retinue included some twenty British and American journalists, plus, with Stormont's cooperation, the three Belfast unionist dailies, and the *Journal*, the *Sentinel* and the *Derry Standard*, with the *Irish News* belatedly invited.[5] Oscar Henderson greeted her on behalf of the government and American and British military commanders, before she lunched at the governor's residence in Hillsborough with the Abercorns, Andrews and various dignitaries.[6] Her first public engagement was at an American military hospital, meeting two-year-old Sally Patterson, who became the hospital's mascot after being hit by an American vehicle, and the First Lady gave the victory sign as she departed to the cheers of well-wishers.[7] Her next stop was, the *News Letter* reported, a 'flying visit' to the Red Cross Club in Chichester Street, where she was loudly cheered by British and American troops and locals. Inside she was given an Ulster damask tablecloth and eighteen napkins, and met the American women working at the club. The weather necessitated her haste as it threatened her flight to Londonderry.[8]

Later in the day large crowds greeted her in Londonderry, and at the city's Red Cross a GI asked her to dance, but she politely demurred: 'I don't think you would enjoy it very much!' That evening she attended a dance for the Marine Corps' 167th anniversary and cut a cake marking the occasion.[9] Where unionist papers covered every detail, the *Journal* was altogether more succinct, '[t]here was a large attendance at the dance. Mrs Roosevelt's visit lasted but a few minutes'.[10] The following day she breakfasted with women's services, including the Auxiliary Territorial Service (ATS), Women's Royal Naval Service (WRENS) and Women's Auxiliary Air Force (WAAF) and, the *News Letter* told readers, 'paused in her whirlwind programme to share in the solemnity of the Two Minutes' Silence' and laid a wreath at the war memorial. She met General Bernard Montgomery's mother, visited the city's famed walls and, having added a shillelagh and an umbrella to her souvenirs, expressed her gratitude for hospitality to American servicemen, before leaving for Scotland.[11] 'Everywhere Mrs. Roosevelt went', the *News Letter* effused, 'she received an enthusiastic welcome, which was no less warm-hearted from the Ulster people in the streets than from the Americans in their clubs and dance halls'.[12] 'Almost every moment of her short stay was accounted for in a crowded programme of visits designed to let her see American soldiers, sailors and marines at work and at play in their Ulster setting', gushed the *Telegraph*.[13] Mrs Roosevelt recounted the trip matter-of-factly in two of her daily 'My Day' newspaper columns, the first of which was reprinted in the *Telegraph*.[14]

The delight at hosting the First Lady masked irritation that officials were only told of the visit when it was imminent, reinforcing the perception that Stormont was either being taken for granted by London and the Americans or not trusted. Commander R. E. Vining of the US embassy and Colonel Arter made the arrangements and communicated these to Abercorn via the Foreign Office.[15] That the trip may have been arranged at short notice and required watertight security did not lessen the sense that Stormont would simply do as it was told. Gransden's first inkling came a few days beforehand when told by Henderson; British General Sir Harold Franklyn then informed him that Vining would chair a conference in Belfast regarding arrangements. Gransden hurriedly notified the police and immediately complained to London 'that these arrangements were made without consultation with the Government of Northern Ireland which would be responsible for the Lady's safety, and I asked that this protest should be conveyed to the proper quarter'.[16] London did not respond. Even after meeting Vining, details remained 'sketchy', with the insinuation – likely unfounded – of information being withheld, which made local security difficult to organize.[17] Gransden rather exaggerated Stormont's wounded pride, and her itinerary was quickly agreed.[18] This was not, however, the first time that Stormont had felt taken for granted, for instance, when Marshall, Harriman and Hopkins visited in April (which resulted in the Clipsham court martial) Gransden found out from press sources. Andrews did attend an inspection of troops at Hartle's invitation, but the party was unable to come to Belfast.[19] Brooke soon complained to Alanbrooke that Stormont had not been properly consulted and that it should be with future distinguished visitors.[20] Mrs Roosevelt's visit implied that this request was ignored.

His wife's niece visiting the UK allowed Gray, alerted at about the same time as Abercorn, to demonstrate America's outward displeasure at Éire's neutrality. This tied in with his and Roosevelt's 'absent treatment', whereby the president largely ignored Éire diplomatically and Mrs Roosevelt's visit permitted, in Gray's eyes, the chance for a very obvious snub. Gray suggested that to reinforce this, '[i]f Eleanor comes back for a night with us on her way home in-cog[nito], we will rub it in. No one will know she is here. It might be a strong hint'.[21] Prior to the announcement of her visit to Northern Ireland, Joseph Walshe, secretary of Éire's Department of External Affairs, inquired if she might return home via Dublin, affording Éire the chance to honour her.[22] Gray with studied politeness replied that she could not accept the invitation 'to recognise her presence here in some appropriate and gracious manner', because she was visiting the UK in an official capacity and would revert to being a private citizen on its completion and, therefore, could not be 'received officially'.[23] Gray sought Roosevelt's approval: 'I hope this is the line [you] would have me take'.[24] When Finance Minister Sean T. O'Kelly, a close associate of de Valera, professed shock that Mrs Roosevelt had not come to Dublin, Gray eliminated any doubt that this was a snub, telling Roosevelt: 'I started to say that as her husband was the Commander in Chief of the United States forces whose presence in Northern Ireland the Irish Government had protested – At this point your aunt shushed me violently but I think the point got over'.[25] O'Kelly also observed that no prominent Americans had visited for a while, which was another element of the 'absent treatment' and proof to Gray that it was working. Gray used a similar approach when Spellman visited a few months later.[26]

The visit's brevity did not diminish its significance to Stormont. Andrews declared his delight and honour at 'having among us so distinguished a lady and bearer of so great a name', praising the friendship between the Americans and locals and predicting closer Anglo-American cooperation 'when the war has passed into history'.[27] He reiterated his appreciation in a subsequent letter, informing Mrs Roosevelt that she was the only first lady to ever visit Northern Ireland, and her presence strengthened the bonds between 'the great English-speaking nations, whose co-operation is so essential for victory'.[28] An interesting aspect of Mrs Roosevelt's visit was Andrews' emphasis on the contemporary Anglo-American link and 'English-speaking nations', rather than the historic Ulster-American dimension (given her uncle Teddy Roosevelt's matrilineal connections to Ulster) and stressing the unionist view that Northern Ireland was simply British and not a place apart within the UK.

In September 1944 three Democratic Congressmen O. C. Fisher, William Poage (both from Texas) and Brooks Hays (Arkansas) arrived in Belfast, courtesy of the MOI, while touring the UK and liberated France. This time Stormont could roll out the red carpet. They lunched with Lord Mayor McCullagh at Belfast's City Hall, where Poage revealed that his ancestors had departed the city two centuries before. They visited the shipyards, the American Red Cross Club, a linen factory and Stormont, where they dined with Brooke and Abercorn.[29] Brooke restated Northern Ireland's privilege in hosting the Americans and hoped for post-war Anglo-American cooperation.[30] Poage declared that 'the whole Allied war effort owes a big debt to Northern Ireland', especially after France fell and when Éire tried 'to play both sides'. 'I believe', he continued, 'this small area has been a whole lot more important to the winning of the war than the world as a whole realises', as without it the Germans would have blockaded American troops and supplies.[31] All three wrote letters of thanks to Brooke on their return to the States.[32] This proved, however, a rare moment of positive interest from American politicians.

'Gladdening the hearts of American mothers': *A Letter from Ulster* and film propaganda

If local newspaper propaganda was necessarily inward-looking, then film provided the opportunity to project a positive image of Northern Ireland to America. Stormont was unable to produce its own film propaganda and relied upon London and MOI to make its case; such assistance and approval, however, were rarely and even then grudgingly granted. A couple of productions dealing with the Americans were made during and immediately after the war, but with little input from Stormont, and none quite promoted the message it desired. Pathé newsreels covered the American presence occasionally with typically jaunty, short features. These included the American arrival, their settling in, and the visits of Winant in March 1942 and Marshall and Harriman in April. Eleanor Roosevelt's trip in November 1942 was also captured, though never broadcast.[33]

One of the Pathé films was *Letters from Home* from April 1942 about the morale-boosting benefits of mail, and the first short documentary-style information film followed a similar theme, involving two Americans writing home about the idiosyncrasies of life in Northern Ireland.[34] William MacQuitty, who had already made a film about Northern Ireland's wartime agriculture, pitched his idea to the head of the MOI's Film Division, Jack Beddington, and Arthur Elton, a key director and producer at the MOI. The local press announced the project in May 1942, to be directed by Belfast-born Brian Desmond Hurst, with fellow Ulstermen MacQuitty as his assistant, and Terence Young as scriptwriter.[35] Hurst, already a renowned filmmaker, was concerned by rumours originating from the German legation in Dublin that the Americans 'were behaving like an army of occupation and beating people up' and wanted to refute these falsehoods.³⁶ The film was made by the ministry's Crown Film Unit as part of a larger series on wartime themes and, therefore, was not under the auspices of Stormont.

The film's premise had two brothers serving in the American armed forces tasked by their commander to write a ten-page letter about life in Northern Ireland.³⁷ The pair embarked upon an odyssey around the countryside, meeting people, accidentally crossing the border, all while documenting their observations for the folks back home. Much of the film was shot around Tynan Abbey in County Armagh and close to the border; however, the training sequences were filmed in Hyde Park, London.³⁸ It featured ordinary people, rather than professional actors, and adopted a quasi-factual approach; in fact, MacQuitty later recalled that soldiers receiving Mass in one scene were actually military prisoners dragged against their will to church.³⁹

Made between May and October 1942 and released in February 1943, it became one of the first films to depict the Americans in the UK, however, because it was intended for American audiences its accompanying publicity there referred to 'Ireland' rather than Ulster, Northern Ireland or Britain.⁴⁰ In seeking the help of the War Office for the training sequences, E. Hudson acknowledged that '[t]he film is being made with the approval of the American authorities and is intended for distribution in America in the form of an illustrated letter home from an American soldier'.⁴¹ The working title of the film was *A Letter Home*, which avoided any mention of place, but 'Ulster' was added to avoid confusion with Carol Reed's *A Letter from Home* (1941).⁴² The film declared itself 'dedicated to those members of the US forces who are guests in these islands' and was shown in some 10,000 US movie theatres.⁴³

On 12 January 1943 the MOI and MGM gave a private screening of *A Letter from Ulster* to Andrews, cabinet members, Colonel I. S. Dierking and other American officers. Andrews believed that the audience 'have been deeply impressed and inspired' and that it gave a 'vivid idea' of the Americans' experience in Northern Ireland. He thought it would fare extremely well in the UK and the US as it depicted 'the unity of two great Democracies'.⁴⁴ Dierking called it 'a first-rate picture' which would be 'highly appreciated' by American audiences.⁴⁵ It would, he continued, 'ease the minds and gladden the hearts of the mothers of America' by demonstrating the 'wonderful hospitality' their sons were receiving.⁴⁶ The trade press saw some merit in the film, but its response was lukewarm. *Today's Cinema* was most positive, highlighting the cooperation of the Americans in the production and complimenting its direction and photography.⁴⁷ The *Motion Picture Herald* offered some praise, noting it was 'made in Ireland by an Irishman for the British Government' and was a 'pleasant and human production' which could prosper on both sides of the Atlantic. It concluded, however, that 'its actual propaganda is a little vague'.⁴⁸ *Kinematograph* was harsher, calling it 'topical and at times human', but 'in spite of its quaint American idiom, somewhat stereotyped' and neither very original nor well edited. It would, nonetheless, 'give pleasure to all Americans with boys on active service', and, perhaps its greatest asset, it would be part of the quota of British films shown in America.⁴⁹

The vagueness of its propaganda message identified by the *Motion Picture Herald* is a useful way of understanding the film. Its makers were conscious of its American and Irish-American audience and avoided engaging with constitutional issues, at a time when protests from Irish nationalists about the Americans were relatively fresh, even though its avowed purpose was to counter negative propaganda. The film downplayed the union, dealt with the border light-heartedly and, as Hill argues, 'provides and image of "Ulster" that represents Catholics (not just Protestants) and draws upon readily recognisable signifiers of "Irish" (rather than "British") culture'.[50] The music used is 'Irish', and its tropes were reliant upon an American and clichéd view of Irishness. Scenes show the happy fraternization between the Americans and the locals, but as a result, Hill notes, 'they also reverberate with associations of Ireland as a simpler, slower, more traditional kind of society. In doing so, they also blur the distinctions between the different parts of the island by invoking a relatively undifferentiated notion of rural "Irishness".[51] When the two soldiers accidentally cross the border, this is treated as entirely trivial (as it likely would have been), but Hurst's underlying message is more subtle and potentially subversive. As Hill argues, it 'dilutes the very distinctiveness' between Northern Ireland and Éire which the former sought to promote.[52] The film, therefore, is motivated by challenging the negative response of nationalism and Irish-Americans to the Americans rather than promoting Northern Ireland as an ally, friend and host.

In an effort to cash in on the American presence, in 1943 Columbia Pictures released the musical comedy *Doughboys in Ireland* directed by Lew Landers. The film, shot on Columbia's backlot in Hollywood, featured a musician called Danny O'Keefe (played by Kenny Baker) leaving one sweetheart in America and finding another in the Emerald Isle. He comes into conflict with the Callahan clan when he offends patriarch Michael's daughter, Molly (Jeff Donnell), resulting in local men threatening American troops. Danny wins everyone over by singing Irish ballads, Molly falls in love with him, but their romance is momentarily complicated when his American girlfriend, Gloria (Lynn Merrick), shows up on a USO tour.[53] The film is unlikely to bother any lists of great movies, including the director's. Untroubled by gritty realism and noteworthy only because it featured a young Robert Mitchum in an early minor role, it is an interesting period piece, revealing details about American perceptions of Ireland. It reinforces to an American audience exactly what they, and Hollywood, already think Ireland is like, with its sultry colleens, angry menfolk and backward ways, and without complicating matters by suggesting that the Americans were in Northern Ireland. Giving the central character an Irish name acknowledges those with Irish heritage in the American forces and also permits him prior knowledge of Irish music. It nods superficially to the conflicts over women, although in this case, an American initially being rude to one, before dating her. It was a reassuring reaffirmation of American-Irish friendship, at a time of poor relations between the States and Éire, but was of little even vicarious propaganda value to Stormont.

A belated indigenous effort at film propaganda appeared in 1946 with Richard Hayward and Donovan Pedelty's documentary *Back Home in Ireland*. Inspired by Eisenhower's visit in August 1945, the pair told Stormont they wanted 'the world to learn about Ulster's role in the war and . . . what Ulster stands for'.[54] The project's title made Stormont reluctant to assist, wanting 'Ireland' changed to 'Ulster', but Hayward and Pedelty felt that the former widened its appeal, especially in America, its principal marketplace.[55] Their plan also raised the possibility of bypassing the usual channels and taking Northern Ireland's message directly to the United States. The Ulster Office in London mustered some positivity arguing the film would 'bring home forcibly the Ulster influence on America' and supporting funding an American trip for Hayward to promote it; Stormont, however, demurred.[56]

The finished product, featuring Hayward giving an unnamed Yank a tour of Ulster's, mainly presidential, links to America and was similar to *A Letter from Ulster* in tone and content. Despite the title, it was clearly about Ulster, even though it relied on 'Irish' tropes such as step-dancing, folk music and a rural setting, all very consciously appealing to an American conception of Ireland. Paradoxically, the makers' unionist sympathies are clear in correspondence with Stormont, even belittling the film's Irish dancing.[57] Stormont's lack of support, however, was compounded by Paramount's attitude, paying much less for it than Hayward hoped, and with a singular lack of enthusiasm.[58] The unfavourable critical, commercial and political assessments of a well-meaning film were harsh but reflected its limited appeal and fuzzy allegiances.

Stormont's insecurities about the title, though far from unreasonable, were part of a larger problem of producing propaganda which foregrounded Northern Ireland's wartime role and underscored the distinction between it and Éire. Some such films had been made about the war generally, with *A Letter from Ulster*, of course, specifically about the Americans; Stormont wanted similar films aimed at both British and American audiences, but this proved particularly difficult as the conflict wore on. Stormont also had to counter anti-partition propaganda as documentaries and newsreels from America and Éire proved troublesome either side of the war's end.[59] This was further exacerbated by perceived hostility at the MOI, with disinterest and excuses illustrating a degree of contempt for the very idea of promoting Northern Ireland.[60] The subtext was that emphasizing Northern Ireland drew attention to partition, potentially reinvigorating the Irish-American lobby and jeopardizing the post-war Anglo-American alliance.[61] Northern Ireland was, therefore, to be hidden away like an embarrassing relative. This was in marked contrast to head of the MOI Brendan Bracken's earlier fulsome appreciation of Stormont and Brooke's handling of the Americans, but this goodwill did not extend to promoting Northern Ireland or propagandizing in its interests.

The difficulty in producing films demonstrates Stormont's subservience to London, preventing it from projecting its preferred image of Northern Ireland and restricted by the prejudices of officials. Stormont controlled the content of neither *A Letter from Ulster* nor *Back Home in Ireland*, and while both depicted the American presence positively, they also offered a generalized 'Irish' view of Northern Ireland that reflected and reinforced their audience's preconceptions of Ireland. Propaganda's job is, of course, to render complex issues simple for a mass audience, and in this regard both films succeed. Just as unionist propaganda presented an unproblematized sense of Northern Ireland as united, stoic and loyal, by depicting an undifferentiated image of Ireland, essentially ignoring partition and the existence of two states on the island, *A Letter from Ulster* was similarly guilty of obscuring huge complexities. *Back Home in Ireland* was closer to Stormont's ideal, but the choice of title rather thwarted its intentions, compounded by its clichéd approach and the post-war circumstances of its release.[62]

The difficulty in generating positive propaganda in America was demonstrated in October 1945. Stormont's publicity committee met Vining and Arter to discuss distributing publicity, and 'it is confidently expected that the information given to Commander Vining and Colonel Arter will be put to effective use when they return to the United States'. The pair spent several days in Northern Ireland and Éire, meeting Adams at Stormont, who outlined the constitutional position, social problems and 'Ulster's post-war prospects'. Vining incorporated this information into a report to Washington, which 'should be brought to the notice of the highest quarters in the United States'. Arter 'was similarly supplied with information which he said he intends to make use of in rebutting anti-Ulster propaganda in his country'.[63] While this semi-official assistance was undoubtedly welcome, it revealed the extent of Stormont's disadvantage. It was rather optimistic to think that two sympathetic, but lowly officials who knew Northern Ireland well held much sway against London's indifference, disinterest in Washington and a remobilizing Irish-American lobby aided by Dublin. Indeed, these discussions coincided with an Irish-American delegation from Boston, including the governor of Massachusetts, arriving in Éire to explain how, contrary to what it dismissed as British propaganda in the States, Éire had actively aided the Allies.[64]

'Preparations for fumigation': Brooke's proposed American trip

In October 1943 Brooke recorded that Gray was 'most anxious that we start propaganda in the United States. He says our position is not fully understood and thinks that we should take steps to increase the knowledge of Americans about ourselves.'[65] Gray, preparing for his 'American Note', demanding the closure of Dublin's Axis legations, lobbied for an invitation to the States for Brooke to put Northern Ireland's case and to politically undermine Irish-America. He told Roosevelt that Maffey, the UK representative in Dublin, had advised him (off the record) to meet Brooke unofficially as he would be 'out of the country to which I was accredited'.[66] They duly spoke off the record (at Brooke's request, claimed Gray) on 9 January 1944 when Gray visited American generals.[67] Gray immediately wrote to Roosevelt asserting that Brooke was 'anxious over this partition question, and what it may do in America, as am I'.[68] Brooke 'asked me' if visiting America was advisable – Brooke's October account infers that it was Gray's idea – but they wanted Roosevelt's endorsement before approaching British officials who had the final say-so on whether Brooke could go. If granted, Gray emphasized, Brooke would avoid partition and stress the great relationship between US forces and civilians, but 'if he were attacked he is prepared to defend religious tolerance and refute the charges of persecution alleged by Éire Catholic leaders'. 'Brooke is first class', he asserted, 'very sensible and would go down well on the Hill'.[69] Adding an element of amateurish espionage, Gray asked Roosevelt to send him a coded telegram with the message 'Your friend would be welcome' if he approved of this scheme.[70] What appears to be Gray's plan was, for the Roosevelt's eyes, reformulated (somewhat misleadingly) as a request from Brooke, to be used by Gray to legitimize his strategy of pressurizing de Valera and undermining the 'hyphen-Americans' who so exercised him.

Gray suggested that the mooted trip begin in Ottawa, before moving to Washington, where Brooke could express his appreciation of the American forces. To create a better understanding between Northern Ireland and America, and explain away anti-Catholic discrimination, Brooke could stress that Stormont 'rests on the tradition of Magna Charta and the same bill of rights that is incorporated into the American Constitution'. He also recommended that Sir Douglas Savory accompany Brooke as an expert in history who could repel attacks from Irish-American groups.[71] It seems unlikely that even the most stalwart unionist would have connected either the Magna Charta or the safeguards enshrined in the Bill of Rights to their own government, but Gray was at least cognizant of the very obvious questions Brooke would be asked.[72]

The unionist government had refrained from officially sanctioned bigotry so far in the war, conscious of the many Catholic American servicemen and an Irish-American bloc poised to exploit any whiff of sectarianism. In a single instant the cultivation of a positive image for American consumption threatened to unravel as a minister reverted to type. At Stormont in February 1944, T. J. Campbell, the only non-absentionist nationalist MP, mentioned Americans celebrating Mass several times in an Orange Hall in Portrush at Christmas which, he observed, was not something 'contemplated by the founders' – in other words, the Orange Order. William Lowry, the Minister for Home Affairs (and seen as a future party leader), immediately quipped, in what Norton aptly describes as a 'preposterously callous interjection', that 'preparations are being made for its fumigation'.[73] This crass attempt at humour immediately attracted widespread condemnation in Ireland and beyond, while at Stormont, anti-partitionist Labour member Jack Beattie demanded Lowry's censure.[74] Quincy Roberts, however, played down the incident telling the State Department that 'one of the opposition speakers attempted to build up a facetious interjection ... into an insult to the Catholics and particularly to Catholics in the armed forces of the United States'.[75] The Bishop of Derry and Vicar Delegate of the US forces, Neil Farren, a senior Catholic cleric who ministered to the Americans without publicly questioning their right to be in Northern Ireland, however, called it a 'gross insult' and demanded an apology.[76]

Lowry unconvincingly claimed ignorance about what Campbell's remark alluded to but soon apologized to Farren: 'speaking with all the reverence for a Faith I do not hold ... I assure your Lordship that no insult was intended by me to the American Catholic chaplains in the exercise of their sacred functions or to those present'.[77] The apology, such as it was, was directed towards American chaplains rather than Catholics more generally; nonetheless, Farren's reply demonstrated admirably good grace: 'I gladly accept the explanation of an unpleasant incident which, I hope, will be forgotten'.[78] When Campbell raised the matter again in Stormont, Lowry claimed he had a 'reputation for respecting other people's religious beliefs for over fifty years', which he feared losing on 'a matter that to me is the most sacred in the eyes of millions of people and secondly that the people most nearly concerned were members of the that gallant Allied nation that has come to our help'.[79] Penitence notwithstanding, it was, as Ollerenshaw argues, an 'ineffective exercise in damage limitation', and such incidents provided manna for Stormont's critics.[80] Lowry, of course, should have known better and had even warned the cabinet against such behaviour. As discussed in Chapter 5, when Archbishop Francis Spellman visited American forces in 1943, Lowry told colleagues not to allow him to portray them as 'a pack of benighted bigots'.[81] Brooke, whose anti-Catholic comments in the 1930s have largely defined his reputation, gave Lowry the benefit of the doubt, calling the remark 'facetious' and claiming that his colleague did not know what Campbell was talking about but had 'written to the Bishop apologizing for a remark which he would not have made had he known what it really meant'.[82] Brooke's explanation, even within the private confines of his diary, was unconvincing and unaware to say the least.

The comments were not widely reported in the States, but they predictably reached Irish-America. A Boston group called the Central Council of Irish County Clubs demanded two senior Massachusetts Democrats, Senator David I. Walsh and House Majority Leader John W. McCormack, 'fully explore this incident and protect our soldiers from repetition of similar incidents ... [which] illustrated the mentality which dominates the Northern Ireland junta'.[83] The council, with earnest overstatement, declared that 'Northern Ireland is one of the problems that must be faced by the world seeking permanent peace' and asserted that 'its existence violates the freedoms for which America is fighting'. In fact, 'world peace is endangered by the narrow blind bigotry' of people such as Lowry.[84] While the group's partisanship grossly exaggerated Northern Ireland's importance for dramatic effect, Lowry nevertheless seemingly provided unimpeachable proof of Stormont's endemic bigotry. Elsewhere, in non-Irish-American circles, Edward P. Morgan, columnist with the *Chicago Daily News*, linked Lowry to the recent banning of the anti-partition pamphlet *Orange Terror*, Brooke's historic bigotry, and 'an endless story of Catholic and Protestant rivalry'.[85] 'Regardless of the merits' of attacks on Stormont, he argued that 'such things provide ammunition for anti-British elements', but, despite damaging their cause, 'the Ulster government itself is less interested in being discreet than venting its venom'.[86] Morgan rightly wondered why unionists lacked the sense to act in their own best interests rather than resorting to sectarian point-scoring, especially when this played so badly in America.

The incident, then, was a gift for Irish-American propagandists, and if the reaction was foreseeable, it was not easily dismissed. Lowry's flippancy threatened Gray's strategy of undermining Éire and neutering Irish-America and could torpedo Brooke's American mission, so he attempted to minimize the harm done. This included informing Washington that Lowry had made a 'full disavowal and a very satisfactory apology' and writing to Farren to thank him for 'generously accept[ing] the apology in the spirit in which it was offered'.[87] He also reassured Irish-American contacts, telling Spellman that the matter was resolved and informing the USO's Frank Matthews of Farren's 'great wisdom, generosity and success. What might have had serious repercussions in American politics ended peacefully thanks to him'.[88] Gray clearly hoped that he could portray the remarks as anomalous.

Stormont still faced negative consequences. In his earlier letter to Roosevelt, Gray stated that Brooke would not approach the British about the visit until the president had approved it.[89] Brooke, acknowledging his comparatively lowly position within the chain of command, shared his reservations with British officials, who were broadly in favour provided an explicit invitation came from Roosevelt. The labyrinthine process of securing approval began when he asked Home Secretary Herbert Morrison's advice, explaining that the trip was 'chiefly with the purpose of telling them about their troops', but 'Ulster's position' might arise in private conversation.[90] Morrison promised to discuss it with colleagues and passed the request onto the Foreign Office via his permanent undersecretary Sir Alexander Maxwell. Maxwell stressed to his Foreign Office counterpart Sir Alexander Cadogan that the idea was Gray's and that Brooke refused to commit until London approved. Brooke, Maxwell reported, recognized 'that he should refrain from making any public utterances of a controversial character on the Irish question' and would restrict his speeches to discussing the US forces in Northern Ireland. Sir Eric Machtig and Lord Cranborne in the Dominions Office believed the visit 'might do some good' and 'there are no objections which outweigh the advantages of a visit, if President Roosevelt wishes to send an invitation'. Eden agreed, but Lord Halifax, the UK ambassador in Washington, had to approve before Churchill would have the final say.[91]

In lieu of any response from the president, in February Gray contacted Harry Hopkins, Roosevelt's key foreign policy advisor and informal conduit to the British, to see if the president was amenable, noting, however, the changed circumstances created by Lowry.[92] 'I have been warning Brooke against just such incidents', he complained, 'and I think they will be more careful not to walk into traps set by the boys down there [in Éire]'.[93] Lowry had hardly walked into a trap, but Gray's paranoia about and hostility towards Éire and nationalism was such that this incident could be attributed to these seemingly pernicious forces, rather than the instinctive bigotry of a Stormont minister. The State Department thought the trip was a bad idea, advising Roosevelt there was 'no advantage to be gained . . . and it might cause embarrassment'.[94] Gray tempered the tone of the rejection, telling Brooke it was 'very friendly but the suggestion was that this was not a good time for such a visit which in the light of developments since the inquiry was made I can well understand', which presumably referred to either the American Note or Lowry, or a combination of the two.[95]

Brooke did not entirely abandon the idea and discussed it with Morrison's successor Chuter Ede in October 1945, with a view to visiting in the spring of 1946.[96] Ede was initially supportive, provided it was unofficial and no invitation solicited from the US government, yet the 'risk of provoking anti-Partition agitation' remained reason for caution. That said, Ede would not object if Halifax approved.[97] In December, however, Ede strongly advised Brooke against the trip. Ede had consulted Halifax and the Foreign Secretary, Ernest Bevin, and both, while reluctant to limit 'your freedom of action', believed that 'such a visit would involve of re-opening the Irish question in the United States again, at a time when we are dealing with the Americans on so many vexed questions'.[98] Ede conceded that Éire's neutrality had quietened Irish nationalism and led to ill-will against the country in the States, but Bevin feared that Brooke would 'be welcomed by some Irish-American politicians and professional agitators as an opportunity to renew anti-British agitation and to organise demonstrations'.[99] While these actions might not be especially widespread or reflect American public opinion more generally they risked being 'most embarrassing to you and prejudice the objects of your visit' and have 'unfortunate repercussions' on Anglo-American relations. Ede concluded: '[i]n all circumstances I am afraid that the disadvantages of the projected visit would outweigh the advantages'.[100]

Brooke persisted, briefly approaching the Dominions Office in mid-1946, but the analysis, stressing its disadvantages, remained unchanged; Stormont also asked Gray, the idea's originator, for his counsel but he too now 'advised strongly against' such a venture.[101] British officials in London and Washington were sufficiently concerned about agitation from the Irish-American lobby and Éire after the war that they discussed methods of countering this, including a fact-sheet to refute anticipated accusations about Northern Ireland.[102] The embassy in Washington worried especially, but Dominions Office officials were privately irritated at its 'supine and unenterprising attitude ... on any matter relating to Irish affairs', suggesting some wanted a more robust line.[103] The strategists appear to have sought no input from Stormont. The injection of realpolitik by Ede and others reflected the continued fear of Irish-America and its ability to damage the nascent, although somewhat shaky, post-war Anglo-American special relationship. Brooke, and Northern Ireland and partition, were to be kept out of sight to avoid undermining Britain's key political and strategic partnership.

Gray's motivation was patently hostility to de Valera rather than support for Stormont, and it was clearly part of his preparations for the 'American Note'. He nevertheless attempted to manufacture a rare, if fraught, opportunity for unionism to make its case in America, although as a tool of American (and specifically his own) foreign policy.[104] Stormont was to be a pawn in this gambit, but both the British and Americans recognized the potential for the trip to backfire. Lowry's indiscretion, therefore, might have spared Stormont an uncomfortable transatlantic spotlight. Brooke could have ended up a stooge in Gray's scheme, as wheeling him out in Washington amid the American Note crisis would have provided de Valera and Irish-America a convenient distraction and the means for a counter-attack by making the dispute about partition. It would be 1950, with Anglo-American relations solidified, before Brooke eventually went, albeit amid a renewed anti-partition campaign from Éire, now a republic. It attracted some protests, and direct questions about the 'fumigation' incident, but these were not nearly as vehement or widespread as anticipated, indicating that Irish-America was perhaps much less influential than all parties suspected.[105]

'The most brilliant spectacle': Landing anniversary column

Stormont wanted to celebrate the landing's first anniversary, and Andrews began by issuing a statement to General Collins at the start of January 1943, noting Northern Ireland's pride at welcoming and hosting his troops and hoping that this was a portent of future friendship.[106] Stormont worked with Crawford McCullagh on the first physical commemoration, a memorial column, featuring the badges of the US Army, Navy and Marines, and a section of Belfast's coat of arms.[107] As Dufferin Quay, the site of the landing, proved impractical, the column was unveiled instead and with great fanfare outside Belfast City Hall on the anniversary.[108] The ceremony, consisting of a military parade, speeches and Abercorn dedicating the column, was broadcast by the BBC, and followed by lunch at the City Hall attended by local dignitaries, representatives from London and the American armed services. It strove to be inclusive and non-sectarian, with invitations to the editor of the *Irish News*, Cardinal MacRory and Bishop Mageean, all prominent nationalist and Catholic figures, but none accepted.[109] As Buhrman remarked, the unionist papers 'carried detailed reports', while the nationalist papers 'ignored it completely'.[110] Remembering the Americans was, then, to be a unionist pursuit.

Brooke believed that it had had the desired effect: 'it was very impressive and I think pleased the Americans'.[111] The *Washington Evening Star* was certainly impressed, lauding 'one of the most brilliant spectacles Britain has seen since the war began'.[112] Initially temporary, Andrews and McCullagh quickly agreed on the memorial becoming a permanent fixture at the City Hall.[113] The *Telegraph* planned to gift Roosevelt a small replica of the stone, something Andrews had also considered but deferred to the *Telegraph*, and this was presented to Buhrman by William Baird of the paper in May (Figure 12.1).[114]

Post-war attempts to memorialize the Americans included maintaining the US military cemetery at Lisnabreeny, a war memorial building, an official wartime history and even repurposing the Armagh Observatory as a 'mecca' for American

Figure 12.1 Landing anniversary, 'The Duke of Abercorn, Governor of Northern Ireland[,] stands at attention alongside the monument, just unveiled, that was dedicated to the landing of the first Amer. troops on foreign soil. Belfast City Hall, Belfast, Ireland'. NARA. Image courtesy of Clive Moore.

astronomers.[115] Stormont offered to maintain the Lisnabreeny cemetery in East Belfast in perpetuity, however, American policy for those who had died in the UK was to bury them in a single cemetery in Cambridge or, if their families preferred, to repatriate them to the United States.[116] The entrepreneurial head of the Armagh Observatory, Eric M. Lindsay, tried to convince Stormont to fund a planetarium as a way of solidifying Ulster-American relations by making 'Armagh the Mecca for all Americans visiting the British Isles'.[117] Funding was not forthcoming, but the planetarium proved a rare instance of cross-border cooperation when it eventually opened in 1968.[118]

A war memorial building emphasizing the American presence was periodically discussed throughout the 1940s, both within the cabinet and among Brooke, Gray and Winant.[119] The US government, however, could not finance or approve foreign memorials; moreover, Congressional sanction was required and Brooke informed the cabinet that he 'was advised that political influences might be brought into motion against the project' – in other words, the omnipresent spectre of the Irish-American lobby.[120] Stormont was again torn between promoting Northern Ireland's wartime contribution to America and drawing its attention to discrimination against Catholics, ultimately concluding that it was not worth the aggravation. The cabinet agreed, nonetheless, to create an American war memorial within the eventual building.[121] It was finally opened to great fanfare in October 1963 on the site of the Queen Anne Hotel, destroyed in the Blitz.[122] Although lacking US support, it contained something of America, featuring Cliffdale marble from Missouri, while its 'Hall of Friendship' had two copper friezes, one depicting the Yanks and the other Northern Ireland during the war.[123]

Stormont had its eye on posterity as early as 1940, when it instructed each department to maintain records of its wartime role. Andrews was conscious that London was already doing this and wanted to ensure that Northern Ireland's voice was heard and 'to prevent the possibility that [its] effort and sacrifices ... should hereafter be discredited or belittled'.[124] Northern Ireland's official wartime history, written by John M. Blake a historian at Queen's University, Belfast, did not appear until 1956.[125] This rather diminished its potential propaganda value and, while painstakingly researched, was not without criticism. The press and critics focused upon German invasion plans and Stormont's poor handling of Belfast's defences prior to the Blitz. The *Times Literary Supplement* questioned the book's necessity, which Blake saw as insulting to Northern Ireland's sacrifices and contribution.[126] Blake found the Americans particularly interesting and meticulously detailed their role, emphasizing their close relationship with the government and people. Blake did not, however, engage critically with the more negative aspects of their presence and reflected the celebratory (and unionist) narrative fostered by Stormont.[127]

'A bridgehead for the American forces': Saying farewell

In June 1944, marking the second anniversary of Chichester Street Red Cross Club's opening, Marcia Mackie, its director, expressed gratitude for the welcome extended to the Americans. G. H. Chater, a senior Red Cross executive, praised Mackie's contribution and those of Abercorn, civilian volunteers and officials, which had allowed Americans to befriend the people of Northern Ireland.[128] The following August, with most Americans long gone and Japan on the cusp of surrender, Chichester Street allowed Northern Ireland and the Americans to bid each other farewell with the formal return of the keys of Langford Lodge to the RAF and the club's closure to mark the official end of the American presence.[129] Brooke used the occasion to recount the welcome given to the Americans, while the American military in turn thanked the people for their hospitality. These speeches, the *Telegraph* enthused, 'so sincere in their expression' of gratitude, are the final instalment in a long list of happy memories'.[130] Alert to the public relations potential, Stormont's Cabinet Publicity Committee noted extensive local newspaper coverage and sent these reports to America and Britain, as it 'reemphasised the unique part played by Northern Ireland in the war effort, particularly in connection with the use of the area as a bridgehead for the American forces'. There was, it believed, 'abundant evidence' that Ulster's contribution in this respect, in contradistinction to Éire's neutrality, is fully realised by public opinion, both in Great Britain and the United States'.[131]

The ceremony at the Belfast Red Cross Club in August 1945 represented a good send-off by Brooke and the government, a celebration of the previous four years and an appropriate closing of this chapter of Northern Ireland's history, but something altogether more special was to follow. In mid-August, indeed on the day Japan's surrender was announced, the *Telegraph* revealed that Eisenhower would visit, to be granted the freedom of Belfast and receive an honorary Doctor of Laws from Queen's University.[132] After landing at the Bishopscourt aerodrome in County Down, reporters immediately accentuated the local angle, and 'Ike' obliged. Alanbrooke was 'one of my best friends. In fact, Northern Ireland has produced three of the great soldiers of this war [Generals Alanbrooke, Bernard Montgomery and Harold Alexander]. They are all good friends of mine, and I have been very lucky that I have had their assistance'.[133] He praised 'North Ireland' saying that it had 'made a whole of a lot of friends', and '[a]ll our boys are very appreciative of the hospitality they received here and of the good-humoured way in which North Ireland people have accepted [them]', sentiments he repeated in a BBC radio broadcast.[134]

Thousands turned out in Belfast to welcome him, with children from state schools given the day off and office and shop-workers taking time out to glimpse the general, greeting him with an improvised ticker-tape parade on Royal Avenue.[135] His first stop was Queen's University, accepting his honorary degree to a cheering standing ovation. His speech mostly emphasized the international cooperation required for victory and his hopes for a better world and made no direct reference to Northern Ireland. As an aside, its content predicted his later concerns as president. He struck a circumspect tone, warning that victory 'was too near a thing. It was a risk we dare not run again'. Anticipating his later desire for a 'peaceful atom' and the warning, in his farewell address as president in 1961, about the 'military industrial complex', he cautioned that the next war would be more devastating than the last. 'The mechanical power of destruction has now become so fearfully devastating that', he declared, 'we must see that a similar menace does not rise again. We must now enlist the same energy and singleness of purpose in developing the institutions of peace which in the time of our necessity we devoted to the prosecution of war'. Moreover, he warned against squandering peace because 'men of narrow vision appeal to prejudice and peace-loving men are tempted to temporise', and it was universities' duty to resist this.[136] Moving on to the City Hall, his speech there was conciliatory towards the vanquished enemy, hoping that Germany could build free institutions.[137] His tone was celebratory; yet it was not triumphalist but rather stressed that victory was not an end in itself.

Eisenhower was presented with a 'handsome silver casket' containing a certificate making him 'an Honorary Burgess of the City of Belfast'. This incorporated a picture of the memorial column, flanked by the US and British flags on the left and a picture of the Statue of Liberty on the right with the dedication: 'in recognition of his brilliant leadership as Supreme Commander of Allied Expeditionary Forces in Europe'.[138] McCullagh, paraphrased by the *Telegraph*, declared Belfast's pride as the first British city to host the Americans and at that moment an unforgettable 'link of friendship with the Ulster people was forged'.[139] The *Irish News*, its coverage altogether briefer, reported thousands giving the general a 'tumultuous reception', almost mobbing him as he alighted from his car for a special performance of the play *Lady from Edinburgh* at the Grand Opera House.[140] The *Whig* illustrated Eisenhower's humanity, publishing a letter he wrote to a Belfastman, Mr R. A. Cockcroft, days before D-Day granting leave to his son, then serving in England. Cockcroft junior immigrated to America in 1928 and the pair had not seen each other since. Eisenhower pulled some strings, and a month later Sergeant Robert A. Cockcroft arrived in Belfast on leave. Cockcroft senior was astonished that amid the preparations for the greatest seaborne invasion in history, Eisenhower found the time to help his son (Figure 12.2).[141]

The unionist press revelled in Eisenhower's presence, with the *Telegraph* going especially overboard dedicating almost the entirety of its 24 August edition to every imaginable detail of the visit, alongside gushing tributes to the general. It called him a 'maker and hater of war' and remarked that on his visit just before D-Day he had exuded a 'consuming purpose, pursued with a quiet mind, a great courage and a persistent patience'. There were, it noted, few accolades to add to the multitude already bestowed upon him, but because of Ulster's 'distinctive contribution to the new Republic of the West' and 'those exciting days of early 1942', there was good reason for him to accept Northern Ireland's appreciation. Eisenhower, it went on, 'has none of the conquering hero about him. The free peoples thrust their fate upon his shoulders and he made war magnificently in a good cause, but at heart he hates war more than anything else in the world'.[142]

Appearing on the balcony at Stormont, before garden party attended by some 3,000 people (making it 'one of the largest ever held in Belfast'), Eisenhower paid his hosts fulsome tribute: '[w]ithout Northern Ireland I do not see how the American Forces could have been concentrated to begin the invasion of Europe. . . . [I]f Ulster had not been a definite co-operative part of the British Empire, and had not been available for our use, I don't see how the build-up could have been carried out in England'.[143] This was, of course, a far cry from his initial objections to sending troops.[144] He had received many honours, 'but never have I been more impressed with the sincerity and friendliness exhibited toward me than in Belfast'. He again gave thanks for '[t]he sojourn of our Forces [which] will remain a cherished memory in the hearts of many Americans. You

Figure 12.2 General Eisenhower reviewing military personnel in front of Belfast City Hall, 24 August 1945. PRONI. Image courtesy of Clive Moore.

received us into your community and into your homes with a generosity which was evident and sincere. You put us at our ease. You gave us your friendship. For this, we are deeply appreciative.'[145] Brooke, in turn, lauded Eisenhower.[146]

In his report to the State Department, William F. Ayer, deputizing for Roberts at the consulate, wrote that never in its history had Belfast given 'greater acclaim to a citizen of another country', remarking how 'unmistakably genuine was the sincerity and warmth' of the large crowds which greeted the general. Indeed, the welcome exceeded that for the King and Queen's recent visit, as among those who 'waited patiently for a fleeting glimpse of the Supreme Allied Commander, there was a hitherto unseen enthusiasm and spontaneity'.[147] Stormont hoped this reception would play well in the States, and wanted the MOI to promote it in the American press.[148] The Eisenhower's visit was America's 'thank you' to Northern Ireland, and it was a welcome and deserved recognition of its wartime role, yet it also acted as a subconscious distraction from the arbitrary ending of Lend-Lease by Roosevelt's successor Harry S. Truman a few days before.[149] Eisenhower's visit lasted barely a day, and it is difficult to argue with Carroll's conclusion that it 'was a gracious and symbolic climax to the story of United States forces in Northern Ireland'. The mood reflected the final end of the conflict, Eisenhower's celebrity status and Northern Ireland's pride in both hosting the Americans and contributing to victory.

Conclusion

'Without Northern Ireland'

When President Bill Clinton visited Northern Ireland in November 1995, one of his tasks was to rededicate the memorial column at Belfast City Hall. The fiftieth anniversary had been marked in 1992, with Henke again the guest of honour, but memories of the Americans, like interest in the column, had begun to fade. The tens of thousands who greeted the president may have wondered why this was significant, but it was a pertinent reminder of a direct and recent connection between Northern Ireland and the 'great republic of the West'. It was also a way of symbolizing America's role as an honest broker in the tentative peace process, at a time when Americans' informal but highly partisan involvement in Northern Ireland made unionists instinctively suspicious of US motivations. Clinton's visit did ultimately herald American stewardship of a peace process which would bring the troubles to an end with the Good Friday Agreement of 1998 and represented another chapter in a historic connection between America and Ulster dating back almost 300 years.

Regardless of the reasons for, or consequences of, selecting Northern Ireland as the first host of American forces, it caused huge logistical problems which would have tested any country and were magnified in a divided society. The central figure in handling all of this was Sir Basil Brooke, ably aided by Sir Robert Gransden and John MacDermott, among many others, representing a rare moment of positivity in his career and arguably its highlight. Brooke's reputation is synonymous with his anti-Catholic bigotry as he forged a political career in the 1930s, but without condoning this, he must be recognized as an excellent organizer, a talent he put to good use to ensure that the Americans' sojourn was as pleasant for them and as undisruptive for the population as possible. Stormont's, and specifically Brooke's, efforts to look after the Americans and minimize the negative aspects of their presence proved largely successful. The numerous hospitality committees Brooke created and the various facilities laid on for the Americans were vital, and if they did not eliminate bad behaviour, they certainly ameliorated the Yanks' worst excesses. These endeavours were aided by a pliant unionist press in Belfast, which, at the behest of Stormont and American and British military officials, celebrated the Americans uncritically.

The American presence in the UK is often referred to as a 'friendly invasion', and for the most part, it was. Some uneasy accommodations and concessions had to be made to facilitate this in the service of the transatlantic alliance and to reflect the UK's status as the junior partner. A prime example of the political problems faced by Stormont was the Visiting Forces Act of 1942, an outwardly reasonable wartime measure ceding of legal jurisdiction over American servicemen. The imposition of US justice meant accepting its negative aspects, particularly discrimination against African Americans, and rendering Stormont a bystander as it took its course. Stormont, nevertheless, had some latitude in managing these often delicate matters, and generally it did so effectively. Where race and American racism are concerned, however, Stormont's policy, like London's, fluctuated between refusing to endorse or enforce segregation and informally facilitating it. At times Stormont, and Brooke, attempted to improve the situation for African American troops, but just as often they found it politically prudent not to interfere.

Brooke was forward-thinking in his (thwarted) desire to take Northern Ireland's case to the States, to capitalize on wartime relationships by tentatively planning a propaganda campaign highlighting its part in the war and hosting the Americans. Stormont's keenness to court the Americans was matched by wariness about provoking Irish-America, resulting in a cautious and defensive approach, reflecting its basic insecurities in simultaneously wanting to celebrate and commemorate the Americans without drawing too much unwanted attention to its treatment of the Catholic minority. Stormont was largely beholden to London but did try to chart its own independent course even if this was largely circumscribed by opposition from London, disinterest in the States and the lack of a politically active Ulster-American diaspora. Shaky post-war Anglo-American relations, demonstrated by the arbitrary ending of Lend-Lease almost as soon as Japan surrendered, meant that London, paralyzed by its fear of provoking the Irish-American lobby, stymied any promotion of Northern Ireland lest it jeopardized the Anglo-American alliance. The 'special relationship', such as it was, overlooked Northern Ireland. The end of the war, despite Northern Ireland's role in it and hospitality towards the Americans, proved an inopportune moment to make its case in America.

The arrival of the US forces necessitated a hasty and complete (if ephemeral) reconfiguration of traditional unionist and nationalist attitudes towards America rendered at least temporarily obsolete by events. Stormont and the unionist press highlighted Ulster's role in American history and its contemporary place in the UK while projecting a generalized sense of Britishness by appealing to a shared 'English-speaking' heritage encapsulated in the Anglo-American alliance. To nationalists, on both sides of the border, the Americans had recognized and legitimized partition by coming to that part of Ireland still governed by Britain and without so much as a courtesy call to Éire's government and duly protested. Nationalist leaders proved incapable of straying from their orthodoxy that everything, including the war, was subservient to the fact of partition, including aiding America in its own hour of need. By ignoring the Americans, nationalism permitted the history of their stay in Northern Ireland to become an essentially unionist narrative.

Nationalism in Northern Ireland had a difficult war, compounded by the American presence. Partition was one issue the various discordant strands of nationalism in Ireland could coalesce around, but it created a constricted, insular and self-righteous world view rooted in hostility towards the British and unionists. This downplayed international crises, crises which threatened democracy, European Catholicism and, in the event of a German invasion, Éire's independence. This ambivalence about the international situation fostered the sense, epitomized by Cardinal Joseph MacRory, that the war was someone else's (and, at times, everyone else's) problem. The histrionic reaction to the American arrival came across as parochial, and the idea that nationalist oppression was equal to any suffered in Europe became increasingly facile as the war wore on and the scale of Nazi atrocities revealed. Nationalism's attitude also implicitly denigrated the ideals America fought for and its sacrifices in pursuit of them. After the initial flurry of condemnation, nationalists stayed largely silent, leaving unionist celebration of historic links largely unchallenged. Sensibly waiting until the war's end before renewing anti-partition agitation suggested that they had made the same calculations as unionists, that the war and the Americans had secured partition for the foreseeable future. The main consequence of the war for nationalists in Northern Ireland was a further undermining of their aspirations. They were the victims primarily of Stormont but also to a lesser degree of Dublin, as the war consolidated the status quo in Northern Ireland, which suited unionists, and Éire's independence, which suited de Valera.

The conflict had barely concluded when nationalists and Irish-Americans began moulding a narrative belittling Northern Ireland's wartime role, exaggerating that of Éire (including outlandish claims of the numbers from Éire who served with British forces) and renewing grievances about partition. Nationalists had the resources of the diaspora in the United States to pressurize the US government, or at least create the impression that they could do this, and hoped, as de Valera predicted, the nascent special relationship would fall apart. De Valera's analysis about Anglo-American frictions proved prescient, if exaggerated and momentary, but beyond Irish-America few in the United States had any interest in what seemed petty insularity as the post-war order took shape. The chimera of the Irish-American lobby's power nevertheless eliminated the meagre prospect of the unionist narrative being heard and was sufficient to douse whatever limited enthusiasm the British could muster to emphasize Northern Ireland's war effort. Yet, although the anti-partition campaign was more strident, it was arguably ineffective in the post-war context. In the end, the fear of emboldening anti-partitionists meant that even Brooke thought better of an American campaign and mothballed it until 1950.

Dublin continued to rhetorically support nationalists north of the border, but only as far as Éire's domestic politics and the broadcasting the injustice of partition required. While de Valera's neutrality might have been subliminally pro-Allied, this did not prevent continued Anglophobia, and this was certainly not designed to wrong-foot the Germans, but, rather, re-advertised his default positions on partition and Anglo-Irish relations. Éire's attitude towards partition hardened, but this proved counterproductive, not least because the issue was less relevant in the UK (and US) than at any time since 1921. Éire justifiably asserted its independence and its right as a sovereign nation to chart its own course, but at the cost of its international reputation and the goal of ending partition. De Valera's focus was very much on maintaining this independence, and his own power, and the cost was worth it. Neutrality was the best, and only, course for Éire, and keeping his country out of the war might in retrospect be de Valera's greatest achievement. That said, the fact, and necessity, of neutrality, and private cooperation with the Allies as the war progressed, was undermined by de

Valera's inability to side even rhetorically with the Allies when their differences with the Nazis were so stark. His desire to treat the belligerents equally in public, and relentless complaints about partition and reminders that Britain was Ireland's traditional enemy, may have been a matter of (misplaced) principle, but it was diplomatically inept and simply antagonized the Americans (and famously, Churchill). The nature of Éire's neutrality meant eliminating the chance, however remote, of American intervention to end partition; Northern Ireland had aided the Americans, and Éire had pointedly refused to.

The upheaval the Americans brought did not encourage far-reaching social change, as they were accepted partially as an expedient necessary to win the war, after which life would return to normal. The liberalization of some women's attitudes towards sex (if not societal attitudes towards female sexuality) associated with the Americans was part of a growing female quest for independence in a patriarchal, conservative and religious society. The Americans, therefore, were part of a transitional, but crucially not transformative, process for Northern Ireland's women, ongoing if slow and moderately accelerated by the war. The Americans, of course, imported their racism, and if African Americans' treatment by their white comrades differed little from the Jim Crow South, then their experiences with local people were broadly, if not universally, positive. A white population recognizing their humanity hinted, however, at the changes to come in the States.

The Americans, from the lowliest private to the loftiest general, made the best of their posting. For ordinary soldiers, an often hectic training regime was interspersed with too much money and too much spare time and too little to do with either, leading to drinking, brawling and casual criminality. The military endeavoured to turn bases into 'little Americas' and provided many comforts to ease the strain of being so far from home in wartime. Wholesome distractions were provided, and most Americans recalled their posting affectionately. The Americans were, as the saying went, 'overpaid, oversexed and over here', but the serious social problems anticipated in 1942 were well managed, if never fully controlled, and, though disruptive, there was no sense, officially at least, that the Yanks outstayed their welcome.

American generals had the space and time to train their men and quickly dispatch them to frontlines, pulling off numerous logistical miracles, including emptying Northern Ireland of nearly 100,000 men in a matter of weeks around D-Day. Northern Ireland was a valuable, if not perfect, training ground, but it was out of harm's way, and the Americans found an indulgent host in Stormont. Highly conscious of the problems their presence brought, the Americans wisely stayed out of politics, cognizant of local divisions and remaining aloof as far as they possibly could. The Americans did, however, provide a convenient catalyst for renewed IRA violence, but, despite threats to embroil GIs, amplified by the unionist press, almost nothing came of this. The Americans, wise to the danger, sensibly watched from the side-lines as the group's campaign flickered briefly; consequently, neither unionists nor nationalists could recruit them as allies or, in the IRA's case, adversaries.

Cautious and pessimistic by nature, Parker Buhrman, the State Department's representative in Belfast in 1942 and 1943, offered analysis which sometimes appears naïve, and his closeness to the unionist establishment is often obvious, but his outsider status provided some interesting insights into political life, the Americans and the war effort. In many ways, he was little different from his predecessors Ernest Ives and John Randolph, or his successor Quincy Roberts, but Americans arrived immediately after he had, and the threats of the IRA against them occurred within months. Even bearing in mind, therefore, that Belfast was a wartime posting, Buhrman had plenty of additional burdens. Roberts, by contrast, despite handling many more Americans, inherited much more stable political conditions, and his principal crisis was arranging transport for war brides wishing to join their husbands in the States, a task completed with admirable energy.

David Gray took an altogether more active approach as America's minister in Dublin. With the zeal of a lapsed believer confronted with an idol's feet of clay, Gray felt that America's best interests were served by plotting against and subverting his host. Gray's original mission, as he defined it, to end partition, was quickly undermined by real and imagined hypocrisies in Dublin, especially de Valera's nurturing of a grievance for his own narrow political ends rather than seeking a realistic solution to partition. Added to this was the danger, undoubtedly exaggerated but openly expressed by its advocates, that nationalists, in league with isolationist Irish-America, would use partition to disrupt American democracy, Roosevelt's Democratic Party and the Anglo-American alliance. Gray made it his mission to prevent this, contrasting Northern Ireland's wartime contribution with what he perceived as de Valera's duplicitous neutrality and trying to destroy Irish-American political influence in the United States. This made him a nuisance in Dublin, which in turn made him a rare, if not necessarily useful, American ally for unionism, but also someone who cultivated his grudges for the rest of his days.

Celebrating shared history during the war was encapsulated by the Ulster-America bond, sentimentalizing Ulster's past and emphasizing its apparently disproportionate and neglected influence on the development of the most powerful nation on earth. In this interpretation, the role of Ulster Protestants, mostly Presbyterian, in the settling of North America was pivotal in forging both a new country and a new kind of country, they would argue, in their image. This largely forgotten connection to the States was evoked the moment the Americans disembarked, with claims of a dozen or more presidents of Ulster descent, alongside various revolutionary-era luminaries, constantly utilized to make an earlier claim to American friendship than Catholic Ireland. Moreover, Ulster not only 'gave' America some of its greatest statesmen, Presbyterians also claimed co-authorship of the doctrine that underpinned the revolution and the fighting spirit – 'the last to quit' – which drove the British out. In addition, Ulster Presbyterians were irked by the perception that this role was now being dishonestly, and shamelessly, appropriated by Catholic Irish-America.

The Catholic Church faced political and cultural dilemmas; the American presence both endorsed partition and was a liberal challenge to the church's social teaching, especially regarding sexual morality, but also the evils of cinema and dancing. The church, personified by Cardinal Joseph MacRory, was blindsided by the international situation, officially resenting the Americans and seemingly ambivalent about the war's outcome. Slackening public morality also exercised Protestant churches, which, sharing concerns about sex, also objected to any loosening of Sabbath observance but otherwise welcomed the Americans. Ordinary people of whatever religion, however, generally embraced the Americans; they provided a morale-boosting break from a grim wartime routine and represented the moment, particularly for unionists, when the war finally seemed winnable.

The importance of Northern Ireland to the war effort could be overstated. Materially, it provided its share (manpower less so), however small in the grand scheme of things, but its main significance was geographical. It was clearly vital from the fall of France in 1940 until victory was claimed in the Battle of the Atlantic in 1943, but once the American forces largely disappeared with D-Day, so too did its strategic importance. It had, however, provided a crucial contribution to the eventual victory. Hopes for a post-war dividend were not forthcoming, however, as Northern Ireland's significance to the United States proved fleeting, unrequired by the tactical and political necessities of the Cold War.

Northern Ireland's inconvenient divisions were ignored by internally generated unionist propaganda depicting the state as loyal and homogeneous, doing its bit without complaint, and promoted regardless of the obvious paradoxes. Stormont tried to control how the war was remembered in anticipation of nationalist efforts to malign Northern Ireland's contribution. Where the Americans were concerned, this involved government and sometimes private efforts to memorialize the American presence. These endeavoured to foreground Ulster-American friendship and highlight the welcome given to the Americans, which both celebrated Northern Ireland in its own right and offered implicit and explicit contrasts to Éire's neutrality. Well-meaning, but essentially inward-looking and self-referential, these efforts went largely unnoticed in the States.

The American presence did nothing to lessen sectarianism or signal a new relationship with Éire; indeed, the gulf between the two Irelands was greater than ever and would continue to widen as unionists consolidated their rule and an increasingly belligerent Dublin took its grievances to the United States after the war. The failure of the 1940 offer to Éire fortified the union and made Northern Ireland indispensable, and along with hardships and experiences shared with the rest of the UK, from the Blitz to hosting the Americans, Northern Ireland became more 'British' than ever. The war was a boon for unionism, and the American dimension was important to this. London's willingness to barter Northern Ireland in 1940 was not forgotten, but paranoia about British intentions was assuaged by the guarantees of the post-war Labour government, not a natural ally for unionism, and a now bipartisan commitment to the union at Westminster.

With the union unassailable, Stormont became less insular in that it sought closer alignment with the rest of the UK and began to look beyond the narrow confines of Commonwealth and Empire, as it attempted to position itself as a vital part of the Western alliance against the new threat of the Soviet Union. Northern Ireland's sense of its 'Britishness' was certainly enhanced by the war, but it was still ill-defined, and the shared experience of Protestants and Catholics did not foreshadow a healing of sectarian divisions, which were generally muted during the war. Not even its desire to court the Americans led to any genuine self-examination by Stormont, and there was no attempt to use the war to create a sense of 'Northern Irishness' that could transcend sectarianism. Depicting nationalists as a potential fifth column and generally disloyal, Stormont, bolstered by its role in the Allied victory, saw no need to alter any of its discriminatory practices and use war as a way of bringing them into the body politic. The slim chance of reshaping the sectarian dynamics of life was lost; with the 1921 settlement copper-fastened, the unionist government felt little incentive to make the state more responsive to nationalist needs. The war, and the American presence, normalized Northern Ireland up to a point, and its experiences mirrored the rest of the UK, but it remained a place apart.

Sending American forces to Northern Ireland made sound military and political sense. In practical military terms, they guarded a potentially vulnerable land border, found time to train and released British troops for other warzones. In some respects, however, the psychological impact of the Americans was as important as the strategic. American troops arrived without the historical baggage of their British counterparts, even while their purpose, defending the border and invading Éire if required, was essentially the same. Unionists welcomed them as allies, potential war-winners and subconscious guarantors of the union; nationalists tolerated them politically (but accepted them generally) due to American-Irish links, underlying sympathy with the Allies and because they were not British. The political dimension was also tied up in Anglo-American, American-Irish, Anglo-Irish and cross-border relationships. It was an unambiguous American endorsement of partition, used by Roosevelt and Churchill to highlight Éire's alleged hypocrisy, pressurize de Valera and demonstrate that the Anglo-American alliance transcended any sentimental American attachment to the Emerald Isle. The publicity surrounding the American presence helped to integrate Northern Ireland within the British war effort and, therefore, within the shared wartime experience of the UK, enhancing unionists' sense of their Britishness, while emphasizing even greater divergence from Éire. The military and strategic problems eased by the Americans and the political needs they served reveal that, in retrospect, sending American troops to Northern Ireland was, in its own way, an act of genius by Roosevelt and Churchill.

Epilogue

'Gray's Great Illusion'

David Gray maintained contacts with Stormont and an interest in Ireland after his departure from Dublin in 1947. In 1957, at Brooke's request, he contributed the introduction to William A. Carson's *Ulster and the Irish Republic: A Brief Survey of Irish Republican Propaganda and an Exposure of Its Fallacies*.[1] This, as the subtitle makes abundantly clear, argued Northern Ireland's case, both historically and in the contemporary context of the Cold War. The book was written with the American market in mind; therefore, choosing Gray to write the introduction was obvious: as a high-profile critic of de Valera and Éire's neutrality his credentials were impeccable. Brooke assisted Gray, re-writing a section on the Cosgrave administration in the Irish Free State in the 1920s which he largely used. Brooke also asked for the omission of a reference to the 1940 deal to end partition, as it would 'give rise to grave misgivings and some anxiety here. I very much doubt the wisdom of mentioning them', and Gray obliged.[2] Gray was impressed with Carson's work, had no suggestions for improvement and 'I shall pilfer from it unconsciously in finishing my book'. Indeed, he had lost none of his capacity for overstatement, offering 'my heartfelt gratitude for having written the most needed book ever written about Ireland', hyperbolic praise at which Carson may have blushed.[3]

By Gray's acerbic standards, and possibly due to the moderating influence of Brooke, the resulting introduction to 'this objective historical outline' was comparatively tame. He offered a potted history of various pre-1921 partitions of Ireland, comparing the Irish to constantly warring Native American tribes and crediting England for uniting them. Beyond this dubiously simplistic interpretation of Irish history, he outlined the economic, political and security benefits (now as part of NATO) of the union, before revisiting his unaltered wartime bugbears about de Valera and Éire. Thus, de Valera thought Hitler would win the war and end partition, and when it became obvious that Germany would lose, he created 'the crime of partition' as a pretext to avoid aiding the Allies. Gray also made public his 1943 claim that de Valera wanted to swap Northern Ireland's Protestants for Irish 'exiles' in Britain.[4] The Republic of Ireland's Department of External Affairs felt sufficiently exercised to include a refutation of Gray's claims in its weekly press release, declaring that they said more about his character than the realities of the period.[5]

In 1942, Gray had written to Winant: '[i]f I had the ability, I might write an interesting book about the pathological mentality that is guiding the destiny of the Irish people'.[6] In retirement Gray penned the aforementioned book as a sprawling account of his time in Dublin and his opinion of the Irish revolution. This offers a fascinating and typically polemical postscript to his tenure, demonstrating the longevity of his grudges as much as it offers insight into wartime Ireland, but it does chart the evolution of his attitudes. Plenty of his wartime Stormont contacts helped out – for example, Carson, Savory and Henderson assisted with his research, fact-checking and sourcing statistics for him.[7] The first part of the work was largely a compendium of the many memoranda sent to Washington repurposed as a tirade against de Valera, while the second attacked Sinn Fein and the IRA and their roles in securing independence between 1919 and 1921. The book's many drafts had several titles, including *Behind the Green Curtain* and *The Emerald Curtain*, as Gray believed that de Valera had 'hung a green curtain' around Éire, hiding the realities of the war from its people, allowing them to hear only a de Valera–approved 'Irish truth'.[8] The 'Green Curtain' notion can also be interpreted in a couple of other ways. Firstly, Gray seems to be applying the concept of the Iron Curtain to the Irish border, with America's friends, and those who shared its values, on the northern side with its adversaries to the south. The titles could also be references to *The Wizard of Oz*, with de Valera playing the part of the wizard, peddling fantasies hidden behind his emerald green curtain, waiting to be exposed as a fraud. The final version was entitled *Sinn Fein: The Great Illusion* (perhaps another reference to the Wizard's trickery) and largely completed by the late 1950s, but the ever-obdurate Gray, now in his late eighties, was unable to find a publisher, partly because he refused to edit his vast manuscript.

Maffey (now Lord Rugby) saw the book in 1958 and was 'deeply impressed with your historical survey and your wonderful analysis of the Great Illusion. This has never been done before and will stir deep thought in many places'. He urged Gray to publish while he and de Valera were still alive.[9] Carson was also impressed, limiting his criticism to clarification and writing conventions, including, ironically, hyphenation, rather than content.[10] Stormont recognized its propaganda value as it kept its vital wartime role in the public eye and, more importantly, provided an opportunity to discredit Éire's neutrality, personified by de Valera. Stormont officials, therefore, gladly aided Gray's quest for a publisher.[11] Brian Faulkner, the Minister for Home Affairs and later Northern Ireland's last prime minister, liaised with Gray over the manuscript, while Savory, Maffey, Eric Montgomery (the Director of Information), and Brooke's secretary A. J. Kelly were all consulted about content, all amid great secrecy lest Stormont's involvement become known.[12] Savory was in regular contact with Gray and seems to have been the first to see it, passing it on to Carson and then Maffey.[13] Such was the incendiary nature of the introduction, however, that Savory 'had made up my mind not to let this copy out of my hands' but relented, lending it to Montgomery.[14] Kelly, who had not read any of it at this point, understood that Gray was writing at the late President Roosevelt's request and that sections on Éire would be 'strongly worded'.[15]

Gray was approached via John Cordner, a former president of the Ulster-Irish Society of New York, who was a near neighbour of Gray – now in retirement in Florida – and, as Faulkner noted, 'a private citizen who is only undertaking the task of contacting Mr Gray because he is a good Ulsterman and is anxious to help us'.[16] Cordner contacted Gray in September 1958 and found him receptive, and the pair met the following month.[17] He reported that Gray 'wants to be assured that his facts are unassailable'; but Cordner suggested to Faulkner that the arrangement gave

Stormont 'an effective measure of control' over the work. He elaborated: '[w]hile Mr Gray's views and opinions must be his own, it seems to me that you should be in a position to channel the facts to guide those opinions and views to a significant extent', thus raising the possibility that Stormont could further manipulate an already sympathetic work.[18] The book was aimed primarily at an American audience, undoubtedly warning about the 'hyphen-Americans' who so exasperated Gray, and the minister did not anticipate difficulty in finding a publisher in either the United States or Britain. Cordner was impressed with Gray, describing him as 'a loveable and congenial personality' whose 'mind is clear, alert and incisive'.[19] Kelly upon reading this, however, advised keeping editing to a minimum, as he put it, 'to preserve the identity of the author unchallenged'.[20] Kelly stressed secrecy, suggesting that he, Faulkner and Montgomery read the manuscript and then compare notes, and if unsatisfactory, it could be returned to Gray and no further action taken; Faulkner was agreeable.[21]

Montgomery was hugely enthusiastic about the introduction, telling Faulkner that if the rest of the manuscript was similar, it would be 'the biggest charge of dynamite that could possibly be exploded under Éire and the great thing is that it comes from a source independent of Northern Ireland and was something of a world standing'.[22] Everything should be done to ensure the book's publication once the remaining chapters had been seen, and they should secure Gray's permission to use the manuscript 'as we see fit' after his death. Montgomery acknowledged that it was a very personal attack on de Valera, the Catholic Church and Sinn Fein but felt that 'so long as a publisher is willing to accept it I do not see that that need matter very greatly to us. In fact, it might only lend interest to the book'. He recognized, however, the need for fact-checking.[23] Maffey, although he had only just received and not yet read the manuscript, was equally enthusiastic and urged Faulkner to 'get the Sputnik airborne as soon as possible' in light of Gray's age, health and 'his incurable habit of constantly re-writing and re-adjusting his script'. 'In short', he concluded, 'I want to see the thing in print!'[24] The end product, however, left much to be desired.

In contrast to his colleagues' enthusiasm, Kelly, seemingly the first person to actually read the whole manuscript, was utterly scathing. He told Faulkner that 'this bitter diatribe and personal animosity diminishes, if it does not destroy, the little merit it possesses'. 'It is a great misfortune', he continued, 'that what could have been a valuable contribution to the history of those days has become an exposition of rancour and pique the publication of which will do harm rather than good'.[25] Kelly reinforced his point in an accompanying note, recording his 'increasing disquiet and disappointment', warning that it was 'disjointed and unbalanced and probably open to challenge and satire'. Gray explained neither his remit in Dublin nor what instructions he had been given, 'instead we have something little better than a diatribe of a personal vendetta which is the measure of Mr Gray's own failure in his mission'. Kelly warned that publication would be detrimental to Northern Ireland's cause and that Gray had passed up the opportunity to offer 'a reasoned, accurate, dispassionate and incontrovertible story'.[26] Despite this damning assessment, Stormont officials, Kelly included, persevered in trying to publish the manuscript and went to great lengths to fact-check it.

Faulkner reported to the Cabinet Publicity Committee in early 1960 that '[t]he book came down strongly against the South and would undoubtedly make a strong impact, particularly in view of the fact that Mr Gray had been initially in opposition to the Ulster view and standpoint'. Yet he urged caution; as the book was 'highly controversial', it was vital that Stormont was not directly associated with it; any sense that the government was encouraging and promoting the book would, therefore, undermine its impact (and, echoing earlier correspondence, allowed it to be disowned).[27] Another cabinet member noted that Frederick Boland was likely to chair the United Nations in the autumn and publication should coincide with this to remind the world of Éire's dubious wartime record.[28] The manuscript did not arrive in time to pursue this but was apparently progressing well by mid-1960; amid concerns about Gray's health and 'his proclivity towards constant revision', Stormont was keen to publish it as soon as possible and in its current form if necessary.[29]

By late 1962, *Sinn Fein: The Great Illusion*, although completed, struggled to find a publisher, partly due to its excessive 300,000-word length. Montgomery created an abridged version of 70,000 words, 'at the same time striking out or revising some parts to make the text more favourable to Northern Ireland'. A London publisher was interested, but on the understanding that Stormont buy 1,000 copies costing 1,000 guineas (just over £1,000). Faulkner urged early publication, while Ivan Neill, the Minister of Education, believed that Gray 'owed it to many surviving individuals from those days to publish soon'. Brooke, still prime minister, agreed and emphasized that 'the public should be given the opportunity of reading an independent authoritative account of a crucial historical period'.[30] Faulkner outlined Gray's thesis, noting that 'he had been completely taken in' by de Valera and his early reports were 'anti-Ulster', but 'he now feels that he owes it to Ulster to try to amend the wrong impression they gave, by setting out the true situation in this book'.[31] Gray believed that Northern Ireland's loyalty saved Britain from defeat; according to Cordner, 'it is now crystal clear to him that Northern Ireland's firm determination to stay with Great Britain during the Second World War saved the British cause from utter defeat in 1941/42 and later provided the only marshalling area anywhere available for the building up of US forces'.[32] Gray, however, lived up to his reputation as a 'testy old gentleman', refusing to countenance publishing anything other than his unabridged manuscript, nor would he allow the release of quotations from it. He also stipulated that, upon his death, the full 300,000-word version was to be published.[33] Despite the efforts of Faulkner and others and the guarantee of 1,000 sales, Gray refused to compromise and, after his death aged ninety-seven in 1968, the manuscript languished in various archives.

Notes

Introduction

1. Derrick Gibson-Harries, *Life-Line to Freedom: Ulster in the Second World War* (Belfast: Ulster Society Publications Ltd., 1990).
2. For unionists using the war to enhance their British identity, previously (and subsequently) hampered by sectarianism, see James Loughlin, *Ulster Unionism and British National Identity Since 1885* (New York and London: Pinter, 1995).
3. For popular histories, see Mary Pat Kelly, *Home Away from Home: The Yanks in Ireland* (Belfast: Appletree Press, 1994) and Ronnie Hanna, *Pardon Me Boy: The Americans in Ulster, 1942-45, A Pictorial Record* (Belfast: Ulster Society, 1991). There are also some good websites recalling the Americans. See, for example, https://wartimeni.com/ and http://www.niwarmemorial.org.
4. John Bowman, *de Valera and the Ulster Question, 1917-1973* (Oxford and New York: Oxford University Press, 1989), 11. Alvin Jackson, *Ireland, 1798-1998: Politics and War* (Oxford: Blackwell 1999), 259.
5. Bowman, *Ulster Question*, 11. Italics in original.
6. For a brief account of the machinations which led to the Government of Ireland Act and the creation of Northern Ireland, see Michael Laffan, *The Partition of Ireland, 1911-1925* (Dundalk: Dundalgan Press, 1983), 61–71. For the sectarian riots and a resultant trade boycott of Belfast instigated by Sinn Fein, see Ronan Fanning, *Fatal Path: British Government and Irish Revolution, 1910-1922* (London: Faber and Faber, 2013), 76–7.

    For an excellent account of British governmental attitudes towards Ireland, and particularly the British political context of partition, the specific refusal to coerce unionist Ulster and negotiations with Sinn Fein, see Fanning, *Fatal Path*.
7. Craig is often misquoted as saying 'Protestant people' rather than 'Protestant state'. Craig prefaced these remarks with the assertion that 'I am the Prime Minister not of one section of the community, but of all, and that as far as I possibly could I was going to see that fair play was meted out to all classes and creeds without favour'. He continued: 'in the South they boasted of a Catholic State. They still boast of Southern Ireland being a Catholic State. All I boast is that we are a Protestant Parliament and Protestant State.' Alvin Jackson, *Home Rule: An Irish History, 1800-2000* (Oxford: Oxford University Press 2004), 229. He also asserted his credentials as an Orangeman.
8. Brian Barton, *Brookeborough: The Making of a Prime Minister* (Belfast: Queen's University, Institute of Irish Studies, 1988), 78. For similar statements, see ibid., 78–89.
9. That de Valera earlier declared 'I was a Catholic first' rarely attracts comment. *Irish Press*, 29 October 1931. Cited in Bowman, *Ulster Question*, 107. Brooke later justified his remarks as a response to kidnap threats against his son (more than ten years earlier). Barton, *Brookeborough*, 87. See also Jackson, *Home Rule*, 229–31. As Jackson

notes, both Craig and Brooke 'were personally more generous than these sentiments might suggest', but they never publicly recanted and the damage was 'incalculable'. Ibid., 231.

Chapter 1

Many of the ideas contained in this chapter appeared in the *Journal of Transatlantic Studies*, and I am grateful to its editor Alan Dobson for allowing me to reprise and incorporate them here. See Simon Topping, '"A hundred thousand welcomes"? unionism, nationalism, partition and the arrival of American forces in Northern Ireland in January 1942', *Journal of Transatlantic Studies*, vol. 16, no. 1 (January 2018), pp. 81–100.

1. Henke also returned for the fiftieth anniversary.
2. 'Government of Northern Ireland Press Release', 25 January 1967. CAB9CD/225/1; *BT*, 23 January 1967.
3. *BT*, 25 January 1967.
4. Ibid.
5. Ibid., 26 January 1967.
6. Prime Minister to President, 20 October 1941. Cited in Winston S. Churchill, *The Second World War, Book VI: The Grand Alliance: War Comes to America, June 23, 1941-January 17 1942* (Geneva: Cassell and Company Limited, 1950 (fifth edition, 1968)), 148. The original document is marked: 'for yourself alone'. Churchill to Roosevelt, 20 October 1941. FDR, Papers as President, Map Room File, 1939–1945. https://catalog.archives.gov/id/194990. NARA. Accessed 5 April 2021.
7. Churchill, *Grand Alliance*, 242.
8. Ibid., 664–5; and Forrest Pogue, *George C. Marshall: Ordeal and Hope, 1939-1942* (New York: Viking Press, 1965), 268. Northern Ireland's official war historian John W. Blake attributes it to Roosevelt. John W. Blake, *Northern Ireland in the Second World War* (Belfast: Her Majesty's Stationary Office, 1956), 252.
9. WM 8 (42) 2nd mtg., 23 December 1941. PRO CAB65/25. Cited in David Reynolds, *Rich Relations: The American Occupation of Britain, 1942-1945* (London: Phoenix Press, 2000), 14.
10. Churchill, *Grand Alliance*, 272–3. The *Bolero* committee was formed in London in May 1942, primarily 'to relieve the German pressure on the Eastern Front especially with regard to Air Forces involved'. 'A History of the First Eisenhower Period, European Theater of Operations', Past Affairs Sub-section, December 1944, 9 (henceforth, 'Eisenhower, ETO'). Administrative History Collection, Historical Section ETOUSA, Folder title: First Eisenhower Period, ETO, Monograph, 1941–43. RG498. ADM NR509. NARA (henceforth RG498/AHC/HS/ETOUSA).
11. Reynolds, *Relations*, 90.
12. Christopher Norton, *The Politics of Constitutional Nationalism in Northern Ireland, 1932-70: Between Grievance and Reconciliation* (Manchester: Manchester University Press, 2014), 35–6. See also Clair Wills, *That Neutral Island: A Cultural History of Ireland During the Second World War* (London: Faber and Faber, 2007), 87–8; Brian Barton, *The Blitz: Belfast in the War Years* (Belfast: The Blackstaff Press, 1989), 92–3.
13. Blake, *Northern Ireland*, 269.
14. Ibid., 270.

15 Blake claims that 'the first step was to get the co-operation' of Stormont. Ibid., 269.
16 'War Cabinet. Defence Committee (Operations) Extract from Minutes of Meeting held on Friday 9th January, 1942'. CAB9CD/255/3. See also, Sir Oscar Henderson to Sir Robert Gransden, 26 January 1942. Ibid.
17 'War Cabinet', 9 January 1942. Ibid.
18 Sir Alexander Maxwell to Grandsen, 10 January 1942, CAB9CD/255/3.
19 L.S.P. Freer (Home Office) to E.W. Scales, 27 January 1942. COM61/568. PRONI. Cited in Robert Fisk, *In Time of War: Ireland, Ulster and the Price of Neutrality, 1939-45* (Dublin: Gill and Macmillan, 1983), 272. Any invasion of Éire would be an Anglo-American operation. Secretary of State for War to GOC BTNI August 1942. PRO ADM1/13031. Cited in Ibid., 272-3.
20 Blake, *Northern Ireland*, 271.
21 For accounts of this offer, see Fisk, *Time of War*, 323-6; T. Ryle Dwyer, *Behind the Green Curtain: Ireland's Phoney Neutrality during World War II* (Dublin: Gill and Macmillan, 2009), 192-3; John P. Duggan, *Neutral Ireland and the Third Reich* (Dublin: Gill and Macmillan Ltd, 1975), 173; Ronan Fanning, *Eamon de Valera: A Will to Power* (London: Faber and Faber, 2015), 214. David Freeman states that, despite claims largely in de Valera historiography, there is no evidence that Churchill was drunk and that it was one of only three messages sent that evening. He also maintains that the offer was serious. David Freeman. 'Leading Churchill Myths (19): "Churchill was drunk and not being serious when he proposed the unification of Ireland in 1941"'. *Finest Hour* 147 (Summer 2010), 57.
22 'SPOBS: The Special Observer Group Prior to the Activation of the European Theater of Operations', (henceforth 'SPOBS'). RG498/AHC/HS/ETOUSA/SPOBS/318. Due to Éire's ambiguous relationship with the UK and the Commonwealth, Maffey could not be a High Commissioner, ambassador or minister; therefore, he was designated a 'representative'. David McCullagh, *De Valera: Volume II Rule 1932-75* (Dublin: Gill Books, 2018), 173.
23 In 1917, for example, de Valera compared unionists to 'the robber coming into another man's house and claiming a room as his'. *Irish Times*, 9 February 1917. In the same year, he described unionists as a 'foreign garrison' and 'not Irish people', and made veiled threats of violence against them. *Freeman's Journal*, 12 November 1917. He told the *Guardian* in 1927 that unionists 'have wilfully assisted in mutilating their motherland [and] can justly be made to suffer for their crime'. *Guardian*, 27 June 1927. Cited in Bowman, *Ulster Question*, 34, 32 and 99. Bowman offers the best analysis of de Valera's attitude towards Northern Ireland and partition.
24 Troy D. Davis, *Dublin's American Policy: Irish American Diplomatic Relations, 1945 1952* (Washington D.C.: The Catholic University of America Press), 1998, 14.
25 *New York Times* (*NYT*), 1 February 1942. Britain had retained three 'Treaty ports' in the Irish Free State for use by the Royal Navy. For the return of the ports, see Fisk, *Time of War*, 40-7.
26 *NYT*, 1 February 1942. Regardless of their official title, the Americans were usually referred to as the AEF.
27 'Eisenhower, ETO', 4. RG498/AHC/HS/ETOUSA/Eisenhower/509.
28 Matoloff and Snell argue that Daley was chosen specifically for this reason. Maurice Matoloff and Edwin M. Snell, *United States Army in World War II: Strategic Planning for Coalition Warfare, 1941-1942* (Washington, D.C.: Center Of Military History, United States Army), 1999, 109.

29 Marshall to Major General Edmund L. Daley, 18 May 1942. *The Papers of George Catlett Marshall*, vol. 3, 'The Right Man for the Job', December 7, 1941-May 31, 1943 (Baltimore and London: The Johns Hopkins University Press, 1991), 204–5.
30 'Eisenhower, ETO', 22. RG498/AHC/HS/ETOUSA/Eisenhower/509.
31 'Developments in Northern Ireland' (henceforth 'Developments'), from Consul General Parker M. Buhrman to the Embassy, 10 January 1942. RG84: Records of the Foreign Service posts of the Department of State; Great Britain: Classified General Records, 1936–1949, Belfast Consulate General; 1936–1942, Confidential File, 1942, file 800 (henceforth RG84/BCG/CF/1942/800).
32 Ibid., 20 January 1942.
33 *Washington Evening Star* (*WES*), 7 January 1942.
34 John P. Duggan, *Herr Hempel at the German Legation, 1937-1945* (Dublin; Portland, Oregon: Irish Academic Press, 2003), 177.
35 Blake, *Northern Ireland*, 272. The State Department released news of the Americans early, causing problems for the British censor. *Minneapolis Morning Tribune* (*MMT*), 27 January 1942, 1.
36 Barton, *Blitz*, 273. Norman Longmate, *The GI's: The Americans in Britain, 1942-1945* (London: Hutchinson of London, 1975), 1.
37 'Q (Movements) Northern Ireland: A Short History covering the period from September 1939 to June 1945', 16. Folder No.18C, Q (Movements) N.I., CAB3/A/52.
38 Francis M. Carroll, 'United States Armed Forces in Northern Ireland During World War II', *New Hibernia Review*, Vol. 12, N. 2 (Summer 2008), p. 24; 'United States Army in World War II: United States Army Forces in Northern Ireland, Chronology', 19 January 1942, U.S. Army Center of Military History. https://history.army.mil/reference/ireland/IRECHR.htm, accessed 4 March 2018 (henceforth 'USAFNI, Chronology').
39 'M.018907/41: Arrival of First US ships in NI, RN, 15th November 1941'. The ships were the *USS Wilkes, Roper, Madison* and *Sturtevant* which had escorted convoy H.X.169 to Liverpool. M.018907/41. Memo. VCNS. 18.1.42. Londonderry Folder No. 2. CAB3A/19.
40 Minnesota took especial pride in its native son. *MMT*, 27 January 1942.
41 Ibid; *Northern Whig* (*NW*), 27 January 1942. 'Northern Ireland War History, File no. 11. American: forces, etc'. CAB3A/47. See also, Barton, *Blitz*, 275.
42 *NW*, 27 January 1942; 'Northern Ireland War History'. CAB3A/47.
43 *NW*, 27 January 1942.
44 Ibid; *Dromore Leader* (*DL*), 31 January 1942, 4; *MMT*, 27 January 1942.
45 *NW*, 27 January 1942.
46 *Stars and Stripes*, London edition (*SSL*), 8 August 1942. Sergeant Alvin C. York was an American hero from the Great War and the subject of a 1941 film starring Gary Cooper.
47 *MMT*, 27 January 1942.
48 *NW*, 27 January 1942.
49 Ibid.
50 Ibid., 29 January 1942.
51 'Northern Ireland premier's greeting to American troops'. 27 January 1942. CAB9CD/225/1.
52 Ibid.
53 'American troops in Northern Ireland: Prime Minister's Welcome in the name of Parliament and People', 27 January 1942. CAB9CD/225/1.

54 *BT*, 27 January 1942.
55 Ibid.
56 *NW*, 29 January 1942.
57 *Londonderry Sentinel (LS)*, 27 January 1942.
58 Ibid.
59 *Derry Journal (DJ)*, 30 January 1942.
60 This is dealt with in detail in Chapter 5.
61 Robert Cole, *Propaganda, Censorship and Irish Neutrality in the Second World War* (Edinburgh: Edinburgh University Press, 2006), 107. Wills, *Neutral Island*, 228. Cole offers an excellent account of the Irish-American press and the war.
62 Cole, *Propaganda*, 109; *NYT*, 27 January 1941. For Éire's press, see, for example, *Irish Independent*, 28 January 1942; *Evening Echo*, 29 January 1942.
63 Telegram Robert Brennan to Joseph P. Walshe, 2 February 1942. *Documents on Irish Foreign Policy*, Volume 7 (*DIFP*). https://www.difp.ie/.
64 Wills, *Neutral Island*, 228.
65 *DJ*, 28 January 1942.
66 Dwyer, *Green Curtain*, 1.
67 *DJ*, 28 January 1942.
68 Longmate, *GI's*, 2
69 Thomas Bartlett, *Ireland: A History* (Cambridge, New York: Cambridge University Press, 2010), 454; *WES*, 1 February 1942.
70 John D. Kearney to Norman Robertson, 20 February 1942. Cited in T. Ryle Dwyer, *Strained Relations: Ireland at Peace and the USA at War, 1941-1945* (Dublin: Gill and McMillan, 1988), 27.
71 As Duggan notes: 'superficially they [the British] were the old enemy: in the public perception the United States was the old friend'. Duggan, *Neutral Ireland*, 176.
72 Reynolds, *Relations*, 118.
73 Dwyer, *Curtain*, 201; Dwyer, *Strained Relations*, 26. Maffey cautioned against the protest, as it could lead to an anti-Irish backlash on both sides of the Atlantic. Cole, *Propaganda*, 109
74 Dwyer, *Curtain*, 201; Fisk, *Time of War*, 529.
75 This was according to Brennan's account of a meeting with Roosevelt in June. Brennan to Walshe, 10 June 1942, cited in John Day Tully, 'Identities and Distortions: Irish Americans, Ireland, and the United States', 1932-1945, unpublished PhD thesis, Ohio State University, 2004, 145, n19.
76 Cole, *Propaganda*, 107. British internees were not necessarily closely guarded, unlike their German counterparts, and often crossed the border without impediment. For the return of airmen, see Fisk, *Time of War*, 327-32.
77 Dwyer, *Relations*, 27.
78 Welles Memo, 6 February 1942. G. Bernard Noble and E. R. Perkins (eds.), *Foreign Relations of the United States, 1942*, (*FRUS*) volume I (Washington: United States Government Printing Office, 1962), 755-6.
79 Brennan to Walshe, 6 February 1942. *DIFP*, 7.
80 Roosevelt told de Valera that the Americans protected the entire British Isles. Dwyer, *Relations*, 29. De Valera thanked Roosevelt for this commitment to respect Éire's neutrality, while complaining that 'Britain's exercise of sovereignty over our six north-eastern counties is repugnant to national sentiment'. De Valera to Franklin D. Roosevelt, 16 April 1942. *DIFP*, 7; Harold Ickes, MS Diary, February 1942, cited in Reynolds, *Relations*, 118.

81 Walshe to Brennan, 9 February 1942. *DIFP*, 7.
82 Walshe to Sean Murphy, 12 February 1942. Ibid.
83 *NW*, 29 January 1942. See also *LS*, 29 January 1942 and CAB9CD/225/1. Andrews was still privately congratulating himself eight years later, remarking that 'when de Valera had the impudence to protest & endeavoured to make trouble, I got the opportunity to set him "back on his traces"'. J.M. Andrews to Ethel, 18 July 1950. D/3655/A/7/2. PRONI.
84 *NW*, 29 January 1942.
85 *LS*, 29 January 1942.
86 Ibid.
87 *LS*, 13 March 1942. Savory discussed the 'three-fold' partition of Poland by Russia, Prussia and Austria at the end of the eighteenth century. Savory became best known for his investigation of the Katyn massacre of 1940.
88 John A. Murphy, 'Irish Neutrality in Perspective', in Brian Girvin and Geoffrey Roberts (eds), *Ireland and the Second World War: Politics, Society and Remembrance* (Dublin: Four Courts Press, 2000), 12.
89 'House of Commons, United States Troops, Northern Ireland (Éire Protest), Questions by Professor Savory, MP', 11 February 1942. CAB9CD225/1.
90 With Savory's consent, Home Secretary Herbert Morrison forwarded this advice to Andrews. Herbert Morrison to Andrews, 7 May 1942. CAB9CD225/1.
91 Ibid.
92 *NW*, 2 February 1942.
93 *DJ*, 30 January 1942.
94 Cole, *Propaganda*, 108.
95 *Bradford Evening Star* (Pennsylvania), 27 January 1942; *Daily Times* (Ohio), 27 January 1942.
96 *MMT*, 27 January 1942.
97 *WES*, 1 February 1942.
98 *NYT*, 27 January 1942.
99 *LS*, 3 February 1942.
100 *The Nation*, 31 January 1942.
101 Ibid., 7 February 1942.
102 Ibid. This piece greatly concerned Buhrman and Gray as it risked involving America in partition. Buhrman to Cordell Hull, Secretary of State, 7 July 1942, and Buhrman to David Gray, 7 July 1942. RG84/BCG/CF/1942/800. Similar issues were raised with *Look* magazine in February 1942, and its article 'Why America can't lose'.
103 See US historian Henry Steele's Commager, 'The Price of Éire's Neutrality', in the *New York Times* (reprinted in the *London Evening Standard*, 21 April 1943). This attack triggered a pamphlet called 'An Invocation of Historical Truth, in reply to Henry Steele Commager', by Henry Harrison, who pointedly noted that neither the Americans nor the Soviets joined the war until attacked and were 'no voluntary crusaders' helping Nazi-conquered countries. Folder No.9, ARCH/11/5/14. Joseph Cardinal MacRory Papers (henceforth JCM).
104 Tom Harrisson, Head of Mass Observation, May-June 1942. Cited in Reynolds, *Relations*, 257.
105 MOI rpt. US forces, 21 April 1943. Cited in ibid., 194.
106 Buhrman to Gray, 26 February 1942. RG84/BCG/CF/1942/800.
107 'Developments', 8 September 1942. Ibid. See Chapter 7.

Notes to pages 20–23

108 Andrews issued a similar greeting to the newer arrivals. Press Release, 26 May 1942. CAB9CD/225/1.
109 Brigadier K. N. Crawford (British Troops Northern Ireland) told Gransden that there would be no formal reception for the second wave of Americans in March 1942. K. N. Crawford to Gransden, 28 February 1942. CAB9CD/225/1.

Chapter 2

1 Eisenhower diary, 30 January 1942. Robert H. Ferrell (ed.), *The Eisenhower Diaries* (New York and London: W.W. Norton and Company), 46. The '45s' is a reference to the flamboyant General George S. Patton, who carried two Colt 45 pistols and was as disruptive a personality as he was a brilliant soldier. For Eisenhower and Patton, see Reynolds , *Relations*, 362–3.
2 'Eisenhower, ETO', 1. RG498/AHC/HS/ETOUSA/Eisenhower/509.
3 Blake, *Northern Ireland*, 254.
4 'Eisenhower, ETO', 3. RG498/AHC/HS/ETOUSA/Eisenhower/509. British intelligence sources, reflecting on the bases in 1943, noted that 'early in 1941 it was agreed that if US came into the war they should take over and operate the Londonderry Naval Base'. 'Case 6321, Vol.3: Londonderry Construction Work – British Naval Base' (item dated 22.5.43). Londonderry Folder No. 2. CAB3A/19.
5 Blake, *Northern Ireland*, 256.
6 The Scottish bases were in Rosneath and Loch Ryan. Having bases in each country meant that if the Germans bombed one, the other would continue to operate, thus minimizing disruption. Ibid., 255.
7 'Preparations for US Naval and Air co-operation with British Naval Forces' [undated]. Londonderry Folder No.2. CAB3A/19. Underlining in original. For an almost identical memo, dated 9 May 1941, see CAB/3/A/22.
8 'Case 6321, Vol.3: Londonderry Construction Work – British Naval Base'. Londonderry Folder No.2. CAB3A/19.
9 Jonathan Bardon, *A History of Ulster* (Belfast: Blackstaff Press Ltd, 1992), 574; *NYT*, 27 and 28 January 1942.
10 *BT*, 11 July 1941. Welles stated that bases were not being built in Siberia or Portugal but did not deny the construction of one in Northern Ireland.
11 Roosevelt offered no comment. *WES*, 11 July 1941. *IN*, 10 July 1941.
12 *NYT*, 11 July 1941.
13 Ibid., 12 July 1941.
14 Kelly, *Home*, 15.
15 *BT*, 11 July 1941. *WES*, 11 July 1941.
16 This quotation was widely reported, see *NW*, 12 July 1941, *DJ*, 14 July 1941, *BT*, 11 July 1941, *WES*, 11 July 1941, and *IN*, 12 July 1941.
17 *BT*, 11 July 1941. *LS*, 12 July 1941. Quotation from *IN*, 11 July 1941.
18 'Q (Movements) N.I.' CAB3/A/52.
19 Blake, *Northern Ireland*, 258.
20 Ibid.
21 Ibid., 259.
22 Ibid.
23 *LS*, 12 July 1941. Quotation from *IN*, 11 July 1941.

24 *LS*, 12 July 1941.
25 Ibid.
26 Brennan, Aide Memoir, to Hull, 15 October 1941. President Franklin D. Roosevelt's Office Files, Part 2, Diplomatic Correspondence File (henceforth FDRP/OF/2/DCF). Wills suggests that to avoid acknowledging partition the bases attracted no attention in the Dáil, and little in its press. Wills, *Neutral Island*, 132.
27 Girvin, *Emergency*, 287.
28 Brennan to Hull, 6 November 1941. FDRP/OF/2/DCF.
29 Sumner Welles to Roosevelt, 14 November 1941. Ibid.
30 Ibid.
31 Girvin, *Emergency*, 287.
32 Blake, *Northern Ireland*, 254.
33 The Americans ultimately never used Lough Erne as a base. Blake, *Northern Ireland*, 263.
34 *NL*, 26 June 1941. *BT*, 11 July 1941; Carroll, *NHR*, 17–18.
35 Blake, *Northern Ireland*, 257.
36 *WES*, 28 January 1942.
37 *BT*, 14 July 1941.
38 *NW*, 26 August 1941. *NW*, 3 September 1941. *WES*, 20 August 1941. *BT*, 20 August 1941. Discretion amounted to most reports being from 'somewhere in Northern Ireland'.
39 *LS*, 31 July 1941. A further 150 workers arrived in September and 200 in October. *WES*, 2 September 1941 and 20 October 1941.
40 *BT*, 14 July 1941.
41 *Indiana Evening Gazette*, (Pennsylvania) 23 September 1941; *Pittsburgh Press*, 24 September 1941.
42 *New York Herald Tribune* cited in *BT*, 11 July 1941. The local press seems to have discovered the base, or been able to make it public, through this *Herald Tribune* report. *BT*, 11 July 1941; *LS*, 12 July 1941.
43 For details on the work, see Carroll, *NHR*, 18–19; Blake, *Northern Ireland*, 46 and Brian Lacey, *Siege City: The Story of Derry and Londonderry* (Belfast: The Blackstaff Press, 1990), 239.
44 *WES*, 28 January 1942.
45 'First Irish GI Bride in the USA', BBC, 15 October 2014. https://www.bbc.co.uk/history/ww2peopleswar/stories/43/a5741543.shtml (accessed 12 April 2019).
46 Blake, *Northern Ireland*, 264. Partially quoted in Lacey, *Siege City*, 239.
47 *BT*, 27 March 1942.
48 Duggan, *Hempel*, 176.
49 'For D. of L.D., 15 August 1941'. M.016597/41. CAB3A/19.
50 *BT*, 2 July 1942.
51 Buhrman to State, 18 July 1942. RG84/BCG/CF/1942/800.
52 Buhrman was referring to 26 February 1942 issue of *Stars and Stripes*.
53 Buhrman to State, 3 March 1943. RG84/BCG/CF/1943-44/800; *SSL*, 26 February 1943.
54 War workers came from the Empire and Commonwealth with, for example, foresters from British Honduras going to Scotland. Neil A. Wynn, '"Race War": Black American GIs and West Indians in Britain During the Second World War', *Immigrants & Minorities*, vol. 24, no. 3 (November 2006), 328.
55 'USAFNI, Chronology', April 1941.

56 'SPOBS', 8. RG498/AHC/HS/ETOUSA/SPOBS/318.
57 Ibid., 113. After Pearl Harbor, he recommended 33,000 troops. Ibid., 52.
58 Ibid., 107-8.
59 Ibid., 109-11. Case believed that if Germany defeated the Soviets, an invasion of Ireland became extremely likely.
60 Ibid., 113.
61 'USAFNI, Chronology', 2 January 1942; 'SPOBS', 118. RG498/AHC/HS/ETOUSA/SPOBS/318.
62 Blake, *Northern Ireland*, 277.
63 'Manuscript G-2 ETOUSA: A History of G-2 HQ ETOUSA', 3-4. RG498/AHC/HS/ETOUSA/G-2/513.
64 'SPOBS', 126-127. RG498/AHC/HS/ETOUSA/SPOBS/318.
65 'A History of Northern Ireland Base Command (Prov.) and Northern Ireland Base Section, from 5 October to 31 December 1943, 25 (henceforth 'Base History'). RG498, Records of HQETO, Box 186, File 597, Folder, Northern Ireland, Base Histories (RG498/AHC/HS/ETOUSA/NIBC/186/597).
66 Quentin Reynolds, *Collier's*, 10 October 1942, 66. Not all Americans agreed with this assessment, one noted: 'Irish fields are good for training, though they have a tendency to be rocky'. *Yank*, 24 June 1942.
67 Blake, *Northern Ireland*, 275; *NW*, 10 July 1942; *WES*, 9 July 1942; *SSL*, 11 July 1942; *SSL*, 22 August 1942. For details of exercises and the units involved, see Kelly, *Home*, 29-58; Carroll, *NHR*, 21-22 and 28.
68 'USAFNI, Chronology', 4 June 1942.
69 Kelly, *Home*, 61.
70 Ibid., 63. For the Rangers time in Northern Ireland, see Kelly, *Home*, 59-95.
71 Mir Bahmanyar, *Darby's Rangers 1942-45* (Oxford: Osprey Publishing, 2003 (Kindle edition)); Robert W. Black, *Ranger Force: Darby's Rangers in World War II* (Mechanicsburg, Pennsylvania: Stackpole Books, 2009 (Kindle edition)).
72 Scott Reeves, 'Andrew Jackson Cottage and US Ranger Centre, County Antrim', *BBC History Extra*, 13 November 2012.
73 Longmate, *GI's*, 55. Legends persist of burning planes returning from missions over Europe.
74 'Aerodromes in Northern Ireland'. 'Draft Conclusions of a Cabinet meeting', 6 March 1941. CAB4/465.
75 Blake, *Northern Ireland*, 278-81.
76 Ibid., 280.
77 'USAFNI, Chronology', May 1942. The US Air Force remained a branch of the army until 1947.
78 For film footage of this process, see *P47s Arrive Sydenham Airfield Belfast, Ireland via USS Block Island*, 14 September 1943. RG428: General Records of the Department of the Navy, 1941-2004, Series: Moving Images Relating to Military Activities, ca. 1947-1980. https://catalog.archives.gov/id/75884. Accessed 5 April 2021.
79 Blake, *Northern Ireland*, 282.
80 Carroll, *NHR*, 27.
81 Blake, *Northern Ireland*, 267 and 279; 'The G.I.'s In Northern Ireland', historical file, U.S. Consulate General, Belfast. Cited in Carroll, *NHR*, 19.
82 'Your Place and Mine', BBC, 16 October 2014. https://www.bbc.co.uk/northernireland/yourplaceandmine/tyrone/cluntoe_airfield_ardboe.shtml (accessed 7 June 2019).
83 *Indiana Evening Gazette*, 23 September 1941; *Pittsburgh Press*, 24 September 1941.

84 'American losses in N Ireland', BBC People's War, 19 August 2005.
85 'B17 41-24451 Crash on Slieveanorra, Co. Antrim', 7 March 2018. https://wartimeni.com/article/b17-crash-on-slieveanorra-co-antrim/ (accessed 6 June 2019).
86 'The Second World War in Northern Ireland: Greater Belfast, part 5'. https://www.ww2ni.com/greaterbelfastpart5.htm (accessed 6 June 2019). *Closing the Ring* (2007).
87 'Chimney Rock B26 Crash 10th April 1944'. http://www.chimneyrockb26crash.com/ (accessed 21 July 2019). For other crashes, see https://wartimeni.com/wwii-timeline/northern-irelands-wartime-airfields/ (accessed 6 June 2019).
88 'Ministry of Information, Northern Ireland Region, Hospitality for American, British and Allied Forces. Activities during March 1944'. CAB9/CD225/19.
89 Brooke Diary, 29 January 1944. D/3004/D/33. PRONI.
90 Carroll, *NHR*, 24.
91 Dwyer, *Strained Relations*, 82–4. For further details, see Fisk, *Time of War*, 327–32. Dwyer, *Strained Relations*, 77–90.
92 Fisk, *Time of War*, 329. Dwyer, *Strained Relations*, 86–7. Hempel heard that Eisenhower was onboard; Boland told him it was a passenger flight and not to believe rumours. Dwyer, *Strained Relations*, 86–7.
93 Dwyer, *Curtain*, 248; Dwyer, *Strained Relations*, 85.
94 Dwyer, *Strained Relations*, 79–82. Wolf made the best of his situation, among other things, riding in the Kildare Hunt dressed as a cowboy! He was eventually released in October 1943 under an agreement between Éire and Allies freeing most remaining internees. Ibid., 81 and 88.
95 'Developments', 22 June 1942. RG84/BCG/CF/1942/800.
96 Reynolds, *Relations*, 119.
97 'Establishment of US Forces in North Ireland', Report by the US-British Joint Planning Committee; US ABC-4/7; British WW12, 11 January 1941. FDRP, Office File, Part One, 'Safe' (henceforth FDRP/OF/1/Safe). See also: 'Foreign Relations of the United States, The Conferences at Washington, 1941–1942, and Casablanca, 1943', document 142. https://history.state.gov/historicaldocuments/frus1941-43/d142 (accessed 9 August 2017).
98 For Éire's defence plans, see Fisk, *Time of War*, 246–64.
99 For the 1940 British plan 'W', to enter Éire after a German landing, see ibid., 235–44. The British expected to be generally welcomed. De Valera told an unofficial Stormont envoy of his preference for Australian or Canadian troops to repel the Germans as 'British troops would not be popular'. Ibid., 244.
100 Mark Willcox Jr., memo, 'Irish situation' [October 1942]. Cited in Reynolds, *Relations*, 118.
101 'Intel. summary', 29 August–13 September 1942, Martin M. Philipsborn Papers, MHI, cited in ibid., 119.
102 The 'American Note' is discussed in Chapter 10.
103 'A few tips' by Major Boyd E. Shriver, 8 June 1942. CAB9CD/225/1. Stormont's copy has 'Great Britain' circled with a margin note correcting it to 'United Kingdom'. No other comments were offered.
104 Ibid. Underlining in original.
105 Ibid.
106 *A Pocket Guide to Northern Ireland*, prepared by Special Service Division, United States, War and Navy Departments, Washington, DC, 1942.
107 *BT*, 4 March 1942.
108 Kelly, *Home*, 38.

109 *Pocket Guide*, 1.
110 Ibid., 2.
111 Ibid., 7. The Irish had apparently been 'engaged for a thousand years in a struggle against English domination', thus adding over 200 years to the conflict. There were also factual errors, twice claiming that Belfast had been bombed in 1940, and Éire was referred to as the Irish Free State.
112 Ibid., 10.
113 Ibid., 10.
114 Ibid., 13; 17–18; 22.
115 Ibid., 29, 31.
116 Ibid., 33.
117 *A Short Guide to Great Britain*, Special Service Division, United States, War and Navy Departments, Washington, DC., 1943.
118 *SS*, 10 April 1944.
119 *DR*, 31 October 1942; *SSL*, 31 October 1942; *NYT*, 25 October 1942. The *Times* later published an extract from the *Guide*. *NYT*, 23 January 1943, vii, 15.
120 *NYT*, 25 October 1942.
121 *SSL*, 31 October 1942.
122 Cole, *Propaganda*, 107
123 Kelly, *Home*, 95.
124 Blake, *Northern Ireland*, 276.
125 'Base History', From: 1 June 1942 to 20 December 1942. RG498/AHC/HS/ETOUSA/NIBC/186/597.
126 Andrews to Russell P. Hartle 9 November 1942; Hartle to Andrews, 14 November 1942. CAB9CD/225/1.
127 Blake, *Northern Ireland*, 286–7.
128 'USAFNI, Chronology', 1 November 1943.
129 'The Day Ulster Became Uncle Sam's Stepping Stone to Berlin', reprinted from the *Belfast Telegraph*. RG498/ETOUSA/HS/AF/Northern Ireland/224.
130 Ibid., 2.
131 Ibid., 3–7.
132 *SS*, 11 December 1943.
133 It should be noted that other regions had proportionately more US troops, often with smaller populations and smaller geographical areas. Devon, for example, with roughly half the size and population of Northern Ireland, hosted 85,000 Americans on the eve of D-Day. Reynolds, *Relations*, 111.
134 *BT*, 20 May 1944; condom reference: Gibson-Harries, *Life-Line to Freedom*, 62.
135 HQ, Northern Ireland Base Section (NIBS), Services of Supply (SOS), ETOUSA, APO 813 US Army, GO #44, 17 May 1944 and GO #45, 18 May 1944 (henceforth 'NIBS'). RG498/ETOUSA/AHC/HS/NIBS/224.
136 *NL*, 8 May 1945.
137 'NIBS', 2 June 1944. RG498/ETOUSA/HS/AF/NIBS/224.
138 Harrisson, 'Report on Americans in Ireland', 8 June 1942, 4. MOI.

Chapter 3

1 Cabinet Meeting, 25 May 1944. CAB9CD/225/2. As governor, the Duke of Abercorn (James Hamilton) was the monarch's official representative in Northern Ireland.

2 *BT*, 14 February 1942.
3 'Conference held at the Home Office on Wednesday 21st January 1942'. J.C. McDermott, 5 February 1942. CAB9CD/225/2.
4 Maxwell to Secretary to the Cabinet, 29 January 1942. CAB9CD/225/2.
5 MacDermott, 19 March 1942. CAB9CD/225/2.
6 Blake, *Northern Ireland*, 292.
7 Graham Smith, *When Jim Crow Met John Bull: Black American Soldiers in World War II Britain* (London: Taurus, 1987), 4.
8 'Conclusions of a Cabinet Meeting', 2 June, 1942. CAB4/511/1. See also, 'United States America (Visiting Forces bill)' Secretary to the Cabinet, 25 August 1942, and Freer to Gransden, 22 December 1942. CAB9CD/225/2.
9 Blake, *Northern Ireland*, 293.
10 'Theirs was largely a conscript army', states Gardiner, 'that had been sent abroad against its will', and as it was permanently 'on duty' it was governed by military law. Janet Gardiner, *Wartime Britain, 1939-1945* (London: Headline, 2004), 518.
11 'NIBS', #813 US Army, Memo #7, 26 October 1943. RG498/AHC/HS/ETOUSA/NIBC/225.
12 Simon, House of Lords, to McDermott, 8 June 1942. CAB9CD/225/2.
13 J. Robert Lilly and J. Michael Thomson, 'Executing US Soldiers in England, World War II', *British Journal of Criminology*, vol. 37, no. 2 (Spring 1997), 264.
14 American military police were often ordinary soldiers with no police training whatsoever who acted as MPs as part of their duties.
15 'Memorandum: Relations between the civil police and the American military police', 31 March 1942. CAB9CD/225/2.
16 Simon Topping, 'Racial Tensions and U.S. Military (In)Justice an Northern Ireland during World War II', *The Journal of African American History*, vol. 102, no. 2 (Spring 2017), 171.
17 *SSL*, 7 June 1943.
18 A. J. Kelly to H. C. Montgomery, 4 October 1944. CAB9CD/225/2. This was taken up with the Home Office and the Foreign Office.
19 For wartime capital cases in Northern Ireland, see Topping, *JAAH*, 157-83.
20 I have located only one reported rape, on 7 June 1944, in government papers at PRONI. 'Inspector General's Office, Royal Ulster Constabulary (RUC), monthly report', Ewing Gilfillan to Gransden, 7 July, 1944. CAB/9/CD/225/18.
21 *DL*, 8 August 1942. There were three types of American court-martial: 'Summary' with a panel of one officer who could hand out punishment of up to thirty days' hard labour and forfeiture of two-thirds pay. 'Special' with a minimum of five officers on panel and punishment of up to six months and forfeiture of pay; and finally, 'General' again with a minimum of five officers, but punishment could include the death sentence. Ibid.
22 'Northern Ireland War History, File No 11. American: forces, etc.'. Supplement to file pr539/w.r. CAB3A/47.
23 *DL*, 8 August 1942.
24 Gilfillan to Gransden, 5 August 1942. CAB/9/CD/225/18. In June 1942, the MOI reported that technicians 'are the focus of particular resentment'. Tom Harrisson, 'Secret: Report on Americans in Ireland', 8 June 1942, 3. MOI.
25 See Freer to Gransden, 22 December 1942; Buhrman to Gransden 13 January 1943; Gransden to Buhrman 14 January 1943; Gransden to A. Robinson 14 January 1943; Montgomery to Gransden 6 February 1943; Gransden to Buhrman 10 February 1943; Buhrman to Gransden, 11 February 1943. CAB9CD/225/2.

26 The *New York Times* reported that the convoy was 'protecting a distinguished military visitor'. *NYT*, 1 May 1942.
27 *LS*, 21 April 1942.
28 Brian Barton, *Northern Ireland in the Second World War* (Belfast: Ulster Historical Foundation, 1995), 102.
29 *BT*, 18 April 1942; *WES*, 18 April 1942.
30 *DJ*, 24 April 1942; *BT*, 20 April 1942; *LS*, 21 April 1942.
31 *BT*, 1 May 1942.
32 Stormont's records include a transcript of the court-martial. CAB9CD/225/2.
33 Barton, *Second World War*, 102.
34 Gilfillan to Gransden, 5 August 1942. CAB9CD/225/18.
35 Ibid.
36 Ibid.
37 Ibid.; Gilfillan to Gransden, 8 September 1942. CAB9CD/225/18.
38 *BO*, 7 August 1942; *BT*, 4 August 1942; *WES*, 4 August 1942; *Board of Review*, volume 1, ETO29: *United States v. Private William E. Davis*, 38042586, 518th Engineer Company, 31 August 1942, 29–30; *BO*, 4 September 1942.
39 Buhrman to State, 11 September 1942. RG84/BCG/CF/1942/823. Gilfillan to Gransden, 8 September 1942. CAB9CD/225/18.
40 Gilfillan to Gransden, 8 September 1942. CAB9CD/225/18.
41 Gilfillan to Gransden, 10 October 1942. Ibid.
42 Several reports suggest Jenkins was stabbed, implying a brawl rather than an encounter with Military Police. See, for example, *BT*, 1 October 1942. A subsequent investigation established that he had been shot. Simon Topping, '"Laying down the law to the Irish and the Coons": Northern Ireland's Response to American Racial Segregation during World War Two', *Historical Research*, vol. 86, no. 234 (November 2013), 750.
43 For further details see Topping, *HR*, 748–51.
44 Gilfillan to Gransden, 8 September 1942. CAB9CD/225/18.
45 *BT*, 23 September 1942. The case made the American press. *WES*, 22 September 1942 and 9 October 1942.
46 'Developments', 25 September, 1942. RG84/BCG/CF/1942/823.
47 *DL*, 26 September 1942.
48 *NL*, 28 September 1942.
49 *BT*, 9 October 1942.
50 Ibid. Buhrman reported the outcome to Washington. Buhrman to State, 14 October 1942. RG84/BCG/CF/1942/823.
51 *BT*, 9 October 1942.
52 Gilfillan to Gransden 10 October 1942. CAB/9/CD/225/18.
53 *NW*, 9 October 1942.
54 *NL*, 21 October 1942; *DR*, 24 October 1942.
55 For the American military's thinking on the case, see *Board of Review*, volume 1, ETO82: *United States v. Technician First Class Lawrence H. McKenzie* (39389670), Company G, 1st Armored Division, 20 October 1942, 10.
56 Gransden to Montgomery, 14 August 1942. CAB/9/CD/225/9.
57 The racial context of the Harris court-martial is discussed in Chapter 9, however, for a full account, see Topping, *JAAH*, 157–83.
58 Cabinet Meeting, 25 May 1944; Gransden to Henderson, 25 May 1944; Duke of Abercorn to General Leroy Collins, 25 May 1944. CAB9CD/225/2.

59 General John C. H. Lee to Abercorn, 10 June 1944. Ibid.
60 General Wade H. Haislip to Michael Coogan, 31 May 1944. A similar letter was sent to the police. Haislip to District Inspector, Royal Ulster Constabulary, York Street, Belfast, 31 May 1944. *Court-Martial Record of Trial of Private Wiley Harris, Jr., 6924547, 626th Ordinance Ammunition Co., ETO2007.*
61 *IN*, 7 November 1944.
62 Niall Glynn, 'American troops, murders and a race riot during World War Two', 3 November 2018. https://www.bbc.co.uk/news/uk-northern-ireland-46033229 (accessed 3 November 2018).
63 Gilfillan to Gransden, 6 October 1944. CAB/9/CD/225/18.
64 Lilly and Thomson, *BJC*, 269–74.
65 Tom Harrisson, 'Ulster Outlooks', 20 May 1944, 8. MOI File Report-2101.
66 'Developments', 17 May 1943. RG84/BCG/CF/1943/800.
67 Barton, *Brookeborough*, 192.
68 Reynolds, *Relations*, 154.
69 Brooke Diary, 12 February 1942.
70 Harrisson, 'Report on Americans', 8 June 1942, 5. MOI.
71 Ibid.
72 Brooke Diary, 19 August 1942 and 2 September 1942. The trip and its purpose were reported by the *Whig*. *NW*, 4 September 1942.
73 'Northern Ireland, Region 13', C. L. Frankland to D. B. Briggs, Director Home Division, 15 December 1945. MOI, Regional Information Officers, Organisation of Work, Regional History. INF1/297. TNA.
74 Brooke Diary, 20 June 1942; 12, 18, 19 July 1942; 31 October 1942; 2 January 1944; 5 March 1944.
75 Ibid., 9 September 1942.
76 Ibid., 16 September 1942. See also, 'An Ulster Welcome', INF1/327B. TNA. 'Hospitality for the forces in Northern Ireland', 'list of chairman and secretaries of local hospitality committees', compiled 6 October 1943. CAB9/CD225/19.
77 Minutes 10 September 1942; Stronge/Adams memo 4 March 1943; MOI report US forces, 21 April 1943 CAB9CD/225/19. Cited in Reynolds, 194. The MOI was wary of Catholic involvement in its religious activities in Northern Ireland and agreed to exclude Catholics from its religious liaison committee. Having met 'a group of ministers of all denominations', on a visit in 1940, Hugh MacLennan reported: 'there was some discussion as to an approach to Roman Catholics in Northern Ireland but it was thought best to confine our efforts to the protestant churches'. Mr MacLennan to Mr (Ivison) McAdam, copy to Mr Rhodes; copy to Sir Kenneth Clark also, 1 May 1940. INF1/404, part A. TNA.
78 A. Dalzell to Brooke, 14 September 1942. COM61/865. PRONI. Dalzell had earlier written to Andrews offering the Ulster Tourist Development Board as a conduit to the Americans. Andrews thanked him, recognizing 'the desirability of ensuring that our visitors are guided along the right lines'. Dalzell to Andrews, 23 May 1942; Andrews to Dalzell 27 May 1942. CAB9/CD225/19.
79 E. Johnston to Brooke 16 May 1944. CAB9/CD225/19. The priest may have been Father Thomas Maguire, a close associate of Cahir Healy and, according to Norton, 'an ardent anti-partitionist and propagandist'. Christopher Norton, 'The internment of Cahir Healy M. P., Brixton Prison July 1941-December 1942', *Twentieth Century British History*, vol. 18 (2007), 176.

80 Clare O'Kane, '"To Make Butter and to Look After Poultry": The Impact of the Second World War on the Lives of Rural Women in Northern Ireland', in Gillian McIntosh and Diane Urquhart (eds.), *Irish Women at War: The 20th Century* (Dublin; Portland Oregon: Irish Academic Press, 2010), 92–3.
81 Reynolds, *Relations*, 193; Leanne McCormick, *Regulating Sexuality: Women in Twentieth-Century Northern Ireland* (Manchester: Manchester University Press, 2010), 241.
82 Rear Admiral King (Royal Navy) to Gransden, 5 September 1942; Hartle to Andrews 25 August 1942. CAB9/CD225/19.
83 'Welfare Committee, first meeting', 10 September 1942. COM61/865. PRONI.
84 Gransden to Turnham, 11 September 1942 CAB9/CD225/19.
85 'Northern Ireland Welfare Committee: Organisation of Hospitality for the Forces', joint memorandum from Lady Stronge and F. H. Adams, 4 March 1943. COM61/865. PRONI.
86 Reynolds, *Relations*, 194.
87 Brooke Diary, 19 November 1942; 'Minutes of the meeting held at the Officers Club Belfast', 25 November 1942. CAB9/CD225/19.
88 Brooke to Brendan Bracken, 19 March 1943. CAB9/CD225/19.
89 'Hospitality for the forces in Northern Ireland', 18 November 1943. CAB9/CD225/19.
90 'Hospitality committee', 10 December 1943. Ibid.
91 'Hospitality for allied forces in Northern Ireland', 25 October 1943. Ibid.
92 Ibid.
93 Ibid.
94 Ibid; Brooke Diary, 19 October 1943; quotation from *SSL*, 27 October 1943.
95 *BT*, 8 July 1942. The MOI in London and Foreign Office argued over who should actually pay for the club, with the FO finally meeting the costs in May 1943. 'Expenditure on American Overseas Club at Belfast'. United States, File no33, pps1925-2651; A1098/33/45. FO371/34124. TNA.
96 *SSL*, 13 January 1943.
97 Brigadier E.H.A.J. O'Donnell, War Office, to Alan Dudley, North American Department, Foreign Office, 15 April 1944. 'Military Base Censorship, NI, Report on relations between British and US Forces, covering period – February 1944'. FO371/38624. TNA.
98 'Secret: Resume of Regional Reports on Anglo-American Liaison for March 1944', HP/943/48. 'Regional Reports on Anglo-American Liaison for March', 28 April 1944, AN1650/275/45. FO371/38624. TNA. 176 hospitality committees provided reports. For the work of committees in Northern Ireland, see Gransden to J.A. Newsam, Under Secretary of State, Home Office, 15 May 1944. CAB9/CD225/19.
99 Bracken stated: 'I have already heard of the successful work of the committee under your chairmanship in coordinating the various welfare activities ... the report from Lady Stronge and Mr Adams makes very encouraging reading'. Bracken to Brooke, 23 March 1943. CAB9CD/225/19.
100 'Secret: Resume of Regional Reports on Anglo-American Liaison for March 1944', 28 April 1944. FO371/38624. TNA.
101 Gilfillan to Gransden 10 October 1942. CAB/9/CD/225/18.
102 Captain Harcourt to Mr N.M. Butler, 9 April 1943. United States, File no. 33, pp. 1925–2651; A3468/33/45: 'United States Troops in Northern Ireland'. FO371/34124. TNA.

103 'Omagh to New York. 24.2.43'. Postal Censorship Report No. 38, 8 April 1943. Harcourt to Butler, 9 April 1943. Ibid.
104 War Office to Butler FO, 6 May 1944, extracts from Army Mail Censorship Report, No.69 for period 11/25 April 1945. FO371/38624. TNA.
105 'Co. Down to Havant, 19.3.43'. Postal Censorship Report No. 38, 8 April 1943. Harcourt to Butler, 9 April 1943. FO371/34124. TNA.
106 Philip Ollerenshaw, *Northern Ireland in the Second World War: Politics, Economic Mobilisation and Society, 1939-45* (Manchester: Manchester University Press, 2013), 16.
107 Ibid. The BBC in Northern Ireland was underfunded, understaffed and struggled to find a voice within the wider corporation. It national output was subservient to the MOI which took a much softer line on Éire's neutrality than either Stormont or the BBC in Belfast would have liked. Rex Cathcart, *The Most Contrary Region: The BBC in Northern Ireland 1924- 1984* (Belfast: The Blackstaff Press, 1984), 106-19.
108 John Hill, *Cinema and Northern Ireland: Film, Culture and Politics* (London: BFI Publishing, 2006), 80. General Sir James Cooke-Collis to Andrews and memorandum, 30 November 1939. COM61/183. PRONI. Cited in Fisk, 181.
109 'Government Publicity: Short Resume since 1922'. CAB9F/123/313, cited in Hill, *Cinema*, 81.
110 MOI, American File, 21 August 1942. CAB9CD/225/19. Arter and Brooke had already discussed this privately. Brooke Diary, 21 July 1942.
111 MOI, American File, 21 August 1942. CAB9CD/225/19.
112 Ibid.
113 *BT*, 28 January 1942 and 11 February 1942.
114 '10. Ref Éire (N. E. Archer) 6.3.45. [handwritten memo], 12 March 1945. WX101/1/69. TNA; Eunan O'Halpin, *Spying on Ireland: British Intelligence and Irish Neutrality During the Second World War* (Oxford: Oxford University Press, 2008), 140.

Chapter 4

1 Floyd Wilson to Mrs Floyd Wilson, Rhode Island, 14 February 1942. CAB9CD/215/1.
2 Tony Canavan, *Frontier Town: An Illustrated History of Newry* (Belfast: Blackstaff Press, 1989), 212.
3 Longmate, *GI's*, 59.
4 *SSL*, 11 July 1942.
5 The weather featured in cartoons, including those by Bruce Bairnsfather, stationed in Northern Ireland in 1942. *Yank* commented: 'the grimmest thing about Ireland is the almost constant rain, which prevents a man from ever feeling completely dry'. *Yank*, 9 September 1942, 9.
6 For positive accounts of Northern Ireland, see Kelly, *Home*.
7 *Yank*, 9 September 1942, 9.
8 Tom Harrisson, 'Secret: Report on Americans in Ireland', 8 June 1942, 5-6. MOI.
9 Ibid.
10 Ibid.

11 *NW*, 31 January 1942; CAB9/CD225/19; 'USAFNI, Chronology', 2 March 1942; *NYT*, 2 March 1942.
12 *LS*, 4 April 1942; *LS*, 7 April 1942; *LS*, 28 May 1942. For a report about the club, see *SSL*, 30 May 1942. For other preparations, see *WES*, 5 May 1942.
13 *SSL*, 18 April 1942.
14 *SSL*, 6 June 1942.
15 'Note of an interview with Mrs Marcia Mackey [sic], undated'. CAB3/A/46 (henceforth 'Mackie interview'); Interview with Marcia Mackey, ARC Chichester Street Belfast, by DAC. FIN17/1/P/23 (2) PRONI.
16 *BT*, 8 October 1942. The opening also saw Miss Brisbane Speers of Belfast chosen as 'Johnny Doughboy's Irish Rose'. *SSL*, 17 October 1942.
17 *SSL*, 26 September 1942; The *Stars and Stripes* called the club 'luxurious'. *SSL*, 17 October 1942.
18 *WES*, 5 May 1942; *SSL*, 30 May 1942. For the number of ARC clubs, see 'Mackie interview' CAB3/A/46. There were committees in Ahgadowny, Antrim, Armagh, Aughacloy, Ballycastle, Ballyclare, Ballymena, Ballymoney, Banbridge, Bangor, Belfast, Bellaghy, Caledon, Castledawson, Clogher, Coleraine, Cookstown, Cultra and Ballyrobert, Downpatrick, Dungannon, Enniskillen, Fivemiletown, Garvagh, Holywood, Irvinestown, Kilkeel, Larne, Limavady, Lisburn, Londonderry, Lurgan, Magherafelt, Moneymore, Moy, Newcastle, Newry, Portadown, Omagh, Portrush, Portstewart, Randalstown, Rostrevor, Upperlands (Co. Londonderry) Warrenpoint. Londonderry had two committees, one for 'home hospitality' and another for 'entertainments'. 'Hospitality for the Forces in Northern Ireland: List of Officers of Local hospitality Committees (up to and including March 31st 1944)'. CAB9CD/225/19.
19 *NL*, 2 September 1942; *DR*, 5 September 1942.
20 *NL*, 2 September 1942; *NW*, 2 September 1942.
21 Brooke Diary, 28 August, 1942.
22 Ibid., 8 September 1942.
23 'Monthly Report', by Louise Farrand, 10 July 1942. Cited in McCormick, *Regulating*, 161.
24 *WES*, 5 March 1943.
25 Ibid., 7 April 1943.
26 *SSL*, 15 and 16 March 1943.
27 Ibid., 13 September 1943.
28 *SS*, 20 March 1944.
29 Ibid., 12 June 1944.
30 Carroll, *NHR*, 31.
31 Joseph R. Healy to G. Romney, 6 April 1943. CAB9/CD225/19.
32 'Bulletin 18', 15 December 1943. 'NIBS'. RG498/AHC/HS/ETOUSA/NIBS/225.
33 NIBS, Memo #19, 9 November 1943 and Memo #45, 17 December 1943. Ibid.
34 'Subject: Officers' Club, Belfast, to RAFNI, 55 Inf. Div., RA NI, from Belfast Sub dist., 11 Dec. 43', Col. Arthur Chitty. Ibid.
35 'US Forces in Northern Ireland'. https://www.flickr.com.
36 Edwin J. Beinecke, 'Notes on Staff Conf', HQ SOS ETO, 30 Aug 43. Cited in Ulysses Lee, *The Employment of Negro Troops*, United States Army in World War II (Washington, DC: Special Studies, Center of Military History United States Army, 1964), 626. Capitalization in original.
37 Ibid.

38 'Extracts from letter from Base Censor Office No. 1', APO 813, US Army, Subject: Special Report (Negro Troops, 1–15 March 1944). RG498: Historical Division, Administrative file, January 1942. 1946, Box 43, file 218.
39 Lee, *Negro Troops*, 626.
40 'Ltr, Hq ETOUSA to CG's and CO's', 16 July 42. Cited in ibid., 624.
41 'Northern Ireland Base Command (Prov) United States Army; Report of Conference on "Rules of Conduct"', 1 August 1942. CAB9CD/225/19.
42 'Hospitality for Allied Forces in Northern Ireland', Belfast, 25 October 1943. CAB9CD/225/19; General David G. Barr to Commanding General, SOS, ETOUSA, 10 Nov.1943, circulated to APO 813. RG107/ASW/Box 36, File 291.2- Race.
43 In January 1945 fifty Americans per day returned to Northern Ireland on leave according to the Red Cross. 'Ministry of Information, Northern Ireland Region, Hospitality for American, British and Allied Forces. Activities during January and February 1945'. CAB9/CD225/19.
44 'Historical Survey of Stars and Stripes, April 1942/January 1944', 1. RG498/ETOUSA/AHC/HS/Stars and Stripes/331.
45 Ibid., 2; 'Brief History [handwritten], the Stars and Stripes' Lt. John S. Howe [handwritten] 10 September 1943. RG498/ETOUSA/AHC/HS/Stars and Stripes/331; *SSL*, 5 July 1944.
46 'Brief History, The Stars and Stripes', 10 September 1943. RG498/AHC/HS/ETOUSA/Stars and Stripes/331.
47 *SSL*, 18 April 1942.
48 *BT* 6 December 1943.
49 'Historical Survey of Stars and Stripes', 12. RG498/ETOUSA/AHC/HS/Stars and Stripes/331; *SSL*, 6 December 1943.
50 *SS*, 6 December 1943.
51 Ibid.
52 Ibid., 17 May 1944.
53 *SSL*, 4 November 1942.
54 Ibid., 15 December 1943.
55 Ibid., 11 March 1944.
56 Ibid., 13 March 1944.
57 Ibid., 14 April 1944. This appeared in the London edition two days earlier. *SSL*, 12 April 1944.
58 *SS*, 14 April 1944.
59 Ibid., 8 July 1944.
60 Egbert White, 'Press in a Citizen's Army', *Journal of Educational Sociology*, vol. 19, no. 4 (December 1945), 236. The idea for *Yank* originated with White, but after editorial disputes he left to edit *Stars and Stripes'* Mediterranean edition.
61 *Yank*, 24 June 1942; 15 July 1942; 13 August 1942.
62 *SS*, 13 December 1943; 27 March 1944.
63 *Yank*, 13 August 1942.
64 *BT*, 5 March 1942.
65 *NYT*, 15 May 1943.
66 *Stars and Stripes* reported that seven newsmen and four photographers had joined US forces in the UK by April 1942. Reporters had similar privileges to officers, but wore no rank. *SSL*, 25 April 1942. The reporters included Fred Vanderschmidt, noted London bureau chief for the AP and *Newsweek*. Another was playwright and journalist Ward Morehouse writing for the *Baltimore Sun*. Ward Morehouse Papers,

1877–1966, The New York Public Library, Archives and Manuscripts. http://archives.nypl.org/the/21501 (accessed 13 March 2020). Ernie Pyle, perhaps the war's most famous correspondent, stayed between June and October 1942 and reported regularly on the troops rather than their surroundings. Cole, *Propaganda*, 108; *LS*, 17 October 1942.
67 *Indiana Evening Gazette*, 23 September 1941; *Pittsburgh Press*, 24 September 1941.
68 *WES*, 13 June 1942.
69 Ibid., 21 June 1942.
70 Ibid., 24 May 1942. Haskin's work appeared in over one hundred newspapers.
71 Quentin Reynolds, 'Letter to a man with a boy in Ireland', *Collier's*, 10 October 1942, 12.
72 Ibid., 66. This portion of the article was reprinted in many American newspapers; see, for example, *Fayette County Leader* (Iowa), 12 November, 1942; *The Hood County Tablet* (Texas) 12 November, 1942; *The Lowndes Signal* (Alabama) 13 November, 1942. The *Armagh Guardian* also published a small extract of this section. *Armagh Guardian*, 2 October 1942.
73 Quentin Reynolds, 'Letter to a man with a boy in Ireland: Letter no.2', *Collier's*, 17 October 1942, 36.
74 Ibid., 10 October 1942, 66.
75 He declared: 'I am for the immediate removal of every Japanese on the West Coast to a point deep in the interior. . . . Personally, I hate the Japanese. And that goes for all of them.' *Seattle Times*, 30 January, 1942.
76 *WES*, 31 March 1943.
77 Ibid., 6 April 1943.
78 Ibid., 6 July 1943; *WES*, 24 July 1943.
79 McLemore also did his bit for morale, hosting quizzes at Red Cross Clubs and military bases. *SSL*, 24 March 1943.
80 See, for example, BBC, 13 April 1942; 23 April 1942; 21 July 1942; 24 August 1942; 10 October 1942; 7 July 1943; 10 October 1943. http://genome.ch.bbc.co.uk/ (accessed 7 February 2018).
81 Melissa Dinsman, *Modernism at the Microphone: Radio, Propaganda, and Literary Aesthetics During World War II* (London: Bloomsbury, 2015), 80–2.
82 Louis MacNeice, 'Halfway House: The AEF in Northern Ireland', BBC Forces Network, 25 September 1942. The following month he wrote and produced 'Salute to the United States Army' for the Home Service, and in 1943 wrote the booklet *Meet the US Army*, published by the Board of Education, with 100,000 copies distributed to schools. Louis MacNeice, 'Salute to the US Army', BBC Home Service, 4 October 1942. MacNeice was not a fan of the BBC and worked there to avoid military service, telling a friend it was a 'v. 2nd rate institution', but it was either that or 'be clapped in uniform forever'. Louis MacNeice to Eleanor Clark, 20 April 1941. Cited in Emily C. Bloom, *The Wireless Past: Anglo-Irish Writers and the BBC, 1931-1968* (Oxford: Oxford University Press, 2016), 67.
83 A. J. Tulip, 'American Presidents of Ulster descent', BBC Home Service, 27 May 1942. Quotations from *NW*, 28 May 1942; 'Workers' Playtime', BBC, Forces Programme, 3 October 1943.
84 Sir Basil Brooke, 'East and West Through an Ulsterman's Eyes', 9 January 1944. Savory Papers, D3015/1A/7/2/1-3. PRONI.
85 *SS*, 11 December 1943.
86 *WES*, 28 February 1942.

87 *BT*, 13 March 1942. In March 1942 Éire prioritized growing wheat over barley and banned the export of beer, leading to a shortage for British troops in Northern Ireland. Their outrage led to Britain renewing wheat exports to Éire. Guinness then complained about the lack of coal, and Éire's export ban was reinstituted until the British agreed to provide more. Bryce Evans, 'A Pint of Plain is your only Man', *History Ireland*, vol. 22 no. 5 (2014), 36–8.
88 'Base History', from: October 5, to December 31, 1943, 23. RG498/AHC/HS/ETOUSA/NIBC/186/597.
89 'Bulletin #26', NIBS, 23 December 1943. RG498/AHC/HS/ETOUSA/NIBC/225. The local brewers included Thomas Caffrey in Belfast. The Americans were also permitted five packets of cigarettes per week from the Post Exchange (PX), which, like alcohol, were often traded. Reynolds, *Collier's*, 10 October 1942, 66.
90 *GI Guide*, 33; *SSL*, 25 January 1945.
91 *Yank*, 9 September 1942, 14.
92 'Bishop Daly in Belleek during the war', *WW2 People's War*, BBC, 15 October 2014. https://www.bbc.co.uk/history/ww2peopleswar/stories/09/a8898709.shtml (accessed 20 October 2020); Kelly, *Home*, 25.
93 *GI Guide*, 13.
94 *Yank*, 24 June 1942.
95 Buhrman, report 65, 27 December 1942, cited in Reynolds, *Relations*, 119.
96 Wills, *Neutral Island*, 6; Carroll, *NHR*, 31.
97 'Base History', from: January 1 1944, to June 15 1944, 8. RG498/ETOUSA/AHC/HS/NIBC/186/597.
98 The *New York Times* observed the 'high cost of whisky' in January 1942. *NYT*, 29 January 1942. The *GI Guide* also remarked upon this. Note: Ireland has 'whiskey' while Scotland has 'whisky'. Guinness aimed some advertisements specifically at the Yanks, including one with the tagline 'To Our American Friends'.
99 'Welfare Committee, first meeting', 10 September 1942. CAB9/CD225/19; Gilfillan to Gransden 8 September 1942. CAB/9/CD/225/18.
100 *LS*, 25 August 1943. The American quoted earlier about beer, said of Irish whiskey: '[s]ome stuff, a fellow might just as well drink plain alcohol'. *Yank*, 9 September 1942, 14.
101 *GI Guide*, 14.
102 Healy to Romney, 6 April 1943. CAB9/CD225/19.
103 Harrisson, 'Americans in Ireland', 8 June 1942, 14. MOI.
104 Buhrman to State, 22 June 1942. RG84/BCG/CF/1942/823; *NL*, 18 June 1942.
105 SPOBS, 161. RG498/AHC/HS/ETOUSA/SPOBS/318.
106 'Base History', October-December 1943, 23. RG498/AHC/HS/ETOUSA/NIBC/186/597; 'Memo #23', NIBS, 12 November 1943. RG498/AHC/HS/ETOUSA/NIBS/225.
107 Sally Edelstein, 'On the Front Lines with Coca Cola Pt I & II', 30 May 2013. https://envisioningtheamericandream.com/ (accessed 27 April 2020).
108 Matt Fratus, 'How Coca-Cola Provided a Fresh Coke to the Front Lines of World War II', 2 April 2019. https://coffeeordie.com/coca-cola-colonels/ (accessed 27 April 2020).
109 'US Forces in Northern Ireland during WW2'. https://www.flickr.com (accessed 27 April 2020).
110 For wartime Coca-Cola advertising, see Edelstein, 'On the Front Lines with Coca Cola Pt I & II', 30 May 2013.

111 *WES*, 31 July 1942.
112 *LS*, 6, 22, 23 and 25 November 1941.
113 *WES*, 7 April 1942. *SSL*, 2 May 1942; for pictures from the game, including of Hartle, see *SSL*, 16 May 1942.
114 *BT*, 3 July 1942; *Yank*, 15 July 1942. For a photo and brief report, see *Yank*, 5 August 1942.
115 *BT*, 4 July 1942; Brooke Diary, 4 July 1942. The following year Belfast hosted the 'champions' of Northern Ireland and England. Brooke 'had to pitch the first ball, which fortunately went in the right direction'. Brooke Diary, 14 August 1943.
116 *SSL*, 8 August 1942.
117 *NW*, 20 July 1942.
118 *NW*, 27 July 1942. See also, *Ottawa Journal*, 5 September 1942.
119 *BT*, 8 October 1942.
120 *SSL*, 16 November 1942; 'Saturday Sport', BBC Forces Programme, 14 November 1942. http://genome.ch.bbc.co.uk/3a0f5e437c354b61b96b55ad6d277a8b (accessed 7 February 2018).
121 *SSL*, 16 November 1942; *NL*, 13 November 1942. The *Belfast Telegraph* carried an advert for the game. *BT*, 12 November 1942.
122 *The Daily Item* (Pennsylvania), 27 November 1942.
123 *SS*, 1 January 1944.
124 *SSL*, 2 and 13 November 1942. The dancefloor in Belfast's Red Cross Club doubled as a basketball court.
125 Prior to the Civil War, cricket was extremely popular in America and the first international match took place between the United States and Canada in 1844. For a brief account of cricket in America, see Ed Smith, 'Patriot Game', *Observer*, 3 July 2006.
126 *BT*, 22 July 1942; *Ottawa Journal*, 5 September 1942 (this report was lifted from the *Telegraph*).
127 *LS*, 23 and 25 November 1941; *SSL*, 4 July 1942. The football match was held alongside the baseball game mentioned earlier.
128 Norton, *Constitutional Nationalism*, 61.
129 *NW*, 9 October 1942.
130 *LS*, 10 October 1942.
131 *NW*, 5 August 1942.
132 *Guide*, 22-23.
133 David Gray campaigned to ban *Ulster Protestant*. See Chapter 10 for a full discussion.
134 See, for example, the remarks of the priest at Edward Clenaghan's funeral, discussed in Chapter 3.
135 Gray to Roosevelt, 19 October 1942; Gray to Spellman, 20 October 1942. David Gray Papers (DGP), Box 8.
136 *LS*, 21 November 1942; *SSL*, 30 November 1942. Farren also encouraged Catholics to join the civil defence services. Barton, *Blitz*, 267.
137 Ollerenshaw, *Politics, Economic Mobilisation*, 193. This incident is discussed in detail in Chapter 12.
138 Rafferty, *Catholicism*, 243.
139 *DR*, 4 December 1943.
140 *SS*, 15 May 1944.
141 Wills, *Neutral Island*, 31.

142 Ibid., 345.
143 Matthew Houston, 'Presbyterianism, Unionism, and the Second World War in Northern Ireland: The Career of James Little, 1939–46', *Irish Historical Studies*, vol. 43 (2019), 264.
144 Buhrman to State, 1 June 1942. RG84/BCG/CF/1942/823.
145 *WES*, 6 April 1942; *Pensacola News Journal*, 6 April 1942.
146 Buhrman to State, 28 May 1942. RG84/BCG/CF/1942/ 823.
147 Ibid.
148 Houston, *IHS*, 265.
149 *IN*, 19 May 1942.
150 'Base History', from: 1 June to 20 December 1942, 9. RG498/AHC/HS/ETOUSA/NIBC/186/597.
151 *BT*, 4 July 1942.
152 *DR*, 11 July 1942. The first reference to the 'Britain and America Circle' appeared in January. *BT*, 22 January 1942.
153 *DR*, 11 July 1942.
154 *BT*, 4 July 1942. This is dealt with in Chapter 11.
155 'Charles Thomson', talk by Jack McQuoid, BBC Home Service, 6 July 1942. Thomson did not sign the Declaration of Independence.
156 Buhrman to State, 6 July 1942. RG84/BCG/CF/1942/823.
157 *SSL*, 28 June 1943; *SSL*, 30 June 1943.
158 *NL*, 27 November 1942.
159 Ibid. Northern Ireland operated, and continues to operate, a segregated school system, divided between state schools, attended largely by Protestants, and Catholic schools.
160 *SSL*, 17 March 1943; *SSL*, 18 March 1943.
161 *SS*, 13 December 1943 (recalling the efforts of the previous year); *SSL*, 17 December 1942 *SSL*, 22 December 1942.
162 *BT*, 23 December 1942. Buhrman included the editorial in a report to Washington. Buhrman to State, 29 December 1942. RG84/BCG/CF/1942/823.
163 *SS*, 20 December 1943.
164 *LS*, 16 December 1943; 'US soldiers' Portrush Christmas treat for local children'. BBC, 23 December 2018. https://www.bbc.co.uk/news/uk-northern-ireland-466 54512 (accessed 23 December 2018).
165 'Re: Christmas celebrations, including toys and parties for children', Signed Webster, Chief, T&S Division. Headquarters Northern Ireland Base Section, APO 813, 19 November 1943. RG498/AHC/HS/ETOUSA/NIBC/224.
166 McCormick, *JHS*, 256.
167 *SSL*, 17 December 1942.
168 'Hospitality for Allied Forces in Northern Ireland: Moneymore'. 7 January 1943. CAB9CD/225/19.
169 'Bulletin #26', NIBS, 23 December 1943. President Roosevelt and various generals also sent seasonal greetings to the troops. 'NIBS, Bulletin #28'. 24 December 1943 and 'Bulletin #29', 25 December 1943. RG498/AHC/HS/ETOUSA/NIBC/225.
170 *SSL*, 25 April 1942.
171 Ibid., 22 March 1943 and 8 August 1942.
172 *Yank* 2 September 1942, 17.
173 *SSL*, 8 August 1942.

174 *Yank*, 24 June 1942. A 'Hillbilly' band, playing the Bluegrass music originating with the Ulster-Scots settlers of Appalachia, also made headlines. *SSL*, 11 July 1942.
175 Wills, *Neutral Island*, 31.
176 Norton, *Constitutional Nationalism*, 61.
177 Reynolds, *Collier's*, 17 October 1942, 36.
178 Kelly, *Home*, 39.
179 *SSL*, 4 July 1942. For the lyrics to 'The Yanks in Ireland', see ibid.
180 Ibid., 8 February 1943.
181 Ibid., 28 December 1942 and 21 January 1943.
182 *SSL*, 13 April 1944 and 13 May 1943.
183 *WES*, 28 October 1944; *SSL*, 31 July 1943 and 13 April 1944. 'Salute the Soldier' events took place across Northern Ireland in the spring of 1944 to celebrate American and British troops and raise money for the war effort. For Londonderry's, see *LS*, 29 January 1944; for Belfast, *SS*, 1 May 1944 and 5 May 1944; *SSL*, 6 May 1944. The *Down Recorder* carried adverts for events throughout County Down. *DR*, 3 June 1944; 17 June 1944; 24 June 1944. Brooke attended the opening of Fermanagh's campaign. *SS*, 5 June 1944.
184 *SSL*, 13 April 1944; *WES*, 28 October 1944.
185 *WES*, 28 October 1944.
186 Carroll, *NHR*, 26. Harry W. Edwards, *A Different War: Marines in Europe and North Africa* (Washington DC: Marine Corps, History and Museums Division, pamphlet, 1994), 14–16, 29. See also, George O. Ludcke, 'WWII Memories Stirred by Londonderry Visit', *Fortitudine* (Winter, 1997–1998), 5–7.
187 *SSL*, 29 August 1942.
188 Brooke Diary, 9 September1942.
189 *SSL*, 26 July 1943. James Cagney, '155 pounds of Irish-American energy under a shock of ginger hair', was scheduled to visit Northern Ireland and Éire in February 1944. *SSL*, 14 February 1944. If Cagney did visit, there was no newspaper coverage.
190 *Larne Times*, 9 December 1943; *SSL*, 6 December 1943.
191 *SS*, 28 December 1943. 250,000 attended the 'This is the Army' tour in London, Glasgow, Liverpool, Birmingham, Manchester, Bristol, Bournemouth and Belfast. Half were servicemen. *SSL*, 7 February 1944.
192 *SS*, 8 January 1944.
193 Ibid., 14 January 1944. American troops had earlier produced their own show, 'Hurry Up and Wait', 'a biting satire on army life'. *SSL*, 25 July 1942.
194 *BT*, 10 June 2017; 'Meeting Glenn Miller', BBC, People's War, 15 October 2014. https ://www.bbc.co.uk/history/ww2peopleswar/stories/82/a2294282.shtml (accessed 13 October 2020); 'Glenn Miller visits Northern Ireland in 1944', https://wartimeni.co m/person/glenn-miller/ (accessed 13 October 2020).
195 *SSL*, 30 December 1942.

Chapter 5

1 Tom Harrisson, 'Secret: Report on Americans in Ireland', 8 June 1942, 1. MOI.
2 Ibid. Underlining in original. Harrisson provided a spiky, forthright assessment of Northern Ireland's divisions, and their impact on the war effort in in 1944, and his exaggerated frankness about the insularity of both unionists and nationalists

offered some harsh truths. 'Ulster Outlooks' *Cornhill* magazine, 8. MOI File Report-2101.
3 *NW*, 23 June 1942.
4 For Irish responses to the Great War see, for example, Richard S. Grayson, *Dublin's Great Wars: The First World War, the Easter Rising and the Irish Revolution*, (Cambridge: Cambridge University Press, 2018); John Horne, *Our War: Ireland and the Great War* (Dublin: Royal Irish Academy, 2008); and Keith Jeffery, *Ireland and the Great War* (Cambridge: Cambridge University Press; 2011).
5 Mervyn O'Driscoll, 'Keeping Britain Sweet: Irish Neutrality, Political Identity and Collective Memory', 3, https://www.academia.edu/. Originally published in N. Keogh and A. Sorokin, *Collective Memory in Ireland and Russia* (Moscow: Rospen, 2006), 98–119.
6 Thomas Hennessey, *A History of Northern Ireland* (London: Palgrave Macmillan, 2000), 85.
7 Barton, *Northern Ireland*, 122.
8 Wills, *Neutral Island*, 397–9.
9 Enda Staunton, *The Nationalists of Northern Ireland, 1918-1973* (Dublin: The Columbia Press, 2001), 147.
10 Ibid., 147–8. This theme, with a stronger undercurrent of anti-Semitism, was also prominent in the Irish-American press. See Brian Hanley, '"No English Enemy . . . Ever Stooped so Low": Mike Quill, de Valera's Visit to the German Legation, and Irish-American Attitudes during World War II'. *Radharc*, vol. 5, no. 7 (2004–2006), 255.
11 Norton, *Constitutional Nationalism*, 37; Paul Bew, *Ireland: The Politics of Enmity, 1789-2006* (Oxford: Oxford University Press, 2007), 470; Barton, *Northern Ireland*, 123.
12 Norton, *Constitutional Nationalism*, 37.
13 Ibid., 54.
14 Grieg estimates that Northern Ireland had 200,000 men aged between 21 and 40; 104,000 in reserved occupations (many undoubtedly outside the 21–40 age bracket) and 28,000 in the military by 1942. Ian Grieg, *The Second World War and Northern Ireland* (London: Friends of the Union, 1990), 14. Patterson suggests that unemployment may have increased Catholic recruitment. Henry Patterson, *Ireland since 1939: The Persistence of Conflict* (Dublin: Penguin Ireland, 2006), 33. The majority in reserved occupations and the military were Protestant, and assuming roughly a third of the population was Catholic (so about 60,000–70,000 men of military age), starkly illustrates how heavily Catholics would have borne the burden of conscription. See also, Norton, *Constitutional Nationalism*, 36.
15 Ollerenshaw, *Politics, Economic Mobilisation*, 44–5.
16 Hennessey, *Northern Ireland*, 91–2.
17 Roosevelt to Churchill, 19 April 1943, cited in O'Halpin, *Spying*, 240.
18 Ernest L. Ives to Joseph Kennedy, 12 April 1939. RG84/BCG/CF/1939/800.
19 Ibid.
20 Ibid., 15 April 1939.
21 Secretary of State to the Chargé in France, 9 February 1940. *FRUS*, 1940, v.i, 4.
22 *IN*, 22 February 1940.
23 ibid.
24 Cahir Healy to Dublin consulate, 22 February 1940. RG84/BCG/CF/1940/800. Farrell describes Cahir Healy as 'a fervent anti-communist, an admirer of Sir Oswald Mosley . . . and a friend of General O'Duffy, the leader of the fascist-style Blueshirts

in the South. He was believed to be sympathetic to the Germans and to have been in contact with them'. Michael Farrell, *Northern Ireland: The Orange State*, revised second edition (London: Pluto Press, 1980), 169. Healy was interned in London between July 1941 and December 1942 for apparent efforts to collaborate with the Germans. Christopher Norton, 'The internment of Cahir Healy M.P., Brixton Prison July 1941-December 1942', *Twentieth Century British History*, vol. 18 (2007), 170–93. An Indian group linked to Gandhi's Congress Party and the Polish government in exile in France also sought audiences with Welles. *NYT*, 24 February 1940; 27 February 1940.

25 Healy to Dublin consulate, 22 February 1940; typed addendum, signed by Francis Styles. RG84/BCG/CF/1940/800.
26 John Randolph to Kennedy, 29 February 1940. Ibid.
27 Ibid.
28 'Voluntary political report (for embassy, London)', from Consul John Randolph, 8 March 1940. RG84/BCG/CF/1940/800.
29 Randolph to Healy, 11 March 1940. Ibid.; *IN*, 11 March 1940.
30 *BT*, 11 March 1940; Randolph to Kennedy, 12 March 1940. RG84/BCG/CF/1940/800. For the press conference more generally, and Welles's terse answers, see, *NYT*, 12 March 1940.
31 *IN*, 13 March 1940; Randolph to Kennedy, 12 March 1940. RG84/BCG/CF/1940/800.
32 Randolph to Kennedy, 12 March 1940. RG84/BCG/CF/1940/800; *IN*, 13 March 1940. The 'refusal to grant interview' was the position of most of the nationalist press. See, for example, *Fermanagh Herald (FH)*, 16 March 1940.
33 *FH*, 16 March 1940.
34 Ibid.
35 *IN*, 13 March 1940. Healy blaming Britain was referred to very briefly by the *New York Times*. *NYT*, 14 March 1940.
36 *IN*, 13 March 1940; *FH*, 16 March 1940.
37 *IN*, 13 March 1940. Stewart's statement appears to have been paraphrased by the *Irish News*.
38 Ibid., 15 March 1940; *IP*, 15 March 1940.
39 *DJ*, 30 January 1942. Capitalization in original.
40 These comments were widely reported. *NW*, 29 January 1942; *DJ*, 30 January 1942; *LS*, 29 January 1942. *NYT*, 29 January 1942.
41 *NYT*, 29 January 1942.
42 Ibid.
43 *Dungannon Observer*, 31 January 1942; *DJ*, 30 January 1942.
44 Norton, *Constitution Nationalism*, 31-32.
45 Thomas Bartlett, *Ireland: A History* (Cambridge and New York: Cambridge University Press, 2010), 454.
46 Ronan Fanning, 'Irish Neutrality: An Historical Review', *Irish Studies in International Affairs*, vol. 1, no. 3 (1982), 32.
47 *Ulster Herald*, 20 October 1926. Cited in Staunton, *Nationalists*, 73.
48 Buhrman to State, 20 January 1943 (enclosing extract from *Irish News*, 20 January 1943). RG84/BCG/CF/1943-44/800.
49 Ibid.
50 Ibid.
51 Farrell, *Orange State*, 164; Norton, *Constitutional Nationalism*, 57.
52 *Irish Times*, 19 February 1941, cited in Wood, *Britain, Ireland*, 221.

53 *DJ*, 4 February 1942.
54 Ibid., 6 February 1942. Moody seems to have later been town clerk of Strabane. *LS*, 14 March 1957.
   Hugh O'Neill Hencken, a Harvard academic and expert on Ireland, expressed similar sentiments: 'the less Mr de Valera insists that his new Constitution already includes Northern Ireland in Eire, and the less enthusiasts elsewhere call the regime in Belfast a puppet, the sooner the union they all want will take place'. *NYT*, 15 March 1942.
55 *NW*, 2 February 1942.
56 Duggan, *Neutral Ireland*, 176.
57 Richard English, *Irish freedom: The History of Nationalism in Ireland* (London: Pan Books, MacMillan, 2007), 344.
58 Brian Spencer, 'Does the Irish rain make us all Irish? Brian John Spencer looking into his soul', 27 May 2015. http://eamonnmallie.com/2015/05/the-irish-rain-makes-us-all-irish-brian-john-spencer-looking-into-his-soul/ (accessed 15 October 2015).
59 J. J. Lee, *Ireland 1912-1985: Politics and Society* (Cambridge: Cambridge University Press, 1989), 254.
60 Michael McCabe, *For God and Ireland: The Fight for Moral Superiority in Ireland 1922-1932* (Sallins, Co. Kildare: Irish Academic Press, 2012), 76.
61 Abercorn to Cardinal Joseph MacRory, 7 December 1939; MacRory to Abercorn, 10 December 1939. Folder No. 4, ARCH/11/5/9. Joseph Cardinal MacRory Papers (JCM). The fund was for various Red Cross charities, including the Duke of Gloucester's Red Cross Fund and the Northern Ireland Branch of the Soldiers', Sailors', and Airmen's Families' association, among others. The Duke of Gloucester was King George VI's younger brother. MacRory viewed Abercorn as 'not a bad sort of a fellow but not by any means intellectual'. MacRory to Gray, 25 September 1941. DGP, Box 5.
62 Fisk, *Time of War*, 457-458.
63 Staunton, *Nationalists*, 145.
64 Wood, *Britain, Ireland*, 177.
65 Duggan, *Hempel*, 134. The lack of military or economic targets may not have saved Armagh. The Germans had launched so-called Baedeker raids in 1942, named after the tourist guides, deliberately targeting historic English cities.
66 Ibid.
67 Gray to MacRory, 15 October 1941. Folder No.4, ARCH/11/5/15. JCM.
68 MacRory to Gray 20 October 1941. Ibid.
69 Gray to MacRory, 23 October 1941. Ibid.
70 Walshe to Brennan, 14 October 1941, cited in Girvin, *Emergency*, 286.
71 'Developments', 12 October 1942. RG84/BCG/CF/1942/800; *FH*, 17 October 1942. https://cunninghamsway.com/2016/12/16/october-1942-fermanagh-herald/ (accessed 11 April 2020).
72 'Developments', 12 October 1942. RG84/BCG/CF/1942/800; *FH*, 17 October 1942.
73 'Developments', 12 October 1942. RG84/BCG/CF/1942/800. Buhrman presumably meant the unionist press.
74 'Joseph, Cardinal Archbishop of Armagh and Primate of All Ireland, Lenten Pastoral', 1943. JCM. See also, 'Developments', 9 March 1943. RG84/BCG/CF/1943-44/800.
75 Staunton, *Nationalists*, 154; *NL*, 28 September 1942.
76 *NL*, 28 September 1942. The statement was widely reported in Ireland. See, for example, *IP*, 28 September 1942; *Kerry Champion*, 3 October 1942; *FH*, 3 October 1942.

77 Gray to Roosevelt, 8 October 1942; Gray to MacRory 7 October 1942. FDRP/OF/2/ DCF; *Impartial Reporter*, 4 October 1945. CAB9CD/225/1.
78 MacRory to Gray, 7 October 1942. Folder No.5, ARCH/11/5/15. JCM. This incident and Gray and MacRory's relationship are detailed in Chapter 10.
79 *NW*, 29 September 1942. The same letter appeared in the *Armagh Guardian*. *Armagh Guardian*, 2 October 1942.
80 *NL*, 30 September 1942.
81 Staunton, *Nationalists*, 154. 'B'-Specials were part-time police mobilized during crises to support the regular police. Almost entirely Protestant, the force was generally hated by nationalists.
82 Paul Lewinkoff to MacRory, 10 October 1942. Folder No. 5, ARCH/11/5/15. JCM.
83 Ibid.
84 'A statement by Bishop Joseph P. Hurley of Florida as quoted in 'The Florida Catholic', newspaper of the Diocese of St. Augustine'. Folder No.5, ARCH/11/5/15. JCM. The statement was reported in *Pensacola News Journal*, 15 October, 1942, and passed onto Stormont by Gray. Henderson to Gransden, 3 November 1942, 'Statement by Bishop Hurley'. CAB9CD/225/1.
85 JCM, Folder No.5; *Pensacola News Journal*, 15 October, 1942, 4; CAB9CD/225/1. Gray thanked Hurley 'heartily' for his comments; he also described MacRory 'a very dear old man'. Gray mentioned leaving the Republican Party in 1928 due to its treatment of Al Smith, that year's Democratic presidential candidate and the first Catholic presidential nominee. Gray to Hurley, 2 November 1942. DGP, Box 9.
86 Hurley to Gray, 28 January 1943. DGP, Box 23.
87 Kennedy to Gray, 8 January 1943. Ibid. Kennedy believed that Hurley had made some foolish statements about the prosecution of the war and consequently was no longer taken seriously.
88 McQuaid congratulated MacRory, noting that Hurley 'has not ceased . . . to make much noise. He will not, I think, effect much'. Archbishop John McQuaid to MacRory, 26 January 1943. Folder No.5. JCM.
89 See, for example, *NYT*, 28 September 1942; *Baltimore Sun*, 28 September, 1942; *Boston Globe*, 28 September, 1942; *Atlanta Constitution*, 28 September, 1942; *Chicago Tribune*, 28 September, 1942.
90 *Richmond Times-Dispatch*, 29 September 1942, 8. See also, Folder no. 4. JCM.
91 *Newark News*, undated. Folder no. 4. JCM. Other newspapers also drew attention to the treatment of Catholic clergy by the Nazis. See, for example, *Ottawa Citizen* (Ontario, Canada) 28 September, 1942.
92 *Newark News*, undated. Folder no. 4. JCM.
93 *Time*, 12 October 1942. *Time* also noted MacRory's attitude to Protestantism.
94 Old IRA reference: *Irish Examiner*, 5 October 1942.
95 John W. Dulanty to Walshe, 18 February 1943. No. 267. NAI DFA 2006/39. *DIFP*, volume 7.
96 *DR*, 26 February 1944; Tim Pat Coogan, *De Valera: Long Fellow, Long Shadow* (London: Arrow Books, 1995), 604.
97 Wilfrid Spender Dairy, 22 February 1944, cited in Staunton, *Nationalists*, 145.
98 Maffey to Machtig, 30 June 1945. 'UK-Éire Political and Constitutional Relations: Cardinal MacRory's observations on Partition'. WX101/1/87 UK-Éire. TNA.
99 Machtig 11 July 1945; Under Secretary of State Paul Emrys-Evans, 12 July 1945. ibid.
100 *NL*, 15 October 1945. For reports on the cardinal's death and funeral, see *BT*, 15 October 1945; *NL*, 16 October 1945; *NL*, 18 October 1945.

101 Staunton, *Nationalists*, 155. In Gray's unpublished memoirs, hugely unreliable in numerous ways and must be viewed with extreme caution, he called the Cardinal 'an honest and warm man but with [a] somewhat constricted outlook' who 'seemed unaware' of the Holocaust. Gray, *Green Curtain*, MSS, Ch.25, 16. DGP, Box 1.
102 *SSL*, 9 February 1943.
103 Ibid., 5 February 1943.
104 Ibid.
105 Buhrman to State, 10 February 1943. RG84/BCG/CF/1943.
106 ibid.
107 Ibid.; *LS*, 4 February 1943; *NL*, 8 February 1943.
108 Spellman, widely believed to have been a closet homosexual, has been implicated as a perpetrator in sexual abuse scandals in the US Catholic Church. Due to ongoing federal investigations, the Archdiocese of New York has closed its archives relating to Spellman to researchers. Repeated requests for information on his trip to Ireland have gone unanswered, leaving me unable to examine some fifty documents relating to it. 'NY archdiocese responds to Cardinal Spellman groping allegation', *Catholic News Agency*, 19 February 2019. 'Covering up for Cardinal Spellman', *Church Militant*, 13 February 2019.
109 John Cooney, *The American Pope: The Life and Times of Francis Cardinal Spellman* (New York: Times Books, 1984), 124.
110 Cooney, *American Pope*, 124.
111 *SSL*, 22 March 1943. The *Telegraph* claimed the tour was on behalf of the Vatican. *BT*, 20 March 1943, 3.
112 *NYT*, 24 March 1943; *Irish Independent*, 23 March 1943. *IP*, 24 March 1943.
113 'Conclusions of a cabinet meeting', 11 March 1943. CAB4/534/11.
114 Lowry to Andrews, 10 March 1943. CAB9CD/225/13.
115 Ibid.
116 'Conclusions of a cabinet meeting', 11 March 1943. CAB 4/534/11. Andrews had more pressing problems and within a month Brooke replaced him as Prime Minister.
117 Spellman's biographer makes no reference to his visit to Northern Ireland and, with Spellman's papers closed to the public, I have been unable to locate any information which sheds light on his attitude.
118 Cooney, *American Pope*, 130.
119 *BT*, 31 March 1943, 1 April 1943, 2 April 1943; *Limerick Leader*, 31 March 1943.
120 'Report no. 55953', Military Intelligence Division, 16 April 1943, cited in Cooney, *America's Pope*, 131. This document is dated after Spellman's visit. Spellman was also briefed that de Valera, according to Cooney, was 'a mystic . . . obsessed with the wrongs done to Ireland over the centuries'. ibid.
121 Gray to State, 8 March 1943. FDRP/OF/2/DCF.
122 Robert I. Gannon, *The Cardinal Spellman Story* (New York: Doubleday and Company, 1962), 208.
123 Spellman's official biographer Gannon believes that it was Roosevelt's 'implied preference' that he stayed with Gray. It was also, he notes, 'a difficult time for a close personal friend of the American President to visit Ireland'. Ibid., 208.
124 Gray to MacRory, 25 March 1943. Folder No.5, ARCH/11/5/15. JCM. Along with MacRory, De Valera, O'Kelly, Archbishop McQuaid and the British and Canadian representatives were also invited.
125 Dwyer, *Curtain*, 258.

126 Ibid.
127 Ibid.
128 *BT*, 2 April 1943.
129 *IP*, 3 April 1943.
130 *Irish Independent*, 3 April 1943. *NL*, 3 April 1943.
131 *BT*, 2 April 1943.
132 *DJ*, 5 April 1943.
133 *BT*, 2 April 1943.
134 *NL*, 3 April 1943. He joked that 'I didn't think there would be any Spellmans in Armagh'. The *Whig* carried a similar report. *NW*, 3 April 1943.
135 *IP*, 1 and 3 April 1943.
136 Dwyer, *Curtain*, 259. *BT*, 2 April 1943.
137 John D. Kearney Diary, 12 April 1943, cited in Dwyer, *Curtain*, 259.
138 'Report no. 55953, Military Intelligence Division', 16 April 1943. Cited in Cooney, *American Pope*, 131.
139 *DJ*, 5 April 1943; *NYT*, 5 April 1943.
140 *DJ*, 5 April 1943. The following year, Cordell Hull rejected any connection between the charter and Ireland, noting that it enshrined responsibilities as well as rights and a nation had to 'fulfil scrupulously its established duties to other nations', which Éire had not. Girvin, *Emergency*, 312.
141 For Spellman's visit to the British Isles, see *BT*, 20 March 1943, 31 March 1943, 2 April 1943; and for a brief report of his visit to American troops see ibid., 3 April 1943.
142 Buhrman to Gray, 6 April 1943. RG84/BCG/CF/1943-44/800.
143 Buhrman to Gray, 29 March 1943. Ibid.
144 Gray to Buhrman, 31 March 1943. Ibid.
145 Buhrman to Gray, 2 April 1943. RG84/BCG/CF1943-44/800. Hill was sympathetic to unionists having visited Ulster prior to partition. For biographical details, see *SS*, 21 January 1943.
146 Gray to Buhrman, 3 April 1943. RG84/BCG/CF1943-44/800.
147 Buhrman to Gray, 6 April 1943. Ibid.
148 ibid.
149 Buhrman, Memorandum to Secretary of State, 3 April 1943. RG84/BCG/CF/1943-44/800. Buhrman's dispatches were sent to Washington, London and, latterly, Dublin, but this one does not appear to have been sent to Dublin.
150 *DJ*, 5 April 1943; *IP*, 3 April 1943; *FH*, 10 April 1943; *Donegal News*, 10 April 1943; *Strabane Chronicle*, 10 April 1943. The *Derry Journal* also complained about 'how grossly this London News Agency [the Press Association] misrepresented the Archbishop's very deliberately and definitely expressed view. A more shocking case of distortion by deletion it would be difficult to find' when it did not publish the full text of a short statement Spellman made. The PA omitted the last couple of sentences, including his view that 'peace is won only by justice. Justice is the mind of civilisation and charity is its heart', which, presumably, was seen as an oblique reference to Ireland. *DJ*, 7 April 1943. The protest was reported in the States. *WES*, 2 April 1943.
151 *IP*, 1 April 1943.
152 *Irish World*, cited in Hanley, *Radharc*, 255
153 *Nenagh Guardian* (Tipperary), 3 April 1943.
154 *BT*, 7 April 1943

155 Spellman, Francis Joseph (4 May 1889–2 December 1967), *American National Biography Online*, http://www.anb.org/articles/08/08-01438.html (accessed 27 November 2015); Pat McNamara, 'The Powerhouse: Cardinal Francis Spellman', *Patheos*, 17 December 2012.
156 'Lurgan to London, 27.2.43'. Postal Censorship Report No. 38, 8 April 1943. Harcourt to Butler, 9 April 1943, M.I.L2/503. United States, File no. 33, pp. 1925–2651; A3468/33/45: 'United States Troops in Northern Ireland'. FO371/34124. TNA.
157 *BT*, 25 October 1945.
158 *NL*, 26 October 1945.

Chapter 6

1 'Developments', 3 September 1942. RG84/BCG/CF/1942/800.
2 Ibid.
3 Ibid.
4 Ibid., 24 July 1942.
5 Maxwell to Grandsen, 10 January 1942. CAB9CD/255/3.
6 'War Cabinet. Defence Committee (Operations) Extract from Minutes of Meeting held on Friday 9th January, 1942'. Ibid.
7 Henderson to Gransden, 26 January 1942. Ibid.
8 Nothing found in US archives suggests that the Americans planned to intervene in Northern Ireland's internal problems.
9 'SPOBS', 112. RG498/AHC/HS/ETOUSA/SPOBS/318. This report was written in October 1944.
10 Ibid., 131. In April 1939, Inspector General Wickham of the Royal Ulster Constabulary claimed to Ernest Ives, US consul in Belfast, that German agents in Dublin funded the IRA. Ives to Kennedy, 1 April 1939. RG84/BCG/CF/1939/800.
11 CG, USAFBI to AGWAR for MAGNET, 7 February 1942. Cited in 'SPOBS', 142. RG498/AHC/HS/ETOUSA/SPOBS/318.
12 'United States Army Northern Ireland Force Bulletin, Number 11', 16 February, 1942. Cited in 'SPOBS', 143. RG498/AHC/HS/ETOUSA/SPOBS/318. See also: CG, USAFBI to AGWAR, 6 February 1942, message number 67. Cited in ibid., 144.
13 'SPOBS', 144. RG498/AHC/HS/ETOUSA/SPOBS/318.
14 Tim Pat Coogan, *Ireland in the Twentieth Century* (London: Arrow Books, 2004), 333; Farrell, *Orange State*, 163. The commander is not named.
15 Bardon, *Ulster*, 582; John O'Neill, *Belfast Battalion: A History of the Belfast IRA, 1922-1969* (Wexford: Litter Press, Kindle Edition, 2018).
16 Brian Hanley, '"Oh Here's to Adolf Hitler"? The IRA and the Nazis', *History Ireland*, vol. 13, no. 3 (May–June 2005).
17 Farrell, *Orange State*, 152.
18 Norton, *Constitutional Nationalism*, 31.
19 John Cudahy to State, 20 January 1939. RG84/BCG/CF/1939/800.
20 HA/20A/1/24. PRONI cited in Wood, *Britain, Ireland*, 127. James Connolly and Patrick Pearse were two leaders of the 1916 rising.
21 Wood, *Britain, Ireland*, 116. For anti-Semitism in *War News*, see Brian Hanley, '"Oh here's to Adolph Hitler"? The IRA's support for the Nazis in context' (unpublished paper, 2004), 3–5. Wood also suggests an anti-Semitic undercurrent to IRA plans to attack cinemas. 'Cinema', Wood argues, 'and its allegedly alien, by which quite often

meant Jewish, cultural influence had been a republican target before and remained one.' Wood, *Britain, Ireland*, 133.
22 Bew, *Enmity*, 478.
23 English, *Irish freedom*, 340.
24 Uinseann Mac Eoin, *The IRA in the Twilight Years 1923-1948* (Dublin: Argenta Publications, 1997), 726.
25 Hanley, *HI*. According to this statement, the Germans wanted a 'free and progressive Europe' and were the 'energising force' of European politics. The statement was heavily criticized by other Irish republican groups.
26 Wood, *Britain, Ireland*, 127; 133. Wood is particularly scathing about Russell, who 'was guilty of the most crass and simplistic self-deception', gave no thought to Ireland's Jews and would have willingly collaborated with a victorious Germany. 'To suggest that Russell occupied a moral vacuum', Wood asserts, 'may even be to flatter him'. Ibid., 117-18. Hanley describes Russell as an 'apolitical militarist', whereas Norton views him as right wing. Hanley, unpublished, 19; Norton, *Constitutional Nationalism*, 31. For a fuller discussion of IRA-Nazi links, anti-Semitism within the organization, and its anti-Nazism in the early 1930s, see Hanley, *HI*.
27 Tom Barry to Sighle Humphreys, 12 June 1976, cited in Hanley, unpublished, 18-19. Hanley states that '[t]he most senior republican figure in the United States, Joseph McGarrity, was not only pro-German, but by 1938 was bemoaning the influence of the "Jewish-controlled press" in America'. McGarrity to J. Brislane, 27 September 1938, cited in ibid. My thanks to Brian Hanley for sharing this unpublished research, which later appeared in revised form in *History Ireland*.
28 Uinseann, *Twilight*, 762.
29 Hennessey, *Northern Ireland*, 86.
30 Cole, *Propaganda*, 23; Bew, *Enmity*, 469; *Irish Times*, 8 May 2017.
31 Uinseann, *Twilight*, 895.
32 Wills, *Neutral Island*, 95; Hanley, unpublished, 20-1.
33 Wood, *Britain, Ireland*, 130. Noted chronicler of Belfast life Sam McAughtry claimed in a 1997 documentary that an IRA member confessed to him that it had aided the Germans in bombing Belfast. *BT*, 21 April 2016.
34 Wood, *Britain, Ireland*, 130.
35 Paul McMahon, *British Spies and Irish Rebels: British Intelligence and Ireland* (Woodbridge: Boydell Press, 2011), 397; Wills, *Neutral Island*, 95. Whether the Germans requested or needed this help is questionable.
36 Cole, *Propaganda*, 24-5; Bew, *Enmity*, 467; Fisk, *Time of War*, 175. Éire's authorities discovered and passed the plans onto British intelligence who gave them to the police in Northern Ireland. Fisk, *Time of War*, 175. There were variants of 'Kathleen', including one so fanciful the Germans wondered if the Irish-born agent who delivered it to Berlin was double-crossing them. Fisk, *Time of War*, 348-9.
37 O'Halpin states: 'Hempel had a trusted intermediary with links to the Northern IRA – the British claimed this to be Sean MacBride, which seems likely.' O'Halpin, *Spying*, 209. MacBride was the son of John MacBride, executed after the Easter Rising, and Maud Gonne, another legendary figure in Irish republicanism. He led the IRA from 1936 until 1939.
38 *LS*, 21 March 1942.
39 *NL*, 20 March 1942.
40 *LS*, 21 March 1942. The letters were reported in the American press. *WES*, 19 March 1942 and *Freeport Journal Standard* (Illinois), 19 March 1942.
41 *LS*, 21 March 1942; *WES*, 20 March 1942.

42 'Irish Republican Army, Chief of Staff, General Headquarters, Dublin, 13 June 1942, for Director of Publicity, Northern Command'. Cited in O'Neill, *Belfast Battalion*.
43 Buhrman to Gray, 3 April 1942. DGP, Box 7.
44 Ibid.
45 Wood, *Britain, Ireland*, 130.
46 The *Irish Press* reported that one of the initial shots fired by the gang hit Murphy's police car. *Irish Press* (*IP*), 29 April 1942.
47 *NYT*, 15 May 1943, 5.
48 *NW*, 2 September 1942; *IP*, 2 September 1942.
49 For a brief account of the circumstances of Murphy's murder, see journalist Hugh Jordan's *Milestones in Murder: Defining Moments in Ulster's Terror War* (Edinburgh: Mainstream Publishing, 2002), chapter four.
50 Brooke, for example, wrote in his diary: '[a]ll morning on the question of the reprieve of any or all of the 6 murderers who shot Constable Murphy. It was a horrible job but I think we did what is right'. Brooke Diary, 26 August 1942.
51 *DJ*, 5 August 1942.
52 *NW*, 2 September 1942; *IP*, 31 August 1942. The trial and subsequent review clearly prove that the condemned man, who was injured in the attack, had wounded but not killed Constable Murphy. Two of his accomplices used the same kind of gun which had killed the officer; however, the police could not establish which had fired the fatal shots. The situation was complicated by the gang insisting on being tried collectively and assuming equal responsibility for the murder, meaning that all or none of them would be guilty. Officials were appalled by this stance and believed that it gave them little choice but to condemn all six. Two were initially reprieved, before the intervention by Abercorn who, supported by the Attorney General, recommended five commutations. Gransden to Abercorn, 27 August 1942; Andrews to Abercorn 30 August 1942; Report of, Trial Judge (E. S. Murphy), *Rex v. Cordner and others*. CAB/4/522A. As Hogan and Walker note, Stormont viewed executing IRA members as counterproductive and operated on 'the pragmatic belief that the death penalty engendered sympathy for the regime's opponents'. Gerard Hogan and Clive Walker, *Political Violence and the Law in Ireland* (Manchester and New York: Manchester University Press; 1989), 154. Williams was the only terrorist ever executed in Northern Ireland. For a report on the reprieves in the United States, see *WES*, 31 August 1942.
53 *BT*, 18 August 1942.
54 Cole, *Propaganda*, 86. Cole also states: '[s]ome in the Éire government feared that a significant portion of the Irish public might back an IRA conspiracy to provoke war between Éire and Britain' if the six were executed. Ibid., 129.
55 *Post Enquirer* (Oakland), 8 September 1942. Clipping sent by J. Miniss to Andrews, 18 November 1942. CAB9F/123/10. If anything, Brennan was jealous of Anglo-American cooperation, which Éire officials believed undermined their influence on Roosevelt's administration. Girvin, *Emergency*, 186.
56 'Developments', 8 September 1942. RG84/BCG/CF/1942/800. US sailors in Londonderry resented IRA efforts to turn them against the British. Buhrman to State, 11 September. RG84/BCG/CF/1942/823.
57 'Developments', 8 September 1942. RG84/BCG/CF/1942/800.
58 Ibid., 11 September 1942.
59 *NW*, 2 September 1942.
60 Ibid.
61 Ibid.

Notes to pages 105–108

62 Ibid.
63 'Developments', 3 September 1942. RG84/BCG/CF/1942/800.
64 NW, 2 September 1942.
65 Wood, *Britain, Ireland*, 116.
66 Cole, *Propaganda*, 110–11.
67 NW, 22 September 1942. Virtually the same quotation appeared in the *Ballymena Observer*. BO, 25 September 1942.
68 NW, 22 September 1942; *Armagh Guardian*, 25 September 1942.
69 NW, 22 September 1942.
70 Ibid., 5 August 1942.
71 Gray to John G. Winant, 27 August 1942. DGP, Box 8. Gray was perturbed by an earlier encounter with the pageantry of Irish republicanism, following the deaths of two hunger strikers in April 1940. The parade for the first included 'bums' and 'down and outs' while the second was 'far more impressive and sinister', Gray calling it a 'dedication not of love of country but to hate of the establishment'. Gray to Roosevelt, 20 April 1940. FDRP/OF/2/DCF.
72 There was a similar response in Éire after the execution of two IRA members for bombing Coventry, with flags flown at half-mast, cinemas closed and sporting events cancelled. Cole, *Propaganda*, 23.
73 Gray to Roosevelt, 3 September 1942. FDRP/OF/2/DCF.
74 'Secret and Confidential, Memorandum on the State of Ireland', 8 September 1942. The *Irish Press* printed the substance of the manifesto. *IP*, 2 September 1942. The US press noted the explicit threat to the Americans. *WES*, 31 August 1942.
75 'Memorandum on the State of Ireland', 8 September 1942. FDRP/OF/2/DCF.
76 Ibid.
77 Ibid.
78 Ibid.
79 'Developments', 22 August 1942. RG84/BCG/CF/1942/800.
80 Ibid.
81 Ibid.
82 Ibid.
83 Ibid, 1 September 1942.
84 Ibid.
85 Ibid.
86 Ibid., 2 September 1942.
87 Ibid.
88 Ibid., 8 September 1942.
89 Ibid., 7 September 1942.
90 Ibid.
91 Ibid., 8 September 1942.
92 Ibid.
93 Ibid.
94 Ibid., 1 October 1942.
95 Ibid., 12 October 1942.
96 Ibid., 10 October 1942. Buhrman referred to a 'series of terrorist activities'.
97 Ibid., 15 October 1942.
98 *WES*, 1 September 1942; *NL*, 2 September 1942; *WES*, 2 September 1942.
99 *Dungannon Observer*, 5 September 1942.
100 *WES*, 2 September 1942.

101 Unattributed newspaper clipping. DGP, Box 8.
102 *WES*, 4 September 1942.
103 The *Boston Globe* and the *Binghamton Press* were among those covering the story on the front page. *Boston Globe*, 2 September 1942; *Binghamton Press*, 2 September 1942. Other regional papers citing the AP report included: *Casper Star-Tribune*, 2 September 1942; *Lancaster News Era*, Pennsylvania, 2 September 1942; *Lansing State Journal*, 2 September 1942; *Pittsburgh Sun*, 2 September 1942.
104 *WES*, 4 September 1942.
105 See, for example, *Fresno Bee*, 1 September 1942.
106 For reports of the 'mild demonstration', see *The Times Tribune*, 2 September 1942; *York Dispatch*, 2 September 1942,
107 *New York Daily News*, 3 and 5 September 1942.
108 *Decatur Daily Review*, 8 November 1942; *Arizona Republic*, 24 November, 1942. King also talked of de Valera's 'cooperative neutrality' and believed that he would never advocate force to end partition as it would repeat the 'fratricidal upheavals' of the period 1916–1923.
109 Coogan, *de Valera*, 530; Bardon, *Ulster*, 583.
110 Bardon, *Ulster*, 583. The collapse of the IRA campaign, according to one member was due to intelligence: '[a]ll information they [the police] got, came from the Catholic population'. Paddy Devlin, interview with Enda Staunton, 17 April 1991, cited in Staunton, *Nationalists*, 154. For the suppression of the IRA in Éire, see Bardon, *Ulster*, 583 and Cole, *Propaganda*, 23.
111 Farrell, *Orange State*, 166.
112 'Developments', 14 January 1943. RG84/BCG/CF/1943/800.
113 Ibid., 16 January 1943.
114 Ibid., 26 April 1946.
115 *NL*, 26 April 1943.
116 'Developments', 26 April 1946. RG84/BCG/CF/1943/800.
117 'Odd Man Out: a story about the Belfast IRA?' Treason Felony Blog, 24 November 2016. https://treasonfelony.wordpress.com/2016/11/24/odd-man-out-a-story-about-the-belfast-ira/ (accessed 19 May 2020). O'Neill, *Belfast Battalion*.
118 OSS 'Report on the Present State of Éire', 27 January 1943. Cited in Wills, *Neutral Island*, 233.
119 'Military Intelligence Division WDGS, Military Attaché Report: Ireland, Subject: Stability of Government – Éire', 1 May 1943, prepared by Lt. Col. J. L. Hathaway, Military Attaché. DGP, Box 10.
120 'Base History', from: 1 January 1942 to 31 May 1942, 14. RG498/AHC/HS/ETOUSA/NIBC/186/597.

Chapter 7

1 Randolph to State, 31 December 1941. RG84/BCG/CF/1941/800. Randolph's prior postings included Moscow at the outset of the Russian Revolution, Baghdad in the 1920s and Quebec in the 1930s. http://politicalgraveyard.com/bio/randolph.html (accessed 6 October 2020).
2 Francis M. Carroll, *The American Presence in Ulster: A Diplomatic History, 1796-1996* (Washington DC: Catholic University of America Press, 2006), 143.

3   For the creation of the consulate, see ibid., 21–45.
4   Ibid., 127.
5   Ives to Kennedy, 1 April 1939. RG84/BCG/CF/1939/800. Ives spent eight years in various German cities, before leaving in 1917 when America declared war, moving to Paris and Alexandria prior to Belfast. http://politicalgraveyard.com/bio/ives.html (accessed 6 October 2020).
6   Carroll, *American Presence*, 132.
7   Randolph to Winant, 16 April 1941; Randolph to Winant, 17 April 1941. RG84/BCG/CF/1941/800.
8   Randolph to Gray, 12 May 1941. DGP, Box 5. Carroll, *American Presence*, 143. Many consular staff ended up living in hotels during the war. Ibid., 155.
9   Randolph to State (May 1941; specific date missing). RG84/BCG/CF/1941/125.6/125.4. The raids' single American casualty was the property of former consul Ives, stored in the heavily bombed docks area. Randolph to Secretary of State, 31 December 1941. RG84/BCG/CF/1941/123.
10 Randolph to Winant, 14 May 1941. RG84/BCG/CF/1941/800.
11 Randolph, 'Voluntary political report: Northern Ireland's reaction to occupation of Iceland by American Forces', 11 July 1941; Randolph, 'Voluntary political report: Northern Ireland comments on American allegations of US Naval Air Base in Ulster', 11 July 1941. Ibid.
12 Randolph, 'Voluntary political report: local reports and appreciation of American help and friendship', 19 September 1941. Ibid.
13 For Buhrman's biographical details, see Randolph to Gransden, 'Historical Data from the Register of the Department of State concerning: Buhrman, Parker Wilson', 2 January 1942. CAB9B/35/9. See also: http://prabook.com/web/person-view.html?profileId=940170 and http://politicalgraveyard.com/bio/buffum-bulloch.html (accessed 7 August 2017).
14 'Developments', 20 January 1942. RG84/BCG/CF/1942/800.
15 Randolph to Ives, 21 February 1940. RG84/BCG/CF/1941/800.1.
16 Randolph to Andrews, 29 December 1941. RG84/BCG/CF/1941/123.
17 Quincy F. Roberts to Brooke, 28 January 1948. CAB9B/35/9.
18 Brooke to Roberts, 29 January 1948. Ibid.
19 'Dept. of State has upgraded Belfast from a consulate to a consulate general from effective from 16 April 1942'. Correspondence, Belfast Consulate General, General Records, 1942 volume 2, Box 46 (RG84/BCG/GR/1942/46).
20 Buhrman to Hull, 15 October 1942. Buhrman had assumed that the embassy forwarded his reports to the State Department but sought clarification. Buhrman to State, 13 October 1942. RG84/BCG/CF/1942/800.
21 'Developments', 20 January 1942. Ibid.
22 Buhrman to Gray, 19 May 1942. Ibid.
23 'Developments', 20 January 1942. Ibid.
24 Ibid., 28 January 1942.
25 Gray to Buhrman, 11 February 1942; Buhrman to Gray, 26 February 1942. RG84/BCG/CF/1942/800.
26 Buhrman to Hull, 11 September 1942. RG84/BCG/CF/1942/823.
27 Ibid. Buhrman noted the potentially negative propaganda these problems could generate.
28 Ibid., 9 March 1942.
29 Ibid., 11 September 1942.

30 Ibid.
31 'Developments', 25 September 1942. RG84/BCG/CF/1942/800.
32 Buhrman to Hull, 21 October 1942. RG84/BCG/CF/1942/823.
33 'Developments', 20 January 1942. RG84/BCG/CF/1942/800. On 6 February, Buhrman submitted a five page memo about conscription debates in 1939. Ibid.
34 Gray to Buhrman, 27 January 1942. Ibid.
35 Buhrman to Gray, 4 February 1942, ibid.
36 Buhrman to Francis H. Styles, 25 February, RG84/BCG/CF/1942/822.
37 Styles to Buhrman, 28 February 1942. Ibid.
38 'Developments', 12 October 1942. RG84/BCG/CF/1942/800.
39 Bardon, *Ulster*, 577.
40 'Developments', 28 February 1942. RG84/BCG/CF/1942/800.
41 Ibid., 11 March 1942. See also, 17 October 1942. Ibid.
42 Ibid., 6 June 1942.
43 Bardon, *Ulster*, 562. See also, Bartlett, *Ireland*, 457-8, and Ollerenshaw, *Politics, Economic Mobilisation*, 33.
44 Ollerenshaw, *Politics, Economic Mobilisation*, 2. Northern Ireland accounted for 10 per cent of working days lost in the UK with only 2 per cent of the workforce. Wood, *Propaganda*, 178-81.
45 Wood, *Propaganda*, 178.
46 Buhrman to State, 12 March, 1942. RG84/BCG/CF/1942/800.
47 Buhrman to State, 15 October 1942. RG84/BCG/CF/1942/850.4.
48 Ibid., 17 October 1942.
49 Ibid., 30 October 1942.
50 Ibid.
51 Wood, *Propaganda*, 179.
52 Ibid. Wood concludes: '[i]t was also a reminder – though one few trade unionists in Belfast needed – of Stormont's fear of solidarity within the Protestant workforce and of how easily Catholic and anti-partitionist influence could be invoked by the authorities'. Ibid., 180.
53 'Labor in Northern Ireland,' prepared by John C. Fuess, 24. RG84/BCG/CF/1942/850.4.
54 Ibid.
55 Ibid.
56 'Developments', 11 February 1942. RG84/BCG/CF/1942/800.
57 Ibid. When Andrews succeeded Craig in November 1940, the hope that he would shake up the government was dashed as he continued Craig's policies with essentially Craig's cabinet. Five of Craig's eight member cabinet had been in office since the state's foundation. Farrell, *Orange State*, 159; Barton, *Blitz*, 55.
58 'Developments', 11 February 1942. RG84/BCG/CF/1942/800.
59 'Developments', 24 September 1942. Ibid.
60 Randolph, 'Voluntary political report (for embassy, London): Confidential: Political Conditions in Northern Ireland. Invitation or Request for a Visit from Mr Sumner Welles', 9 March 1940. ('Copies sent to American Embassy London, Department of State, Consulate General, London'). RG84/BCG/CF/1940/800.
61 'Developments', 29 September 1942. RG84/BCG/CF/1942/800.
62 Ibid.
63 'Developments', 24 July 1942. RG84/CF/1942/800.

64 Buhrman to Hull, 8 December 1942. RG84/BCG/CF/1942/800. Buhrman's attitude to national minorities, or his reporting of perceptions of them, appears in a report from Syria in the mid-1920s, amid the refugee problems created by the Ottoman Empire's collapse: '[t]he present deportees are Armenians who are politically objectionable, and Assyrians. Both groups are unassimilable national minorities, and are therefore considered undesirable by the nationalists'. Buhrman to Secretary of State, 7 April 1924, cited in Shamiran Mako and Sargon Donabed, 'Harput, Turkey to Massachusetts: Immigration of Jacobite Christians', *CHRONOS Revue d'Histoire de l'Université de Balamand*, Numéro, vol. 23 (2011), 21.
65 Buhrman to State, 20 January 1943 (enclosing extract from *Irish News*, 20 January 1943). RG84/BCG/CF/1943-44/800.
66 'Developments', 11 February 1943. RG84/BCG/CF/1943-44/800. See also, 'Developments', 18 February 1943; 25 February 1943; 26 February 1943. Ibid.
67 Buhrman to State, 1 March 1943. Ibid.
68 Ibid., 20 January 1943.
69 Ibid., 30 April 1943; 17 May 1943.
70 Ibid., 17 May 1943.
71 'Developments', 18 September 1942. RG84/BCG/CF/1942/800.
72 Ibid. This nominally referred to the British but also alluded to unionists.
73 De Valera encouraged people to learn Irish; in 1944 he condemned English as 'the language of the conqueror'. Cole, *Propaganda*, 165.
74 'Developments', 18 September 1942. RG84/BCG/CF/1942/800.
75 Glenn A. Abbey, American Consul London, to Randolph, 15 December 1941; Telegram from American Consulate General London, December 15 1941, to John Randolph American Consulate Belfast. RG84/BCG/CF/1941/123.
76 *BT*, 7 May 1943.
77 Ibid. Sir Robert Baird's father and uncle founded the *Telegraph* in 1870, and he was managing director from 1886 until his death in 1934. 'Poor Richard' was a reference to Benjamin Franklin's *Poor Richard's Almanac*. The State Department later appointed Buhrman to inspect prisoner of war camps. Carroll, *American Presence*, 154. He then became consul in Munich after the war. James F. Tent, *Mission on the Rhine: 'Reeducation' and Denazification in American-Occupied Germany* (Chicago and London: University Of Chicago Press, 1984), 110–12.
78 Carroll, *American Presence*, 154.
79 *BT*, 7 May 1943; Christian G. Appy, *Cold War Constructions: The Political Culture of United States Imperialism, 1945-1966* (Amherst: University of Massachusetts Press, 2000), 278. Roberts began service in 1915, and was posted to Venice, Genoa and Salonika, before reaching Western Samoa in 1928. He had most recently served in the Far East and Pacific, including Fiji, French Indo-China and Chefoo in China. Political Graveyard: http://politicalgraveyard.com/bio/roberts7.html#670.32.86 (accessed 19 April 2018).
80 See, for example, Roberts to State, 'Developments', 27 March 1944. This report dealt with Éire's forthcoming general election, MacRory's Lenten Pastoral about Éire deserving credit for not siding with the Axis and Lowry's 'fumigation' remark. RG84/BCG/GR/1944/63.
81 Henry Stubbins, US embassy, to Roberts, 14 April 1944. Ibid.
82 Not all American soldiers were citizens; for example, there was a citizenship ceremony for 72 American servicemen, two from Northern Ireland, at the consulate in May

1944. SS, 29 May 1944. See also, *Belfast Weekly Telegraph*, 19 May 1944. For other ceremonies, see *BT*, 29 February 1944, 29 March 1944 and 11 May 1944.
83 William F. Ayer, 'Northern Ireland Political Developments during August', 1945, 31 August 1945. RG84/BCG/GR/1945/73. Ayer also noted that VJ Day had been an anti-climax as most saw VE Day as the end of the war.
84 See Chapter 8.
85 J.C. Homes to American Diplomatic and Consular Officers, 14 July 1945 and Secretary of State to certain American Diplomatic and Consular Officers, 1 November 1945 RG84/BCG/CF/1945-46/811.11 and 851.

Chapter 8

1 *Guide*, 27.
2 Ibid., 29.
3 Dehra Parker to Gransden, 3 January 1944. CAB9CD/225/19.
4 *NW*, 22 September 1942; McCormick, *JSH*, 231.
5 *IN*, 16 October 1942.
6 Harrisson, 'Americans in Ireland', 8 June 1942, 4. MOI.
7 'WW2, People's War: American Servicemen in Northern Ireland', BBC, 15 October 2014. https://www.bbc.co.uk/history/ww2peopleswar/stories/24/a2094824.shtml (accessed 16 April 2019).
8 Joseph McCain, quoted in Bardon, *Ulster*, 576.
9 Campbell to author, 17 June 2009.
10 'Dehra Parker's notes on "Black and White" problem', 13 December 1943. CAB9CD/225/19.
11 Parker to Gransden, 3 January 1944. Ibid.
12 Isobel Kennedy to Eleanor Roosevelt, 10 September 1942. RG107: Office of the Secretary of War: General Correspondence of John J. McCloy, 1941–45, Box35, File ASW291.2, Negro Troops, 1942. Eleanor Roosevelt to Kennedy, 22 September 1942. Ibid. Underlining in original.
13 Eleanor Roosevelt wrote: 'the young Southerners were very indignant to find that the Negro soldiers were not looked upon with terror by the girls in England and Ireland and Scotland'. Eleanor Roosevelt to Secretary of State, 22 September 1942, ibid.
14 For example, see 'Extracts from letter from Base Censor Office No. 1', APO 813, US Army, Subject: Special Report (Negro Troops, 1–15 March 1944). RG498/HQ/ETOUSA/HD/AF/Censor, Box 43, file 218.
15 Longmate, *GI's*, 63.
16 No African American soldier was executed for rape in Northern Ireland, but five were on the mainland (the other soldier executed for rape was Latino). For a full discussion on this topic in the context of Northern Ireland, see Topping, *JAAH*. See also, Lilly and Thomson, *BJC*, 269–76.
17 'Base Censor', 1–15 March 1944. RG498/HQ/ETOUSA/HD/AF/Censor/43/218.
18 Ibid.
19 'Army Mail Censorship Report, No. 48', 12–26 April 1942. RG338, File 250.1. Cited in McCormick, *JSH*, 244.

20 For more on this, see Sonya O. Rose, 'Girls and GIs: Race, Sex and Diplomacy in Second World War Britain', *International History Review*, vol. 19 (1997), 141–60, and 'Sex, Citizenship and the Nation in World War II Britain', *The American Historical Review*, vol. 103 (1998)1147–76. Some English newspapers explicitly linked African American troops and immorality among young women. See, for example, *Huddersfield Daily Examiner*, 10 July 1943, cited in Sonya O. Rose, *Which People's War? National Identity and Citizenship in Wartime Britain, 1939-1945* (Oxford and London: Oxford University Press, 2003), 76.

21 Rose, *People's War*, 78; Rose argues that interracial sex was regarded as a 'as a kind of sexual perversion'. Rose, AHR, 103 (1998), 1159.

22 Censorship Report No. 79, 11–25 November 1943, 27. FO371/34126. TNA.

23 Lucy Bland, *Britain's Brown Babies: The Stories of Children Born to Black GIs and White Women in the Second World War* (Manchester: Manchester University Press, 2019), 3. Graham Smith's earlier study put the figure as low as 550. Smith, *Jim Crow*, 208. For further discussion of 'brown babies', see Plummer, 'Brown Babies: Race, Gender and Policy after World War Two', in *Window on Freedom: Race, Civil Rights and Foreign Affairs, 1945-1988*, Plummer (ed.) (Chapel Hill: University of North Carolina Press, 2003). Neither Plummer nor Bland discuss Northern Ireland.

24 Juliet Gardiner, *Wartime Britain, 1939-1945* (London: Headline Book Publishing, 2004), 481. Valerie Hill-Jackson estimates that between 70 and 100 women from Cardiff's Tiger Bay black community area married African American servicemen and were able to move the States. http://www.gibrides.com/the-welsh-war-brides-of-tiger-bay/ (accessed 23 June 2015). Hill-Jackson and 15th Floor Productions have made a documentary on this subject, *Tiger Brides* (2013).

25 Roberts to State, 30 July 1945. This was in reply to a confidential request from the State Department, which also asked for an estimate of 'the number of Negroes who have married white members of the American Armed Forces'; the answer in Northern Ireland was 'none'. 'Confidential: Additional Information Required on Form 258', 26 June 1945. RG84/BCG/CF/1945-1946/811.11.

26 'The Problem of Marriages in ETO', 2 and 14 April 1944. MSS. Monograph prepared by Pfc. William F. Sprague, Past Affairs Department, History Sub-section ETOUSA, ADM NR: 518, RG498. (henceforth RG498/AHC/HS/ETOUSA/Marriages/518).

27 Reynolds, *Relations*, 23; Rose, *AHR*, 1159. Only nineteen states did not have anti-miscegenation laws. Laws banning interracial marriage were finally repealed in 1967 by the *Loving v. Virginia* Supreme Court decision.

28 'Accosting of United States Troops by British Women', 5 March 1943. Venereal disease was a huge problem in the UK: '[i]t is worth pointing out that the total number of men infected during the period between January and November 1942 was almost exactly equal to the strength of a normal British division'. United States, File no. 33, pp. 1925–2651; A2283/33/45. FO371/34124. TNA.

29 McCormick, *Regulating*, 159.

30 In France, when Americans confronted the same sort of problems, prostitution around Belfast City Hall was specifically mentioned, alongside the notorious 'Piccadilly Commandos' of London. *SSL*, 15 June 1944.

31 Clare O'Kane, '"To Make Butter and to Look After Poultry": The Impact of the Second World War on the Lives of Rural Women in Northern Ireland', in McIntosh and Urquhart, *Irish Women*, 95.

32 Myrtle Hill, *Women in Ireland: A Century of Change* (Belfast: The Blackstaff Press, 2003), 124.
33 *Mid-Ulster Mail*, 27 November 1943.
34 McCormick, *Regulating*, 159.
35 Ibid. Female police officers had to be single, childless, aged between 21 and 35 and had to resign if they married. *Portadown News*, 29 May 1943, cited in Ollerenshaw, *Politics, Economic Mobilisation*, 147–8. For a report on female officers, see *Belfast Weekly Telegraph*, 12 May 1944.
36 Medical Superintendent of Health, Belfast Annual Report of Health, 1943, 2–5, LA7/9DA/28. PRONI. Cited in McCormick, *JSH*, 248.
37 McCormick, *JSH*, 249.
38 'General Orders of the Headquarters of the United States Army, Northern Ireland Forces', No. 31, 2 February 1945, CAB9/CD/225/6. Cited in McCormick, *JSH*, 251.
39 McCormick, *JSH*, 252.
40 Fisk, *Time of War*, 449. A VD hospital was set up in Lurgan. Longmate, *GI's*, 282.
41 'General Orders', 2 February 1945, Civil Defence, CAB/9CD/225/6. Cited in McCormick, *JSH*, 251.
42 Derrick Gibson-Harries, *Life-Line to Freedom: Ulster in the Second World War* (Belfast: Ulster Society Publications Ltd., 1990), 61.
43 CID, Exhibit 'D', Statement of Eileen Mildred Megaw, 9 March 1944, Statement taken by the RUC. *Court-Martial Record of Trial of Private Wiley Harris, Jr., 6924547*, 626th Ordinance Ammunition Co., ETO2007 (*CMR-Harris*).
44 *BT*, 17 March 1944.
45 Ibid., 21 March, 1944.
46 *IN*, 22 March 1944. See also, *NW*, 22 March 1944.
47 Rose, *AHR*, 1150.
48 For examples of this kind of behaviour, see McCormick, *Regulating*, 156.
49 Harrisson, 'Americans in Ireland', 8 June 1942, 4. MOI.
50 'Postal Censorship Report No.38', 8 April 1943. Harcourt to Butler, 9 April 1943, M.I.L2/503. United States, File no33, pps1925-2651; 'United States Troops in Northern Ireland'. A3468/33/45. FO371/34124. TNA. The accompanying official note says: 'both white and coloured personnel are indicted'.
51 Hill, *Women in Ireland*, 122.
52 'Inspector General's Office, Royal Ulster Constabulary (RUC), monthly report', 7 July 1944. CAB/9/CD/225/18.
53 The Board of Review only confirmed convictions and was supposed to ensure that defendants had had a fair trial. For details on the case resulting in execution, see *Dungannon Observer*, 11 November 1944. Private Thomas Bush was convicted of the attempted rape in March 1944 in Ardglass, County Down, and sentenced to eight years' hard labour. ETO2500, *United States v. Private Thomas Bush* (35152781), *Branch Office of the Judge Advocate General with the European Theater of Operations, Board of Review: ETO Board of Review: Opinions CM ETO 2452-CM ETO 3153*, vol. 7–8, 87.
54 ETO82: *United States v. Technician First Class Lawrence H. McKenzie* (39389670), 20 October 1942. Ibid., *CM ETO 24-CM ETO 439*, vol. 1, 69. For local newspaper reports, see *NL*, 21 October 1942; *DR*, 24 October 1942
55 Leanne McCormick et al., *Mother and Baby Homes and Magdalene Laundries in Northern Ireland, 1922-1990: Report for the Inter Departmental Working Group on Mother and Baby Homes, Magdalene Laundries and Historical Clerical Child Abuse* (Department of Health, 2021), 159.

56 See, for example, the case of two Londonderry sisters who accused a sailor of sexual assault. McCormick, *Regulating*, 157.
57 *SSL*, 30 May 1942.
58 Ibid., 31 October 1942.
59 Letter home from Bob Reed of New York, 28 March 1942. Cited in Kelly, *Home*, 40.
60 'WW2, People's War: The Chaperone', BBC, 15 October 2014. https://www.bbc.co.uk/history/ww2peopleswar/stories/01/a3967301.shtml (accessed 19 December 2018)
61 *WES*, 5 March 1943.
62 Adams to Secretaries of local hospitality committees, 12 January 1944. CAB9/CD225/19.
63 *SSL*, 27 June 1942.
64 'Marriages', 1–2. RG498/AHC/HS/ETOUSA/Marriages/518.
65 Telegram No. 122, USNIF to USLON, 22 March 1942, in AG291.1 (1942). Ibid, 4.
66 'Eisenhower, ETO' 364. RG498/AHC/HS/ETOUSA/Eisenhower/509. See also, 'Marriages', 5. RG498/AHC/HS/ETOUSA/Marriages/518.
67 'Northern Ireland War History, File No 11'. CAB3A/47.
68 *BT*, 3 April 1942.
69 *WES*, 11 April 1942.
70 Ibid.; *BT*, 11 April 1942; Carroll, *NHR*, 33.
71 *WES*, 13 April 1942.
72 'Base History', from 1 January 1942 to 31 May 1942, 28. RG498/ETOUSA/HD/AF/NIBC/186/597; *BT*, 16 April 1942.
73 The couple's granddaughter told Leanne McCormick that the media attention spared Cooke from disciplinary action. Leanne McCormick email to author, 25 November 2019. My thanks to Leanne for passing on this information.
74 McCormick, *JSH*, 247.
75 'Eisenhower, ETO' 366. RG498/AHC/HS/ETOUSA/Eisenhower/509. There was actually a blatantly racist context to this; the problem had emerged when Americans were posted to Trinidad: 'the native population there was largely Negro and considered to be socially and mentally inferior to the average American soldier'. Marriage to local women was, therefore, actively discouraged. 'Marriages', 6. RG498/AHC/HS/ETOUSA/Marriages/518. The later 'Eisenhower' history of the ETO cut the phrase 'largely Negro', but included the rest of the quotation about the alleged inferiority of the population. 'Eisenhower, ETO', 366.
76 'Eisenhower, ETO' 367. RG498/AHC/HS/ETOUSA/Eisenhower/509; *BT*, 19 August 1942.
77 'Marriage of US Military Personnel stationed in European Theater of Operations' to Commanding General, SOS, ETOUSA. Headquarters European Theater of Operations United States Army, AG291.1, 6 October 1943. RG498/AHC/HS/ETOUSA/NIBC/225.
78 'Eisenhower, ETO', 369 and 383. RG498/AHC/HS/ETOUSA/Eisenhower/509.
79 'Base History', from 1 January 1942 To 31 May 1942, 28. RG498/ETOUSA/HD/AF/NIBC/186/597. Hartle continued to grumble that '[g]ullible men are readily seduced by British girls, whose ulterior motive may be that of extra remunerations on the part of our Government as well as that of the soldier'. Hartle to General Frank M. Andrews, 23 April 1943. Cited in Reynolds, *Relations*, 213.
80 'Marriages', 13. RG498/AHC/HS/ETOUSA/Marriages/518.
81 'Copy of memorandum from Col. C.E. Brand to Chaplain O'Connor', 29 May 1942. Folder No.4, ARCH/11/5/15. JCM. Brand also warned that girls marrying bigamists had 'no rights whatsoever' beyond helping to prosecute the offender. See also, *Yank*, 24 June 1942, 8.

82 *DR*, 20 June 1942. See also, Reynolds, *Relations*, 210.
83 *BT*, 16 April 1942.
84 *SSL*, 3 August 1943.
85 McCormick, *Regulating*, 253–6.
86 'WW2, People's War: First Irish GI Bride in the USA', BBC, 15 October 2014. https ://www.bbc.co.uk/history/ww2peopleswar/stories/43/a5741543.shtml (accessed 12 April 2019)
87 Barbara G. Friedman, *From the Battlefront to the Bridal Suite: Media Coverage of British War Brides, 1942-1946* (Columbia and London: University of Missouri Press, 2007), 28.
88 Lt. Col. Dell King Steuart, JAGD, 'On Marital Problems, Arising In ODB', *The Judge Advocate Journal*, vol. 1, no. 5 (December 1944), 13. 'ODB' stands for 'Office of Dependency Benefits'. The Red Cross attempted to arrange telephone weddings for soldiers with pregnant girlfriends back in America, however, the British complained that these phones should be reserved for the war effort and in February 1943 demanded the practice be stopped. The ARC complained to General Marshall who allowed it 'only in cases of pregnancy or illegitimacy' but was concerned about the legality of these marriages in some states. 'Marriages', 16–17. RG498/AHC/HS/ETOUSA/Marriages/518.
89 Melanie Friscia Ippolito recalls that her grandparents 'were convinced that nothing but unhappiness would follow their daughter; they knew many "mixed marriages" that had ended in heartache. They were very fond of my father but believed strongly that it could never work. That was the reality in Northern Ireland in the 1940s'. Melanie Friscia Ippolito, *I'll Be Back When Summer's in the Meadow: A World War II Chronicle, Volume I, 1942-1943* (Bennington, Vermont: Merriam Press, Military Monograph 137, 2011), 7. Ippolito discovered a treasure trove of over 2,000 of her parents' letters to each other during the war, correspondence which beautifully encapsulates how their love overcame every barrier put before them.
90 Bob Reed, 28 March 1942. Cited in Kelly, *Home*, 40.
91 Figure for marriages from McCormick, *Regulating*, 255; figure for births from Carroll, *NHR*, 35. Some 70,000 British women married Americans. Friedman, *War Brides*, 3.
92 'Memo #2, Children Born in Northern Ireland whose fathers are American Citizens', APO #813, 2 January, by order of General Collins. RG498/ETOUSA/HD/AF/History/44/225.
93 Kelly to Montgomery, 26 October 1944. CAB9CD/225/2.
94 Carroll, *NHR*, 35, *n*61. *Stars and Stripes* reported that US casualty lists featured in Northern Ireland's newspapers 'because many of the men who married Irish girls had become well known there'. *SSL*, 7 November 1944
95 Hill, *Women in Ireland*, 125. For a child raised by his grandparents as his mother's brother, see 'World War Two GI baby: Albert Gilmour reunites with family', BBC, 29 September 2019.
96 McCormick emails to the author, 25 November 2019 and 16 June 2020; McCormick, *JSH*, 149; McCormick et al, *Mother and Baby Homes*, 159. Some of these laundries secured lucrative military contracts. Ibid., 289. From the 1940s to the 1970s, some children from Catholic homes were adopted by American couples, often illegally facilitated by the church. Ibid., 79.
97 The correspondence between Muriel and Ray Friscia illustrates how frustrating this process could be. See, for example, Ippolito, *I'll Be Back When Summer's in*

Notes to pages 131–133   253

the Meadow: A World War II Chronicle, Volume III, 1945-1946 (Bennington, VT: Merriam Press, Military Monograph 137, 2012), 308.
98 BT, 28 July 1944. See also, 'Hospitality for American, British and Allied Forces, Activities during July 1945', MOI, Northern Ireland Region. CAB9/CD225/19.
99 NL, 25 September 1942.
100 BT, 3 February 1945. The Telegraph claimed that the couple met in 1941 and married six months later, however, they married in September 1942.
101 Ippolito, Meadow, III, 308.
102 Ibid., 7; NW, 7 September 1945.
103 Yank, 21 September 1945. See also, Jenel Virden, Good-Bye, Piccadilly: British War Brides in America (Urbana and Chicago: University of Illinois Press, 1996), 47.
104 Yank, 21 September 1945, 19.
105 Carroll, NHR, 35.
106 Friedman, War Brides, 28.
107 WES, 21 March 1943.
108 Virden, Piccadilly, 55–6.
109 Friedman, War Brides, 28.
110 NYT, 6 September 1944, cited in Friedman, War Brides, 34. WES, 6 September 1944; BT, 6 September 1944. Thirty-five of the women were from Northern Ireland. Carroll, NHR, 35.
111 NYT, 6 September 1944, cited in Friedman, War Brides, 34.
112 'People's War: First Irish GI Bride', BBC, 15 October 2014. Mathes was even able to travel with her husband Bob who was returning to the States having served at the US Naval base in Londonderry.
113 Friedman, War Brides, 28.
114 BT, 24 January 1946.
115 Roberts to Col. John Easton Assistant Military Attaché, American Embassy, London, 20 February 1946. RG84/BCG/GR/1946/81/800.
116 NL, 17 September 1945.
117 BT, 24 January 1946; NL, 25 January 1946. The press gives no indication of how they organised the protest.
118 BT, 24 January 1946; NL, 25 January 1946.
119 Ippolito, Meadow, III, 283. Friscia explained to her frustrated husband that the situation was not of her making, and later that she had not secured a place on the first ship. Ibid., 290–7. She at least felt supported by consulate staff, one of whom, Miss Bell, sent her 'a wee note to cheer you up and to wish you a good crossing'. Miss J.M. Bell (consulate) to Murial Friscia, 3 April 1946. Ibid., 299.
120 NL, 30 January 1946
121 BT, 27 February 1946; BT, 5 March 1946; BT, 6 March 1946; NW, 5 March 1946.
122 NL, 5 March 1946. The Telegraph declared that the Gibbins, 'sailed to form another link in Ulster-American friendship'. BT, 6 March 1946.
123 NL, 3 April 1946. The News Letter reported that thirty three of the brides and twenty children were from Éire.
124 Ibid., 3 April 1946. BT, 4 April 1946.
125 BT, 26 and 27 April 1946. The Telegraph reported that the SS Thomas H. Barry, with the capacity to take 526 women and children, would sail from Belfast on 21 March, however, no newspaper subsequently reported this actually happening. Ibid., 27 February 1946. The Telegraph refers to the Parker as both the 'third bride ship' and carrying the 'third contingent'. Ibid., 26 and 27 April 1946. The Whig described

the *Parker* as 'the third and last bride ship expected leave Northern Ireland', *NW*, 20 April 1946. Carroll states, however, that 448 wives sailed on the *Barry* but I have been unable to confirm this. Carroll, *NHR*, 35. Incidentally, on a previous visit, in January 1944 the *Parker* brought troops to Northern Ireland. 'USAFNI, Chronology', 9 January 1944.
126 *NL*, 3 April 1946.
127 *BT*, 6 March 1946; *NL*, 3 April 1946.
128 Virden, *Piccadilly*, 136.
129 'Publicity Committee: Report on the work of the Government Publicity Office during March 1946'. CAB9F/123/37.
130 *BT*, 4 April 1946.
131 Ibid., 4 April 1946. *IN*, 6 April 1946.
132 *BT*, 27 April 1946.
133 *IN*, 6 April 1946.
134 *BT*, 5 March 1946.
135 Leanne McCormick. '"Filthy little girls": Controlling Women in Public Spaces in Northern Ireland during the Second World War', in McIntosh and Urquhart (eds.), *Irish Women*, 104. McCormick argues that the presence of all foreign, not just American, soldiers caused these anxieties.

Chapter 9

This chapter is based on three articles I have published on African American troops in Northern Ireland: 'The Dusky Doughboys: Interaction between African American Soldiers and the Population of Northern Ireland during the Second World War', *Journal of American Studies*, vol. 47, no. 4 (Autumn 2013), 1131–54; '"Laying down the law to the Irish and the Coons": Northern Ireland's Response to American Racial Segregation during World War Two', *Historical Research*, vol. 86, no. 234 (July 2013), 741–59; and 'Racial Tensions and U.S. Military (In)Justice in Northern Ireland During World War II', *Journal of African American History*, vo. 102, no. 2 (2017), 157–83. I am grateful to the editors of each for allowing me to reuse material from these pieces here.

1 *Newry Journal*, 2 August 2005. http://www.newryjournal.co.uk/content/view/888/39/ (accessed 2 July 2011).
2 Reynolds, *Relations*, 217.
3 Memorandum for the Chief of Staff from Secretary of War, 30 April 1942. RG107: Office of the Secretary of War: General Correspondence of John J. McCloy, 1941–1945 (RG107/OSW/McCloy) Box35, File 291.21. The US military, nevertheless, only reluctantly sent African American troops to the Caribbean as they would be much better paid than locals, and Australia, which had a whites' only immigration policy. Stimson had no love of African Americans, later decreeing that they were 'unable to master the techniques of modern weapons' and that 'leadership is not embedded in the Negro race yet, and to try to make commissioned officers to lead men into battle- colored men- is only to work disaster to both'. *Crisis*, 51, April 1944, 115.
4 Longmate, *GI's*, 121–2.
5 For accounts of these debates, see Reynolds, *Relations*, 216–37; Longmate, *GI's*, 117–28 and Smith, *Jim Crow*, chapter 3.

Notes to pages 137–140   255

6   James Warburg to Elmer Davis, 1 September 1942. RG107/OSW/McCloy, Entry 47, Box 124.
7   Buhrman to Gray, 19 May 1942. RG84/BCG/CF/1942/800.
8   Reynolds, *Relations*, 217.
9   Brooke Diary, 21 July 1942.
10 Ibid., 18 August 1942.
11 Ibid.
12 Ibid., 19 August 1942.
13 'MOI, American File', 21 August 1942. CAB9CD/225/19.
14 Brooke Diary, 2 and 3 September 1942. Unfortunately, Brooke does not outline what was agreed and no record of the meetings has been found.
15 'Memorandum, 4 September 1942 From the Home Office to the Chief Constable', forwarded by Freer to Gransden, 5 September 1942. CAB9CD/225/19.
16 'Confidential', Gransden to Turnham 8 September 1942. CAB9CD/225/19.
17 For details on numbers of African American troops in Northern Ireland, see http://www.history.army.mil/reference/ireland/nistat.htm (accessed 1 July 2011). In May 1942 the US military predicted only 12,887 African American servicemen would go to the UK. Marshall to Secretary of War, 13 May 1942. 'Records of the War Department; Department General and Special Staffs', RG165, Box 189, File 291.21. At this point, no African American troops were currently in the UK but 811 were 'en route'.
18 'Hospitality for Allied Forces in Northern Ireland: Moneymore'. 7 January 1943. CAB9CD/225/19.
19 'Northern Ireland Troop Welfare Committee', Joint Memorandum by Lady Stronge and Mr F.M. Adams, 4 March 1943. CAB9CD/225/19.
20 Bracken to Brooke, 23 March 1943. CAB9CD/225/19.
21 'Note on Anglo-American (Army) Relations Committee, Appendix 'A', Military Base Censorship, NI', February 1944. FO371/38624. TNA.
22 This was not always true in England. Rose, *AHR*, 103 (1998), 1158.
23 *DR*, 20 June 1942. Most black troops were in service roles as US generals did not trust them in combat.
24 *Mid-Ulster Mail*, 25 July 1942.
25 *Dungannon Observer*, 25 July 1942.
26 Smith, *Jim Crow*, 61.
27 *BT*, 31 July 1942.
28 *BT*, 12 October 1942.
29 *Mid-Ulster Mail*, 27 July 1942.
30 For coverage in the African American press, see *Washington Tribune*, 17 October 1942; *Amsterdam News*, 8 August 1942; *Pittsburgh Courier*, 29 August 1942 and *Chicago Defender*, 8 August 1942. African American newspapers feared that Jim Crow would be introduced in the UK and they featured many racist incidents in England.
31 *Chicago Defender*, 8 August 1942.
32 *NYT*, 29 July 1942.
33 Reynolds, *Collier's*, 10 October 1942, 12.
34 BBCMR 24 July 1942. CAB9CD/207, cited in Fisk, *Time of War*, 404.
35 *Amsterdam News*, 20 July 1942.
36 'Morale Rpts (colored troops) 16–31 August, and 1–15 September 1942', cited in Smith, *Jim Crow*, 135. For similar quotations, see McCormick, *JHS*, 244.

37 'Morale Report (ColoredTroops) September 1-15, 1942', cited in Allison J. Gough, "Messing Up Another Country's Customs: The Exportation of American Racism During World War II," *World History Connected*, October 2007.
38 'Extracts from letter from Base Censor Office No. 1, APO 813, US Army', Subject: Special Report (Negro Troops, 1-15 March 1944). RG498/HQETOUSA/HD/AF/Censor, Box 43, file 218.
39 Longmate, *GI's*, 119.
40 'Censorship Report No. 79', 11-25 November 1943, 27. FO371/34126. TNA.
41 African American veterans participated in the civil rights movement of the 1950s and 1960s. The parallels with Northern Ireland's own civil rights movement are obvious, however, Bob Purdie, for example, urges caution in comparing the two. Bob Purdie, *Politics in the Streets: The Origins of the Civil Rights Movement in Northern Ireland* (Belfast: The Blackstaff Press, 1990). For the role of veterans in civil rights see, Christopher Parker, *Fighting for Democracy: Black Veterans and the Fight Against White Supremacy in the Post-War South* (Princeton: Princeton University Press, 2009).
42 Anonymous, undated letter. CAB9CD/225/19.
43 Ibid.
44 Smith, *Jim Crow*, 135.
45 'Morale Report (Colored Troops)', 1-15 September 1942. Cited in Gough, *WHC*.
46 Smith, *Jim Crow*, 140.
47 Ibid.
48 Gilfillan to Gransden, 8 September 1942. CAB9CD/225/18.
49 Longmate, *GI's*, 63.
50 'Base Censor Office', Special Report (Negro Troops, 1-15 March 1944). RG498/HQETOUSA/HD/AF/Censor/43/218.
51 'Army Mail Censorship Report, No. 48, 12-26 April 1942'. Cited in McCormick, *JHS*, 244. Italics in original.
52 Roi Ottley, 'Jim Crow in Britain', *Negro Digest*, vol. II, no. 1 (November 1942).
53 Harold L. Stark to Frank Knox, Secretary of the Navy, 1 July 1942. Cited in Reynolds, *Relations*, 219.
54 Northern Ireland Base Command (Prov) United States Army; 'Report of Conference on "Rules of Conduct"', 1 August 1942. CAB9CD/225/19.
55 Ibid.
56 Ibid.
57 Ibid.
58 Ibid.
59 Robert (Bob) Fawcett, email to author, 19 June 2009.
60 For Bamber Bridge, see, for example, Ken Werrell, 'The Mutiny at Bamber Bridge', *After the Battle* (No. 22, 1978), 1-11 and Smith, *Jim Crow*, 141-4. For Bristol, see Wynn, *I&M*, 333, and for Launceston, Kate Werren, *An American Uprising in Second World War England: Mutiny in the Duchy* (Yorkshire and Philadelphia: Pen and Sword History, 2020).
61 Smith, *Jim Crow*, 140.
62 Fawcett to author, 19 June 2009.
63 Romie Lambkin, *My Time in the War: An Irishwoman's Diary* (Dublin: Wolfhound Press, 1992), 42. Lambkin vowed not to go back to the Ulster Hall, Belfast's main concert venue, because of this. Eamon McGale, whose grandmother owned a café in Omagh, says: 'I was told that they [black troops] were not allowed to mix with other troops in places like my granny's, the Rix Café, Nardone's, the one ballroom in the

town, the Star, or in any of the two cinemas'. Eamon McGale to the author, February 2011.
64 *People's Voice*, 26 September 1942.
65 John Campbell, email to the author, 17 June 2009. Campbell also recollects a woman being beaten up by an African American soldier. Ibid., 18 June 2009.
66 Gilfillan to Secretary, Home Affairs, 5 November 1943. HA/8/593. PRONI. The police report suggests that the locals started the trouble. Ibid.
67 Col. W. M. Lanagan, to Crawford McCullagh, 25 May 1943. LA/7/3A/115: Crawford McCullagh. PRONI
68 Lord Mayor's Secretary to Lanagan, 27 May 1943. Ibid.
69 See Rose, *Which People's War?* 263–5.
70 'Record of Trial Proper, 17 March 1944. Cross examination of Eileen Megaw by 1st Lt. Dewitt D. Irwin, Jr., Counsel for the Defense'. *CMR-Harris*.
71 Ten of the eighteen US soldiers executed in the United Kingdom during the war were African American, despite making up only 10 per cent of personnel. Three of the remaining five were Latino. For further details, see J. Robert Lilly, 'Dirty Details: Executing US Soldiers during World War II', *Crime and Delinquency*, vol. 42 (1996), 497 and Alice Kaplan, *The Interpreter* (Chicago and London: University of Chicago Press, 2005), 156.
72 On the day after the murder, for example, the *Telegraph*'s sub-headline read: 'Negro Soldiers Held'. *BT*, 7 March 1944. This was the only mention of race in a *Telegraph* headline; similarly, only one *Irish News* headline noted Harris's race. *IN*, 18 March 1944.
73 *IN*, 22 March 1944.
74 'A Loyal and Law-Abiding Citizen' to Brooke, 25 May 1944. CAB9CD/225/2.
75 See, for example, R. Morrow, Belfast and District Trade Union Council, to Brooke, 24 May 1944 and Gransden to J. Malcolm, National Union of General and Municipal Workers, 25 May 1944. Ibid.
76 Cabinet Meeting, 25 May 1944. CAB4/585. For a full account of Harris's court-martial, see Topping, *JAAH*, 157–83.
77 Campbell to author, 17 and 18 June 2009.
78 'Meeting of Representatives of Hospitality Committees', 25 October 1943. CAB9CD/225/19. Collins was also expecting black Red Cross workers.
79 Gransden to Brunskill, 7 October 1943. CAB/9/CD/225/18.
80 'Hospitality Committee', 25 October 1943. CAB9CD/225/19.
81 Ibid.
82 Devers suggested the 'rotation of pass days in towns near which two or more different units are stationed [and] [A]llocation of public recreational facilities such as dance halls and public houses to units through control of pass privileges or by placing such places off limits for certain units'. General Jacob L. Devers to Commanding General, SOS, ETOUSA, 25 October 1943. RG498/HQETOUSA/HD/AF/Censor/43/218.
83 Hopkins to Gransden, 13 December 1943. See also: Hopkins to Gransden, 12 January 1944. CAB/9/CD/225/18.
84 'Dehra Parker's notes on "Black and White" problem', 13 December 1943. CAB9CD/225/19.
85 Ibid. Underlining in original.
86 Brunskill to Gransden 20 December 1943. CAB9CD/225/19.
87 Ibid.

88 Ibid.
89 Ibid.
90 Gransden seemed satisfied by their inquiries: 'my records about the coloured question are fairly complete'. Secret: Gransden to Brunskill, 28 December 1943. CAB9CD/225/19.
91 Lilly and Thomson, *BJC*, 282.
92 Gardiner, *Wartime Britain*, 485.
93 Mary Pat Kelly, *Proudly We Served: The Men of the USS Mason* (Annapolis, Maryland: Bluejacket Books, Naval Institute Press, 1995), 92. For similar quotations, see ibid., 90–4.

Chapter 10

1 *Behind the Green Curtain*, chapters 1, 2. Unpublished MSS. DGP, Box 1. See also, Bew, *Enmity*, 479.
2 'Early Chapters', *Green Curtain*, MSS. DGP, Box 20. O'Halpin speculates that Brennan said publicly that Governor Earle of Pennsylvania would be chosen and Gray's appointment may have been due to 'White House indignation at this egregious faux pas'. O'Halpin, *Spying*, 155.
3 John Day Tully, *Ireland and Irish Americans 1930 to 1945: The Search for Identity* (Dublin and Portland, Oregon: Irish academic Press, 2010), 80.
4 Gray to Roosevelt, 28 May 1941. FDRP/OF/2/DCF.
5 Coogan notes that Roosevelt 'made quite clear, everything Gray did was done with his approval'. Coogan, *de Valera*, 595. Girvin observes that Gray was a stalwart of the Democratic Party's progressive wing, suggesting the appointment was not solely nepotistic and, more than once, Gray offered to resign if Roosevelt felt that he had outlived his usefulness. Girvin, *Emergency*, 287; 295.
6 Fisk, *Time of War*, 542. For Marlin's role, see Dwyer, *Strained Relations*, 71–6 and Tully, *Irish Americans*, 143 n48. The two men did not get along: Marlin believed Gray leaked stories to newspapers and Gray purportedly sought Marlin's recall. Fisk, *Time of War*, 530–1. Marlin was summarily removed in December 1942 after only a few months. O'Halpin, *Spying*, 221. O'Halpin states that Gray 'wished to be the sole conduit of information from Dublin to Washington, and he eventually forced Marlin out'. The OSS and Walshe both praised Marlin's role liaising between Éire and America's intelligence services. O'Halpin, *Defending*, 230.
7 Paul Bew, *A Yankee in de Valera's Ireland: The Memoir of David Gray* (Dublin: Royal Irish Academy, 2012), i.
8 Ibid., ii.
9 Fisk, *Time of War*, 326.
10 Tully, *Irish Americans*, 80.
11 Dwyer, review of Bew, *Yankee*, *History Ireland*, vol. 21, no. 1 (January/February 2013).
12 Tully, *Irish Americans*, 72.
13 Bew, *Enmity*, 465. Gray called Craig 'the perfect Bourbon'. Gray to Roosevelt, 19 June 1940. DGP, Box 4.
14 Bartlett, *Ireland*, 454.
15 Gray's 'importance, or nuisance value to de Valera may be gauged from the fact that there are more references to him in de Valera's official biography, covering his seven

years in Ireland, than there are to Sean Lemass, who shared a lifetime with de Valera'. Coogan, *de Valera*, 541.
16 Girvin, *Emergency*, 316.
17 Welles, Hull and Hull's successor, Edward Stettinius had little time for Éire's complaints about partition. Ibid., 212; 312 and 317.
18 Gray to Secretary of State (John F. Byrnes), 26 November 1945. Cited in Troy D. Davis, *Dublin's American Policy: Irish American Diplomatic Relations, 1945 1952* (Washington D.C.: The Catholic University of America Press, 1998), 13.
19 De Valera to Roosevelt, 25 January 1938; Roosevelt to de Valera 22 February 1938. FDRP/OF/2/DCF.
20 Cudahy to Roosevelt, 1 March 1938. Ibid.
21 Brennan to Walshe, 7 March 1940. *DIFP*, v6.
22 William J. B. Macaulay to Walshe, 20 March 1940. *DIFP*, v6.
23 Michael MacWhite to Walshe (Confidential) Rome, 21 March 1940. Ibid. Gray's determination included wishing to discuss partition with the Pope.
24 As Fanning notes, the war 'affirmed rather than altered the priorities in de Valera's Ireland: independence first, unity a poor second'. Ronan Fanning, *Eamon de Valera: A Will to Power* (London: Faber and Faber, 2015), 214.
25 Gray, 'Memorandum on the Irish Situation', 16 August 1943. DGP, Box 11. As Dwyer convincingly argues: '[t]hroughout his long career de Valera talked a great deal about Irish unity, but never made any gestures to try to win over the support of the Protestant unionist majority in Northern Ireland. He was essentially demanding a solution on his own terms of unionist capitulation, or ethnic cleansing. In the process he essentially abandoned the nationalist population of Northern Ireland'. Dwyer, *Curtain*, 347.
26 Gray to Robert Stewart, Division of European Affairs, Department of State, 5 May 1943. DGP, Box 10. Gray to Abercorn, 19 October 1942. DGP, Box 8; Gray to Brooke, 14 January 1944. DGP, Box 12.
27 Bew, *Yankee*, vi-vii.
28 Ibid., vii.
29 Bew, *Yankee*, xxi.
30 Ibid., vii; Bew argues: 'Irish critics of Gray rarely acknowledge his most substantive points: for example, his critique of Dublin offers to manipulate mainstream American politics in the German interest through the utilisation of the Irish lobby. Gray's anger at discovering this offer being made to Berlin is absolutely inevitable, given his own strong anti-isolation stance.' Ibid., xxvii. See also British official Malcolm MacDonald's conversations with de Valera, Aiken and Lemass in 1940. Ibid., xxix.
31 See, for example, Gray to Winant, 7 January 1944. DGP, Box 12.
32 Gray note, 9 November 1942. Cited in Girvin, *Emergency*, 297.
33 British diplomats were more measured about towards Éire's neutrality and there was a good deal of informal cross-border cooperation over security.
34 Gray to Winant, 7 January 1944. DGP, Box 12. There were 678,000 Irish-born people in the United States in 1941, and some 30 million more with Irish heritage. English, *Irish Freedom*, 315.
35 US Legation, Dublin, April 8, 1940. FDRP/OF/2/DCF. In *Behind the Green Curtain*, Gray quoted Churchill as saying: 'if you have come here to offer me a bribe to sell-out Ulster for any kind of American support you had better go back'. Gray, *Green Curtain*, MSS, ch2, 11. DGP, Box 1.
36 Gray to Roosevelt, 15 April 1940. FDRP/OF/2/DCF.

37 Ibid., 16 May 1940.
38 Ibid.
39 Ibid., 6 June 1940.
40 Ibid.
41 Ibid.
42 Ibid.
43 Gray to Abercorn, 16 June 1940. FDRP/OF/2/DCF
44 Gray to Roosevelt, 28 June 1940. Ibid.
45 Ibid. O'Kelly became Finance Minister in 1941, and president of Éire from 1945 to 1959. In 1934, while minister of local government, O'Kelly had threatened a 'bloody march on the border'. Paul Bew, 'Review: Varieties of Irishness? Some New Explanations', *The Historical Journal*, vol. 33, no. 3 (September, 1990), 751. In 1955, O'Kelly conceded to writer Shane Leslie that he did not understand Northern Ireland and had no idea how to cope with the reality of partition ending, a stunning confession from someone who had dedicated his life to this cause. Girvin, *Emergency*, 26-7.
46 Gray to Roosevelt, 7 August 1940. FDRP/OF/2/DCF. Bew argues: 'in the end, Gray concluded that de Valera had no intention of supporting Britain, even if Irish unity was delivered, and that Lord Craigavon's suspicions were entirely justified'. Bew, *Enmity*, 465.
47 Gray to Roosevelt, 25 September 1940. FDRP/OF/2/DCF.
48 Ibid., 18 March 1941.
49 Ibid., 28 July 1941,
50 Ibid., 21 October 1941.
51 Ibid., 28 July 1941, 169; Roosevelt to Gray, 28 August 1941. Ibid.
52 Gray to Roosevelt, 21 October 1941. Gray visited the Londonderry base in September. Gray to Roosevelt, 12 September 1941. Ibid.
53 Aide Memoir, 15 October 1941; Brennan to Hull, 6 November 1941; Welles to Roosevelt, 14 November 1941. Ibid.
54 Gray to Roosevelt, 27 January 1942. ibid. De Valera, like many statesmen, did not foresee war between America and Japan, but Gray predicted a Japanese attack after it joined the Rome-Berlin Axis, which Dwyer concedes was an 'astute assessment'. T. Ryle Dwyer, *De Valera: The Man and his Myths* (Dublin: Poolberg Press, Ltd, 1991), 255.
55 Gray to Roosevelt, 27 January 1942. FDRP/OF/2/DCF.
56 *NL*, 28 September 1942.
57 Gray to Roosevelt, 8 October 1942. DGP, Box 8.
58 Gray to MacRory, 7 October 1942. FDRP/OF/2/DCF. *Impartial Reporter*, 4 October 1945. CAB9CD/225/1.
59 MacRory to Gray, 7 October 1942. Folder No.4, ARCH/11/5/15. JCM.
60 *Impartial Reporter*, 4 October 1945. CAB9CD/225/1.
61 Henderson to Gransden, 3 November 1942. CAB9CD/225/1. As noted, Henderson's family owned the *News Letter*.
62 As well as Roosevelt, O'Kelly, Abercorn, Winant and Hartle, Gray forwarded the letter to McInerny, Spellman and Hurley. McInerny to Gray, 28 October 1942; Gray to Spellman, 20 October 1942; Gray to Hurley, 2 November 1942. DGP, Box 8.
63 Gray to Roosevelt, 19 October 1942. FDRP/OF/2/DCF.
64 Gray to Winant, 16 October 1942. Gray to Hartle, 16 October 1942. DGP, Box 8.
65 Gray to Winant, 16 October 1942. ibid.

66 McInerny to Gray, 28 October 1942, Ibid. McInerny, stationed in Northern Ireland, gleaned this information from a colleague who had met with MacRory.
67 'Postal and Censorship Report, United Kingdom, From Letter 1. J.C. Musgrave, Drogheda, 30-6-43'. W.X101/1/21, 'UK-Éire Political Relations, misc. matters: Mr D. Gray's Letter to Cardinal McCrory' [sic]. DO35/1228. TNA.
68 'Postal and Censorship Report, United Kingdom, From Letter 1. J.C. Musgrave, Drogheda; Letter 2. Grand Central Hotel, Royal Avenue, Belfast, to Capt. G. S. Elliston, House of Commons, London, 30-6-43'. Ibid.
69 'NW. JN.3.6.43. Confidential, Branch or Unit: Liverpool. Report no: Live/T/1869; Date 28.5.43. Northern Editor, Daily Mirror to American Legation'. Examiner G. Tait, Officer in Charge. Dominions Office, Ibid. How the Dominions Office came into possession of the transcript of this conversation is not revealed.
70 'Postal and Censorship Report, United Kingdom, From Letter 1. J.C. Musgrave, Drogheda', 30-6-43. This writer was a conspiracist who believed that de Valera had arranged the German bombings of Dublin in January and May 1941 to frighten Éire's population and believed that it would be a 'good and holy thing for Éire to shake off priest domination and take a stride from the middle ages'. The Dominions Office commented with typically bureaucratic understatement that the writer 'shows strong loyalist sympathies'. 'Postal and Censorship Report, United Kingdom', Hugh Alexander Boyd to Professor D. L. Savory, 29 June 1943. Ibid. Savory did not publicize the letter. 'UK-Éire Political Relations, misc. matters: Mr D. Gray's Letter to Cardinal McCrory'. WX101/1/21. DO35/1228. TNA.
71 Gray to MacRory, 31 May 1943. DGP, Box 10.
72 *Impartial Reporter*, 4 October 1945. CAB9CD/225/1.
73 Ollerenshaw, *Politics, Economic Mobilisation*, 196. For another account of the Ulster Protestant controversy, focusing on the attitudes of Stormont and London, as well as Gray, see Graham Walker, 'Northern Ireland, British-Irish Relations and American Concerns, 1942-1956', *Twentieth Century British History*, vol. 18, no. 2 (2007), 195-205.
74 Abercorn to Gray, 25 September 1941. DGP, Box 5.
75 Gray to MacRory, 25 September 1941. Ibid.
76 Gray to Roosevelt, 19 October 1942. FDRP/OF/2/DCF.
77 Gray to Abercorn, 19 October 1942. Ibid.
78 Ibid.
79 Gray to Spellman, 20 October 1942. DGP, Box 8. Gray to Roosevelt, 19 October 1942. FDRP/OF/2/DCF.
80 Gray to Roosevelt, 28 December 1942. Ibid.
81 Gray to Maffey, 4 January 1943. Ibid.
82 Cole, *Propaganda*, 147-8.
83 Wood, *Britain, Ireland*, 186.
84 Five radical, anti-partition Éire newspapers were banned. Cole, *Propaganda*, 22.
85 Herbert Morrison to Clement Atlee, 14 December 1942. CAB9B/261. Cited in Ollerenshaw, *Politics, Economic Mobilisation*, 195.
86 Ollerenshaw, *Politics, Economic Mobilisation*, 195-6.
87 Gray to Maffey, 10 September 1943. DGP, Box 11.
88 Montgomery to Gransden, 10 January 1944. CAB9B/261, cited in Ollerenshaw, *Politics, Economic Mobilisation*, 196.
89 Graham Walker, '"Protestantism before Party!": The Ulster Protestant League in the 1930s', *Historical Journal*, vol. 28, no. 4 (1985), 964-6; Ollerenshaw, *Politics, Economic Mobilisation*, 196.

90 Gray to Brooke, 14 January 1944. DGP, Box 12.
91 Ibid.
92 Buhrman to State, 10 February 1943. RG84/BCG/CF/1943/800.
93 Brooke Diary, 18 April 1944
94 Buhrman to Gray, 9 January 1943; RG84/BCG/CF/1943/281.
95 Ibid.
96 Gray to Buhrman, 11 January 1943. RG84/BCG/CF/1943/800. For Gray's advice to Ireland, see Gray to Denis Ireland, 3 January 1942. DGP, Box 6.
97 See Bew, *Yankee*, iii; Dwyer, *de Valera*, 250; Tully, *Irish Americans*, 80; and Coogan, *de Valera*, 572. In May 1941 he met Dan Breen, telling Roosevelt he was the 'gunman who started the Black and Tan war', and 'has over a dozen bullet holes in him and has probably killed about twenty cops'. Gray to Roosevelt, 28 May 1941. FDRP/OF/2/DCF. Gray and Betjeman, then a British civil servant in Dublin, enjoyed an enduring friendship. In July 1948 Betjeman sent Gray a handwritten copy of his poem 'The Empty Pew', which only appeared in print after the poet's death. The poem dealt his wife's conversion to Catholicism and he confided in Gray: 'Penelope joined the church of Rome this Easter. I was not pleased & have expressed my sentiments in a sonnet which I have transcribed overleaf. . . . I don't feel so sorry about the Roman business now, but am still vain enough to be proud of the sonnet!' John Betjeman to Gray, xix.vii.mcmxlviii (19 July 1948). DGP, Box 20.
98 Gray to Stewart, 5 May 1943. DGP, Box 10.
99 Ibid.
100 Ibid.
101 Ibid.
102 'Developments', 24 September 1942. RG84/BCG/CF/1942/800.
103 Tully also makes this connection. Tully, *Irish Americans*, 120-134. For a full account of the 'American Note', see Dwyer, *Strained Relations*, 118-55.
104 Gray to Hurley, 2 November 1942. DGP, Box 9.
105 Joseph Kennedy to Gray, 8 January 1943. DGP, Box 18.
106 Girvin stresses Gray's efforts to facilitate the trip, including trying to secure a meeting with Eleanor Roosevelt. Girvin, *Emergency*, 193-4. O'Kelly was the initial choice, but declined. There are various accounts of the 'Aiken mission'. See for example, Joseph L. Rosenberg, 'The 1941 Mission of Frank Aiken to the United States: An American Perspective', *Irish Historical Studies*, vol. 22, no. 86 (September 1980), 162-77; Dwyer, *Curtain*, 146-56; Fisk, *Time of War*, 306-10; Coogan, *de Valera*, 573-83. Girvin, *Emergency*, 195-219. Aiken was from Armagh so partition left his home in Northern Ireland.
107 Rosenberg, *IHR*, 164; Dwyer, *Curtain*, 141.
108 Girvin, *Emergency*, 201-4.
109 Coogan, *de Valera*, 575. German foreign minister Joachim von Ribbentrop told German diplomats to court the Irish-American press, and large amounts of money were dedicated to this. Ibid.
110 Girvin, *Emergency*, 207.
111 Ibid., 210-11.
112 Gray to Roosevelt, 7 May 1941. FDRP/OF/2/DCF.
113 Maffey to Machtig, 15 May 1941. Cited in Fisk, *Time of War*, 310.
114 Gray to Roosevelt, 28 May 1941. FDRP/OF/2/DCF.
115 The AFIN's closeness to Éire's government led to the appearance that it was run by it, and the legation in Washington warned the group to avoid giving this impression.

Girvin, *Emergency*, 186–7. Lindbergh wrote: 'when we were alone, Aiken told me he was very much in accord with the stand I have taken on the war'. Rosenberg, *IHR*, 176.
116 For some insights into the Irish-American press, see Hanley, *Radharc*, 255–62; and Cole, *Propaganda*, 107 and 169.
117 Dwyer, *Curtain*, 155.
118 Gray told the State Department: 'my impulse would be to bring the issue to a head and thrash it out while the war is on'. Gray to Stewart, 5 May 1943. DGP, Box 10.
119 Gray to Winant, 24 May 1943. Ibid. This came after a de Valera speech demanding the 'liberation' of 'the six counties'.
120 'Memorandum by the Minister in Ireland (Gray) on Recommendations for the Adoption of a Joint Anglo-American Economic Policy Toward Eire Shaped With Reference to Political Considerations', 14 May 1943. *FRUS*, 1943, volume III, 134.
121 This was an umbrella group of around twenty-five anti-partition Irish-American organizations founded in 1933. For details, see Dennis Clark, *The Irish Relations: Trials of an Immigrant Tradition* (London and Toronto: Associated University Presses, Fairleigh Dickinson University Press, 1982), 127–8.
122 'Memorandum by the Minister in Ireland', 14 May 1943. *FRUS*, 1943, volume III, 138.
123 Ibid., 139.
124 There is no written record of this meeting but in a 1971 letter Averill Harriman noted that Churchill 'seemed unimpressed' with Gray's plans to coerce Éire. Tully, *Irish Americans*, 123. See also, Dwyer, *Strained Relations*, 107.
125 'Irish Situation', 16 August 1943. DGP, Box 11.
126 Ibid; Gray to Archbishop Edward Rooney, Detroit, 25 August 1943. DGP, Box 11.
127 'Irish Situation', 16 August 1943; Gray to Rooney, 25 August 1943. DGP, Box 11. Girvin believes that it is highly unlikely that de Valera would have contemplated a population exchange to end partition. Brian Girvin to the author, 28 April 2020. For all his hostility to unionists and refusal to engage with them at any meaningful level, he did nominally regard them as fellow Irishmen with a place in an all-island state.
128 Ibid.
129 As it turned out, de Valera was not far wrong, for example, the Americans' unilateral and unanticipated cancellation of Lend-Lease almost as soon as the Japanese surrendered soured Anglo-American relations.
130 'Irish Situation', 16 August 1943. DGP, Box 11.
131 Ibid.
132 Ibid.
133 He met Archbishop Samuel Stritch of Chicago, Bishops Joseph Hurley (Florida), John O'Hara (New York), and Joseph McCarthy (Portland), along with Monsignor Michael Ready in Washington DC, and corresponded with Archbishop Edward Mooney of Detroit. Ibid. Kennedy had to postpone his meeting as his son John F. Kennedy, serving in the navy, had just been posted as missing in action. Tully, *Irish Americans*, 123. Gray and Kennedy did, however, have 'a long talk' in Boston. Gray to John McCormack, 4 August 1943. DGP, Box 11.
134 Sean Nunan to Brennan, 20 August 1943. *DIFP*, v7.
135 Davis suggests that Gray's hostility originated from his perception that Irish-Americans, united with isolationists, stopped America entering the League of Nations, which, in turn, helped cause the current conflict. Davis, *American Policy*, 17–18.

136 Gray to Mooney, 25 August 1943. DGP, Box 11.
137 Ibid.
138 Ibid.
139 'Irish Situation', 16 August 1943. DGP, Box 11.
140 Gray to Hull, 28 September, 1943. *FRUS*, 1943, v.III, 153.
141 Bowman, *Ulster Question*, 251; Tully, *Irish Americans*, 141.
142 'Irish Situation', 16 August 1943. DGP, Box 11.
143 Ibid.
144 Gray to Roosevelt, 10 January 1944. FDRP/OF/2/DCF.
145 O'Halpin, *Spying*, 240.
146 Cecil Liddell, diary, composite entry for 23–7 November 1943. Cited in O'Halpin, *Spying*, 243,
147 O'Halpin, *Spying*, 240.
148 *Sunday Independent* (Dublin), 12 March 1944. Folder No.4, ARCH/11/5/15. JCM.
149 Davis, *American Policy*, 28. Hull initially saw 'considerable usefulness' in the bases, but was wary of America being seen to take sides between the British and Irish and, therefore, would defer to the Joint Chiefs of Staff. Secretary of State to Roosevelt, 29 June 1943. The chiefs believed the bases would only be useful in as yet unforeseen circumstances (for example, *after* the invasion of Europe), and with British approval. Secretary of State to Roosevelt, 13 September 1943; 'Memorandum from Joint Chiefs of Staff for President Roosevelt, 11 August 1943. Hull communicated his misgivings to Gray a few days later. Hull to Gray, 18 September 1943. *FRUS*, 1943, v.iii, 142–5; 151.
150 O'Halpin, *Spying*, 247. The Germans surrendered their transmitter in December 1943 when two of their parachutists were captured and after British pressure on Dublin. Dwyer, *Strained Relations*, 119.
151 O'Halpin, *Spying*, 245.
152 Davis, *American Policy*, 16. Dwyer, *Strained Relations*, 112. Davis argues that Churchill's earlier statement about not needing Éire's help actually emboldened Gray 'to pursue an even more antagonistic policy' towards Éire. Any need to maintain good relations in Dublin in case the bases were needed had gone and with it the necessity for even the semblance of politeness on Gray's part. Davis, *American Policy*, 16.
153 Gray to Hull, 15 and 18 March 1944. Cited in Bowman, *Ulster Question*, 251.
154 'United States attitude to Éire-Axis Relations', 11 March 1944; 'American News Summary', 11 March 1944. Radio Trends and Content. America 1944, File No. 550. FO371/38646. TNA.
155 Fisk, *Time of War*, 532.
156 Reynolds, *Relations*, 118; Coogan, *De Valera*, 602.
157 Fanning, *De Valera*, 214–15.
158 Extract of letter from Maffey to Machtig, 25 February 1943. FDRP/OF/2/DCF; Dwyer, *Strained Relations*, 141.
159 Maffey to Machtig, 25 February 1943. FDRP/OF/2/DCF. *The Playboy of the Western World* was a 1907 play by Irish playwright John Millington Synge. There may be a deeper meaning for Maffey choosing this phrase, but the play, about attempted patricide and the fickleness of Irish womanhood, sparked riots by republicans on its opening night due to its portrayal of rural Ireland, and Synge's questionable commitment to Irish nationalism given his Anglo-Irish roots. *Guardian*, 23 September 2011.

160 Maffey to Machtig, 25 February 1943. FDRP/OF/2/DCF.
161 Fisk, *Time of War*, 441.
162 'Postal and Censorship Report, United Kingdom', Norman E. Riches, UK representative to Éire 5 June 1943. DO35/1228. TNA.
163 Henderson to Gray, 24 May, 1957. DGP, 18.

Chapter 11

1 'Hi! Uncle Sam!' W. F. Marshall, *Ulster Sails West* (Belfast: The Quota Press, 1943). Reprinted in W. F. Marshall, *Livin' in Drumlister* (Belfast: Blackstaff Press, 1983), 120. Reprinted with the kind permission of the W.F. Marshall estate.
2 John Walker Dinsmore, *The Scotch-Irish in America: Their History, Traits, Institutions and Influences: Especially as Illustrated in the Early Settlers of Western Pennsylvania, and Their Descendants* (Chicago, IL: Winona Publishing Company, 1906), 1–2. Also quoted in, *NW*, 8 June 1942.
3 'Diaspora' is used here in fairly generally, with the interrogation of what does and does not constitute a diaspora left to others. For the use of the term in the context of Ulster-Scots and America, see, for example, Patrick Fitzgerald, 'Mapping the Ulster Diaspora, 1607–1960', *Familia* 22: 3 and Gary Peatling, 'The "Irish", the "Scots-Irish" and the unionists of America in the Twentieth Century: Some Patterns of Exchange', *Etudes Irlandaises*, vo. 2,no. 28 (2003), 88.
4 'American Presidents of Ulster descent', talk by A. J. Tulip, BBC Home Service, 27 May 1942. http://genome.ch.bbc.co.uk/78719959389a494fbc4cf279b3ef0c93 accessed 5 February 2018. Quotations from *NW*, 28 May 1942. Tulip wrote *A Short History of Modern Ireland (1780-1914)*, published by John Adams, King Street, Belfast, 1930, and 'printed for private circulation only'.
5 To pre-partition unionists, the colonial and Revolutionary eras represented a 'golden age' for the diaspora, according to Flewelling. Lindsey Flewelling, *Two Irelands Beyond the Sea: Ulster Unionism and America, 1880-1920* (Liverpool: Liverpool University Press, 2018), 131.
6 See, for example, David Noel Doyle, 'Scots Irish or Scotch-Irish', in J. J. Lee and Marion R. Casey (eds), *Making the Irish American: The History and Heritage of the Irish in the United States* (New York and London: New York University Press, 2006), 162–8.
7 'Scotch-Irish' was used rarely in either Ireland or America in the eighteenth century. Doyle, 'Scots Irish or Scotch-Irish', in Lee and Casey, *Making*, 151; Kerby A. Miller, 'Ulster Presbyterians and the Two Traditions in Ireland and America', in Terry Brotherstone, Anna Clark and Kevin Whelan (eds), *These Fissured Isles, Ireland Scotland and the Making of Modern Britain 1798-1848* (Edinburgh: John Donald Publishers, 2005), 270. For the perils of nomenclature, see Miller in Brotherstone et al., *Fissured Isles*, 260–77, and also his article 'What's in a Name? Presbyterian Identity and Experience in Ulster and America', *Radharc*, vol. 3 (2002), 17–28. See also: Oren F. Morton and Oren F., *A History of Rockbridge County, Virginia* (Westminster, MD: Heritage Books, 2007, copyright 1920), 14 and Peatling, *Etudes Irlandaises*, 82. In this discussion, for simplicity's sake, 'Ulster-Scots' is used when contemporary figures in Northern Ireland are talking about these links and 'Scotch-Irish', when Americans of Irish Protestant descent are speaking.

8. For a brief explanation of Anglo-Saxonism, see Will Kaufman, and Heidi Slettedahl Macpherson (eds), *Britain and the Americas: Culture, Politics, and History, Volume 2* (Santa Barbara, Denver, Oxford: ABC-CLIO, 2005), 90–2. Blatt says of 'germ theory': '[f]or Teutonists, the U.S. political system represented the highest development of an Anglo-Saxon "genius for liberty". Political life was the expression of a racial soul and history was the record of racial development; some races had the capacity and were destined to develop free political institutions'. Andy Seal, 'Teutonic Germs and Race Realism: An Interview with Jessica Blatt', Society for U.S. Intellectual History Blog, 5 August 2019. https://s-usih.org/2019/08/teutonic-germs-and-race-realism-an-interview-with-jessica-blatt/ (accessed 11 May 2020).
9. Doyle, 'Scots Irish or Scotch-Irish', in Lee and Casey, *Making*, 365–6. These were echoed within late nineteenth-century Irish unionism, as Lee asserts: 'Orangeism was racism and essentially impervious to economic change. It retained a tenacious hold on Scotch-Irish loyalties throughout the whole period fiercely resisting the contamination of equality of opportunity for Catholics'. J. J. Lee, *The Modernisation of Irish Society, 1848-1918* (Dublin: Gill and MacMillan, 1989), 166. Lee uses 'Scotch-Irish' in the context of Ireland, rather than the United States.
10. Dinsmore, *Scotch-Irish*, 7. The Celts were, according to Dinsmore, apparently descended from Aryans, and the Scotch-Irish 'were of Teutonic or Anglo-Saxon origin'. Ibid., 9.
11. See Kevin Kenny, 'Violence and Anti-Irish Sentiment in the Nineteenth Century', in Lee and Casey, *Making*, 364–8.
12. Many immigrant groups, not least the Irish, formed lodges and fraternal associations. Jason Kaufman, *For the Common Good? American Civic Life and the Golden Age of Fraternity* (Oxford: Oxford University Press, 2002), 8–9.
13. Col. Thomas T. Wright obituary, The Twenty-sixth Annual Meeting and Dinner of the Pennsylvania Scotch-Irish Society, Philadelphia, 19 February, 1915, Appendix A, 37–8. http://www.archive.org/details/annualmeetingban02penn (accessed 20 January 2020). Wright appears to have been in the Confederate Army.
14. Flewelling, *Two Irelands*, 97–101.
15. 'There, for four crowded days', wrote T.W. Moody in 1945, 'a mixed multitude of Americans who were, or believed themselves to be, descendants of Ulster settlers, revelled in a Turkish bath of sentimentality and mutual edification'. T. W. Moody, 'The Ulster Scots in Colonial and Revolutionary America', *Studies: An Irish Quarterly Review*, vol. 34, no. 133 (March 1945), 85.
16. Flewelling, *Two Irelands*, 108.
17. Ibid; Jones derides Ford for giving 'the Scotch-Irish the almost exclusive credit' for these and other claims. Maldwyn A. Jones, 'The Scotch-Irish and Colonial America', in J. W. Blake (ed.), *The Ulster American Connection, A Series of Lectures Delivered in the Autumn of 1976* (Coleraine: The New University of Ulster, 1981), 10.
18. Flewelling, *Two Irelands*, 135–7.
19. Ibid., 149; 154–5; 220.
20. Ibid., 208; 232.
21. Theodore Roosevelt, *New York* (Delray Beach, FL: Levenger Press, 2004), 106. This edition is an abridgment of the Longmans, Green and Co., edition of the book published in 1891. https://books.google.co.uk/books?id=dcjkPwybiY0C&printsec=frontcover#v=onepage&q&f=false (accessed 3 January 2020).
22. Owen Wister, *A Straight Deal or The Ancient Grudge* (New York: Macmillan and Company, 1920), 259.

23 Ibid., 255-66.
24 Wayland Fuller Dunaway, *The Scotch-Irish of Colonial Pennsylvania* (Chapel Hill: University of North Carolina Press, 1944), 181-2. Dinsmore makes similar claims. Dinsmore, *Scotch-Irish*, 16-18; 47-9.
25 Speaking at a symposium in Northern Ireland marking the US bicentennial in 1976, Esmond Wright departed little from this characterization of the Ulsterman, describing him as 'the best of Americans . . . outgoing and gregarious, reliable and trustworthy; adventurous and pioneering; querulous and experimental; democratic to the point of lawlessness; church going and education addicted; haters of Indians and haters of the Establishment; at once sentimental but pragmatic'. Esmond Wright, 'Ulster and the United States A Prologue', in John W. Blake (ed.), *The Ulster American Connection: A Series of Lectures Delivered in the Autumn of 1976* (Coleraine: The New University of Ulster, 1981), 9. At the same symposium, Maldwyn Jones argued: 'essentially a race of individualists, the Scotch-Irish were tough, unprincipled, pugnacious, stern and intolerant. As seen by others these were unattractive traits but most of them were qualities needed in a new country. Even if much of it has been self-conferred, a good deal of the praise of the Scotch-Irish was not undeserved.' A. Jones, 'The Scotch-Irish and Colonial America', ibid., 17-18.
26 Blake, 'Preface', 'Ulster American Connection'. Denis Brogan: 'as much nonsense has been written about the Scotch-Irish as about any other groups taking its claim to an important part in the achievements of the American people', cited in Jones, 'The Scotch-Irish and Colonial America', in ibid, 10, *n*5.
27 James G. Leyburn, 'The Scotch-Irish: The Melting Pot: The ethnic group that blended', *American Heritage*, vol. 22, no. 1 (December 1970). https://www.americanheritage.com/content/scotch-irish (accessed 7 February 2018).
28 Aviotte argues that in eighteenth-century America, treatment of the Scotch-Irish 'despite their loyalty, their social status became comparable to the Catholics' in the nineteenth. Elodie Aviotte, 'Ulster Presbyterian Emigration to America: The Absence of a Unionist Political Dimension in America', *Familia: Ulster Genealogical Review*, vol. 19 (2003), 83. Peatling asserts: '[i]ronically, while a "Scotch-Irish" identity was intended to create a distinction between those of Ulster-Scots descent and more recent Catholic immigrants, the "Scotch-Irish" and the "Irish" shared the experience of encountering prejudice from this American establishment at several stages of the nineteenth century'. Peatling, *Etudes Irlandaises*, 88. Doyle argues that most Scotch-Irish identified solely as American by 1828 (coincidentally, the year Andrew Jackson was elected president). David Noel Doyle, 'The Irish in North America 1776-1845', in Lee and Casey, *Making*, 178.
29 For an overview of the plantation of Ulster and subsequent Protestant Ascendancy, see Bartlett, *Ireland*, 79-143.
30 Stormont's later official war history did make this connection. Blake, *Second World War*, 298.
31 As Peatling notes, this perspective is problematic in that 'this supposedly underprivileged narrative itself has repeatedly involved the suppression of inconvenient facts. Most obviously, this interpretation of a debt to "Ulster" involves a denial of the existence or significance of nationalists and Catholics in Ulster'. Peatling, *Etudes Irlandaises*, 87.
32 Marshall, *Ulster Sails West*, 48-9. Frontiersmen from Ulster, for example, killed twenty Native Americans in the Conestoga massacre of 1763, during the Seven Years' War (1756-63). Jones, 'The Scotch-Irish and Colonial America', in Blake, *Ulster*

American Connection, 16. Gary Peatling, 'Scotch Irish Rebellion? The Ulster Scots, the Scotch-Irish, and Revolution, 1688- 2003', *Journal of Scotch-Irish Studies*, vol. 2, no. 3 (2007), 37.

33 Aviotte, *Familia*, 88. Aviotte argues: 'Unionists therefore could not seek help in America, as it was perceived as the shelter of republicanism and Irish nationalism. This strongly contributes to the understanding of Unionists' reluctant attitude toward the US involvement, as America had symbolically become a shelter for their opponents.' Ibid., 88. For more on the lack of American political support for unionism, see ibid., 83–9.

34 As Peatling argues, both the unionist and the nationalist narratives have 'a tendency to reaffirm unreconstructed forms of United States nationalism'. Peatling, *Etudes Irlandaises*, 94. He also notes that '[t]hose who espouse crude theories (especially where racial in nature) are never short of an alibi for the failures of their "own" group'. Ibid., 90.

35 In 1900, 21 States had Orange lodges, by 1920 it was 40. The order was strongest in Pennsylvania, Michigan and New York, but also found in Georgia, Louisiana, Colorado, Arizona, Idaho, and even Alaska. Flewelling, *Two Irelands*, 118. For more on the Orange Order in America, see Ibid., 111–25. When Brooke eventually visited the States in 1950 he refused to formally meet Orange lodges, but he did attend the Ulster-Irish Society of New York's annual banquet. 'Visit by the Prime Minister and Lady Brooke to America in 1950'. Gransden, 24 October 1949. CAB9F/127/23.

36 Poem by Mrs Samuel Evans, cited in Dunaway, *Scotch-Irish*, 155.

37 *DJ*, 30 January 1942.

38 O'Byrne was a key confidant of many leading figures of the Irish revolution including Patrick Pearse and Roger Casement and, like Cardinal MacRory, bore witness to the bloody sectarian rioting in Belfast in 1920 and 1921, which left hundreds, primarily Catholics dead. For O'Byrne's life and career, see Richard Kirkland, *Cathal O'Byrne and the Northern Revival in Ireland, 1890-1960* (Liverpool: Liverpool University Press, 2006). For brief biographical details: http://www.newulsterbiography.co.uk/index.php/home/viewPerson/1273 (accessed 9 March 2018).

39 *IN*, 27 May 1942. The previous year, Henry II of England landed in Ireland, beginning eight centuries of Anglo-Irish conflict.

40 *IN*, 27 May 1942.

41 For Ireland and slavery, see Grace McGrath, *Ulster and Slavery: The Story from the Archives* (Belfast: Public Record office of Northern Ireland, 2007) and Bill Rolston, 'A Lying Old Scoundrel', *History Ireland*, vol. 11, no. 1 (Spring 2003). http://www.historyireland.com/18th-19th-century-history/a-lying-old-scoundrel/ (accessed 5 November 2015).

42 Rolston, *HI*.

43 *IN*, 27 May 1942.

44 Ibid. Cunningham abandoned his scheme due to local opposition. 'Hidden Connections: Slavery and Belfast'. http://www.culturenorthernireland.org/article/101/hidden-connections-slavery-and-belfast (accessed 5 November 2015). McCracken was the grandson of the Henry Joy, founder of the *News Letter*.

45 Russell and Tone were Anglicans, while most United Irishmen were Presbyterians.

46 *IN*, 1 June 1942.

47 *IN*, 30 January 1946.

48 Ibid.

49 Ibid.

50 Ibid.
51 Ibid.
52 For post-war anti-partition agitation within Northern Ireland, see Wood, *Propaganda*, 192; Farrell, *Orange State*, 177–80; Ollerenshaw, *Politics, Economic Mobilisation*, 217.
53 *IN*, 28 May 1942. Protestants could, however, make a strong counter-claim for an abolitionist heritage with W. F. Marshall crediting the Reformed Presbyterians of South Carolina and East Tennessee as being among the earliest Southern abolitionists, debarring all slave-holders from communion some forty years before anti-slavery agitation in New England. Marshall, *Ulster Sails West*, 48–9.
54 *BT*, 6 October 1942.
55 *NW*, 8 June 1942. This text seems to be from a sermon given by Marshall, which was published the following year in a pamphlet entitled: 'Three Hundred Years of Presbyterianism: Sermon and Address Delivered on the Occasion of the Tercentenary Commemoration of the Founding at Carrickfergus of the First Presbytery (18th June 1642-10th June 1942)'.
56 *NW*, 8 June 1942.
57 Ibid.
58 Ibid. Fitzgerald and Lambkin argue that Presbyterian emigration was motivated more by economics than persecution, and put the numbers arriving in what became the United States from Ireland as a whole at between 100,000 and 250,000 from 1700 and 1775, with some 40,000 to 80,000 leaving Ulster between 1750 and 1775, two-thirds of whom were Presbyterian. Patrick Fitzgerald and Brian Lambkin, *Migration in Irish History, 1607-2007* (London: Palgrave Macmillan, 2008), 90, 123, 124, and 144.
59 Marshall misattributes this quotation to Thomas Newenham, but it is lifted verbatim from Lecky. William Edward Hartpole Lecky, *A History of England in the Eighteenth Century, Volume II* (New York: D. Appleton and Company, 1891), 285–6. Lecky also claims that Protestants in Ireland were displaced by the 'Catholic cottier population, sunk in the lowest depths of ignorance and poverty', forcing them to emigrate. Ibid, 284. https://ia800301.us.archive.org/1/items/historyofengnew02leck/historyofengnew02leck.pdf (accessed 1 February 2018).
60 *NW*, 8 June 1942.
61 Marshall, *Ulster Sails West*, 8. For biographical details on Marshall, see http://www.ulster-scots.com/uploads/USCNWFMarshall.pdf (accessed 8 March 2018).
62 Marshall, *Ulster Sails West*, 8.
63 Ibid., 29. Marshall's view tallied with much existing historiography, however, more modern historians do not see the Battle of Alamance as part of the wider revolution, suggesting that the 'War of Regulation' was a limited regional conflict and rebels did not seek a break from Britain, and it was retrospectively and erroneously connected to the revolution. For details, see Sarah Sadlier, 'Prelude to the American Revolution? The War of Regulation: A Revolutionary Reaction for Reform', *The History Teacher*, vol. 46, no. 1 (November 2012), 98. Earlier historiographical suggestions that Alamance was the revolution's first battle, 'are quite simply false', in fact, the Regulators were often loyalists, while their opponents became fervent patriots. Sadlier, *History Teacher*, 101.
64 *NW*, 8 June 1942. During the election of 1896, the *Scranton Tribune* (Pennsylvania) reprinted an article from the *Herald Tribune* reporting that the next president 'is sure to be a Scotch-Irishman' as both McKinley and his Democratic opponent William

Jennings Bryan were 'Celtic' and 'some of the greatest sons of this sturdy race who have figured prominently in American history. . . .. Uncle Sam will have to do a lot of figuring to find out how much he owes the Scotch-Irish race'. *Scranton Tribune*, 5 August 1896.
65 Marshall, *Ulster Sails West*, 33.
66 Ibid., 44–6.
67 Ibid., 38.
68 Ibid., 51.
69 Ibid., 53.
70 Ibid., 50.
71 Ibid., 53.
72 Ibid.
73 'Minutes of the Cabinet Publicity Committee', 8 March 1944. CAB9F/123/34.
74 Ibid., 11 April 1944.
75 *BT*, 4 July 1942. These claims may have some credence. Leyburn notes that 'no other immigrants were so patriotically unanimous in support of the American cause as the Scotch-Irish. One group of patriotic settlers in Mecklenburg County, North Carolina, drew up a set of resolutions on 20 May 1775, declaring the people of that county free and independent of the British Crown. This predominantly Scotch-Irish assemblage thus anticipated by more than a year the Declaration of Independence. The Revolutionary War might not have been won without Scotch-Irish fighting men'. Leyburn, *American Heritage*. Dinsmore also cites Mecklenburg as a pivotal moment. Dinsmore, *Scotch-Irish*, 30.
76 *BT*, 4 July, 1942.
77 *NL*, 13 February 2012. 'The *News Letter* was heavily involved in publicizing the emigration trek to America through the 18th century by Ulster Presbyterians, publishing daily advertisements with times the ships were leaving the ports of Belfast, Larne, Londonderry, Newry and Portrush and the fares charged'. Ibid.
78 *BT*, 15 October 2013.
79 Brooke, 'Dominion Day speech in Canada', Broadcast 1 July 1950. CAB9F/123/34. Underlining in original.
80 Kelly, *Home*, 98.
81 Dozens of papers carried this story. See, for example, *Bend Bulletin* (Oregon), 30 July 1942; *Hartford Courant* (Connecticut) 11 July 1942; *Brooklyn Citizen* (New York) 23 July 1942.
82 *Dayton Daily News* (Ohio), 30 July 1942.
83 *NW*, 10 October 1942.
84 Ibid.
85 Buhrman to State, 19 December 1942. RG84/BCG/CF/1942/823.
86 *LS*, 27 January 1944. The *Sentinel's* transcription uses the British-English spelling of 'honour'.
87 *BT*, 7 August 1945.
88 Ian Paisley, *America's Debt to Ulster* (Belfast: Martyrs Memorial Publications, 1976), preface. http://www.lisburn.com/books/americas-debt/debt-a.htm (accessed 14 October 2020).
89 For Paisley's connection to the *Ulster Protestant* see, Walker, *TCBH*, 204. The Republican Party waged a shameless campaign of anti-Catholic bigotry against Smith, helping it win some Southern states for the first time since Reconstruction.
90 Paisley, *America's Debt*, foreword.
91 Ibid., epilogue.

Chapter 12

1. Daniel Cunningham to Andrews, 8 June 1942. Underlining and Capitalisation in original. CAB9CD/225/1. *NW*, 8 June 1942. Cunningham details: https://www.len nonwylie.co.uk/DAYB1943photos1.htm (accessed 11 February 2019).
2. Andrews to Cunningham, 11 June 1942. CAB9CD/225/1
3. *BT*, 10 November 1942.
4. Carroll, *NHR*, 22.
5. Deputy Regional Information Officer to Gilfillan, 7 November 1942; Gransden to Robinson, 7 November 1942. For the full itinerary, see memorandum, 'Mrs Roosevelt's Visit'. CAB9CD/225/10
6. *NL*, 11 November 1942.
7. Ibid.
8. Eleanor Roosevelt, 'My Day, 12 November 1942'. *The Eleanor Roosevelt Papers Digital Edition* (2017). https://www2.gwu.edu/~erpapers/myday/1942/ (accessed 20 August 2019).
9. *NL*, 11 November 1942.
10. *DJ*, 11 November 1942. A later report showed further disinterest and even referred to the Siege of Derry with 'siege' in inverted commas. Ibid., 13 November 1942.
11. *BT*, 11 November 1942; *NL*, 12 November 1942.
12. *NL*, 11 November 1942.
13. *BT*, 10 November 1942. For American press coverage, see, for example, *WES*, 11 November 1942; *SSL*, 11 November 1942.
14. Eleanor Roosevelt, 'My Day, November 12, 1942'; 'My Day, November 13, 1942'; *BT*, 12 November 1942.
15. Deputy R.I.O. to Gilfillan, 7 November 1942. CAB9CD/225/10.
16. Gransden to Robinson, 7 November 1942. Ibid.
17. Deputy R.I.O. to Gilfillan, 7 November 1942. Ibid.
18. Gransden to Robinson, 7 November 1942. Ibid.
19. 'Visit to Northern Ireland of General Marshall, Chief of Staff, USA Army, Mr H. Hopkins, and Mr A. Harriman', 23 April 1942. CAB9CD/225/1.
20. Basil Brooke to Alan Brooke, 15 July 1942. CAB9CD/225/1. Brooke thought that Major Douglas Beresford-Ash, from one of Ulster's oldest Protestant families, was a very poor choice as local host. Brooke met Marshall in 1950 where the general 'repeated the discomfort he had suffered with Beresford-Ash'. Brooke Diary, 24 April 1950.
21. Gray to Roosevelt, 19 October 1942, DGP, Box 8
22. Gray to Walshe, 26 October 1942. DGP, Box 8.
23. Gray to Roosevelt, 30 October 1942. FDRP/OF/2/DCF. This was while she was in England and before the announcement of her Northern Ireland trip.
24. Ibid.
25. Gray to Roosevelt, 6/9 November 1942. 'Later his wife told Maude: "Of course you know we would do the same thing for Hitler or Mussolini." Maude wanted to say that was the reason why Eleanor did not come here'. Ibid.
26. Ibid.
27. *NL*, 11 November 1942. See also, press release 10 November 1942, CAB9CD/225/10.
28. Andrews to Eleanor Roosevelt, 19 November 1942. The First Lady thanked him for his kind words. Eleanor Roosevelt to Andrews, 14 December 1942. Ibid.
29. *BT*, 27 September 1944.

30 Ibid., 28 September 1944.
31 Ibid., 29 September 1944.
32 'Publicity Committee Report', December 1944. CAB9F/123/38A. Another Congressional delegation arrived on a fleeting visit in July 1945. *BT*, 25 July 1945; *NL*, 26 July 1945.
33 To see this footage, visit: https://www.britishpathe.com/video/eleanor-roosevelts-tour-of-northern-ireland (accessed 20 August 2019).
34 Mail was vital to morale and soldiers sent 500,000 letters from Northern Ireland each month during 1942. 'Base History', from 1 June 1942 to 20 December 1942, 8. RG498/AHC/HS/ETOUSA/NIBC/186/579.
35 *LS*, 12 May 1942. All three would have stellar careers. Hurst had already directed films such as *Dangerous Moonlight* (1941) and in 1951 would direct the definitive version of Charles Dickens' *A Christmas Carol*. MacQuitty somewhat stumbled into film but later produced *A Night to Remember* (1958), about the sinking of the Titanic (whose launch he watched as a child), while Young directed several James Bond films.
36 Brian Desmond Hurst, *Autobiography*, unpublished, 123. BFI Library, cited in Hill, *Cinema*, 90.
37 'A Letter from Ulster': Synopsis, Crown Film Unit, Pinewood Studios. 'A Letter from Ulster- CFU222'. F256/656 Crown. INF6/347.TNA.
38 E. Hudson to W. E. Edwards (Ministry of Works and Buildings), 11 August 1942. 'Letter from Ulster, American Troops in North Ireland File'. INF5/87. TNA.
39 Hill, *Cinema*, 88–9; Brian McIlroy, 'British Filmmaking in the 1930s and 1940: The Example of Brian Desmond Hurst', in Wheeler Winston Dixon (ed.), *Re-viewing British Cinema 1900–1992: Essays and Interviews* (New York: State University of New York Press, 1994), 35.
40 Hill, *Cinema*, 89.
41 Hudson to C. H. Ward (War Office), 7 August 1942. INF5/87. TNA.
42 Hill, *Cinema*, 89. It was still referred to as *A Letter Home* in August 1942. Hudson to Ward, 5 August 1942. INF5/87. TNA.
43 'A Letter from Ulster', by Shaun Terence Young. INF6/347. TNA; MacQuitty to Brooke, 19 April 1943, COM61/661. PRONI. Cited in Hill, *Cinema*, 89.
44 'Short statement on film', E. P. Northwood to Hudson, 13 January 1943. INF5/87 TNA.
45 Ibid.
46 'A Letter from Ulster' shown in Northern Ireland'. INF6/347. TNA.
47 *Today's Cinema*, vol. 59, no. 4818, 23 December 1942
48 *Motion Picture Herald*, vol. 50, no. 1, 2 January 1943.
49 *Kinematograph Weekly*, no. 1863, 31 December 1942.
50 Hill, *Cinema*, 90.
51 Ibid., 91.
52 Ibid., 91–2. Pettitt's description of the film as 'overtly propagandistic' is accurate at a fairly superficial level and reflects its intentions, but this rather neglects the nuance of Hill's analysis. Lance Pettitt, 'Irish exilic cinema in England', *Irish Studies Review*, vol. 19, no. 01 (2011), 46.
53 *Doughboys in Ireland* (1943), [film]; Dir. Lew Landers, USA, Columbia. https://www.imdb.com; https://www.allmovie.com/movie/doughboys-in-ireland-v89869 (accessed 20 May 2020).

54 'Back Home in Ireland' [Mr Adams to see. RG 26/3/46. Seen 27/3/46]. CAB9/F/123/81. Hayward and Pedelty had made Northern Ireland's first feature film *The Luck of the Irish* in 1935.
55 Adams to Northwood, 19 November 1945; Brooke handwritten note to Northwood, 22 November 1945. CAB9F/123/81.
56 'Government of Northern Ireland, Information Services, London Office, report for September 1945', 'Report for November 1945' and 'Report for December 1945'. CAB/9F/123/34. Hayward to Grandsen, 12 April 1946. CAB9F/123/81.
57 Hayward to Grandsen, 9 April 1946. CAB9F/123/81.
58 Hayward to Grandsen, 12 April 1946. CAB9F/123/81; Paul Clements, *Romancing Ireland: Richard Hayward, 1892-1964* (Dublin: Lilliput Press, 2014), 196; Hill, *Cinema*, 111–12.
59 Sir Ernest Cooper, for example, complained about a *March of Time* film entitled *The Irish Question*. Sir Ernest Cooper to Bracken, 14 June 1944. CAB9/F/123/81.
60 'Proposed MOI film on Ulster's War Activities and Strategic Importance; Memorandum by Government Press Officer on Interview at MOI Headquarters, 30th January 1945', memo from 2 February 1945. CAB9/F/123/81
61 For correspondence between Stormont, the Ulster Office and the MOI on this, see CAB9/F/123/81.
62 I am hoping to write an article about *Back Home in Ireland* and Stormont's conflicts with London over propaganda.
63 'Publicity Committee Report', October 1945'. CAB9F/123/38A.
64 *BT*, 25 October 1945; *NL*, 26 October 1945. This is discussed in more detail in Chapter 5.
65 Brooke Diary, 28 October 1943
66 Gray to Roosevelt, 10 January 1944. FDRP/OF/2/DCF.
67 This was a phone conversation, as Brooke thanked Gray 'for ringing me' regarding a radio address the Prime Minister made, and 'I appreciated our own talk that night very much'. Brooke to Gray, 10 January 1944. DGP, Box 12.
68 Gray to Roosevelt, 10 January 1944. FDRP/OF/2/DCF.
69 Ibid.
70 Ibid. Brooke's diary entry makes no mention of an American trip, but Gray did tell him about demands to close the Axis legations in Dublin, which Brooke thought 'might raise a whole lot of other issues'. Brooke Diary, 9 January 1944.
71 Gray to Brooke, 14 January 1944, DGP, Box 12.
72 Ibid. Gray believed his mail was being opened, so advised Brooke to contact him via the Belfast consulate.
73 Norton, *Constitutional Nationalism*, 60; *Fermanagh Times* (*FT*), 10 February 1944. Another nationalist MP, Richard Byrne, took his seat from 1937 until his death in 1942.
74 *Manchester Guardian*, 5 February 1944.
75 Roberts to State, 'Developments', 27 March 1944. RG84/BCG/GR/1944/63.
76 Ollerenshaw, *Politics, Economic Mobilisation*, 193.
77 William Lowry to Bishop Neil Farren, 4 February 1944, cited in Oliver P. Rafferty, *Catholicism in Ulster 1603-1983: An Interpretative History* (London: Hurst, 1994), 243.
78 *FT*, 10 February 1944.
79 Ibid.

80 Ollerenshaw, *Politics, Economic Mobilisation*, 193. Ironically, in 1945, Farren warned Catholic parents about letting their children befriend those of other faiths and talked of the 'shame and the disgrace of Catholic people who had gone into Masonic and Orange halls'. *IN*, 5 May 1945.
81 Lowry to Andrews, 10 March 1943. CAB9CD/225/13.
82 Brooke Diary, 4 February 1944.
83 *Boston Globe*, 7 February 1944. The group was later involved in Congressional anti-partition hearings in 1950. Walsh was a former member of America First and a pre-Pearl Harbor isolationist, he shared a platform with Charles Lindberg at an America First rally in May 1941 (only weeks after the second bombing of Belfast) where many gave Nazi salutes and expressed anti-Semitic views. Dwyer, *Curtain*, 155.
84 *BG*, 7 February 1944.
85 *Chicago Daily News* services (*Ottawa Journal*, 19 February 1944).
86 Ibid.
87 Gray to Harry Hopkins, 15 February 1944; Gray to Farren, 11 February 1944. DGP, Box 12.
88 Gray to Bishop John F. O'Hara (Military Ordinariate), 18 February 1944; Gray to Francis Matthews, 16 February 1944. Ibid.
89 Gray to Roosevelt, 10 January 1944. FDRP/OF/2/DCF.
90 Brooke Diary, 21 January 1944.
91 Alexander Maxwell to Lord Cadogan, 2 February 1944. Handwritten notes from Cadogan to Eden and reply, 3 February 1944. FO954/6A/74. TNA.
92 Gray to Harry Hopkins, 15 February 1944. FDRP/OF/2/DCF.
93 Ibid.
94 'Memo for president', 18 February 1944. FDRP/OF/2/DCF.
95 Gray to Brooke, undated. DGP, Box 12. Gray stated that 'last Sunday was Easter', which would mean this letter was from sometime between 10 and 16 April (Easter fell on the 9th).
96 By this point, the Churchill-led wartime national government had been replaced by a Labour administration under Clement Atlee.
97 R. Price to Archer, 6 June 1946. WX101/120: DO35/1228. TNA.
98 Chuter Ede to Brooke, 21 December 1945. CAB9F/123/34. One vexed question was the sudden end of Lend-Lease in August 1945.
99 Ibid.
100 Ibid.
101 'Conversation between Lord Addison and Sir Basil Brooke, May 1946'. 'UK-Éire Political and Constitutional Relations'. WX101/146: DO35/1228. TNA; 'Cabinet Publicity Committee, Minutes of the Twenty-First meeting', 26 July 1946. CAB9F/123/37.
102 For details of these discussions, involving the Commonwealth Office and the embassy in Washington among others, see, for example, Bernard Sullivan (British consulate, Boston) to Ben Cockram (British embassy, Washington DC), 17 May 1946, and 'Confidential: Note on Principal Éire Propaganda Claims with Answers Thereto': WX101/1/69: DO35/1228. TNA.
103 '10. Ref Éire (N. E. Archer) 6.3.45, 12 March 1945. Ibid.
104 This is discussed in more detail in Chapter 10.
105 Brooke Diary, 17 May and 22 June 1950; Seamus Smyth, 'In Defence of Ulster: The Visit of Sir Basil Brooke to North America, Spring 1950', *The Canadian Journal of Irish Studies*, vol. 33, no. 2 (Fall 2007), 10–18.

106 Press release: 'PM Andrews message to American Brigadier General Collins', 1 January 1943. CAB9CD/225/10.
107 *SSL*, 22 January 1943; *BT*, 25 January 1943. R. M. Sayers (*Belfast Telegraph*) to H. V. V. Thompson, 4 February 1943. CAB9CD/225/20.
108 'American Landing Celebration', 14 January 1943. CAB9CD/225/20; *SSL*, 22 January 1943. Londonderry had its own ceremony in February, unveiling of plaque to mark the commissioning of the US naval base. Buhrman reported 'considerable local interest' in the event. Buhrman to State, 6 February 1943. RG84/BCG/GR/1943/58/841.5. In May a bronze plaque was presented by the US Marines to the city of Londonderry 'as a token of lasting friendship'. 17 May 1943, ibid. See also, US Naval Headquarters, London, 30 January 1943. CAB9CD/225/20.
109 'Landing of United States Forces in Ulster: Unveiling of Commemorative Stone, Tuesday 26th January 1943, Order of Ceremony'; 'List of Guests, to Luncheon in the Grand Central Hotel', 26 January 1943. For the role of the BBC, see Gransden to Henderson, 21 January 1943. CAB9CD/225/20. Mageean, like MacRory, was a strident anti-partitionist. Norton, *Constitutional Nationalism*, 56–7.
110 Buhrman to State, 27 January 1943. RG84/BCG/GR/1943/58/841.5.
111 Brooke Dairy, 26 January 1943.
112 *WES*, 26 January 1943; *NYT*, 27 January 1943.
113 Andrews to Crawford McCullagh, 29 January 1943; 'Extract from Minutes of the Estates Committee', 4 February 1943. CAB9CD/225/20.
114 The *Telegraph* first asked Stormont's permission. Sayers to Thompson, 4 February 1943. Gransden to Thompson, 9 February 1943. CAB9CD/225/20. *Stars and Stripes* reported the presentation. *SSL*, 4 May 1943.
115 I am developing this material into an article on memorialization of the Americans.
116 For further details on Lisnabreeny cemetery, see 'Memorial ceremony to be held at Lisnabreeny on 25 May 1945' and W. J. Gallman, Charge d'Affaires ad interim, to Brooke, 20 October 1947. CAB/9CD/225/5; 'USAFNI, Chronology', 28 January 1942; 'Lisnabreeny American Cemetery, Rocky Road, Belfast, Co. Antrim', https://wartimeni.com (accessed 21 July 2019); 'Lisnabreeny cemetery tribute to fallen US servicemen', https://www.bbc.co.uk (14 September 2013).
117 *NL*, 9 June 1944.
118 E. M. Lindsay to Brooke, 13 August 1943 (original memorandum dated 24 February 1943). CAB9CD/225/20; E. M Lindsay 'The Story of the Armagh Planetarium' (draft), E. M. Lindsay to K. P. Bloomfield, 10 April 1968. CAB9A/57/1.
119 Winant to Brooke, 18 December 1944; Brooke to Gray, 31 May 1946. CAB9CD/225/20.
120 'Cabinet Publicity Meeting: American War Memorial', 21 July 1946. Ibid. See also: 'Minutes of the Twenty-First Meeting of the Cabinet Publicity Committee', 25 July 1946. CAB9F/123/37.
121 'Cabinet Conclusions', 1 July 1947. CAB9CD/225/20.
122 *BT*, 29 October 1963.
123 Ibid. For details on the building, see Northern Ireland War Memorial Museum, https://www.iwm.org.uk/memorials/item/memorial/13218 (accessed 18 January 2019).
124 Andrews, 11 December 1941. CAB4/493. Cited in Barton foreword to Blake, *Second World War*, xiii.
125 For the gestation of the book, see Barton foreword, Blake, *Second World War*, xv–xvi.
126 Ibid., xvi–xvii.
127 For a full discussion of the book, see Tina Nelis, 'Northern Ireland in the Second World War', unpublished MPhil thesis, 2012, 143–90. As she notes, 'the official

history would act as a testament – a lasting memorial – to the role Northern Ireland had played', and it was self-consciously propagandistic in a way that other official British war histories were not. Nelis, 153. Blake, she argues, 'presented an uncomplicated, patriotic narrative that described how 'Ulster' and 'Ulstermen' contributed to the war. This was a narrative, not about the people of Northern Ireland as a whole, but about unionists'. Ibid., 187.
128 *NL*, 5 June 1944.
129 'US Army's Farewell to Ulster'. 'Report on the Work of Government Publicity Office during August 1945' (dated 1 September) CAB9F/123/34.
130 *BT*, 7 August 1945.
131 'US Army's Farewell to Ulster'. CAB9F/123/34.
132 *BT*, 15 August 1945. The visit was announced in America several days earlier. *Wilmington Morning Star*, 11 August 1945. See also, *SSL*, 22 August 1945; *SSL*, 25 August 1945.
133 *BT*, 23 August 1945. None of the three were actually born in Ulster. Alanbrooke, Sir Basil Brooke's cousin, was born and grew up in France, while Montgomery and Alexander were both born in England. Montgomery's roots were in Donegal, part of Ulster but not Northern Ireland, where his mother still lived during the war. Alexander was born in London into a family from County Tyrone and was an officer in the Irish Guards in the Great War.
134 *BT*, 23 August 1945.
135 The Ministry of Education announced a school holiday on the day of the visit. Ibid., 20 August 1945 and 24 August 1945. It is not clear whether Catholic schools also gave children a day off.
136 'Text of General Eisenhower's speech at Queen's University, Belfast, today, Friday, August 24, 1945'. RG84/BCG/GR/1945/70.
137 The *Irish News*'s muted coverage emphasised Eisenhower's conciliatory tone towards the Germans. *IN*, 25 August 1945. See also, WES, 24 August 1945.
138 'Order of Ceremony: Presentation to General Dwight D. Eisenhower of Certificate of his Election and Admission as an Honorary Burgess of the City of Belfast, City Hall Belfast, Friday 24th August 1945' RG84/BCG/GR/1945/70.
139 *BT*, 24 August 1945.
140 *IN*, 26 August 1945.
141 *NW*, 24 August 1945.
142 *BT*, 24 August 1945.
143 Ibid.; *LS*, 25 August 1945. See also, Ronnie Hanna, *Pardon Me Boy: The Americans in Ulster, 1942-45, A Pictorial Record* (Belfast: Ulster Society, 1991), viii.
144 Eisenhower diary, January 30, 1942. Ferrell (ed.), *The Eisenhower Diaries*, 46.
145 *BT*, 24 August 1945.
146 Ibid.
147 'General Dwight D. Eisenhower's Visit of August 23 and 24, 1945, to Belfast, Northern Ireland', prepared by William F. Ayer. RG84/BCG/GR/1945/70.
148 The Publicity Committee stated: '[a] special account was sent by the Regional Information Officer to American Division, MOI for transmission to the United States Press'. Publicity Committee: Report on the Work of Government Publicity Office during August 1945 (dated 1 September). CAB9F/123/34.
149 In 2013 a signed photo of Eisenhower was found in Belfast City Hall's basement by the incoming deputy mayor. *NL*, 29 June 2013. Truman suddenly and unexpectedly ended Lend-Lease on 21 August 1945. *NYT*, 23 August 1945. The now ex-President

Eisenhower returned to Northern Ireland in August 1962, on a European tour, to a similarly ecstatic welcome. The *Telegraph* once again provided extensive coverage. *BT*, 19 July 1962, 28 July 1962, 30 July 1962, 8 August 1962, 16 August 1962, 17 August 1962, 20 August 1962.

Epilogue

1. William A. Carson to Gray, 11 January, 1957. Ibid.
2. Brooke to Gray, 16 October 1956. DGP, 18.
3. Gray to Carson, 18 January 1957. Ibid
4. William A. Carson, *Ulster and the Irish Republic: A Brief Survey of Irish Republican Propaganda and an Exposure of Its Fallacies*, with an Introduction by David Gray, United States Minister to Éire, 1940-1947 (Belfast: William W. Cleland Ltd, 1957), i-ix. The book was distributed by the Ulster Unionist Council. Oscar Henderson to Gray, 27 June 1957. DGP, Box 18.
5. Tully, *Irish Americans*, 149.
6. Gray to Winant, 26 June 1942. DGP, Box 8.
7. Henderson, for example, tried to verify Gray's claim about population swaps in the event of the end of partition. Henderson to Gray, 27 June 1957. DGP, Box, 18.
8. Gray, *Green Curtain*, MSS, Ch. 26, p 29a-b. DGP, Box 1.
9. Lord Rugby (Maffey) to Gray, 8 August 1958. DGP, Box 18.
10. Carson, to Gray, 20 August 1958. Ibid.
11. 'Memoirs of Mr David Gray', Cabinet Publicity Committee, 10 July 1958. CAB9F/123/137.
12. A.J. Kelly to Brian Faulkner, 6 November 1958; Rugby to Faulkner, 31 March 1959. Ibid.
13. Savory to Gray, 4 August 1958; Savory to Gray, 17 September 1958. DGP, Box 18.
14. Savory to Montgomery, 15 September 1958. CAB9F/123/137. Montgomery would later go on to found the Ulster American Folk Park in Omagh. *Irish Times*, October 18, 2003.
15. 'Memoirs of Mr David Gray', Cabinet Publicity Committee, 30 September 1958. CAB9F/123/137.
16. Faulkner to Kelly, 18 May 1959. Ibid.
17. John Cordner to Gray, 21 September 1958. Cordner did offer something of a qualification: '[t]here is no doubt that Mr Gray stands emphatically on our side on the Partition issue. But it should not be expected that he will paint Ulster all white and the Republic all black, and, I am sure, you would not want it that way'. Ibid.
18. Cordner to Faulkner, 22 October 1958. Ibid.
19. Ibid. This is at odds with Tully's assessment that Gray was now suffering from dementia. Tully, *Irish Americans*, 149.
20. Kelly to Faulkner, 6 November 1958. CAB9F/123/137.
21. Ibid; Faulkner to Kelly 12 November 1958. Ibid.
22. Montgomery to Faulkner, 24 March 1959. Ibid.
23. Ibid.
24. Rugby to Faulkner, 31 March 1959. Ibid.
25. Kelly to Faulkner, 13 April 1959. Ibid.
26. Ibid. '(with accompanying note)'.

27 Publicity Committee, 10 February 1960. Ibid.
28 Ibid.
29 Ibid., 3 June 1961.
30 'Memorandum by Minister of Home Affairs: The David Gray manuscript', 2 October 1962. Ibid.
31 Ibid.
32 Ibid.
33 Ibid.

Primary sources

Public Record Office of Northern Ireland (PRONI), Belfast

Personal Papers
D/3004/D/33: Sir Basil Brooke Diary, 1940–1945
D/3015: Papers of Sir Douglas Savory

Government of Northern Ireland: Official papers and copies of official papers
CAB/3/A/30: Folder no. 73, 'The Battle of the Atlantic' (BBC script of broadcast on 25 September and 2 October 1949)
CAB/3/A/46: N. Ireland War History. File no 11 Americans, pr539/w.r.
CAB/3/A/47: Northern Ireland War History, FILE NO 11. American: forces, etc. Supplement to file pr539/w.r
CAB3/A/52: Folder No.18C, Q (Movements) N.I.
CAB3/A/96: BBC Scripts. Broadcast from N.I. during War Period, Folder No. 15

Government of Northern Ireland: Cabinet conclusion files ('topics discussed')
CAB/4/483/3: 30 September 1941, Letter from President Roosevelt
CAB/4/511/1: 2 June 1942, United States of America (Visiting Forces) Bill
CAB/4/534/11: 11 March 1943, Visit of Monsignor Spellman
CAB/4/540/6: 28 April 1943, Conscription
CAB/4/542/3: 12 May 1943, Conscription
CAB/4/543/4: 18 May 1943, Conscription
CAB/4/585: 25 May 1944, Capital sentence on court-martialled US Army private
CAB/4/631: 26 July 1945, American forces on leave

Government of Northern Ireland: Cabinet secretariat
CAB/9/CD/215/1: Additional Construction Work for War Purpose in NI
CAB/9/CD/225: Entry of America into the War:
CAB/9CD/225/1: Arrival of American troops in NI
CAB/9CD/225/2: Jurisdiction over Members of US forces in NI
CAB/9CD/255/3: Sub-series: Foreign (Allied) Troops in Northern Ireland
CAB/9CD/225/5: Provision of Cemetery near Belfast for American forces

CAB/9CD/225/9: Attachment of Police Liaison Officers to US Army
CAB/9CD/225/10: Visit of Mrs Roosevelt
CAB/9CD/225/11: Accommodation in Belfast for 'Stars and Stripes'
CAB/9CD/225/13: Visit of Most Rev. Dr Spellman- RC Archbishop of New York
CAB/9CD/225/17: Independence Day
CAB/9CD/225/18: Miscellaneous
CAB/9CD/225/19: Social Centres for US Troops
CAB/9CD/225/20: Commemoration Ceremonies
CAB/9F/123: Sub-series: Political publicity (Government Propaganda and Publicity)
CAB/9F/123/10: Northern Ireland Publicity: Correspondence
CAB/9F/123/34: Cabinet Publicity Committee, Minutes of Meetings, 1943–1945
CAB/9F/123/38A: Reports on work of the Publicity Officer, 1943–1947
CAB/9/F/123/81: Films featuring Northern Ireland
CAB/9F/123/90: Ulster Handbook
CAB/9F/123/137: Memoirs of Mr David Gray

National Emergency 'NE' files, 1939–1952

COM/61/865: Welfare of Armed Forces, Ministry of Commerce

Records of Public Record Office

FIN/17/1/P/23 (2): Miscellaneous Files

Belfast Corporation/County Borough Council

LA/7/3A/115: Crawford McCullagh
LA/7/3A/120: Crawford McCullagh

National Archives and Records Administration (NARA) College Park, Maryland

RG84: Records of the Foreign Service Posts of the Department of State, Great Britain: Classified General Records, 1936–1949, Belfast Consulate General
Confidential Files, 1939 to 1946
Correspondence, American Consulate General, Belfast, 1942.
RG84: Records of the Foreign Service Posts of the Department of State; Records of the US Embassy, London, England. Records Maintained by Ambassador John G. Winant, 1938–46. Box 3, Ireland file
RG107: Office of the Secretary of War: General Correspondence of John J. McCloy, 1941–45
RG107: Records of the Adjutant General's Office 1917 – WWII Operations Reports, 1941–48, Quartermaster
RG165: Records of the War Department; Department General and Special Staffs
RG218: Records of the US Joints Chiefs of Staff; Geographic File, 1942–45
RG332: ETO PR Sect. ETO Public Relations Section, Decimal File, 1943–1945

RG338: Records of US Army Operational, Tactical and Support Organizations (World War Two and thereafter) V Corps, Adjutant General Section, Central Decimal File, 1940–1945
RG407: Records of the Adjutant General's Office, WWII Operations Reports, 1940–48, European Theater
RG498: Records of the Headquarters, European Theater of Operations United States Army (World War Two); European Theater of Operations Historical Division, Administrative File, 1942–1946, 219 Netherlands, Gen To 225 No. Ireland Base.
RG498: Records of the Headquarters, European Theater of Operations United States Army (World War Two); European Theater of Operations Historical Division, Administrative File, 1942–Jan. 1946

Fold3: https://www.fold3.com/ digitized from NARA

RG498: US Army, US Forces, European Theater, Historical Division: Records, 1941–1946
Administrative history collection, historical section, ETOUSA, folder titles:
Northern Ireland, ADM NR (administrative number): 224
Northern Ireland Base Command (Directives), ADM NR: 225
Ports -Northern Ireland, ADM NR: 254
SPOBS (Special Observers), ADM NR: 318
Stars and Stripes – General, ADM NR: 331
First Eisenhower Period, ETO, Monograph, 1941–43, ADM NR: 509
Manuscript G-2 ETOUSA: A History of G-2 HQ ETOUSA, ADM NR: 513
Monograph: The Problem of Marriages in ETO. April. 1944. MSS. ADM NR: 519.
Northern Ireland Base Command Histories, ADM NR: 597

The National Archives (TNA) London

Dominions Office

DO35/1228: UK-Éire Political and Constitutional Relations

Foreign Office

FO371/34124: United States Forces in the United Kingdom
FO371/38624: United States Forces in the United Kingdom, File No.275
FO371/38646: American, 1944, File No.550
FO954/6A/74: Eire: Volume 6, folio(s) 74. 2 February 1944

Ministry of Information

INF1/297: Histories of Regional Information Offices
INF1/327A: Co-operation with U.S. Information Service (Anglo-American relations in Britain)
INF1/404: Ministry of Information Northern Ireland, Part A

Roosevelt Institute for American Studies (RIAS) Middelburg

President Franklin D. Roosevelt's Office Files, 1933–1945, Part 1, Safe File, Reels 1, 3, 15, 34
President Franklin D. Roosevelt's Office Files, 1933–1945, Part 2, Diplomatic Correspondence File, Reels 18, 19, 34 and 35

National Archives Catalog

FDR: Papers as President, Map Room File, 1939–1945 https://catalog.archives.gov/id/194990

Belfast Newspaper Library

Armagh Guardian
Ballymena Observer
Belfast Telegraph
Belfast Weekly Telegraph
Derry Journal
Down Recorder
Dromore Leader
Dungannon Observer
Fermanagh Times
Irish News
Londonderry Sentinel
Mid-Ulster Mail
News Letter
Northern Whig
Stars and Stripes (Northern Ireland edition)

British Library

Tuskegee File

Irish Newspaper Archive

https://www.irishnewsarchive.com/
Donegal News
Fermanagh Herald
Irish Examiner
Irish Independent
Irish Press
Kerry Champion
Limerick Leader

Nationalist and Leinster Times
Nenagh Guardian
Strabane Chronicle
Ulster Herald

Library of Congress (Chronicling America)

https://chroniclingamerica.loc.gov/
Detroit Tribune
Washington Evening Star
Washington Sunday Star

Newspaperarchives.com

Stars and Stripes (London)
Biddeford Daily Journal (Maine)

Newspapers.com

Arizona Republic
Atlanta Constitution
Baltimore Sun
Bend Bulletin (Oregon)
Binghamton Press
Boston Globe
Bradford Evening Star and the Bradford Daily Record (Pennsylvania)
Brooklyn Citizen
Calgary Herald
Casper Star Tribune Charlotte News (North Carolina)
Chicago Tribune
Daily Item (Pennsylvania)
Daily Times (Ohio)
Dayton Daily News
Decatur Daily Review
Fayette County Leader (Iowa)
Freeport Journal Standard
Fresno Bee The Republican
Hartford Courant
Hood County Tablet (Texas)
Indiana Evening Gazette (Pennsylvania)
Lancaster News Era (Pennsylvania)
Lansing State Journal
Lowndes Signal (Alabama)
Minneapolis Morning Tribune

Ottawa Journal
Pensacola News Journal
Pittsburgh Press
Pittsburgh Sun Telegraph
Richmond Times Dispatch
Scranton Tribune
Times Tribune
York Dispatch

Other

New York Times
Yank

Bibliography

Books

Appy, Christian G. (2000), *Cold War Constructions: The Political Culture of United States Imperialism, 1945-1966*, Amherst: University of Massachusetts Press

Bahmanyar, Mir (2003), *Darby's Rangers 1942-45*, Oxford: Osprey Publishing, (Kindle edition)

Bardon, Jonathan (1992), *A History of Ulster*, Belfast: Blackstaff Press Ltd

Bartlett, Thomas (2010), *Ireland: A History*, Cambridge and New York: Cambridge University Press

Bartlett, Thomas (2018), *The Cambridge History of Ireland: Volume 4: 1880 to the Present* Cambridge and New York: Cambridge University Press

Barton, Brian (1988), *Brookeborough: The Making of a Prime Minister*, Belfast: Queen's University, Institute of Irish Studies

Barton, Brian (1989), *The Blitz: Belfast in the War Years*, Belfast: Blackstaff Press,

Barton, Brian (1995), *Northern Ireland in the Second World War*, Belfast: Ulster Historical Foundation

Bew, Paul, Gibbon, Peter, and Patterson, Henry (1979), *The State in Northern Ireland, 1921-72: Political Forces and Social Classes*, Manchester: Manchester University Press.

Bew, Paul (2007), *Ireland: The Politics of Enmity, 1789-2006*, Oxford: Oxford University Press

Bew, Paul (2012), *A Yankee in de Valera's Ireland: The Memoir of David Gray*, Dublin: Royal Irish Academy

Black, Robert W. (2009), *Ranger Force: Darby's Rangers in World War II*, Mechanicsburg, Pennsylvania: Stackpole Books, (Kindle edition)

Blake, John W. (1956), *Northern Ireland in the Second World War*, Belfast: Her Majesty's Stationary Office

Blake John W., ed. (1981), *The Ulster American Connection, A Series of Lectures Delivered in the Autumn of 1976*, Belfast: The New University of Ulster

Bland, Lucy (2019), *Britain's 'Brown Babies': The stories of children born to black GIs and white women in the Second World War*, Manchester: Manchester University Press

Bloom, Emily C. (2016), *The Wireless Past: Anglo-Irish Writers and the BBC, 1931-1968* Oxford: Oxford University Press

Bowman, John (1989), *de Valera and the Ulster Question, 1917-1973*, Oxford and New York: Oxford University Press

Brotherstone, Terry, Clark, Anna and Whelan, Kevin, eds. (2005), *These Fissured Isles, Ireland Scotland and the Making of Modern Britain 1798- 1848*, Edinburgh: John Donald Publishers

Canavan, Tony (1989), *Frontier Town: An Illustrated History of Newry*, Belfast: Blackstaff Press

Carroll, Francis M. (2006), *The American Presence in Ulster: A Diplomatic History, 1796-1996*, Washington D.C.: Catholic University of America Press

Carson, William A. (1956), *Ulster and the Irish Republic, A Brief Survey of Irish Republican Propaganda and an Exposure of its Fallacies*, Belfast: William W. Cleland Ltd

Cathcart, Rex (1984), *The Most Contrary Region: The BBC in Northern Ireland 1924-1984*, Belfast: Blackstaff Press

Churchill, Winston S. (1950), *The Second World War, Book VI: The Grand Alliance: War comes to America, June 23, 1941-January 17 1942*, Geneva: Cassell and Company Limited (fifth edition, 1968)

Clark, Dennis (1982), *The Irish Relations: Trials of an Immigrant Tradition*, London and Toronto: Associated University Presses, Fairleigh Dickinson University Press

Clements, Paul (2014), *Romancing Ireland: Richard Hayward, 1892-1964*, Dublin: Lilliput Press

Cole, Robert (2006), *Propaganda, Censorship and Irish Neutrality in the Second World War*, Edinburgh: Edinburgh University Press

Coogan, Tim Pat (1995), *De Valera: Long Fellow, Long Shadow*, London: Arrow Books

Coogan, Tim Pat (2004), *Ireland in the Twentieth Century*, London: Arrow Books

Cooney, John (1984), *The American Pope: The Life and Times of Francis Cardinal Spellman*, New York: Times Books

Davis, Troy D. (1998), *Dublin's American Policy: Irish American Diplomatic Relations, 1945 1952*, Washington D.C.: Catholic University of America Press

Dinsman, Melissa (2015), *Modernism at the Microphone: Radio, Propaganda, and Literary Aesthetics During World War II*, London: Bloomsbury

Dinsmore, John Walker (1906), *The Scotch-Irish in America: Their History, Traits, Institutions and Influences: Especially as Illustrated in the Early Settlers of Western Pennsylvania, and Their Descendants*, Chicago: The Winona Publishing Company

Dixon, Wheeler Winston (1994), *Re-Viewing British Cinema: Essays and Interviews*, New York: State University of New York Press

Duggan, John P. (1975), *Neutral Ireland and the Third Reich*, Dublin: Gill and Macmillan Ltd

Duggan, John P. (2003), *Herr Hempel at the German Legation, 1937-1945*, Dublin and Portland, Oregon: Irish Academic Press

Dunaway, Wayland Fuller (1944), *The Scotch-Irish of colonial Pennsylvania*, Chapel Hill: University of North Carolina Press (Genealogical Publishing Company, 2012 Original from Pennsylvania State University Digitized 2009)

Dwyer, T. Ryle (1988), *Strained Relations: Ireland at Peace and the USA at War, 1941-1945*, Dublin: Gill and McMillan

Dwyer, T. Ryle (1991), *De Valera: The Man and his Myths*, Dublin: Poolberg Press, Ltd,

Dwyer, T. Ryle (2009), *Behind the Green Curtain: Ireland's Phoney Neutrality During World War II*, Dublin: Gill and McMillan

English, Richard (2007), *Irish Freedom: The History of Nationalism in Ireland*, London: Pan Books, MacMillan

Fanning, Ronan (2013), *Fatal Path: British Government and Irish Revolution, 1910-1922*, London: Faber and Faber

Fanning, Ronan (2015), *Eamon de Valera: A Will to Power*, London: Faber and Faber

Farrell, Michael (1976), *Northern Ireland: The Orange State*, London: Pluto Press (second revised edition, 1980)

Ferriter, Diarmaid (2007), *Judging Dev: A Reassessment of the Life and Legacy of Eamon De Valera*, Dublin: Royal Irish Academy

Ferrell, Robert H., ed. (1981), *The Eisenhower Diaries*, New York and London: W. W. Norton and Company

Bibliography

Fisk, Robert (1983), *In Time of War: Ireland, Ulster and the Price of Neutrality, 1939–45*, Dublin: Gill and Macmillan
Fitzgerald, Patrick and Lambkin, Brian (2008), *Migration in Irish History, 1607–2007*, London: Palgrave Macmillan
Flewelling, Lindsey (2018), *Two Irelands Beyond the Sea: Ulster Unionism and America, 1880–1920*, Liverpool: Liverpool University Press
Friedman, Barbara G. (2007), *From the Battlefront to the Bridal Suite: Media Coverage of British War Brides, 1942–1946*, Columbia and London: University of Missouri Press
Friscia Ippolito, Melanie (2011), *I'll Be Back When Summer's in the Meadow: A World War II Chronicle, Volume I, 1942–1943*, Bennington, Vermont: Merriam Press, Military Monograph 137
Friscia Ippolito, Melanie (2013), *I'll Be Back When Summer's in the Meadow: A World War II Chronicle, Volume III, 1945–1946*, Bennington, Vermont: Merriam Press, Military Monograph 137
Gannon, Robert I. (1962), *The Cardinal Spellman Story*, New York: Doubleday and Company
Gibson-Harries, Derrick (1990), *Life-Line to Freedom: Ulster in the Second World War*, Belfast: Ulster Society Publications Ltd
Gardiner, Juliet (2004), *Wartime Britain, 1939–1945*, London: Headline Book Publishing
Girvin, Brian and Roberts, Geoffrey, eds. (2000), *Ireland and the Second World War: Politics, Society and Remembrance*, Dublin: Four Courts Press
Girvin, Brian (2006), *The Emergency: Neutral Ireland 1939–45*, London: Pan Books MacMillan
Grayson, Richard S. (2018), *Dublin's Great Wars: The First World War, the Easter Rising and the Irish Revolution*, Cambridge: Cambridge University Press
Grieg, Ian (1990), *The Second World War and Northern Ireland*, London: Friends of the Union
Hanna Ronnie (1991), *Pardon Me Boy: The Americans in Ulster, 1942–45, A Pictorial Record*, Belfast: Ulster Society
Hanna, Ronnie (1992), *Land of the Free: Ulster and the American Revolution*, Belfast: Ulster Society
Hennessey, Thomas (2000), *A History of Northern Ireland*, London: Palgrave MacMillan
Hill, John (2006), *Cinema and Northern Ireland: Film, Culture and Politics*, London: BFI Publishing
Hill, Myrtle (2003), *Women in Ireland: A Century of Change*, Belfast: Blackstaff Press
Hogan, Gerard and Walker, Clive (1989), *Political Violence and the Law in Ireland*, Manchester and New York: Manchester University Press
Horne, John (2008), *Our War: Ireland and the Great War*, Dublin: Royal Irish Academy
Jackson, Alvin (1999), *Ireland, 1798–1998: Politics and War*, Oxford: Blackwell
Jackson, Alvin (2004), *Home Rule: An Irish History, 1800–2000*, Oxford: Oxford University Press
Jeffery, Keith (2011), *Ireland and the Great War*, Cambridge: Cambridge University Press
Jordan, Hugh (2002), *Milestones in Murder: Defining Moments in Ulster's Terror War*, Edinburgh: Mainstream Publishing
Kaplan, Alice (2005), *The Interpreter*, Chicago and London: University of Chicago Press
Kaufman, Jason (2002), *For the Common Good? American Civic Life and the Golden Age of Fraternity*, Oxford: Oxford University Press
Kaufman, Will and Slettedahl Macpherson, Heidi, eds. (2005), *Britain and the Americas: Culture, Politics, and History, Volume 2*, Santa Barbara, Denver, Oxford: ABC-CLIO

Keegan, Nicholas M. (2018), *US Consular Representation in Britain since 1790*, New York and London: Anthem Press
Kelly, Mary Pat (1994), *Home Away from Home*, Belfast: Appletree Press
Kelly, Mary Pat (1995), *Proudly We Served: The Men of the USS Mason*, Annapolis, MD: Bluejacket Books, Naval Institute Press
Lacey, Brian (1990), *Siege City: The Story of Derry and Londonderry*, Belfast: Blackstaff Press
Laffan, Michael (1983), *The Partition of Ireland, 1911–1925*, Dundalk: Dundalgan Press
Lambkin, Romie (1992), *My Time in the War*, Dublin: Wolfhound Press
Lecky, Edward Hartpole (1891), *A History of England in the Eighteenth Century, Volume II*, New York: D. Appleton and Company
Lee, J. J. (1989), *Ireland 1912–1985: Politics and Society*, Cambridge: Cambridge University Press
Lee, J. J. (1989), *The Modernisation of Irish Society, 1848–1918*, Dublin: Gill and MacMillan
Lee, J. J. and Casey, Marion R., eds. (2006), *Making the Irish American: The History and Heritage of the Irish in the United States*, New York and London: New York University Press
Lee, Ulysses (1964), *The Employment of Negro Troops*, Washington D.C.: United States Army in World War II Special Studies, Center of Military History United States Army. Available online: http://www.history.army.mil/books/wwii/11-4/
Longmate, Norman (1975), *The GI's: The Americans in Britain, 1942–1945*, London: Hutchinson
Loughlin, James (1995), *Ulster Unionism and British National Identity Since 1885*, New York and London: Pinter
Mac Eoin, Uinseann (1980), *Survivors: The Story of Ireland's Struggle as Told Through Some of Her Outstanding Living People*, Dublin: Argenta Publications (second edition, 1987)
Mac Eoin, Uinseann (1997), *The IRA in the Twilight Years 1923–1948*, Dublin: Argenta Publications
Marshall, W. F. (1943), *Ulster Sails West*, Belfast: The Quota Press
Matoloff, Maurice and Snell, Edwin M. (1999), *United States Army in World War II: Strategic Planning for Coalition Warfare, 1941–1942*, Washington D.C.: Center Of Military History United States Army, the War Department. https://www.ibiblio.org/hyperwar/USA/USA-WD-Strategic1/USA-WD-Strategic1-5.html
McCabe, Michael (2012), *For God and Ireland: The Fight for Moral Superiority in Ireland 1922–1932*, Sallins, Co. Kildare: Irish Academic Press
McCormick, Leanne (2010), *Regulating Sexuality: Women in Twentieth-Century Northern Ireland*, Manchester: Manchester University Press
McCullagh, David (2018), *De Valera: Volume II Rule 1932–75*, Dublin: Gill Books
McIntosh, Gillian and Urquhart, Diane, eds. (2010), *Irish Women at War: The 20th Century*, Dublin and Portland Oregon: Irish Academic Press
McMahon, Paul (2011), *British Spies and Irish Rebels: British Intelligence and Ireland, 1916–1945*, Woodbridge: Boydell Press
Miller, Kerby A. (2008), *Ireland and Irish America: Culture, Class, and Transatlantic Migration*, Dublin: Field Day
Morton, Oren F. (1920), *A History of Rockbridge County, Virginia*, Westminster, MD: Heritage Books (2007)
Noble, G. Bernard and Perkins, E. R., eds. (1962), *Foreign Relations of the United States, 1942*, (*FRUS*) volume I, Washington: United States Government Printing Office
Norton, Christopher (2014), *The Politics of Constitutional Nationalism in Northern Ireland, 1932–70: Between Grievance and Reconciliation*, Manchester: Manchester University Press
O'Halpin, Eunan (2001), *Defending Ireland: The Irish State and its Enemies since 1922*, Oxford: Oxford University Press

O'Halpin, Eunan (2008), *Spying on Ireland: British Intelligence and Irish Neutrality During the Second World War*, Oxford: Oxford University Press
Ollerenshaw, Philip (2013), *Northern Ireland in the Second World War: Politics, Economic Mobilisation and Society, 1939-45*, Manchester University Press
O'Neill, John (2018, *Belfast Battalion: A History of the Belfast IRA, 1922-1969*, Wexford: Litter Press (Kindle Edition)
Paisley, Ian (1976), *America's Debt to Ulster*, Belfast: Martyrs Memorial Publications, http://www.lisburn.com/books/americas-debt/debt-a.htm
Parker, Christopher (2009), *Fighting for Democracy: Black Veterans and the Fight Against White Supremacy in the Post-War South*, Princeton: Princeton University Press
Patterson, Henry (2006), *Ireland since 1939: The Persistence of Conflict*, Dublin: Penguin Ireland
Phoenix, Éamon, ed. (1995), *A Century of Northern Life: The Irish News and 100 Years of Ulster History 1890s-1990s*, Belfast: Ulster Historical Foundation
Purdie, Bob, ed. (1990), *Politics in the Streets: The Origins of the Civil Rights Movement in Northern Ireland*, Belfast: The Blackstaff Press
Rafferty, Oliver P. (1994), *Catholicism in Ulster 1603-1983: An Interpretative History*, London: Hurst
Reynolds, David (2000), *Rich Relations: The American Occupation of Britain, 1942-1945*, London: Phoenix Press
Rose, Sonya O. (2003), *Which People's War? National Identity and Citizenship in Wartime Britain, 1939-1945*, Oxford and London: Oxford University Press
Roosevelt, Theodore (2004), *New York*, Delray Beach, FL: Levenger Press
Smith, Graham (1987), *When Jim Crow Met John Bull: Black American Soldiers in World War II Britain*, London: Taurus
Staunton, Enda (2001), *The Nationalists of Northern Ireland, 1918-1973*, Dublin: The Columbia Press
Tent, James F. (1984), *Mission on the Rhine: "Reeducation" and Denazification in American-Occupied Germany*, Chicago and London: University Of Chicago Press
Tully, John Day (2010), *Ireland and Irish Americans 1930 to 1945: The Search for Identity*, Dublin and Portland, OR: Irish academic Press
Virden, Jenel (1996), *Good-Bye, Piccadilly: British War Brides in America*, Urbana and Chicago: University of Illinois Press
Werren, Kate (2020), *An American Uprising in Second World War England: Mutiny in the Duchy*, Yorkshire and Philadelphia: Pen and Sword History
Wills, Clair (2007), *That Neutral Island: A Cultural History of Ireland During the Second World War*, London: Faber and Faber
Wilson, Tom (1989), *Ulster: Conflict and Consent*, Oxford and New York: Basil Blackwell
Wister, Owen (1920), *A Straight Deal or the Ancient Grudge*, New York: Macmillan and Company. http://www.gutenberg.org/files/1379/1379-h/1379-h.htm
Wood, Ian S. (2010), *Britain, Ireland and the Second World War*, Edinburgh: Edinburgh University Press, 'Societies at War Series'

Articles

Aviotte, Elodie (2003), 'Ulster Presbyterian Emigration to America: The Absence of a Unionist Political Dimension In America', *Familia: Ulster Genealogical Review*, Vol. 19, pp. 75-91
Bergreen, Laurence (1996), 'Irving Berlin: This Is the Army', *Prologue Magazine*, Vol. 28, No. 2, National Archives

Bew, Paul (1990), 'Review: Varieties of Irishness?: Some New Explanations', *The Historical Journal*, Vol. 33, No. 3, pp. 747–754

Carroll, Francis M. (2008), 'United States Armed Forces in Northern Ireland During World War II', *New Hibernia Review*, Vol. 12, No. 2, pp. 15–36

Dwyer, T. Ryle (2013), Review: Paul Bew, *A Yankee in de Valera's Ireland: The Memoir of David Gray*, *History Ireland*, Vol. 21, No. 1. http://www.historyireland.com/20th-centu ry-contemporary-history/a-yankee-in-de-valeras-ireland-the-memoir-of-david-gray/ (accessed 11 January 2018)

Evans, Bryce (2014), 'A Pint of Plain is your only Man', *History Ireland*, Vol. 22, No. 5, pp. 36–38

Fanning, Ronan (1982), 'Irish Neutrality: An Historical Review', *Irish Studies in International Affairs*, Vol. 1, No. 3, pp. 27–38

Fitzgerald, Patrick (2006), 'Mapping the Ulster Diaspora, 1607–1960', *Familia*, Vol. 22, pp. 1–17.

Freeman, David (2010), 'Leading Churchill Myths (19): "Churchill was drunk and not being serious when he proposed the unification of Ireland in 1941"'. *Finest Hour*, Vol. 147, p. 57. https://winstonchurchill.org/publications/finest-hour/finest-hour-147/ leading-churchill-myths-19-churchill-was-drunk-and-not-being-serious-when-he-pro posed-the-unification-of-ireland-in-1941/ (accessed 6 March 2020)

Hanley, Brian (2005), 'Oh Here's to Adolf Hitler: The IRA and the Nazis', *History Ireland*, Vol. 13, https://www.historyireland.com/20th-century-contemporary-history/oh-heres -to-adolph-hitler-the-ira-and-the-nazis/ (accessed 4 August 2017)

Hanley, Brian (2004–2006), '"No English Enemy . . . Ever Stooped so Low": Mike Quill, de Valera's Visit to the German Legation, and Irish-American Attitudes during World War II'. *Radharc*, Vol. 5, No. 7, pp. 245–264

Henderson, Ian (1981), 'The G.I.s in Northern Ireland', *After the Battle*, No. 34, p. 140. https://www.afterthebattle.com/magazine/issues26-50.html

A History of United States Army Forces Northern Ireland (USAFNI), War Department, The Adjutant General's Office, Washington, War Department Records Branch, Historical Records Section

Houston, Matthew (2019), 'Presbyterianism, Unionism, and the Second World War in Northern Ireland: The Career of James Little, 1939–46', *Irish Historical Studies*, Vol. 43, pp. 252–268

Johnston, Maria (2008), '"This Endless Land": Louis MacNeice and the USA', *Irish University Review*, Vol. 38, No. 2, pp. 243–262

Leyburn, James G. (1970), 'The Scotch-Irish: The Melting Pot: The Ethnic Group that Blended', *American Heritage*, Vol. 22, No. 1. https://www.americanheritage.com/co ntent/december-1970 (accessed 7 February 2018)

Lilly, J. Robert (1996), 'Dirty Details: Executing U.S. Soldiers During World War II', *Crime & Delinquency*, Vol. 42, No. 491, pp. 491–516

Lilly, J. Robert and Thomson, J. Michael (1997), 'Executing US Soldiers in England, World War II', *British Journal of Criminology*, Vol. 37, No. 2, pp. 262–288

Mako, Shamiran and Donabed, Sargon (2011), 'Harput, Turkey to Massachusetts: Immigration of Jacobite Christians', *CHRONOS Revue d'Histoire de l'Université de Balamand*, Numéro, Vol. 23, pp. 19–42.

McCormick, Leanne (2006), '"One Yank and They're Off": Interaction between U.S. Troops and Northern Irish Women, 1942–1945', *Journal of the History of Sexuality*, Vol. 15, No. 2, pp. 228–57.

McNamara, Pat (2012), 'The Powerhouse: Cardinal Francis Spellman', *Patheos*, 17 December
Miller, Kerby A. (2002), 'What's in a Name? Presbyterian Identity and Experience in Ulster and America', *Radharc*, Vol. 3, pp. 17–28
Ludcke, George O. (1997–1998), 'WW II Memories Stirred by Londonderry Visit', *Fortitudine*, Vol. 27, No. 3, pp. 5–7.
Moody, T. W. (1945), 'The Ulster Scots in Colonial and Revolutionary America', *Studies: An Irish Quarterly Review*, Vol. 34, No. 133, pp. 85–94
Moody, T. W. (1946), 'Irish and Scotch-Irish in Eighteenth-Century America', *Studies: An Irish Quarterly Review*, Vol. 35, No. 137, pp. 85–90
Norton, Christopher, (2007), 'The Internment of Cahir Healy M.P., Brixton Prison July 1941–December 1942', *Twentieth Century British History*, Vol. 18, No. 2, pp.170–193
Peatling, Gary (2007), 'Scotch Irish Rebellion? The Ulster Scots, the Scotch-Irish, and Revolution, 1688–2003', *Journal of Scotch-Irish Studies*, Vol. 2, No. 3, pp. 37–56.
Pettitt, Lance (2011), 'Irish exilic cinema in England', *Irish Studies Review*, Vol. 19, No. 01, pp. 41–54
Rolston, Bill (2003), 'A Lying Old Scoundrel', *History Ireland*, Vol. 11, No. 1. http://www.historyireland.com/18th-19th-century-history/a-lying-old-scoundrel/ (accessed 5 November 2015)
Rose, Sonya O. (1997), 'Girls and GIs: Race, Sex and Diplomacy in Second World War Britain,' *International History Review*, Vol. 19, pp. 146–160
Rose, Sonya O. (1998), 'Sex, Citizenship and the Nation in World War II Britain,' *American Historical Review*, Vol. 103, pp. 1147–1176
Rosenberg, Joseph L. (1980), 'The 1941 Mission of Frank Aiken to the United States: An American Perspective', *Irish Historical Studies*, Vol. 22, No. 86, pp. 162–177
Sadlier, Sarah (2012), 'Prelude to the American Revolution? The War of Regulation: A Revolutionary Reaction for Reform', *History Teacher*, Vol. 46, No. 1, pp. 97–126
Smyth, Seamus (2007), 'In Defence of Ulster: The Visit of Sir Basil Brooke to North America, Spring 1950', *The Canadian Journal of Irish Studies*, Vol. 33, No. 2, pp. 10–18
Topping, Simon (2013), '"Laying down the law to the Irish and the Coons": Northern Ireland's Response to American Racial Segregation during World War Two', *Historical Research*, Vol. 86, No. 234, pp. 741–759
Topping, Simon (2013), 'The Dusky Doughboys: Interaction between African American Soldiers and the Population of Northern Ireland during the Second World War', *Journal of American Studies*, Autumn, pp. 1131–1154
Topping, Simon (2017), 'Racial Tensions and U.S. Military (In)Justice in Northern Ireland during World War II', *Journal of African American History*, Vol. 102, No. 2, pp. 157–183
Topping, Simon (2018), '"A Hundred Thousand Welcomes"? Unionism, nationalism, partition and the arrival of American forces in Northern Ireland in January 1942', *Journal of Transatlantic Studies*, Vol. 16, No. 1, pp. 81–100
Walker, Graham (2007), 'Northern Ireland, British–Irish Relations and American Concerns, 1942–1956', *Twentieth Century British History*, Vol. 18, No. 2, pp. 194–218
Werrell, Kenneth P. (1978), 'The Mutiny at Bamber Bridge', *After the Battle*, No. 22, pp. 1–11
White, Egbert (1945), 'Press in a Citizen's Army', *Journal of Educational Sociology*, Vol. 19, No. 4, pp. 236–248

Wynn, Neil A. (2006), '"Race War": Black American GIs and West Indians in Britain During The Second World', *War, Immigrants & Minorities*, Vol. 24, No. 3, pp. 324–46

Miscellaneous

Government reports

McCormick, Leanne, O'Connell, Sean, Dee, Olivia and Privilege, John (2021), *Mother and Baby Homes and Magdalene Laundries in Northern Ireland, 1922–1990*, Report For the Inter Departmental Working Group on Mother and Baby Homes, Magdalene Laundries and Historical Clerical Child Abuse

Pamphlets

Edwards, Harry W. (1994), *A Different War: Marines in Europe and North Africa*, Washington D.C.: Marine Corps, History and Museums Division

Falls, Cyril (1951), 'Northern Ireland as an Outpost of Defence,' first appeared in *World Review*

McGrath, Grace (2007), *Ulster and Slavery: The Story from the Archives*, Belfast: Public Record office of Northern Ireland

Montgomery, Ian (undated), 'Researching the United States Military Presence in the Public Record Office of Northern Ireland', Belfast: Public Record office of Northern Ireland

Smith, Allan Esler (2012), 'Revisiting *A Letter From Ulster*', Belfast: Northern Ireland War Memorial, Home Front Exhibition

PhD theses

Tina Nelis (2012), 'Northern Ireland in the Second World War', A thesis submitted to The University of Manchester for the degree of Master of Philosophy (MPhil) in the Faculty of Humanities

Tully John Day (2004), 'Identities and Distortions: Irish Americans, Ireland, and the United States', 1932–1945, unpublished PhD thesis, Ohio State University

Conference proceedings

O'Driscoll, Mervyn (2005) 'Keeping Britain Sweet: Irish Wartime Neutrality, Political Identity and Collective Memory'. In: N. Keogh and A. Sorokin eds. *Collective Memory in Ireland and Russia. Proceedings of a conference* held on *11–12 November 2005 in the State Library of Foreign Literature*, Moscow State Library of Foreign Literature, Moscow, 11–12 November 2005, pp. 98–119

Unpublished material

Hanley, Brian (2004) '"Oh here's to Adolph Hitler"? : The IRA's support for the Nazis in context'.

Bibliography

Websites and online resources

Online journals, articles and blogs

Draper, John (2008), 'Letters, "A Protestant Parliament for a Protestant People"?' *History Ireland*, No. 2. https://www.historyireland.com/20th-century-contemporary-history/a-protestant-parliament-for-a-protestant-people/ (accessed 4 November 2020)

Edelstein, Sally (2013), 'On the Front Lines with Coca Cola Part I & II', 30 May 2013. https://envisioningtheamericandream.com/2013/05/30/on-the-front-lines-with-coca-cola-pt-ii/ (accessed 27 April 2020)

Fratus, Matt (2019), 'How Coca-Cola Provided a Fresh Coke to the Front Lines of World War II', 2 April 2019. https://coffeeordie.com/coca-cola-colonels/ (accessed 27 April 2020)

Hill-Jackson, Valerie (2014), 'The Welsh War Brides of Tiger Bay', 28 January 2014. http://www.gibrides.com/the-welsh-war-brides-of-tiger-bay/ (accessed 4 November 2020)

O'Driscoll, Mervyn (2017), 'Ireland and the Nazis: A Troubled History', *Irish Times*, 15 May 2017. https://www.irishtimes.com/culture/books/ireland-and-the-nazis-a-troubled-history-1.3076579 (accessed 04 August 2017)

O'Neill, John (2016), 'Odd Man Out: a story about the Belfast IRA?' *Treason Felony Blog*, 24 November 2016. https://treasonfelony.wordpress.com/2016/11/24/odd-man-out-a-story-about-the-belfast-ira/ (accessed 19 May 2020)

Reeves, Scott (2012), 'Andrew Jackson Cottage and US Ranger Centre, County Antrim', *BBC History Extra*, 13 November 2012. https://www.historyextra.com/period/georgian/andrew-jackson-cottage-and-us-ranger-centre-county-antrim/ (accessed: 21 March 2020)

Seal, Andy (2019), 'Teutonic Germs and Race Realism: An Interview with Jessica Blatt', Society for U.S. Intellectual History Blog, 5 August 2019. https://s-usih.org/2019/08/teutonic-germs-and-race-realism-an-interview-with-jessica-blatt/ (accessed 11 May 2020)

Spellman, Francis Joseph (4 May 1889–2 December 1967), *American National Biography* Online, http://www.anb.org/articles/08/08-01438.html (accessed 27 November 2015)

Spencer, Brian (2015), 'Does the Irish rain make us all Irish? Brian John Spencer looking into his soul', 27 May 2015. http://eamonnmallie.com/2015/05/the-irish-rain-makes-us-all-irish-brian-john-spencer-looking-into-his-soul/ (accessed 15 October 2015)

Online news sources

Derry Journal, 6 June 2008. https://www.derryjournal.com/news/springtown-camp-the-l and-of-the-free-and-the-home-of-the-brave-1-2126079 (accessed 21 January 2019)

Derry Journal, 7 May 2010. https://www.derryjournal.com/news/tin-huts-a-hollywood-star-and-one-big-family-1-2145661 (accessed 21 January 2019)

'Energetic pioneer of Scotch-Irish folk history', *Irish Times*, 18 October 2003. https://www.irishtimes.com/news/energetic-pioneer-of-scotch-irish-folk-history-1.385039 (accessed 21 July 2018)

Jones, Kevin, 'NY Archdiocese Responds to Cardinal Spellman Groping Allegation', Catholic News Agency, 19 February 2019. https://www.catholicnewsagency.com/news/ny-archdiocese-responds-to-cardinal-spellman-groping-allegation-36449 (accessed 11 May 2019)

Kiberd, Declan (2011), 'The Riotous History of The Playboy of the Western World', *Guardian*, 23 September. https://www.theguardian.com/stage/2011/sep/23/playboy-western-world-old-vic (accessed 3 April 2020)

McLemore, Henry (1942), 'This Is War! Stop Worrying About Hurting Jap Feelings', *Seattle Times*, 30 January 1942. http://densho.org/wp-content/uploads/2016/06/Documents_SPW.pdf (accessed 2 November 2018)

McNamara. Pat (2012), 'The Powerhouse: Cardinal Francis Spellman', *Patheos*, 17 December 2012 . http://www.patheos.com/Catholic/Powerhouse-Spellman-Pat-McNamara-12-18-2012 (accessed 27 November 2015)

Neumayr, Charles (2019), 'Covering up for Cardinal Spellman', *Church Militant*, 13 February 2019. https://www.churchmilitant.com/news/article/covering-up-for-cardinal-spellman (accessed 11 May 2019)

Ottley, Roi (1942), 'Jim Crow in Britain', *Negro Digest*, Vol. II, No. 1, November 1942. http://www.bulldozia.com/projects/index.php?id=275. (accessed 12 June 2020)

Websites (Alphabetical by URL)

Cathal O'Byrne (1876–1957), *Dictionary of Ulster Biography* http://www.newulsterbiography.co.uk/index.php/home/viewPerson/1273 (accessed 9 March 2018)

Cunninghamsway. https://cunninghamsway.com/2016/12/16/october-1942-fermanagh-herald/ (accessed 11 April 2020)

Doughboys in Ireland, (1943) https://www.allmovie.com/movie/doughboys-in-ireland-v89869 (accessed 19 June 2020)

Doughboys in Ireland (1943). https://www.imdb.com/title/tt0035824/plotsummary?ref_=tt_ov_pl (accessed 19 June 2020)

'Eisenhower Pier, Bangor, Co. Down'. https://wartimeni.com/location/eisenhower-pier-bangor-co-down/ (accessed 25 April 2019)

GI Jive festival. https://medium.com/@MediaKristina/retrace-the-footsteps-of-the-gis-in-northern-ireland-with-the-gitrail-and-commemorate-dday-with-6d75960d26a8 (accessed 21 July 2019)

'Glenn Miller visits Northern Ireland in 1944'. https://wartimeni.com/person/glenn-miller/ (accessed 13 October 2020)

'Hidden Connections: Slavery and Belfast'. http://www.culturenorthernireland.org/article/101/hidden-connections-slavery-and-belfast (accessed 5 November 2015)

Lennon Wylie. https://www.lennonwylie.co.uk/DAYB1943photos1.htm (accessed 11 February, 2019)

'Lisnabreeny American Cemetery, Rocky Road, Belfast, Co. Antrim'. https://wartimeni.com/location/lisnabreeny-american-cemetery-rocky-road-belfast-co-antrim/ (accessed 21 July 2019)

'Northern Ireland National War Memorial'. Imperial War Museum. https://www.iwm.org.uk/memorials/item/memorial/13218 (accessed 18 January 2019)

Northern Ireland War Memorial Museum. http://www.niwarmemorial.org/about/#more-6 (accessed 18 January 2019)

Political Graveyard: Quincy Roberts. http://politicalgraveyard.com/bio/roberts7.html#670.32.86 (accessed 19 April 2018)

'Red Cross in NI'. https://sites.google.com/site/americansinulster/a-r-c-ulster

Springtown Camp, 1946–1967. http://www.springtowncamp.com/ (accessed 21 January 2019)

Bibliography 295

'The Day an American Actress Dropped by an Ulster Town to See Her Ancestral Home'. https://heritageandcultureblog.wordpress.com/2019/02/01/the-day-an-american-actress-dropped-by-an-ulster-town-to-see-her-ancestral-home/ (1 February 2019)
'The Life, Work and Legacy of Rev. W.F. Marshall', Ulster-Scots Community Network. http://www.ulster-scots.com/uploads/USCNWFMarshall.pdf (accessed 8 March 2018)
'US Forces in Northern Ireland'. https://www.flickr.com/photos/usani4245/21452049033/in/album-72157659654375196/ (accessed 15 July 2019)

BBC sources

BBC general

'American Troops, Murders and a Race Riot During World War Two', 3 November 2018. https://www.bbc.co.uk/news/uk-northern-ireland-46033229 (accessed 7 June 2019)
'Lisnabreeny Cemetery Tribute to Fallen US Servicemen', 14 September 2013. https://www.bbc.co.uk/news/uk-northern-ireland-24085462 (accessed 14 January 2019)
'Springtown Camp: Plans for Naval Base Tribute Gets Go Ahead', BBC, 18 January 2019. https://www.bbc.co.uk/news/uk-northern-ireland-foyle-west-46916098 (accessed 13 May 2019)
'US Soldiers' Portrush Christmas Treat for Local Children', BBC, 23 December 2018. https://www.bbc.co.uk/news/uk-northern-ireland-46654512 (accessed 23 December 2018)
'World War Two GI baby: Albert Gilmour Reunites with Family', BBC, 29 September 2019. https://www.bbc.co.uk/news/uk-northern-ireland-49727021 (accessed 29 September 2019)
'Your Place and Mine', BBC, 16 October 2014. https://www.bbc.co.uk/northernireland/yourplaceandmine/tyrone/cluntoe_airfield_ardboe.shtml (accessed 7 June 2019)

BBC 'People's War'

'American losses in N Ireland', 19 August 2005. https://www.bbc.co.uk/history/ww2peopleswar/stories/87/a5212487.shtml (accessed 6 June 2019)
'American Servicemen in Northern Ireland', 15 October 2014. https://www.bbc.co.uk/history/ww2peopleswar/stories/24/a2094824.shtml (accessed 16 April 2019)
'Bishop Daly in Belleek During the War', 15 October 2014. https://www.bbc.co.uk/history/ww2peopleswar/stories/09/a8898709.shtml (accessed 12 April 2019)
'First Irish GI Bride in the USA', 15 October 2014. https://www.bbc.co.uk/history/ww2peopleswar/stories/43/a5741543.shtml (accessed 12 April 2019)
'Meeting Glenn Miller', 15 October 2014. https://www.bbc.co.uk/history/ww2peopleswar/stories/82/a2294282.shtml (accessed 13 October 2020)
'The Chaperone', 15 October 2014. https://www.bbc.co.uk/history/ww2peopleswar/stories/01/a3967301.shtml (accessed 19 December 2018)
'US Army in Ulster', 15 October 2014. https://www.bbc.co.uk/history/ww2peopleswar/stories/78/a2058978.shtml (accessed 14 January 2019)

BBC Genome Project

MacNeice, Louis (1942), 'Halfway House: The AEF in Northern Ireland', BBC Forces Network, 25 September 1942. http://genome.ch.bbc.co.uk/ff7747f6a7d14664b1a6673 9f0e1f0f6 (accessed 18 February 2018)
MacNeice, Louis (1942), 'Salute to the US Army', BBC Home Service, 4 October 1942. http://genome.ch.bbc.co.uk/947c43971eb64c4a88dcfc9b1e745566 (accessed 18 February 2018)
Tulip, A. J. (1942), 'American Presidents of Ulster Descent', BBC Home Service, 27 May 1942. http://genome.ch.bbc.co.uk/78719959389a494fbc4cf279b3ef0c93 (accessed 5 February 2018)
'Saturday Sport' (1942), BBC Forces Programme, 14 November 1942. http://genome.ch .bbc.co.uk/3a0f5e437c354b61b96b55ad6d277a8b (accessed 7 February 2018)
'Workers' Playtime' (1943), BBC Forces Programme, 3 October 1943. http://genome.ch .bbc.co.uk/6dcff53ef0154e629e9da2c022ca2a30 (accessed 18 February 2018)

Films

A Letter from Ulster (1943), Brian Desmond Hurst, UK, Crown Film Unit
American Troops in Northern Ireland (1942), British Pathé. Media Urn: 43605; Film ID: 1316.09; Canister: 42/9; Sort Number: 42/009. https://www.britishpathe.com/video/american-troops-in-northern-ireland
Back Home in Ireland (1946), Donovan Pedelty, UK. https://www.youtube.com/watch?v =D4mcyNItywQ (accessed 15 February 2019)
Closing the Ring (2007), Richard Attenborough, UK, Canada, US, Prospero Pictures
Eleanor Roosevelt's Tour of Northern Ireland (1942), British Pathé. Media Urn: 61023; Film Id: 1857.07; Canister: UN730 A; Sort Number: UN0730 A. https://www.britishpathe.com/video/eleanor-roosevelts-tour-of-northern-ireland
Letters From Home (1942), British Pathé. Media Urn: 43774; Film Id: 1324.05; Canister: 42/30; Sort Number: 42/030. https://www.britishpathe.com/video/letters-from-home-3.
More Americans Arrive In Belfast (1942), British Pathé. Media Urn: 60523; Film ID: 1695.08; Canister: UN312 B; Sort Number: UN312 B. https://www.britishpathe.com/video/more-americans-arrive-in-belfast-1942
Mr Winant Visits US Army Camps in Northern Ireland (1942), British Pathé. Media Urn: 43660; Film ID: 1318.28; Canister: 42/18; Sort Number: 42/018. https://www.britishpathe.com/video/mr-winant-visits-us-army-camps-in-northern-ireland
P47s Arrive Sydenham Airfield Belfast, Ireland via USS Block Island, 14 September 1943. RG428: General Records of the Department of the Navy, 1941–2004, Series: Moving Images Relating to Military Activities, ca. 1947–1980. https://catalog.archives.gov/id /75884
Settling In–American Troops In Northern Ireland (1942), British Pathé. Media Urn: 43635; Film ID: 1318.03; Canister: 42/14; Sort Number: 42/014. https://www.britishpathe.com /video/settling-in-american-troops-in-northern-ireland
US Chief of Staff Reviews American Troops in Northern Ireland (1942), British Pathé. Media Urn: 43793; Film ID: 1324.24; Canister: 42/34; Sort Number: 42/034. https://www.britishpathe.com/video/us-chief-of-staff-reviews-american-troops-in-north

Index

ABC-1 (American, British, Canadian) Report (1941) 22, 100
Abercorn, James Hamilton, Duke of
  attends baseball matches 67, 68
  Eleanor Roosevelt visit 182, 183
  Governor's Fund and Cardinal MacRory 85
  Gray and 149, 153, 156–7
  Harris case 37, 44–5, 144
  links to *News Letter* 51
  meeting US Congressmen 184
  memorial column ceremony 193
  opening of Officers Club, Belfast 49
  Opening of Red Cross club Belfast 57; attends events at 59, 197
  opening of Red Cross Welfare Centre, Portrush 54
  Spellman visit 94
  Thanksgiving message 72
  upholding death penalty 103–4
Adams, F. M. 47–8, 51, 127, 133, 188
Aghalee, County Antrim 43
Aiken, Frank 151, 160, 161
Air Raid Protection (ARP) 43
Alabama 159
Alamance, Battle of 177
Albatross, US FWS 13
Alexander, Harold 195
Alien Fiancées and Fiancés Act (1946) 132
'The Ambassadors of Swing' 74
Amelia Street, Belfast 54, 125
America First 161
American Expeditionary Force (AEF) 7, 38, 64
American Forces Network (AFN) 34
American Friends of Irish Neutrality (AFIN) 161
'American Note'
  criticism of Gray 150
  Gray and 153, 158, 160–6, 188, 191–2
  invasion scare and 30
  Stars and Stripes reports on 59–60

American Red Cross (ARC) clubs
  American volunteers working at 54, 123
  celebrity visits to 76
  Christmas parties at 72
  colored Red Cross and segregation 57, 141–2
  confused with 'Green Cross' 61
  congressional visit to 195
  departure of the Americans and 195
  Eleanor Roosevelt visit to 182, 194
  at Kensington Hotel, Belfast 57
  in Londonderry 66, 89
  Matthews visit to 89
  pictures of 55, 74, 142
  at the Plaza, Belfast 54, 55
  press stories about 56
  prostitution near 124–5
  Red Cross Welfare Centre, the Northern Counties Hotel, Portrush 54
  role of 46, 49, 54–8
  rules for female guests 127–9
  second anniversary of founding 194–5
  war brides and 131–3
American Revolution
  Pennsylvania Rangers 27
  R. L. Marshall, Presbyterians and 176, 177, 181, 203
  A Short Guide to Great Britain and 33
  Ulster and 3, 169, 171–3, 179
  unionist celebration of 175
Amicable Society of Belfast 175
Ancient Order of Hibernians 177
Anderson, Mary 127
Andrews, General Frank M. 129
Andrews, John M.
  attacks de Valera and reaction in Éire to Americans 17, 18
  attends baseball 67
  Brooke, African American troops and 138

Index

clemency appeals to 103
concerns about workers from
  Éire 115
creating an official history of the war
  and 194
creation of hospitality committees 46
departure of Americans in late 1942 34
Eleanor Roosevelt visit and 182, 183
fears of civil unrest 100
first anniversary of American
  landing 192-3
4th July 1942 71
Gray, *Ulster Protestant* and 157
Gray and 149
informed of American arrival by
  London 11-12, 100
John Randolph's praise for 113
opening of Red Cross club in
  Belfast 55
praises *A Letter from Ulster* 185
proposed American bases in Northern
  Ireland 23
related to Bob Montgomery 76
resigns 118-19
Ulster-American links and 181
visit of Spellman 91, 92, 94-5
welcome to Americans 14-15
'And They Called It Ireland' 33
Anglo-American Army Relations
  Committee 49
Anglo-Irish treaty (1921) 16
Anglo-Saxonism 168-70
Anti-Partition Council 81
Antrim town 28, 42, 57, 58, 131, 143
Arcadia conference 9
Armagh Observatory 193-4
Armagh town
  condom 'harvest' 126
  fear of air-raids 85-6
  General Patton in 34
  Mass for American troops at
    St Patrick's cathedral 70
  Spellman visit to 91, 93
  Thanksgiving 72
Armstrong, Louis 73
Arter, Col. Theodore 51, 123, 137-8,
  182, 188
As I Roved Out: A Book of the North
  (1946) 174

Associated Press (AP)
  reports 'American Note' 164
  reports arrival of Americans 13, 19
  reports IRA activity 61, 62, 64, 108-9
Atlantic, Battle of 6, 20, 34, 204
Atlantic Charter 93-4, 110, 162
Attenborough, Richard 28
Auxiliary Territorial Service (ATS) 182
Ayer, William F. 120, 197

Back Home in Ireland (1946) 186, 187
Baird, William 51, 60, 119, 193
Baker, Kenny 186
Balkans 160
Ballygawley, County Tyrone 85
Ballymena, County Antrim 34, 76
Bamber Bridge, Lancashire 143
Banbridge, County Down 59
Bangor, County Down 13, 72
Barry, John J. 96, 97
Barry's amusement arcade, Portrush 72
baseball 13, 61, 63, 67-9, 71, 75
basketball 55, 68
Beattie, Jack 14, 69, 118, 189
Beddington, Jack 184
beer 64-6
Behind the Green Curtain 149, 208
Belfast blitz (1941)
  Aiken mission coinciding with 162
  alleged IRA involvement 102
  American press reports on 63
  concern about air-raid on
    Armagh 85
  impact on building of US bases 22,
    25, 26
  impact on civilian morale 112
  Northern Ireland and Britain, shared
    experience of 3, 204
  Stormont preparedness for 194
  US Consuilate and 111
Belfast Hospital for Sick Children 67
Belgium 78
Belleek, County Fermanagh 65
Berlin 25, 75, 101, 112
Berlin, Irving 76
Berlin Radio 110
Bessbrook, County Armagh 135, 146
Betjemen, John 159
Bevin, Ernest 191

Index

Bill of Rights, The 159, 189
Bishopscourt aerodrome, County Down 195
Blake, John M. 194
Blake, Vice-Admiral Geoffrey 136
Bob Jones University 180
Boland, F. H. (Frederick) 78, 150, 210
Bonner, Robert 169, 171
Boston 173, 188, 190
'Boston air party' 96–7
Boundary Commission 4, 5
Bourgeois, Anna 133
Boyne, Battle of (1690) 177
Bracken, Brendan 48–50, 187
Brandywell stadium, Londonderry 67
Breen, Dan 159
Brennan, Robert
    Gray and 151, 162, 163
    IRA campaign and 104–5
    Irish America and 154, 160
    Roosevelt and 161
    US bases and 23, 24
    US landing and 15–17
Bristol 62, 143, 175
Britain-America Circle 71
British Broadcasting Corporation (BBC)
    American complaints about programming 51, 54
    baseball coverage 68
    broadcasts to US 74
    Eisenhower visit 195
    4th July celebrations 71
    memorial column coverage 193
    programming for Americans 64
    Stormont distrust of 54
    talk on US presidents 167
British Red Cross 54
British Troops Northern Ireland (BTNI) 34, 48, 51
Brooke, Colonel Arthur 178
Brooke, Field Marshall Alan (Viscount Alanbrooke) 11, 100, 183, 195
Brooke, Sir Basil
    African American troops and 137–8, 145, 147
    Alanbrooke and 11
    American departure and 195
    attempts to suppress *Ulster Protestant* 157–8, 164

attends baseball 67
becomes Prime Minister 118–19
Bracken praise for 187
construction of US bases and 23
departure of the Americans in late 1942 and 34
Eisenhower visit and 197
Gray, IRA and 158
Gray's *Great Illusion* and 208, 210
Gray praise for 149
Harris court martial and 44, 144
leadership qualities of 46
Louise Farrand and 55–6
Lowry 'fumigation' controversy 190
management of and hospitality for the Americans 3, 34, 37, 46–50, 52, 66, 72, 199–200
Marshall, Harriman and Hopkins and 183
memorial column 193
memorial to US forces 194
mooted wartime visit to the US 159, 188–92, 201
1950 visit to North America 178, 201
parachutists in Fermanagh and 29
radio broadcasts to US 64
relationships with US consuls 113
sectarian comments of 5
US dignitaries' visit to Northern Ireland 183, 184
US generals and 52
visiting US celebrities and 75–6
War of 1812 and 178
Brooke, Lady Cynthia 113
Brooks, Clairce 141
Brundick, Chaplain William T 71
Brunskill, General G. S. 145–6
'B'-Specials 87, 106
Buhrman, Parker S.
    Archbishop Spellman visit and 92, 94
    arrival of African American troops and 137
    arrival of Americans and 12, 20, 29, 113
    background and arrival in Belfast 3, 112–13
    bombing of Hippodrome cinema and 71

comments on conscription and
  recruitment in Northern
  Ireland   115
concerns about behaviour of
  Americans   33, 42, 66, 114
concerns about publicity surrounding
  American bases   25
departure and award of the badge of
  'The Poor Richard Club'   119–20
discusses discrimination against
  Catholics   117–19
Francis Matthews visit and   89–90
insights of   202–3
landing memorial service   193
positive response to Americans   179
replacement of Andrews with
  Brooke and views of unionist
  politics   118–19
reports on IRA campaign   99, 103,
  104, 106–10, 114
security concerns about David
  Gray   158–9
view of Brooke   46
views on nationalism   83
views on the Catholic Church and
  Cardinal MacRory   71, 86
war effort and strikes in Northern
  Ireland   116–17

Cadogan, Sir Alexander   191
California   133
California Eagles   68
Campbell, John   122, 143
Campbell, T. J.   189–90
Carrickfergus, County Antrim   27,
  29, 141
Carrickmore, County Tyrone   41
Carson, William A.   207, 208
Case, Lt. Col. Homer   26
Castledawson, County Londonderry   145
Castlewellan, County Down   44, 126
Cave Hill, County Antrim   28
Central Council of Irish County
  Clubs   190
Chamberlain, Neville   6
Chaney, Major General James E.   12, 26,
  28, 66, 100, 135
Chateau Thierry, USS   13
Chater, G. H.   194

Chitty, Colonel Arthur   57
Christmas   70, 72, 138, 189
Christmas Under Fire (1941)   62
Churchill, Winston S.
  'American Note'   136, 162, 164
  Andrews and sending troops   11
  asks Brooke to look after
    hospitality   46
  Brooke's American trip   191
  critical of Northern Ireland's
    airfields   27–8
  discusses conscription with
    Roosevelt   79
  discussions with Roosevelt over
    sending troops   9, 10, 21, 26
  Éire's neutrality   202, 205
  Gray and   89, 153–4
  meets Spellman   92
  offer to de Valera to end partition   11
  praise for Northern Ireland   1
Church of Ireland   71, 173, 176
Clenaghan, Edward   42–5, 115
Clinton, Bill   199
Clipsham, Sgt. William   40–1, 183
Clonnard Monastery, Belfast   70
Closing the Ring (2007)   28
Cluntoe, County Tyrone   28
Coca-Cola   66–7
Cockcroft, R.A.   196
Cockcroft, Sgt. Robert A.   196
Cold War   204, 207
Colebrooke, County Fermangh   47
College Square Presbyterian Church,
  Belfast   128
Collier's   62, 139
Collins, General Leroy
  African American troops and   58,
    144–5
  assumes command   34
  children of US servicemen   130
  Harris case   45
  hospitality for US forces   49
  landing anniversary   192
  Red Cross   57
  Stars and Stripes   58
  Thanksgiving   72
Colonial Office   136
Colored Red Cross Clubs   57, 141
Columbia, Tennessee   169

Columbia Pictures   186
Connecticut   59
Connolly, James   101
conscription in Northern Ireland   19, 78–9, 111, 113, 115
Continental Congress   71, 177
Coogan, Henry   44, 45, 126, 143, 144
Cooke, Pvt. Herbert   128–9
Cookstown, County Tyrone   138, 142 (image), 145, 146 (image)
Cooper, Sir Ernest   51, 178
Cordner, John   208–9, 210
Cosgrave, William T.   84, 207
Count Basie   73
Craig, Sir James (Lord Craigavon)   5, 113, 149, 152–4, 159
Cranborne, Lord   191
cricket   67, 68
Criminal Investigation Division (CID)   40
Crown Film Unit (CFU)   62, 185
Cudahy, John   101, 149
Cunningham, Daniel   181
Cunningham, Waddell   175
Curragh internment camp, Dublin   29
Czechoslovakia   79

Dahlquist, General J. H.   58
Dáil Éireann   4, 5, 16
Daley, General Edmund L.   12
Daly, Jean   132
Dalzell, A   48
Darby, Major William O.   27
Darby's Rangers   27
Davis, General Benjamin O.   42, 63
Davis, Pvt. Elmer   136
Davis, Pvt. William E.   42
Davison, Sir Joseph   157
Dawson Bates, Richard   156
'The Day Ulster Became Uncle Sam's Stepping Stone to Berlin'   34
D-Day   27, 28, 50, 57, 60, 196, 202, 204
Declaration of Independence   31, 176–8
Deleo, Sgt. Frederick S.   131
Democratic Party   160, 163, 166, 174, 180, 184, 203
Derry, *see* Londonderry
Derrymore, County Antrim   146
Derry Standard   157, 182

de Valera, Éamon
  'American Note'   30, 59, 60, 160–6
  Americans warned not to comment on   14, 100
  anti-partition agitation in America   161–2, 164, 166
  British offers to end partition   6, 11
  David Gray hostility towards   2, 4, 107, 109, 113, 149–55, 159, 161, 189, 192, 203
  David Gray's *The Great Illusion* and   207–10
  IRA and   102, 106, 109, 110
  Irish Language and   119
  McLemore refers to   64
  mooted visit to US in 1939   79
  neutrality of Éire   83, 84, 153, 201–3
  1919–1920 visit to America   171
  partition and   5, 15, 97, 152, 201–2
  Pocket Guide to Northern Ireland and   32, 33
  protest against US troops   11, 12, 15–19, 77, 82, 85, 88, 96, 114, 154
  Roosevelt and   17, 30, 149–51, 176, 205
  Sean T. O'Kelly and   183
  Spellman visit   92, 93
  US press comment on   63
Devers, General Jacob   29, 58, 145, 146
Dierking, Col. I. S.   185
Dillon, James   78, 160
Dinsmore, John Walker   167, 169
Dominions Office   18, 89, 156, 164, 165, 191, 192
Donegal   63, 66, 169
Donnell, Jeff   186
Donnelly, Eamon   79
Doughboys in Ireland, The, (1943)   186
Dowler, General Arthur   136
Down and Connor, Diocese of   129
Downpatrick, County Down   63, 72
Downpatrick Cathedral   63
Dromora, County Down, pipe band competition   75
Dufferin Quay, Belfast   1, 13, 192
Dulanty, John W.   88
Dunaway, Wayland Fuller   172
Dundon, S. Sgt. Lawrence   28
Dungannon, County Tyrone   103, 125

302 Index

Dungiven, County Londonderry 40
Dunkirk 21
Dunlap, John 177

East Anglia 28, 34
Easter Rising 103, 106, 109
Ede, Chuter 191–2
Eden, Anthony 38, 164, 191
Eden, Carrickfergus, County Antrim 29
Eglinton, County Londonderry 28
VIII Army Air Force 28
80th Airborne Division 86
Eisenhower, General Dwight D.
  appointed ETO commander 12
  attitude to *Stars and Stripes* 58
  opposes sending troops to Northern Ireland 21
  supports distribution of Coca-Cola to troops 67
  23rd anniversary greetings 9
  views on discrimination against African American troops 57
  visit to Belfast 1945 1, 61, 186, 195–7
  visit to Northern Ireland before D-Day 34
Elton, Arthur 184
Emerald Curtain, The 208
Empire Windrush, SS 147
Entertainments National Service Association (ENSA) 48

Falls Road, Belfast 67, 101, 102, 122
Farley, Pvt. Embra 43, 44
Farrand, Louise 55–6
Farren, Neil, Bishop of Derry 69, 70, 89, 189–91
Faulkner, Brian 208–10
Fawcett, Bob 143
Federal Bureau of Investigation (FBI) 40
Federation of American Societies for Irish Independence 162
female police officers 125
Fianna Fáil 79, 110
Fine Gael 84, 93
Fisher, Congressman O. C. 184
Fleming, Pvt. George 13
Flynn, Edward J. 149
Forbes, Constable Thomas 103
Ford, Henry Jones 169

Foreign Office
  attitude towards Northern Ireland 52
  Bracken praise for Brooke 50
  Brooke's proposed trip to US 191
  concerns about behaviour of British women 124
  Eleanor Roosevelt visit 182
  jurisdiction over American personnel 39
  Maffey warns of plots against Gray 161
  reports on race relations 138
4th July 67, 71–2, 178
France
  fall of 6, 21, 85, 184, 204
  German occupation compared to Northern Ireland 82
  mooted invasion 10
  Stars and Stripes in Great War and 58
  US forces depart for 35
Frankland, C. L. 47
Franklin, Jay 88
Franklyn, General Sir Harold 182
Friscia, Ray 130, 131
Fuess, John C. 117
Fullerton, Hugh Jr. 67

Gaelic Athletic Association (GAA) 68–9, 73
Gallagher, Mick 9
Gartree parish church, County Antrim 76
Georgia 141, 159
German-American Bund 101, 160
Germany
  alleged agents in Northern Ireland 62–3, 115–17, 157–8
  American soldiers with German ancestry 13–14
  British declaration of war on 111
  Buhrman's prior postings 112
  de Valera and 106, 155, 161, 201
  Fall of France 85
  Éire's neutrality and 152–4, 164
  Eisenhower comments on 196
  Gray's *The Great Illusion* and 207
  impact of American presence in Northern Ireland on 10, 11, 15, 21

IRA links to 100-3, 105, 108-10
Irish Americans and 140, 160-1
MacRory's attitude towards 85-7, 94
nationalist attitudes towards 78-80, 82
radio propaganda against African American troops 140
threat to Ireland 10, 17, 19, 24-6, 28-30, 34, 184, 194, 200
gerrymandering 5-6, 17, 117-18, 159
Gilbert, Billy 76
Gilfillan, County Inspector Ewing 41-3
Glasgow 26, 112, 116
'G-men' 40
Good Conduct Committee 58, 142
Good Friday Agreement (1998) 199
Goodman, Benny 73
Government of Ireland Act (1921) 4, 17
Grand Central Hotel, Belfast 11, 63, 112, 119
Grand Opera House, Belfast 76, 196
Gransden, Sir Robert
   African American troops 138, 144-5
   arrival of the Americans 100
   Eleanor Roosevelt visit 182-3
   hospitality and welfare for the Americans 47-9, 199
   policing and the Americans 41, 44
Grant, General Ulysses S. 167
Gray, David
   Abercorn and 149
   'American Note' 161-6, 188, 191-2, 203
   appointment to Éire 4, 149
   attitude towards Catholics in Northern Ireland 117-18, 158-9
   bases in Éire 26
   Behind the Green Curtain 149
   Buhrman sends reports to 113
   campaign against *Ulster Protestant* 69, 156-8
   Dan Breen and 159
   Denis Ireland and 158-9
   departure from Éire 165
   efforts to end partition 151-4
   Eleanor Roosevelt vist 183, 189
   foreword to *Ulster and the Irish Republic* 207

historiography on 150-1
informed of arrival of African American troops 137
IRA 99, 103, 105-6, 108-10, 118
Irish-Americans and post-war anti-partition campaign in US 96, 149, 166
John Betjemen and 159
Lord Craigavon and 153
Lowry controversy 188
MacRory and 86-9, 154-6
Maffey view of 165
mooted Brooke visit to America 188-92
relationship with and hostility towards de Valera 2, 4, 16, 107, 113, 149-55, 161-2, 166, 192
return of US airmen from Éire 29
Sinn Fein: The Great Illusion 207-10
Spellman visit 89-94
Stormont support for *The Great Illusion* 207-10
support for war memorial building sought 194
US troops in Northern Ireland 114
views on conscription in Northern Ireland 115
Gray, Maud 149, 183
Great War
   African Americans in 139, 141
   Brooke and 47
   Denis Ireland in 83
   Gray and 150, 163
   Henry Lundborg and 102
   Irish-Americans and 172
   Irish nationalists and 11, 78-9
   MacRory attitude towards 86
   Quincy Roberts in 119
   songs of 74
   Stars and Stripes in 58
   unionists and 115
   United States in 1, 33
Greencastle, County Down 28
Green Cross 61
Grigg, Sir James 136
Grosvenor Presbyterian church, Belfast 71
Guildhall, Londonderry 17, 72
Guinness 64-5

'Hale' and 'Yarvard' 68
Halifax, Lord 81, 191
Hancock, John 177
Harchar, Major H. A. 59
Harland Shorts 116
Harriman, W. Averell 30, 183, 184
Harris, Pvt. Wiley 44–5, 126, 144, 147
Harrison, President Benjamin 183
Harrison, Pvt. William 45
Harrisson, Tom 46, 77–8
Hartle, General Russell P.
  appointed 12
  attends baseball 67–8
  attitude to marriages 63, 127–8
  departure 34
  Good Conduct Committee 142
  Gray letter regarding MacRory's
    protest 155
  Red Cross 55
  relationship with Stormont 52
  response to IRA threat 100
Haskin, Frederic J. 62
Hathaway, Lt. Col. J. L. 110
Hays, Arthur Sulzberger 136
Hays, Brooks 136
Hayward, Richard 186–7
Healy, Cahir 80–3
Hempel, Edouard 12, 29, 79, 85–6, 102, 160
Henderson, Alderman Thomas 72
Henderson, Sir Oscar 51, 100, 155, 166, 182, 208
Henke, Pvt. Milburn Herman 9, 13–14, 20, 21, 32 (image), 52, 132, 199
Henry Gibbins, SS 133
'Hi! Uncle Sam!' 167
Hill, General Edmund 52, 89, 94
Hinsley, Archbishop Arthur 91
Hitler, Adolf 18, 33, 86–8, 99, 101, 161, 207
Home Guard 29, 125
Home Office 11, 38, 100, 130, 138, 157
Home Rule 78, 89, 170
Hoover, Desmond 133
Hope, Bob 76
Hopkins, Harry 30, 183, 191
Hudson, E. 185
Hull, Cordell 59, 60 (image), 162, 164
Hurley, Bishop Joseph 87–8, 155
Hurst, Brian Desmond 184, 186

Iceland 10, 12, 21, 22, 25, 28, 112
'In the Mood' 76
Ireland, Denis 83, 158
Irish-America
  Aiken Mission and 161
  execution of Williams 104
  Gray's attitude towards 4, 157–8, 161–4, 203
  Irish Americans in US military 14, 33, 63, 107, 114
  A Letter from Ulster and 185–6
  mooted wartime Brooke trip
    and 188–92, 200
  Owen Wister, *A Straight Deal*
    and 172
  patriotism of 84, 91, 96, 160
  perceived influence on US
    politics 2, 3, 5, 12, 22–3, 51–2, 80–1, 96, 174, 186–8, 190, 192, 200–1, 203
  plans for a post-war anti-partition
    campaign 96, 120, 160, 164–6, 194, 201
  response to arrival of Americans 15, 18
  R. L. Marshall on 176–8
  role in 1970s 180
  Spellman visit and 95
  Teddy Roosevelt on 171
  'Ulster revivalism' and 203
Irish civil war 4–5
Irish Famine 168, 173, 178
Irish Free State 4–5, 18, 31, 151, 207
Irish language (Gaelic) 17, 69, 119
Irish Republican Army (IRA)
  activities in Éire 78, 102
  alleged involvement in Hippodrome
    bombing 70–1
  alleged involvement in strikes 117
  British campaign of 101
  Buhrman's concerns about 90, 99, 103, 107–8, 110, 113–16, 118, 120, 203
  campaign linked to US
    forces 3, 4, 26, 32–3, 41, 44, 46, 69, 86–7, 100, 102–10, 121, 122, 126, 202
  Cathal O'Byrne and 174
  Cork Old IRA Association 88

Dan Breen and 159
execution of Williams 43, 84, 103
German links of 101–2, 105
Gray's attitude towards 105–7, 155, 158, 208
Green Cross 61
Irish American support for in 1970s 180
manifesto refers to American presence 104–5
Mass Observation report on 77
murder of Constable Murphy 99
suppression of 109
Ulster Union Club and 83, 158
US press and 108–9
Italy 27, 80, 140
Ives, Ernest L. 79, 111–13, 203

Jackson, Andrew 167, 175
Jacobs, Pvt. Herbert 43–4
James Parker, SS 133
Japan 1, 9, 63, 82, 119, 195, 200
Jenkins, Allan 75
Jenkins, Pvt. William 42–3, 143
'Jim Crow' 118, 123, 135–7, 141–5, 147, 202
jitterbugging 73, 121
'Jive Bombers', swing band 73, 74 (image)
'Johnny Doughboy Found a Rose in Ireland' 74
Johnson, Pvt. Silas 13
Johnson, William 'Wariaghejaghe' 176
Joint Council of the Irish Union Association 81
Jolson, Al 75
Jones, Bob III 180
Jones, Bob Sr 180
Judge Advocate General Department (JAGD) 129

Kearney, John D. 16
Kelly, A. J. 208–9
Kennedy, Isobel 123
Kennedy, Joseph 80–1, 87–8, 90, 112, 160, 162
Kentucky Wildcats 67
Keyser, Kay 74
Kinematograph 185

King, William B. 109
King George III 178
King William III 177
Kirkpatrick, Helen 12
Knights of Columbus 89, 158, 177
Krock, Arthur 22
Kuh, Frederick R. 142

Lady From Edinburgh, The 196
Lander, Col. 51
Landers, Lew 186
landing memorial column 192–3, 196, 199
Langford Lodge 25, 28, 76, 182, 195
Launceston, Cornwall 143
League of Nations 163
Lee, General John C. H. 179
Lend-Lease 21–2, 24, 26, 197, 200
Letter from Ulster, A, (1943) 185, 187
Letters from Home (1941) 184
Lexington, Battle of (1775) 177
Limavady, County Londonderry 41
Lincoln, Abraham 16, 83, 95
Lindberg, Charles 161
Lindsay, Eric M. 194
Lisahally, County Londonderry 24, 25
Lisburn, County Antrim 48
Lisnabreeny cemetery, Belfast 29, 193–4
Little, Memmi 131
Little, Rev. James 131
Liverpool 175
Llewellyn, Major E. M. 58–9
Lockheed Overseas Corporation (LOC) 25, 28, 72, 74 (image)
London Can Take It (1940) 62
Londonderry (Derry)
  alleged IRA activity in 107
  arrival of Americans 13, 17
  'Base One Europe' 25
  Battle of the Atlantic and 34
  behaviour of US technicians in 40–1, 52, 66
  Buhrman on gerrymandering 117–18
  building of US base in 1941 22, 24–5, 154
  Declaration of Independence and 178
  'disorderly houses' in 125

Eleanor Roosevelt visit 182
Francis Matthews visit 158
links to America 179
Mass celebrated at US base 69
nationalism in 77, 80, 82, 120
Officers Club 49
racial incidents in 142, 145
Red Cross Club 54, 57, 58, 66, 89
sport in 68
Sunday opening in 48
tensions between British and American personnel in 51
Thanksgiving and Christmas in 72
US Marines in 63, 65 (image), 74
war brides 129, 132, 133
Long Kesh, County Down 28
Lord Craigavon, *see* Craig, Sir James
Lord Rugby, *see* Maffey, Sir John
Lough Erne, County Fermanagh 24, 154
Lowe, Dr Herbert P. 126
Lowry, William 70, 91, 119, 157, 189–91
Lundborg, Henry 102–3
Lurgan, County Armagh 48, 96

McAteer, Hugh 109
MacBride, Sean 102
McCabe, Thomas 175
McCarthy, Joseph 90
McCleary's Bar, Belleek, County Fermanagh 65
McCormack, John 162, 190
McCracken, Henry Joy 175
McCracken Memorial Presbyterian church 71
McCullagh, Crawford 184, 192–3, 196
McDaniel, Essa Anne 133
McDaniels, Pvt. George 42
MacDermott, John 38–9, 119, 199
McHugh, Frank 75
McIntyre, Jane 133
MacKenzie, Ella 76
McKenzie, Pvt. Lawrence 44
McKinley, William 169, 177
McLaughlin, Senator Thomas 79
McLemore, Henry 56, 63–4
McLoughlin, Pvt. Owen 42, 44, 51
McMichael, Frederick 41
MacNamee, Padraig 119
MacNeice, Louis 64

McPherson, John W. 179
McQuaid, Archbishop John 88
MacQuitty, William 184–5
McQuoid, Jack 71
MacRory, Cardinal Joseph
attitude to the war 85–6, 88–90, 162
background 85
Buhrman on 117
celebrating Mass for Americans 69–70
correspondence with Gray 154–6, 165
friendship with Hempel 85
Gray's *Ulster Protestant* campaign and 157
image 90
invited to memorial column unveiling 193
IRA campaign and 108
Lenten pastorals 86
protest against American troops 33, 43, 85, 87–8, 94, 115, 155, 201, 203
Spellman visit 91–5
Thomas McLaughlin and 79
Macaulay, William J. B. 151
Machtig, Sir Eric 89, 165, 191
Mackie, Marcia 54, 131, 194–5
Maffey, Sir John (Lord Rugby)
Aiken Mission and 160
'American Note' and 164
Brooke's mooted American trip and 188
burning of Union Jack in Dublin and 106
Gray's campaign against the *Ulster Protestant* and 157–8
Gray's *The Great Illusion* and 208–9
informs de Valera of arrival of Americans 11, 155
on MacRory 89
1940 deal to end partition and 152, 153
relationships with de Valera and Gray 161, 165
Magdalene Laundries 130
Magee, Evelyn 122
Mageean, Bishop Daniel 108, 129, 193
Magee College, Londonderry 176

Maghaberry, County Antrim 28
Maghera, County Londonderry 122
Magherafelt, County Londonderry 146
Magheralin, County Down 128 (image)
Magna Charta 159, 189
Manning, Paul 62
'Marching Through Georgia' 13
Marlin, Ervin 'Spike' 150
Marshall, General George C.
   Darby's Rangers and 27
   General Daly and 12
   sending African American troops to UK 135
   sending troops to Northern Ireland 10, 12, 27
   view on Treaty Ports 164
   visit to Northern Ireland 30, 40, 183, 184
Marshall, Robert Lyons (R. L.) 176, 180, 181
Marshall, William Forbes (W. F.) 176–8, 180
Martin, Edwin T. 'Lefty' 55
Martin, Mary Jane 'Minnie' 44, 115
Mason, USS 148
Mason-Dixon Line 7
Mass Observation 19, 66, 77
Mater Dei home 126
Mathes, Maureen 129, 132
Matthews, Francis (Frank) 88, 89–90, 90 (image), 158, 190
Maxwell, Patrick 81, 82
Maxwell, Sir Alexander 11, 191
Maydown, County Londonderry 28
Mays, Lt. J. O. 133
Medal of Freedom 70
Meeks, Eleanor 133
Megaw, Eileen 44, 126
Merrick, Lynn 186
Metro-Goldwyn-Mayer (MGM) 185
Midgley, Harold (Harry) 14, 117
Midland Station Hotel, officers club, Belfast 49
Mid-West Giants 67–8
Miller, Glenn 76
Ministry of Aircraft Production 28
Ministry of Information (MOI)
   African Americans 138–9
   films and 62, 184–5, 187

F. M. Adams and 127
Harrisson and 46
hospitality for Americans 46–7
links to Stormont 50–2, 123, 178, 184, 197
popularity of Americans 122, 126
'Report on Americans in Ireland' (1942) 35, 54, 77
reports welcome given to Americans 19–20
visit of US congressmen 184
Mitchell, Muriel (Friscia) 130–3
Mitchum, Robert 186
Mohawk tribe 176
Moneymore, County Londonderry 72, 138
Montgomery, General Bernard 182, 195
Montgomery, Eric 208–10
Montgomery, Robert 24, 76
Moody, W. S. 83–4, 97
Mooney, Archbishop Edward 163
Morgan, Edward P. 190
Morrison, Herbert 157, 191
Morrison, Patricia 75
Motion Picture Herald 185
Mullaghmore, County Londonderry 28
Murney, Peadar 78, 79
Murphy, Constable Patrick 87, 103–4, 106, 109
Murrow, Edward 62

National Geographic Bulletin 179
Navy Day 75
Neill, Ivan 210
Newfoundland 28
New Orleans, Battle of (1815) 175
Newtownbreda, County Down 175
Newtownbutler, County Fermangh 48
New York
   civilian correspondence to 50
   construction firm awarded contract for Londonderry base 24
   Irish in 173
   Spellman and 90
   Theodore Roosevelt's history of 171
   war brides going to 133
   Yank and 61
New York Lions 68

North Africa
  British troops sent to   26
  General Devers crash lands en route from   29
  invasion of   10, 31, 34, 50, 62, 119
  Spellman visits Irish troops in   93
  US Rangers in   27
North Atlantic Treaty Organization (NATO)   207
Northern Ireland Base Section (NIBS)   34–5
Northern Ireland Labour Party (NILP)   14, 69, 117, 118, 189
Norway   15, 82
Nunan, Sean   162–3
Nutt's Corner airfield, County Antrim   28

Oberon, Merle   75
O'Brien, Joseph J.   18
O'Byrne, Cathal   174–5
O'Donnell, Cardinal Patrick   85
Office of Strategic Services (OSS)   70, 110
Office of War Information (OWI)   136
Officers' Club, Belfast   49, 57, 179
Officers' Club, Londonderry   49
O'Kelly, Sean T.   153–5, 183
Omagh, County Tyrone   34, 50, 72, 143
O'Neill, Terence   9
Operation Bolero   34
Operation Magnet   10, 26, 54, 135
Operation Torch   34
Orange Order   5, 157, 174, 189
'Orange Terror' (1943)   97, 190
Ormeau baths, Belfast   57
Ottawa   189

Paisley, Rev. Ian   180
Paramount Pictures   187
Parker, Dehra   48, 122, 124, 145
Pathé   184
Patterson, Sally   182
Patton, General George S.   34
Pearl Harbor
  American attitudes after   19, 79, 84, 111
  American attitudes before   21, 25, 28, 62, 88, 91, 126, 154, 161, 174

  attack on   1, 9, 11, 12, 15
  David Gray and   151–3
  internment of American pilot and   29
  prejudice against Japanese-Americans after   63
Pearse, Patrick   101
Pedelty, Donovan   186
Pennsylvania   27, 68, 71, 169, 172
'Pennsylvania Line'   167, 176
Pennsylvania Scotch-Irish Society (PSIS)   169, 179
Pitzer, T/5 Keith T. K.   33
Playboy of the Western World, The   165
Plaza, Belfast, Red Cross Club   54, 55 (image)
Poage, Congressman William   184
Pocket Guide to Northern Ireland (1942)   31–4, 59, 65, 121, 127
Polk, James K.   167
Pollen, Fr. Daniel   43
Pollock dock   13
'Poor Richard Club'   119
Portadown, County Armagh   34
Portrush, County Antrim   70, 72, 189
poteen   32, 55, 64, 66
Presbyterians
  alcohol and   66
  in colonial America   3, 167–8, 171–3, 176, 178, 179, 203
  in Londonderry   25
  'Ulster Revivalism' in Second World War   176–7
  welcome to Americans   69, 71, 72
Prestwick, Scotland   28
Price, Norman   67
prostitution   44, 49–50, 54, 124–6
Putnam McCabe, William   175

Queen Anne Hotel   194
Queen's University Belfast   194, 195
Quintrell, F. M.   51

'Rainbow-5' plan   26
Randalstown, County Antrim   42
Randolph, John   80–1, 111–13, 118–19, 203
Ravenhill, Belfast   67–8, 75
Reuters   70
Reynolds, Quentin   62–3, 139–40

Index 309

Roberts, Quincy
 arrival 119-20
 assisting war brides 120, 131-3, 203
 departure 113
 Lowry 'fumigation' comment 189
 William Ayer deputising for 197
Rodden, Albert 40-1, 45
'Roll Out the Barrel' 74
Roosevelt, Eleanor 34, 58, 89, 123, 149, 157, 181-4
Roosevelt, Franklin D.
 Aiken mission and 161
 'American Note' and 162, 164-6
 Andrews sends greetings on arrival of troops 14-15
 attitude towards conscription in Northern Ireland 79
 Axis propaganda against African American troops 140
 Bishop Hurley support for 88
 building of bases in Northern Ireland 22, 24
 decision to send African American troops 136
 de Valera's protest 16-17, 30, 151
 gifting replica of landing memorial proposed 193
 gifts copy of Declaration of Independence to de Valera 176
 Gray-MacRory dispute 155
 Gray's *Great Illusion* and 208
 mooted Brooke visit 188, 190-1, 205
 nationalists and the Welles visit 80-1
 relationship with Gray 149-54, 160, 203
 reprieve sought from for condemned IRA member 104, 106
 sending troops to UK 9-11, 21, 26
 Spellman visit to Ireland 90-2
Roosevelt, Theodore 'Teddy' 171, 183
Ross, General Robert 178
Rostrevor, County Down 179
Royal Air Force (RAF) 16, 22, 26, 27, 29, 131, 195
Royal Black Institution 135
Royal Hippodrome cinema 70-1
Royal Naval War Amenities Committee 49
Royal Navy (RN) 13, 24, 25

Rugby 67-9
Russell, Sean 101
Russell, Thomas 175

St Anne's Cathedral, Belfast 71
St Patrick's Cathedral, Armagh 70
St Patrick's College, Cavan 86
St Patrick's Day 31, 57, 72, 93, 161
Salvation Army 54
Savory, Sir Douglas 17-18, 156, 189, 208
Sayers, R. M. 119
Schafer, PFC. Jack 74
Scotch-Irish 7, 167-74, 176-7, 179
Scotch-Irish Society of America (SISA) 169, 179
Scotch-Irish Society of the United States of America, *see* Pennsylvania Scotch-Irish Society (PSIS)
Scottish Provident Building 111
Seven Years' (French and Indian) War (1756-1763) 27, 176
Short Guide to Great Britain, A, (1943) 33
Shriver, Major Boyd 30-1
Sikorski, General Władysław 27
Simmons, Sir Frederick James 17-18
Sinn Fein 4, 151, 172, 208, 209
Sinn Fein: The Great Illusion 207-10
slavery, Ulster's role in 173-6
Slieveanorra Mountain, County Antrim 28
Smith, Alfred (Al) E. 160, 180
Smith, Thelma 128-9
Soldiers', Sailors' and Airmen's Families Association 67
Somme, Battle of the (1916) 115
Soviet Union 21, 204
'Spam Circuit' 76
Special Observer Group (SPOBS) 22, 26, 100
Special Powers Act (1922) 157-8
Spellman, Cardinal Francis 89-96, 157, 183, 190
Spender, Sir Wilfrid 89
Stark, Admiral Harold L. 136, 142
Stars and Stripes
 'American Note' 59-60, 60 (image)
 Matthews visit 89
 Northern Ireland edition 58-61

report on *Guide* 33, 127
report on Lockheed facility 25
report on marriages between US servicemen and local women 129
report on St Patrick's Day 72
reports on life in Northern Ireland 53, 54, 61, 68, 69, 73–5
Stewart, Joseph F. 81, 82
Stimson, Henry L. 135
Strabane, County Tyrone 69, 83
Straight Deal, A 171–2
Strathaird, HTMS 13
strikes 6, 113, 116
Stronge, Lady Gladys 47–8
Styles, Francis 80, 115
Sulzberger, Arthur Hays 136
Sunday opening
  cinemas and 53
  Guide on 32
  MOI concerns 54
  pubs and 66
  restrictions eased 37, 48
  Royal Hippodrome cinema and 70–1
Sunday working 116
Sunnylands, Carrickfergus, County Antrim 27

Taft, Robert 23
Teutonic 'germ theory' 168–9
Thanksgiving 68, 72
This is the Army 76
Thomson, Charles 71, 177
Tiger Bay, Cardiff 124
Time 61, 88
Tobin, Governor M. J. 96–7
Today's Cinema 185
Tone, Wolfe 175
Toner, Mrs 125
Toome, County Antrim 28, 125
Treaty ports
  'American Note' and 60, 154, 163
  return of in 1938 6, 12
  wartime rumours surrounding 29, 114
Truman, Harry S. 197
Truscott, Major General Lucian 27
Tulip, A. J. 64, 167–8
Turnham, Colonel Alexander Smith 48, 51, 137–8
Tynan Abbey, County Armagh 185

U-Boats 24, 26, 101
Ulster-American Hospitality Committee 49
Ulster and the Irish Republic (1957) 207
Ulster Hall 143
Ulster Hospital for Children and Women 67
Ulster-Irish Society of New York 174, 208
Ulster Office 51, 52, 187
Ulster Protestant, The 69, 150, 156–8, 180
Ulster Protestant League 156–8
Ulster Sails West (1943) 177–8
Ulster Television (UTV) 9
Ulster Tourist Development Association 54
Ulster Union Club 83, 158
Ulster Unionist Party 14, 51
United Irishmen 171, 173, 175
United Services Organization (USO) 75–6, 88, 89, 158, 186, 190
United States Army Air Force (USAAF) 9 (map of bases), 28, 45
United States Army Forces in the British Isles (USAFBI) 12
United States Army Northern Ireland Force (USANIF) 12
United States Marine Corps 63, 65, 74–5, 132, 182, 192
US Civil War
  baseball in 68
  compared to partition 16, 17, 175
  Scotch-Irish revival and 169, 171–2
  A Short Guide to Great Britain on 33
  Ulstermen in 179
US Consulate, Dublin 80, 115
US Consulate General, Belfast
  becomes a Consulate General 113
  children born to American servicemen 130
  Eisenhower's visit to Northern Ireland 197
  foundation of, 1796 111
  jurisdiction over Americans 40
  location 54, 120
  marriages of African Americans to local women 124
  opening and development of 111

role in Belfast   2, 3, 111, 112
routine functions of   119-20
rumoured Welles visit   80
war brides   132

Vatican   87, 90
VE Day (1945)   35, 120
Venereal Disease (VD)   122, 124-5
Vichy France   17
Vining, Commander R. E.   136, 182-3, 188
Virginian, The   171
Viscount Alanbrooke, *see* Alan Brooke
Viscount Simon   39
Visiting Forces Act (VFA) (1942)   37-41, 43, 44
VJ Day (1945)   1, 120

Walsh, James G.   77
Walsh, Senator David I.   190
Walshe, Joseph   17, 86, 88, 151, 160, 183
War Brides Act (1945)   132
Warburg, James   136
War memorial building, Belfast   193-4
War News   101
War Office   11, 136, 185
Washington, George   149, 176
Waterbury, Lt. Clair M.   131
Waterloo, Battle of (1815)   175
Wayne, General Anthony   177
Welfare Committee   46-50, 66
Welles, Sumner   17, 22, 23, 79-81, 112, 160
Wheeler, Burton K.   22

whiskey   42, 44, 54, 66, 72, 105, 143
Wickham, Sir Charles   44, 48
Williams, Thomas   104
Willkie, Wendell   22-3
Wilmont House, County Antrim   26, 71
Wilson, Harold   116
Wilson, Pvt. Floyd   53
Winant, John   105-6, 155, 157, 184, 194, 207
Windsor Park, Belfast   67, 68, 71
Wister, Owen   171-2
Wizard of Oz, The   208
Wolf, Roland   29
Women's Auxiliary Air Force (WAAF)   182
Women's Patrol   125
Women's Royal Naval Service (WRENS)   182
Women's Voluntary Service (WVS)   29, 47-9
Woodrow Wilson   16, 167, 170
Woodruff, Robert   67
World Series, 1919   67
Wright, Colonel Thomas T.   169-70

Yahner, Rice   13, 62
Yank   53, 61, 65, 72, 73, 131
'The Yanks Are Coming'   74
'The Yanks in Ireland'   74
'Yarvard'   68
York Road, Belfast   143
Young Men's Christian Association (YMCA)   54, 72, 108

www.ingramcontent.com/pod-product-compliance
Lightning Source LLC
Chambersburg PA
CBHW052148300426
44115CB00011B/1572